Shojo Beat

honey and clover

Vol. 3
Story & Art by
Chica Umino

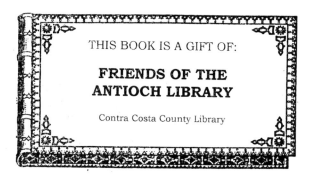

honey and clover

Volume 3
CONTENTS

honey and clover

honey and clover

chapter 16

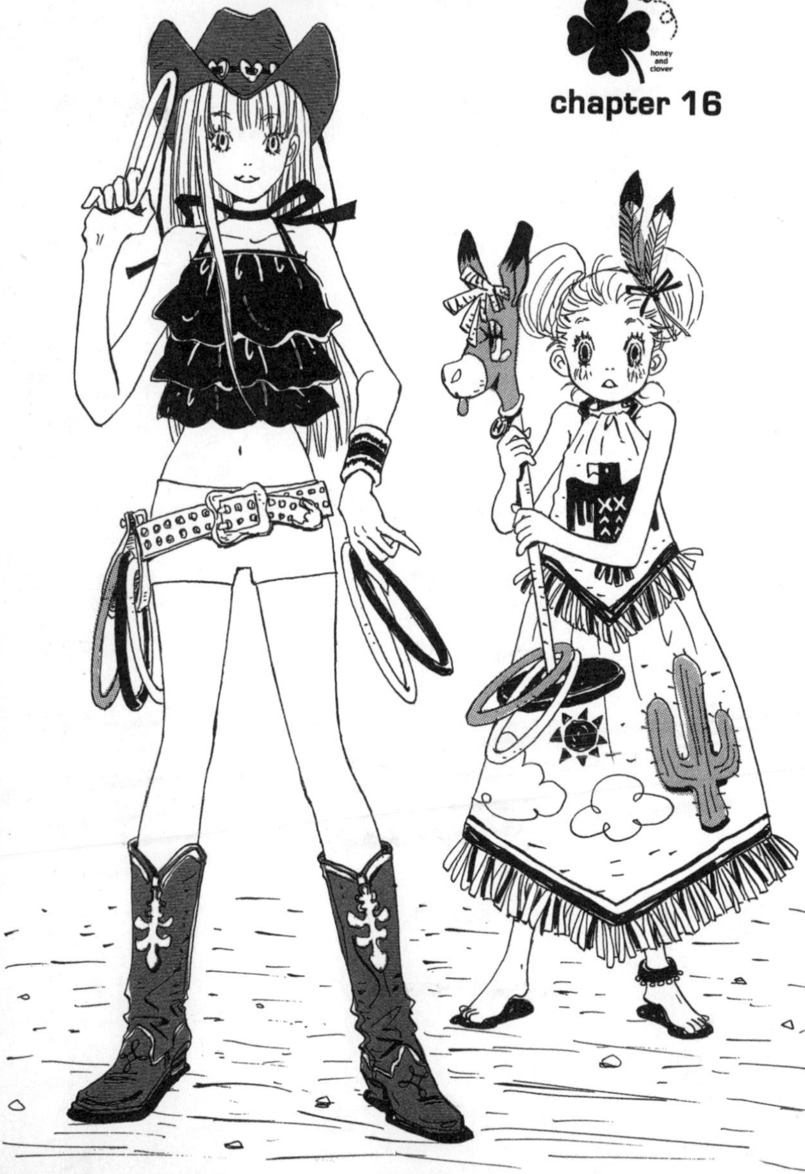

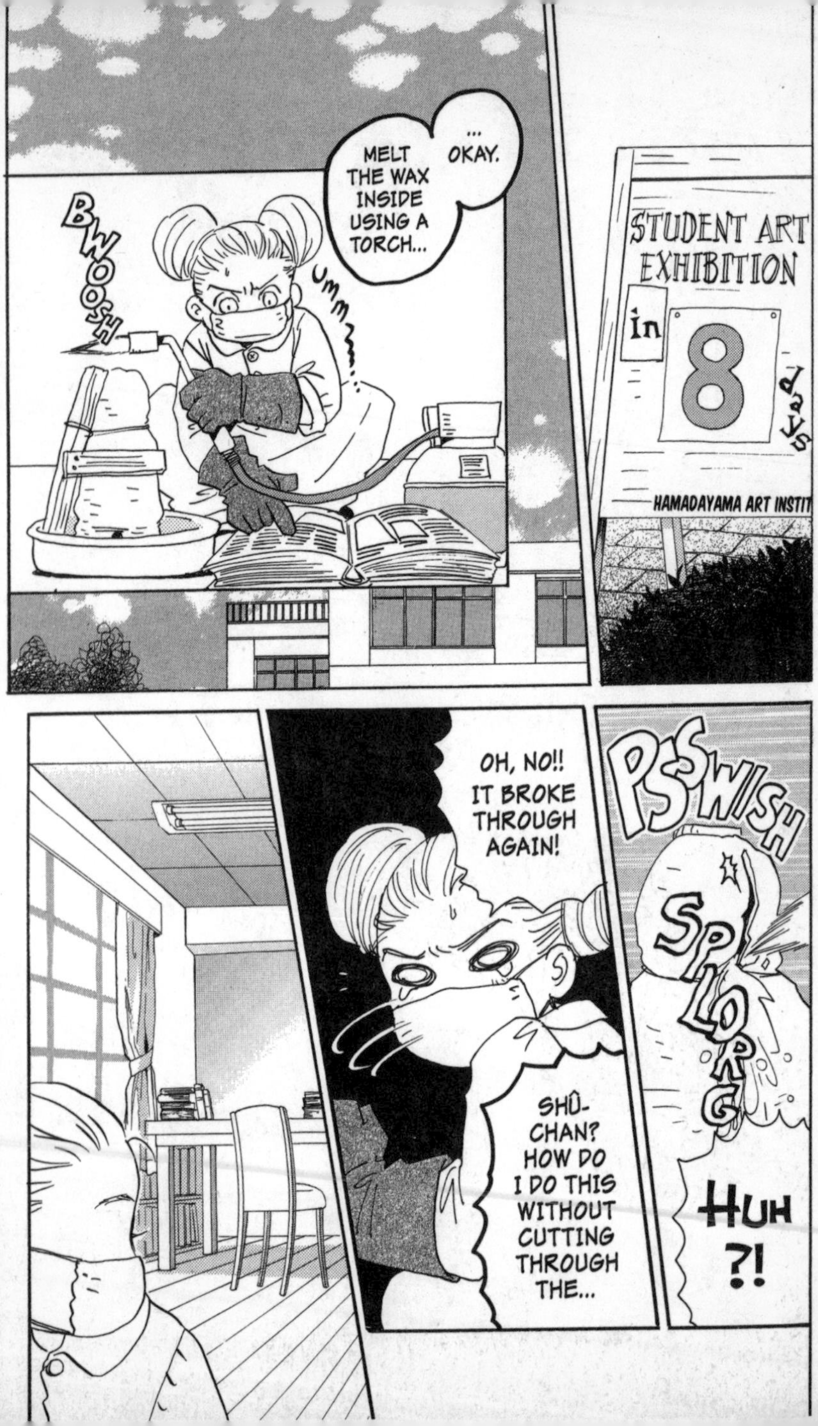
STUDENT ART EXHIBITION
in 8 days
HAMADAYAMA ART INSTIT
... OKAY.
MELT THE WAX INSIDE USING A TORCH...
BWOOSH
UMMMM...
PSSWISH
SPLORG
HUH ?!
OH, NO!! IT BROKE THROUGH AGAIN!
SHÛ-CHAN? HOW DO I DO THIS WITHOUT CUTTING THROUGH THE...

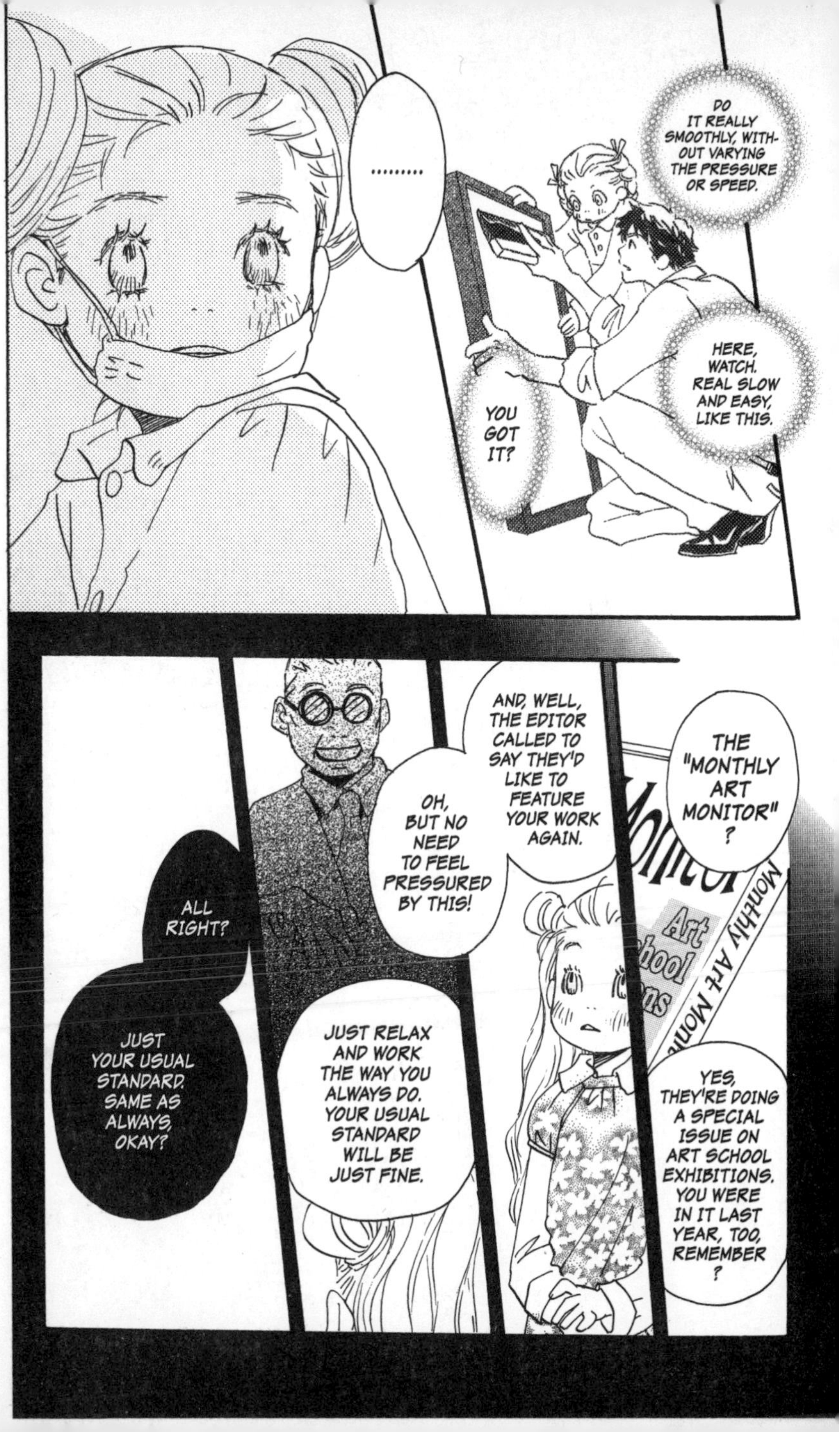
DO IT REALLY SMOOTHLY, WITH-OUT VARYING THE PRESSURE OR SPEED.
HERE, WATCH. REAL SLOW AND EASY, LIKE THIS.
YOU GOT IT?
....
THE "MONTHLY ART MONITOR"?
YES, THEY'RE DOING A SPECIAL ISSUE ON ART SCHOOL EXHIBITIONS. YOU WERE IN IT LAST YEAR, TOO, REMEMBER?
AND, WELL, THE EDITOR CALLED TO SAY THEY'D LIKE TO FEATURE YOUR WORK AGAIN.
OH, BUT NO NEED TO FEEL PRESSURED BY THIS!
JUST RELAX AND WORK THE WAY YOU ALWAYS DO. YOUR USUAL STANDARD WILL BE JUST FINE.
ALL RIGHT?
JUST YOUR USUAL STANDARD. SAME AS ALWAYS, OKAY?

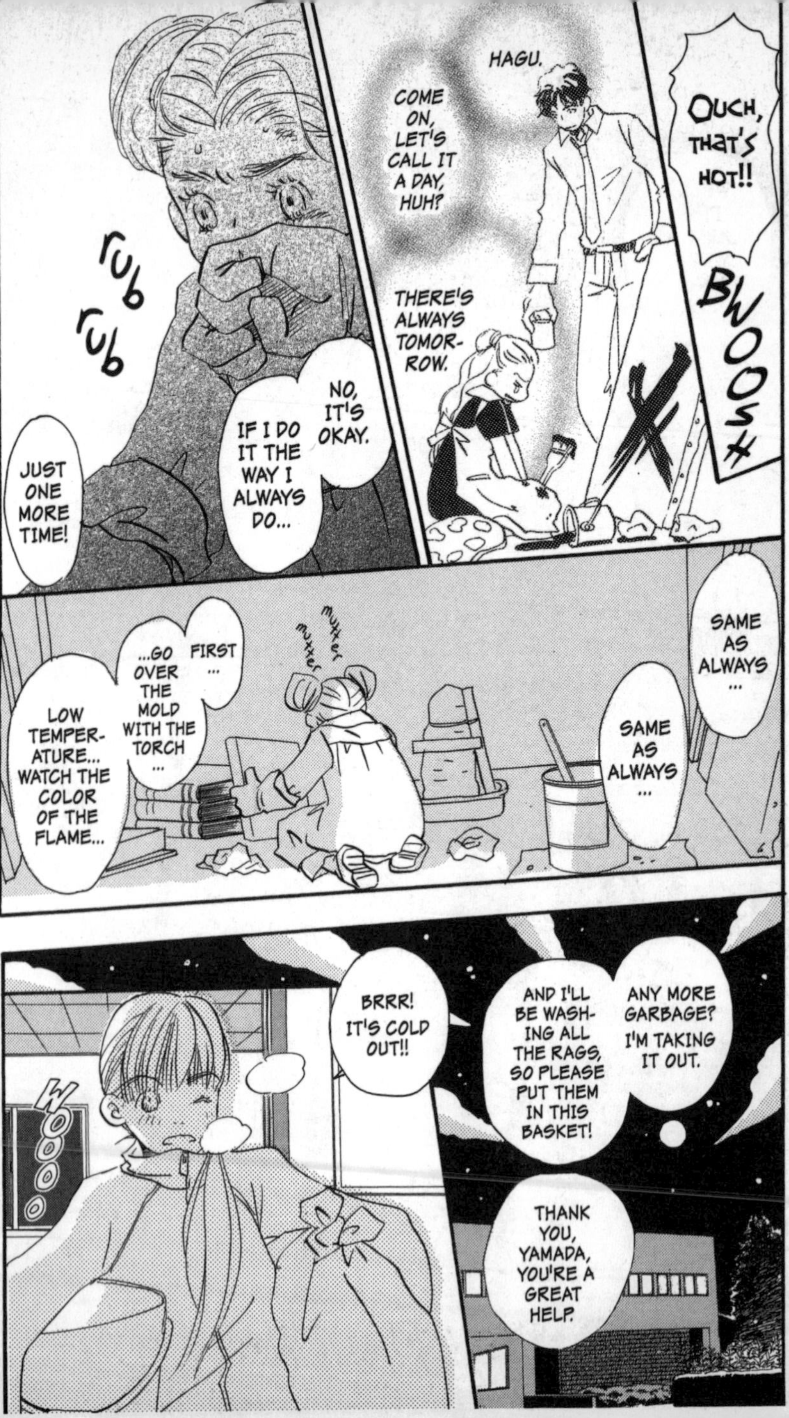

OUCH, THAT'S HOT!!
BWOOSH
HAGU.
COME ON, LET'S CALL IT A DAY, HUH?
THERE'S ALWAYS TOMORROW.
NO, IT'S OKAY.
IF I DO IT THE WAY I ALWAYS DO...
JUST ONE MORE TIME!
rub rub
SAME AS ALWAYS ...
SAME AS ALWAYS ...
FIRST ...
...GO OVER THE MOLD WITH THE TORCH ...
LOW TEMPERATURE... WATCH THE COLOR OF THE FLAME...
mutter mutter
ANY MORE GARBAGE? I'M TAKING IT OUT.
AND I'LL BE WASHING ALL THE RAGS, SO PLEASE PUT THEM IN THIS BASKET!
THANK YOU, YAMADA, YOU'RE A GREAT HELP.
BRRR! IT'S COLD OUT!!
WOOOO

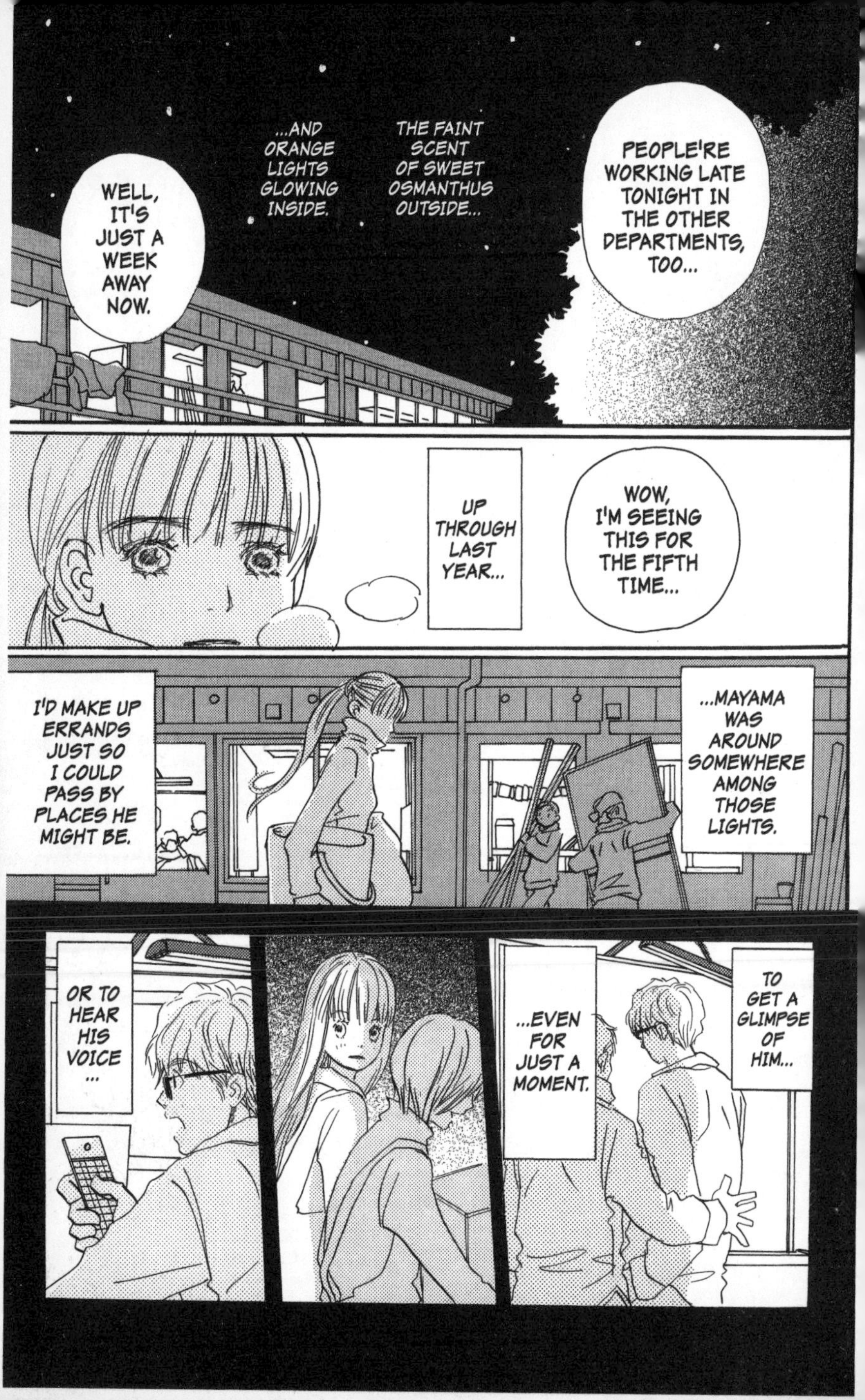
PEOPLE'RE WORKING LATE TONIGHT IN THE OTHER DEPARTMENTS, TOO...
THE FAINT SCENT OF SWEET OSMANTHUS OUTSIDE...
...AND ORANGE LIGHTS GLOWING INSIDE.
WELL, IT'S JUST A WEEK AWAY NOW.
WOW, I'M SEEING THIS FOR THE FIFTH TIME...
UP THROUGH LAST YEAR...
...MAYAMA WAS AROUND SOMEWHERE AMONG THOSE LIGHTS.
I'D MAKE UP ERRANDS JUST SO I COULD PASS BY PLACES HE MIGHT BE.
TO GET A GLIMPSE OF HIM...
...EVEN FOR JUST A MOMENT.
OR TO HEAR HIS VOICE ...

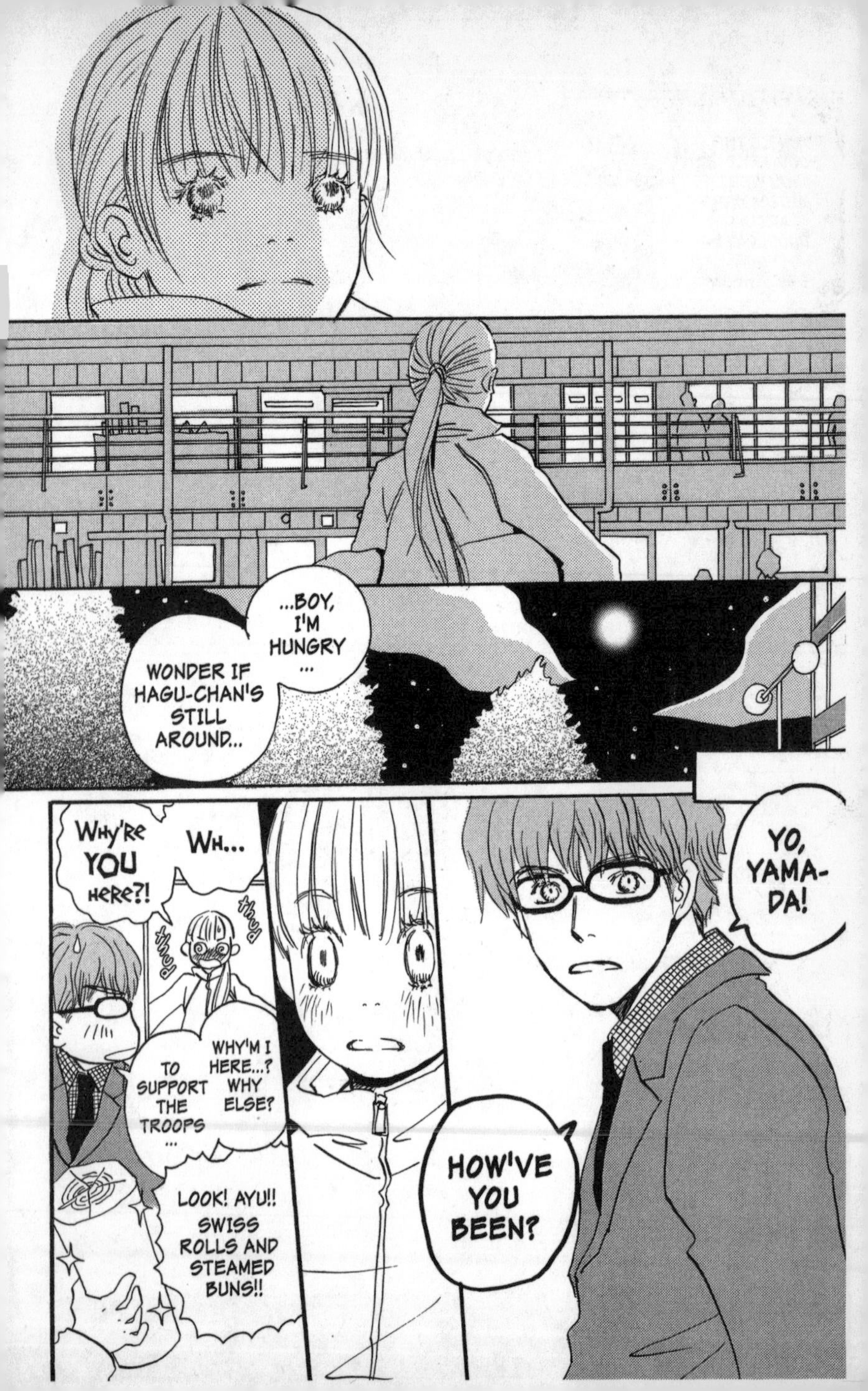
...BOY, I'M HUNGRY ...
WONDER IF HAGU-CHAN'S STILL AROUND...
YO, YAMADA!
HOW'VE YOU BEEN?
WH...
WHY'RE YOU HERE?!
WHY'M I HERE...? WHY ELSE?
TO SUPPORT THE TROOPS ...
LOOK! AYU!! SWISS ROLLS AND STEAMED BUNS!!

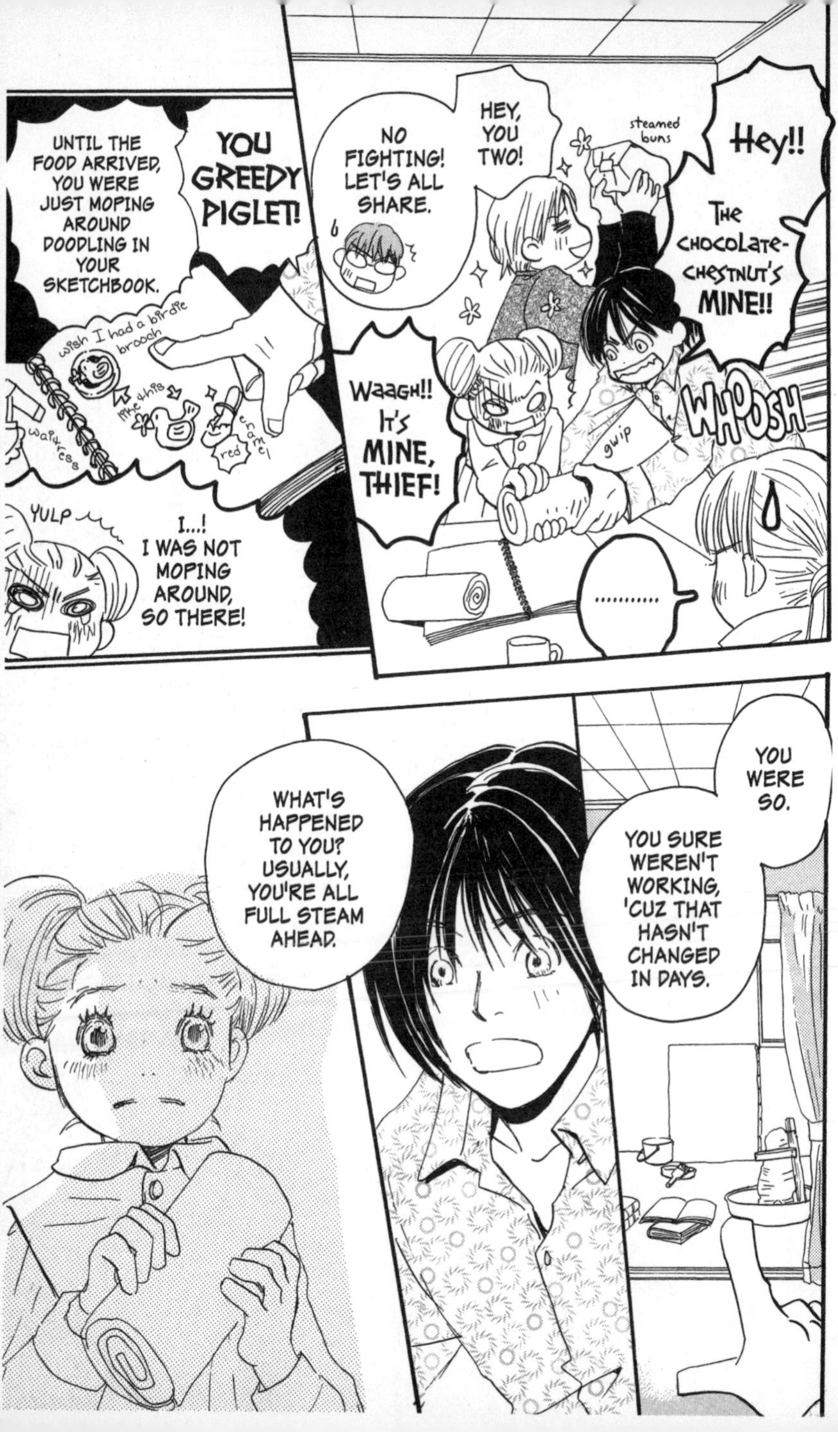
Hey!! The chocolate-chestnut's MINE!!
steamed buns
HEY, YOU TWO!
NO FIGHTING! LET'S ALL SHARE.
WHOOSH
Waagh!! It's MINE, THIEF!
gwip
....
YOU GREEDY PIGLET!
UNTIL THE FOOD ARRIVED, YOU WERE JUST MOPING AROUND DOODLING IN YOUR SKETCHBOOK.
wish I had a birdie brooch
like this
waitress
enamel
red
YULP
I...! I WAS NOT MOPING AROUND, SO THERE!
YOU WERE SO.
YOU SURE WEREN'T WORKING, 'CUZ THAT HASN'T CHANGED IN DAYS.
WHAT'S HAPPENED TO YOU? USUALLY, YOU'RE ALL FULL STEAM AHEAD.

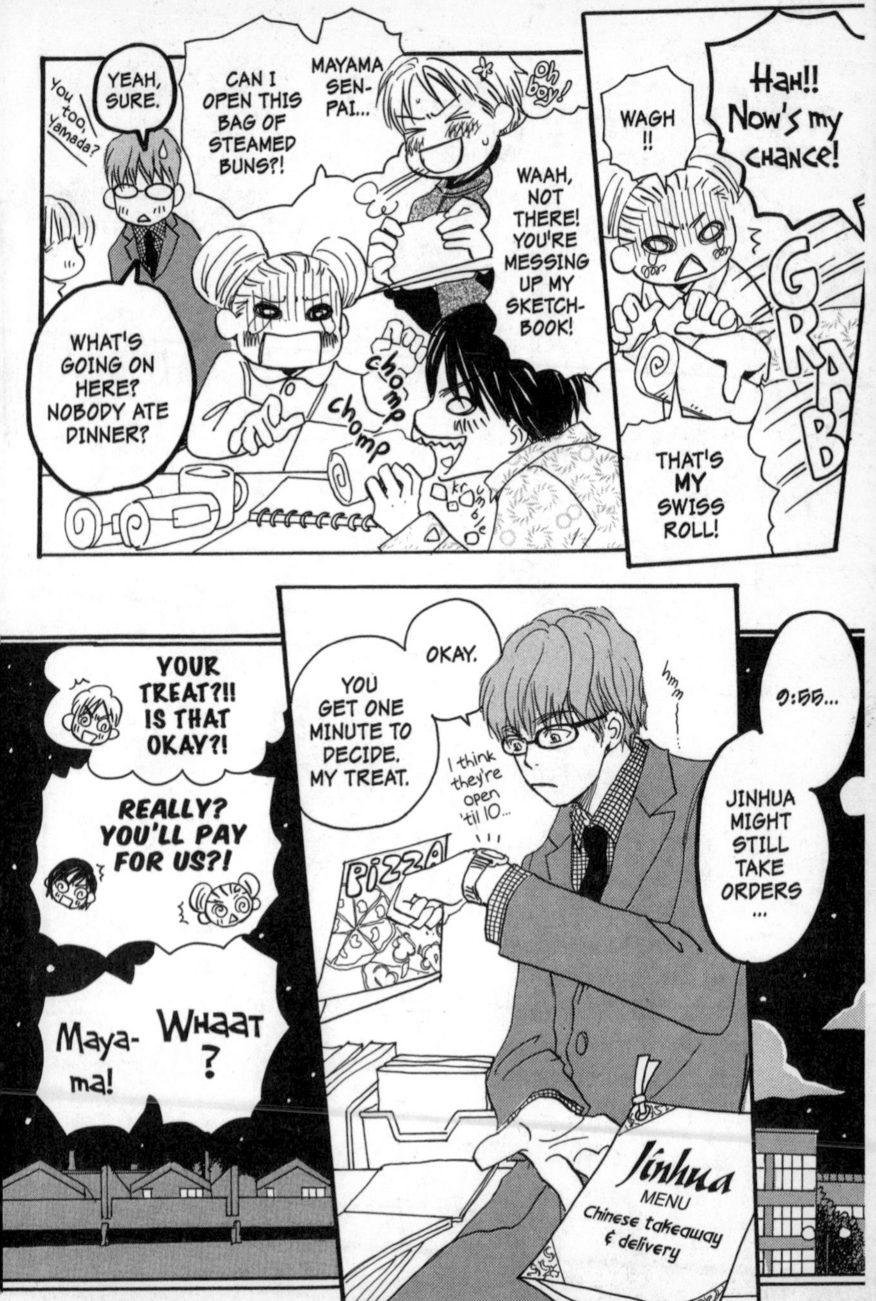
HAH!! NOW'S MY CHANCE!
WAGH !!
GRAB
THAT'S MY SWISS ROLL!
Oh boy!
MAYAMA SEN-PAI...
CAN I OPEN THIS BAG OF STEAMED BUNS?!
YEAH, SURE.
You too, Yamada?
WAAH, NOT THERE! YOU'RE MESSING UP MY SKETCH-BOOK!
chomp chomp
WHAT'S GOING ON HERE? NOBODY ATE DINNER?
9:55...
JINHUA MIGHT STILL TAKE ORDERS ...
hmm...
I think they're open 'til 10...
OKAY.
YOU GET ONE MINUTE TO DECIDE. MY TREAT.
PIZZA
Jinhua MENU Chinese takeaway & delivery
YOUR TREAT?!! IS THAT OKAY?!
REALLY? YOU'LL PAY FOR US?!
WHAAT ?
Maya-ma!

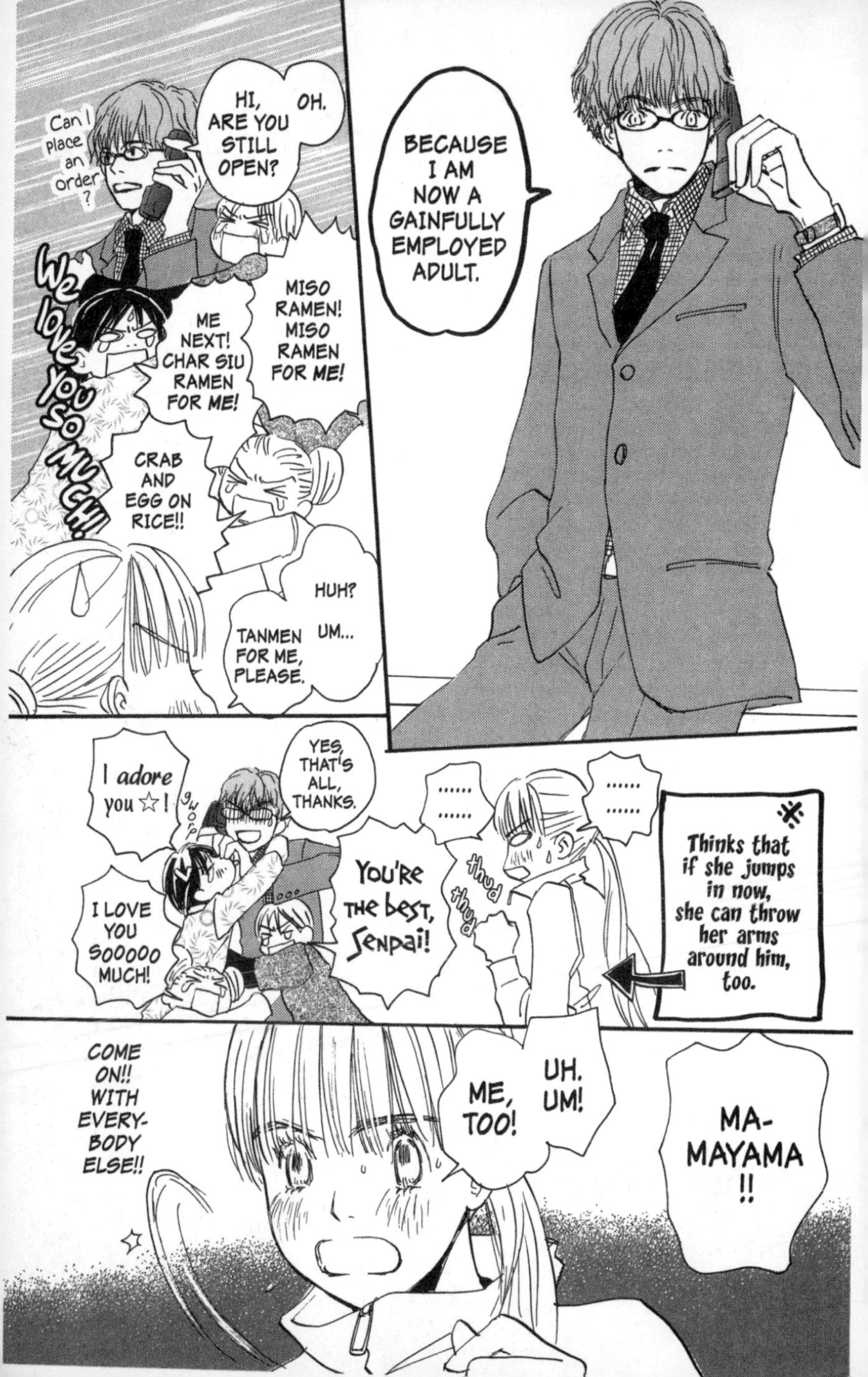
BECAUSE I AM NOW A GAINFULLY EMPLOYED ADULT.
OH.
HI, ARE YOU STILL OPEN?
Can I place an order ?
MISO RAMEN! MISO RAMEN FOR ME!
ME NEXT! CHAR SIU RAMEN FOR ME!
We love you so much!!
CRAB AND EGG ON RICE!!
HUH?
UM...
TANMEN FOR ME, PLEASE.
※ Thinks that if she jumps in now, she can throw her arms around him, too.
....
....
thud thud
You're the best, Senpai!
YES, THAT'S ALL, THANKS.
I adore you☆!
I LOVE YOU SOOOOO MUCH!
MA-MAYAMA !!
UH. UM!
ME, TOO!
COME ON!! WITH EVERY-BODY ELSE!!

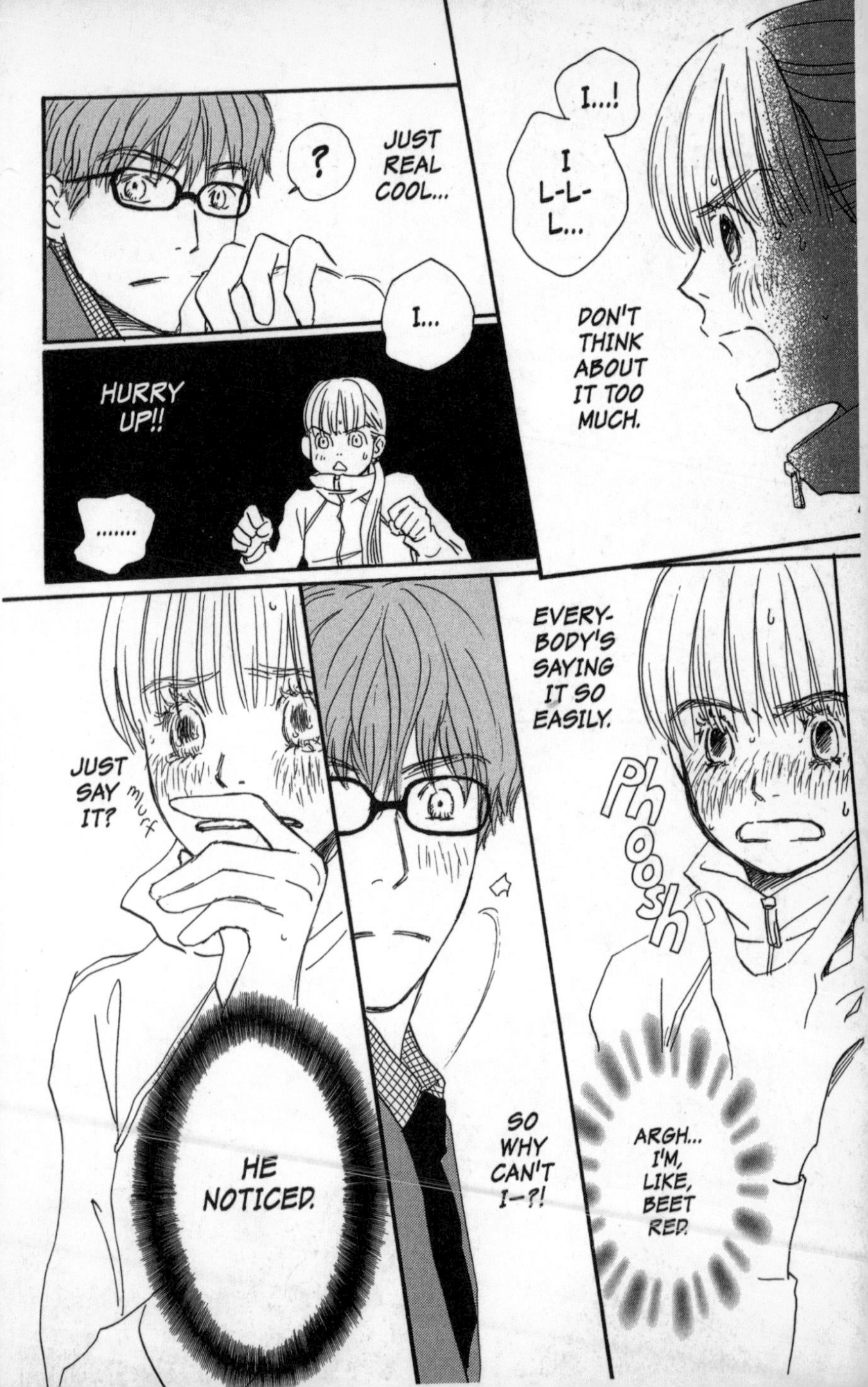
I...!
I L-L-L...
DON'T THINK ABOUT IT TOO MUCH.
?
JUST REAL COOL...
I...
HURRY UP!!
....
EVERY-BODY'S SAYING IT SO EASILY.
Phoosh
ARGH... I'M, LIKE, BEET RED.
SO WHY CAN'T I—?!
JUST SAY IT?
mlurf
HE NOTICED.

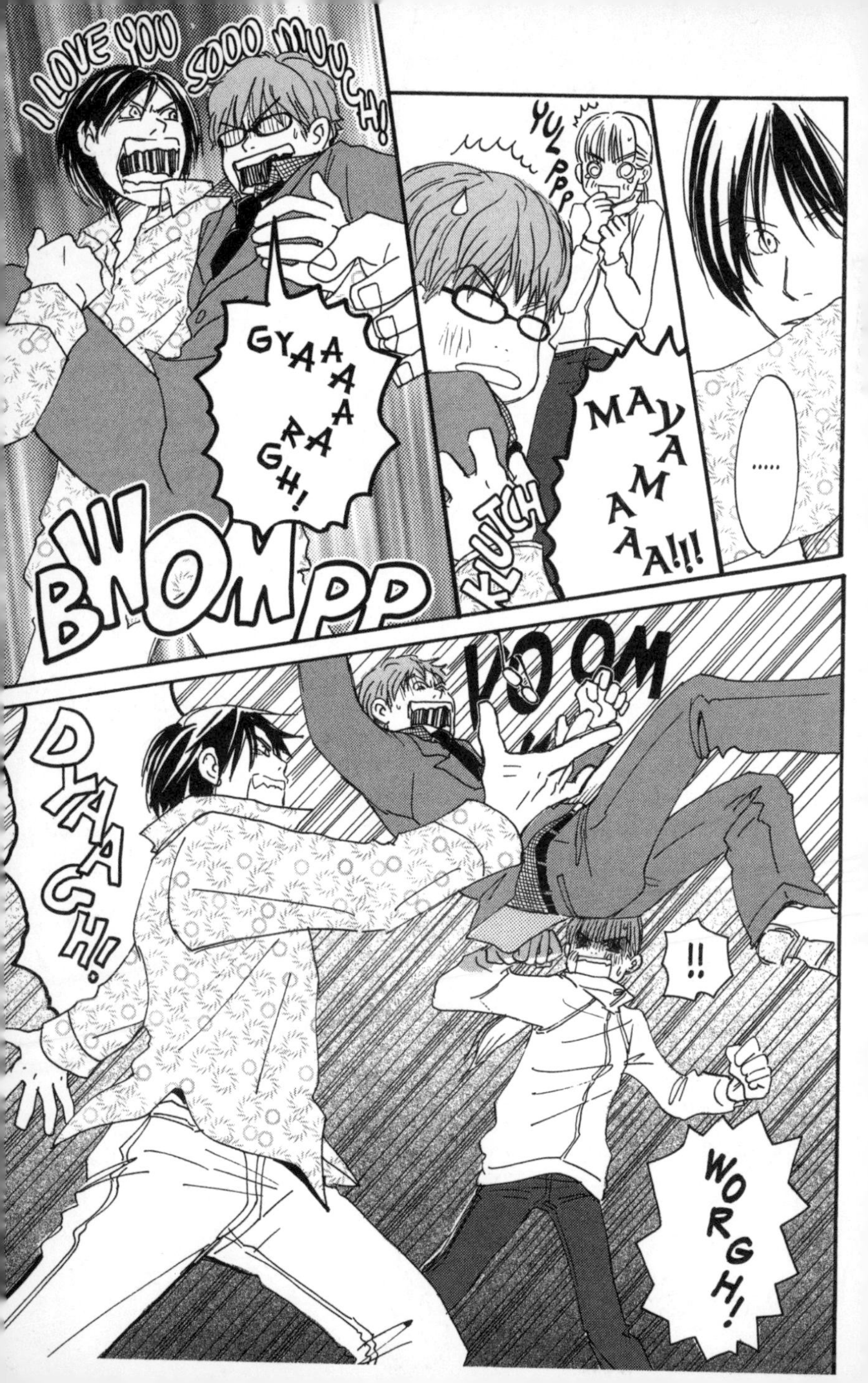
.....
YULPPP
MAYAMAAAA!!!
KLUTCH
I LOVE YOU SOOO MUUUCH!
GYAAAAAARAGH!
BWOMPP
VOOM
!!
WORGH!
DYAACH!

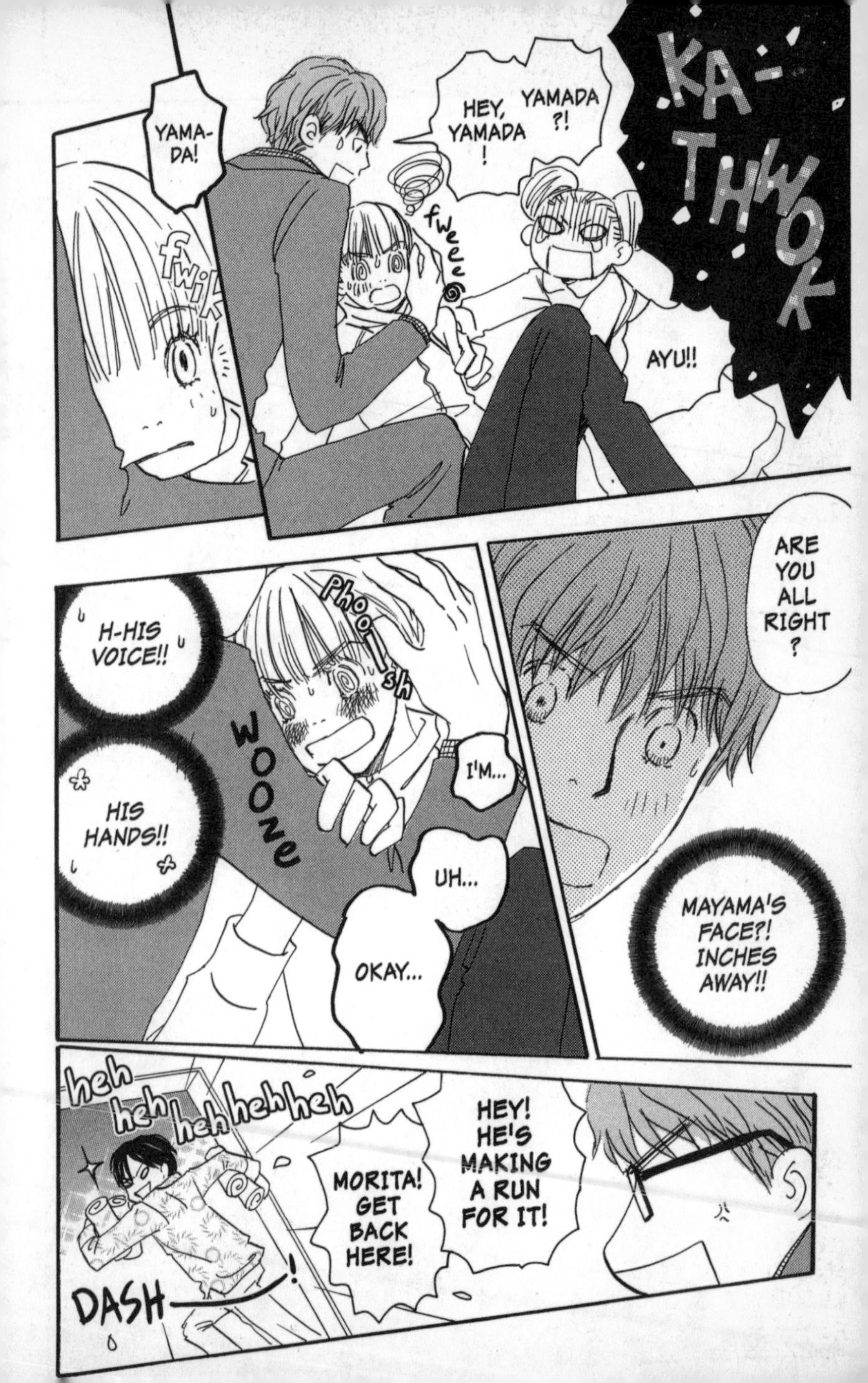
KA-THWOK
AYU!!
YAMADA?!
HEY, YAMADA!
fweee
YAMA-DA!
fwik
ARE YOU ALL RIGHT?
MAYAMA'S FACE?! INCHES AWAY!!
Phooish
H-HIS VOICE!!
HIS HANDS!!
WOOZE
I'M...
UH...
OKAY...
HEY! HE'S MAKING A RUN FOR IT!
MORITA! GET BACK HERE!
heh heh heh heh heh heh
DASH!

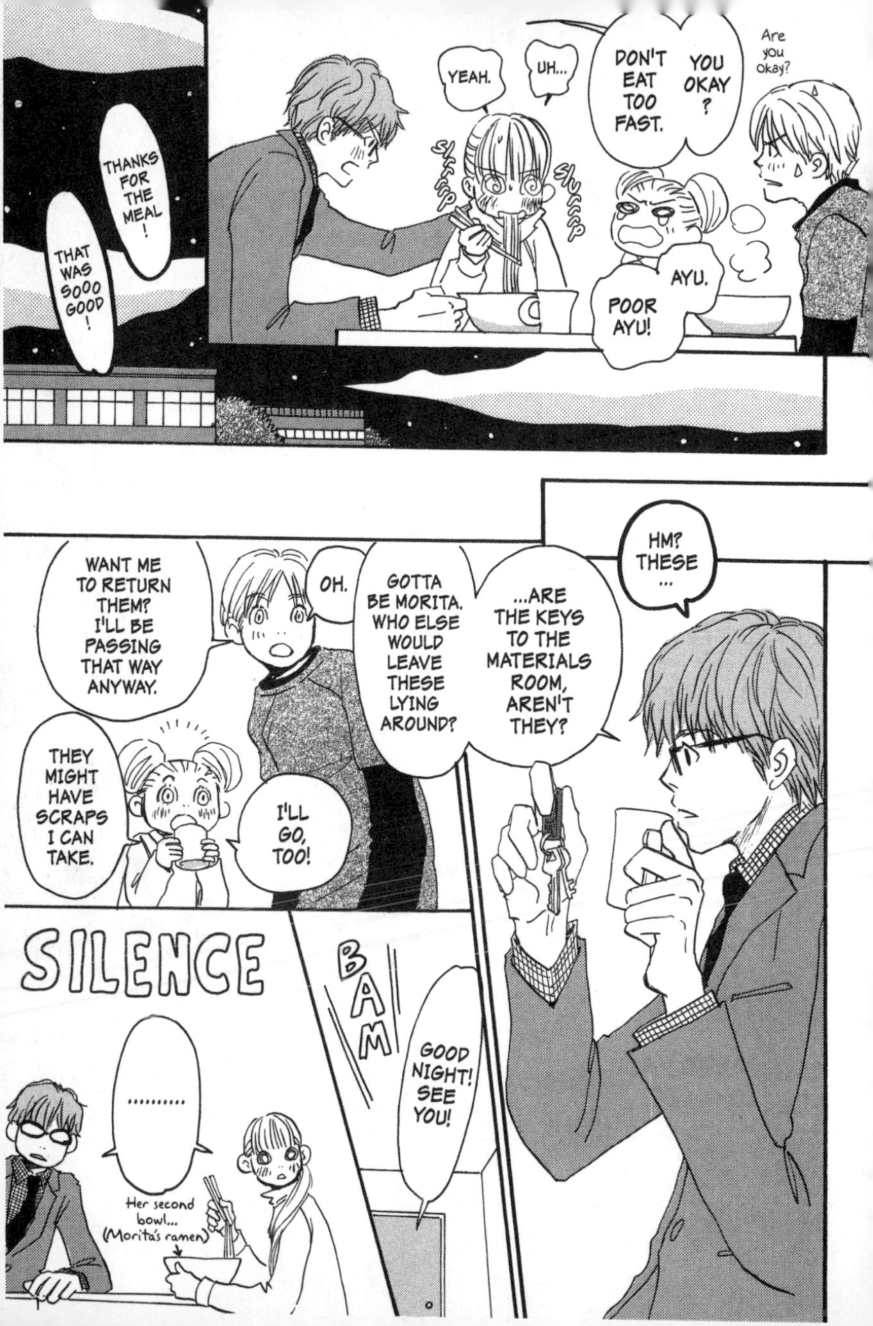
Are you okay?
YOU OKAY ?
DON'T EAT TOO FAST.
UH...
YEAH.
AYU.
POOR AYU!
THANKS FOR THE MEAL!
THAT WAS SOOO GOOD!
HM? THESE ...
...ARE THE KEYS TO THE MATERIALS ROOM, AREN'T THEY?
GOTTA BE MORITA. WHO ELSE WOULD LEAVE THESE LYING AROUND?
OH.
WANT ME TO RETURN THEM? I'LL BE PASSING THAT WAY ANYWAY.
I'LL GO, TOO!
THEY MIGHT HAVE SCRAPS I CAN TAKE.
BAM
GOOD NIGHT! SEE YOU!
SILENCE
....
Her second bowl... (Morita's ramen)

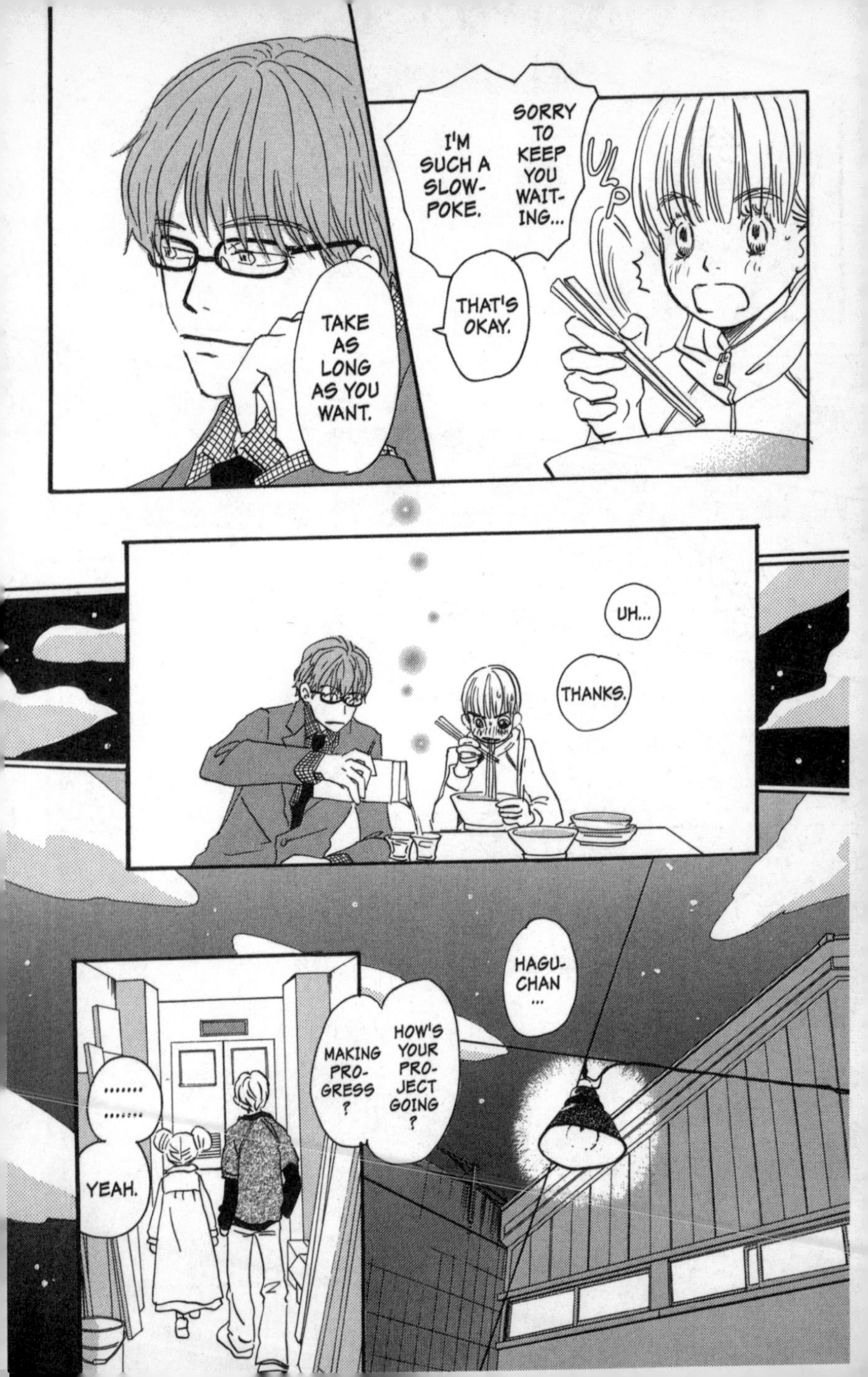
ULP
SORRY TO KEEP YOU WAIT-ING...
I'M SUCH A SLOW-POKE.
THAT'S OKAY.
TAKE AS LONG AS YOU WANT.
UH...
THANKS.
HAGU-CHAN ...
HOW'S YOUR PRO-JECT GOING?
MAKING PRO-GRESS?
....
....
YEAH.

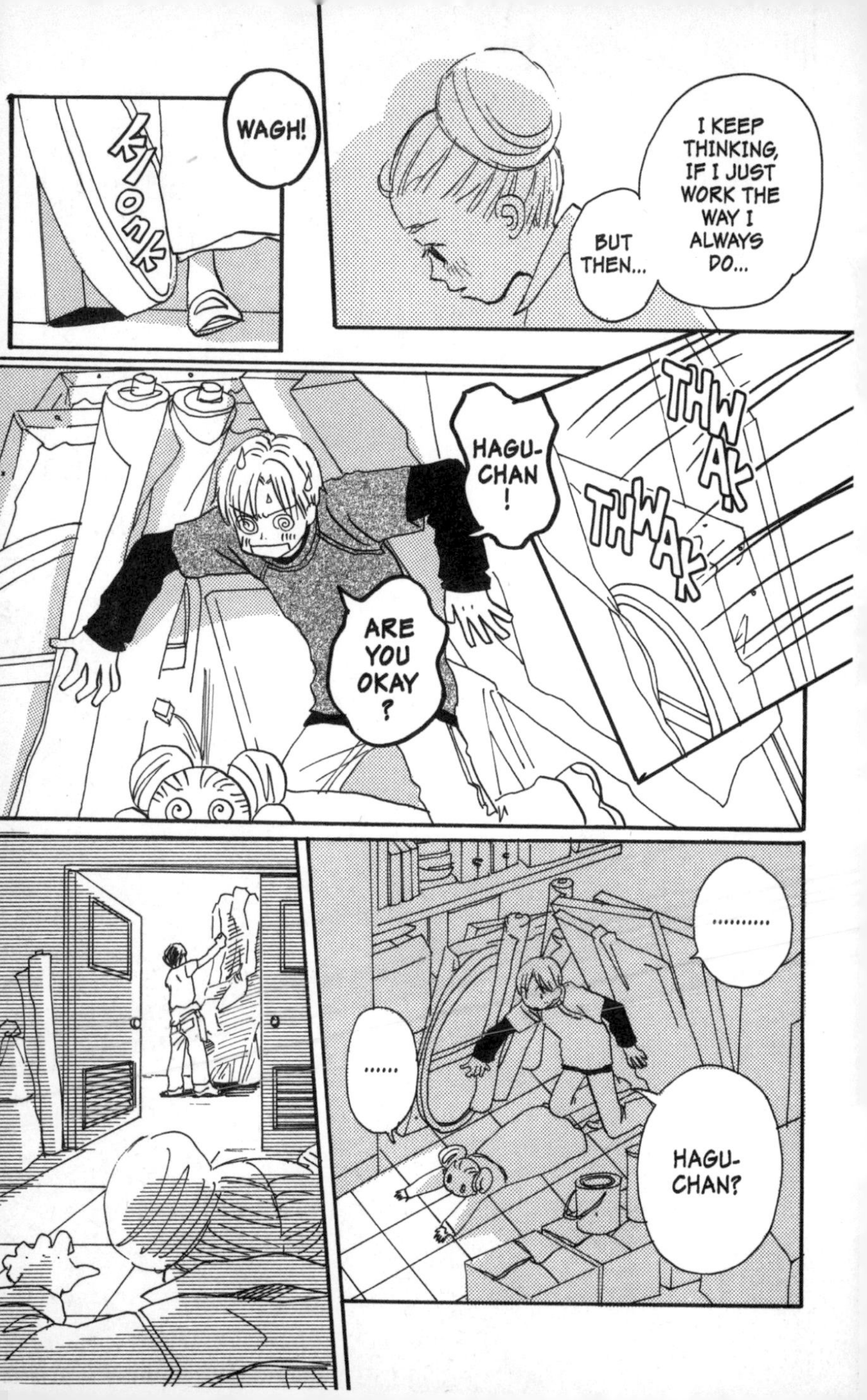
I KEEP THINKING, IF I JUST WORK THE WAY I ALWAYS DO...
BUT THEN...
KLONK
WAGH!
THWAK
THWAK
HAGU-CHAN!
ARE YOU OKAY?
....
......
HAGU-CHAN?

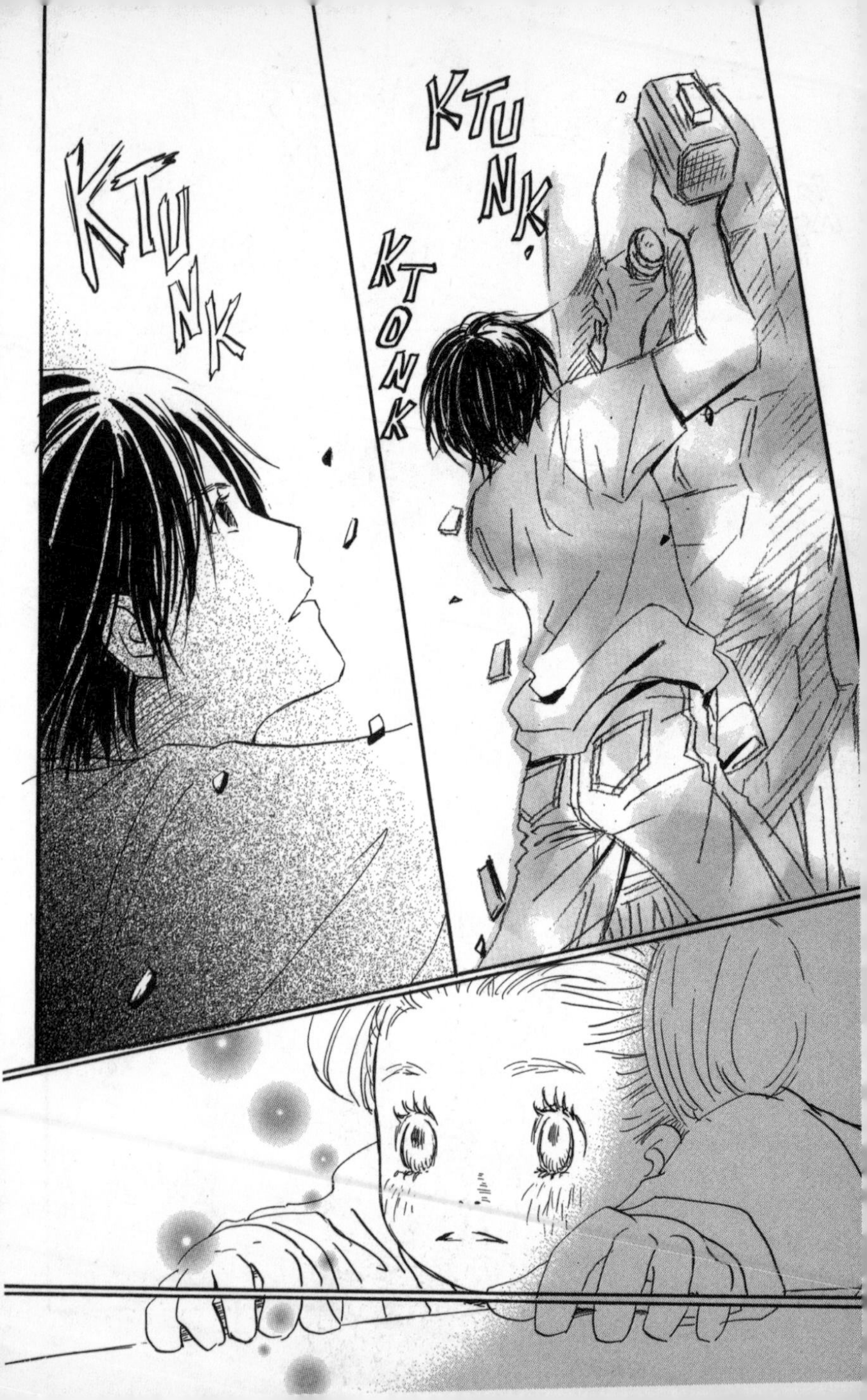
KTUNK
KTONK
KTUNK

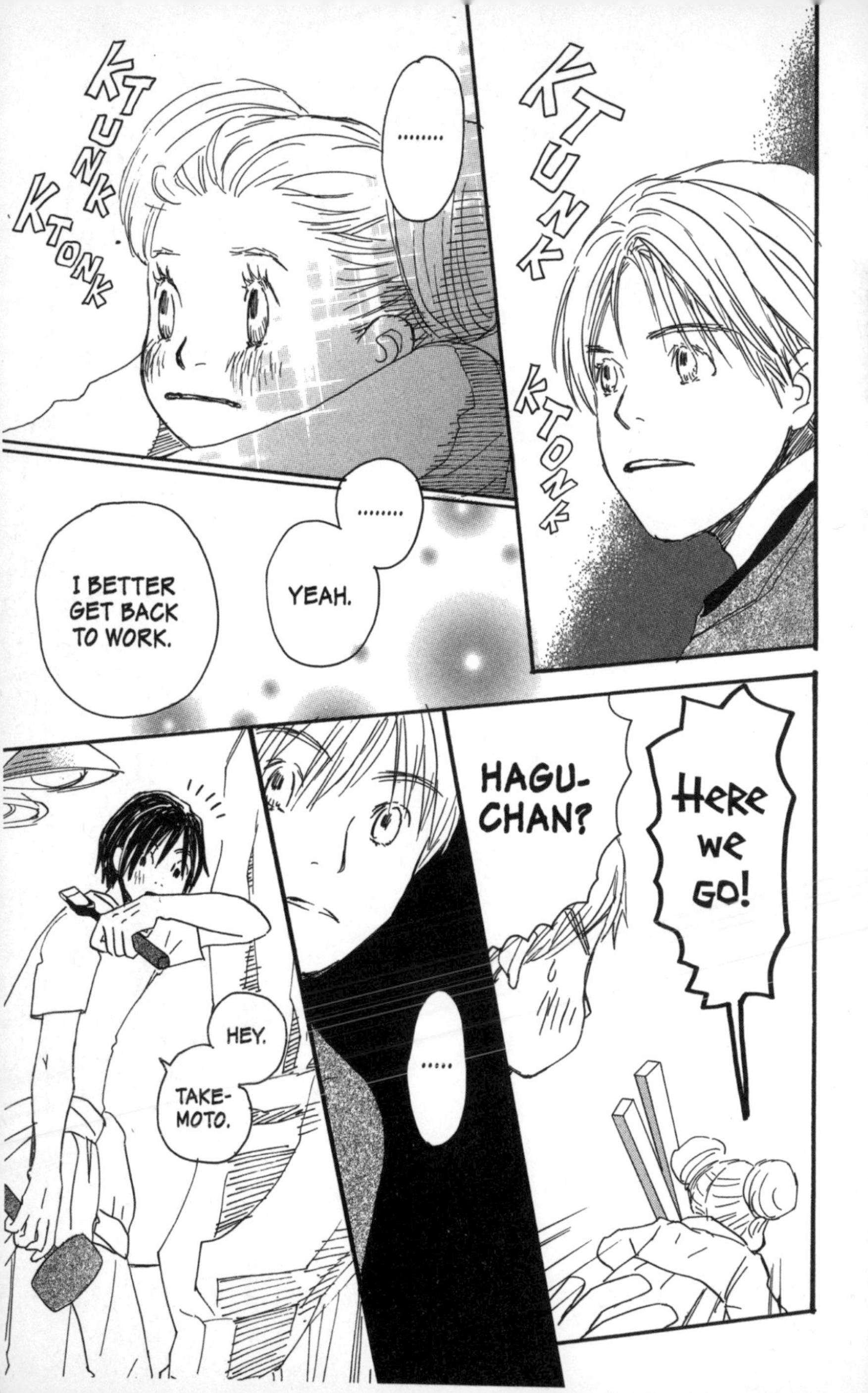
KTUNK
KTONK
KTUNK
KTONK
....
....
YEAH.
I BETTER GET BACK TO WORK.
Here we go!
HAGU-CHAN?
......
HEY.
TAKE-MOTO.

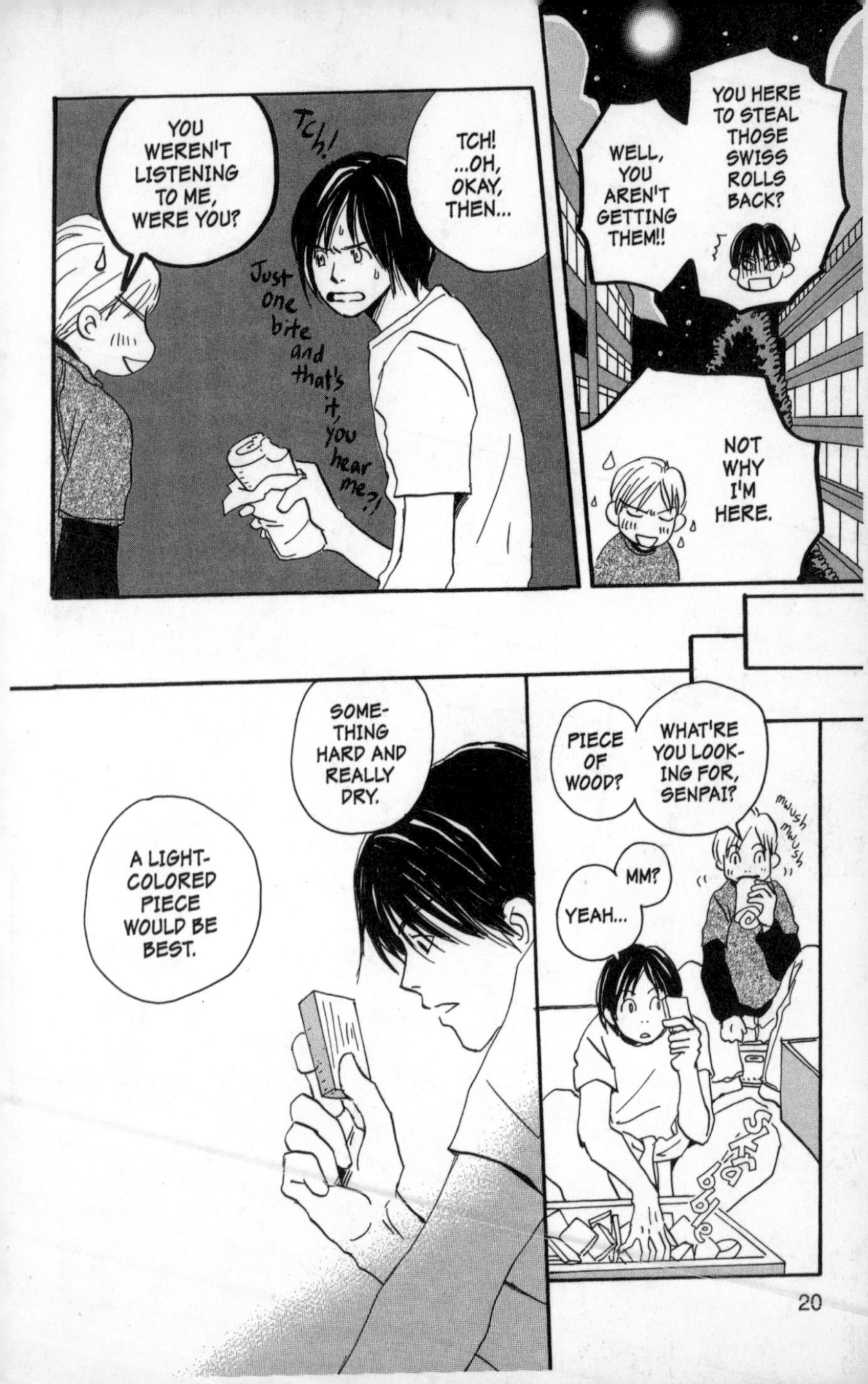
YOU HERE TO STEAL THOSE SWISS ROLLS BACK?
WELL, YOU AREN'T GETTING THEM!!
NOT WHY I'M HERE.
TCH! ...OH, OKAY, THEN...
Tch!
Just one bite and that's it, you hear me?!
YOU WEREN'T LISTENING TO ME, WERE YOU?
WHAT'RE YOU LOOKING FOR, SENPAI?
mwush mwush
PIECE OF WOOD?
MM? YEAH...
SKRabble
SOME-THING HARD AND REALLY DRY.
A LIGHT-COLORED PIECE WOULD BE BEST.

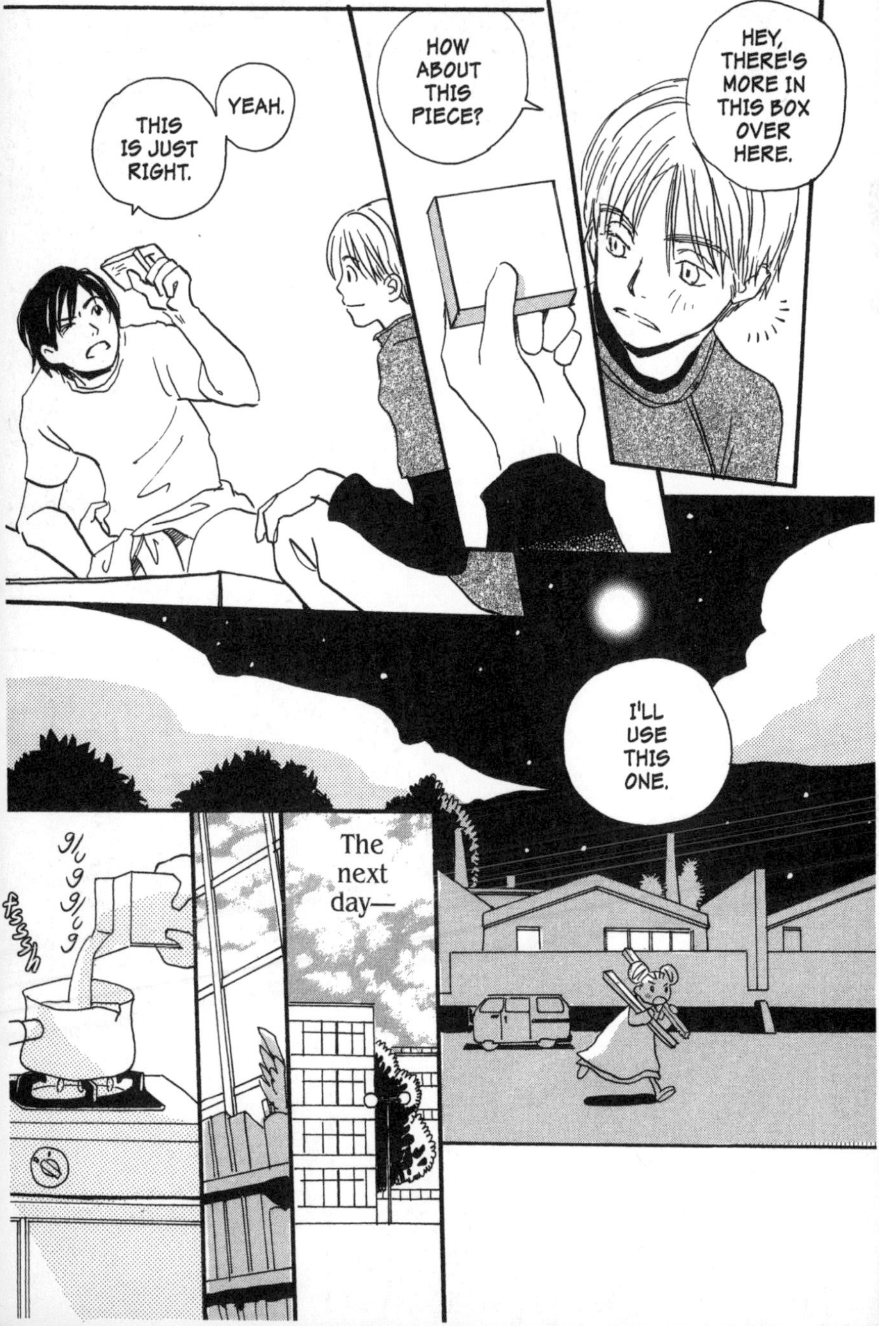
HEY, THERE'S MORE IN THIS BOX OVER HERE.
HOW ABOUT THIS PIECE?
YEAH.
THIS IS JUST RIGHT.
I'LL USE THIS ONE.
The next day—

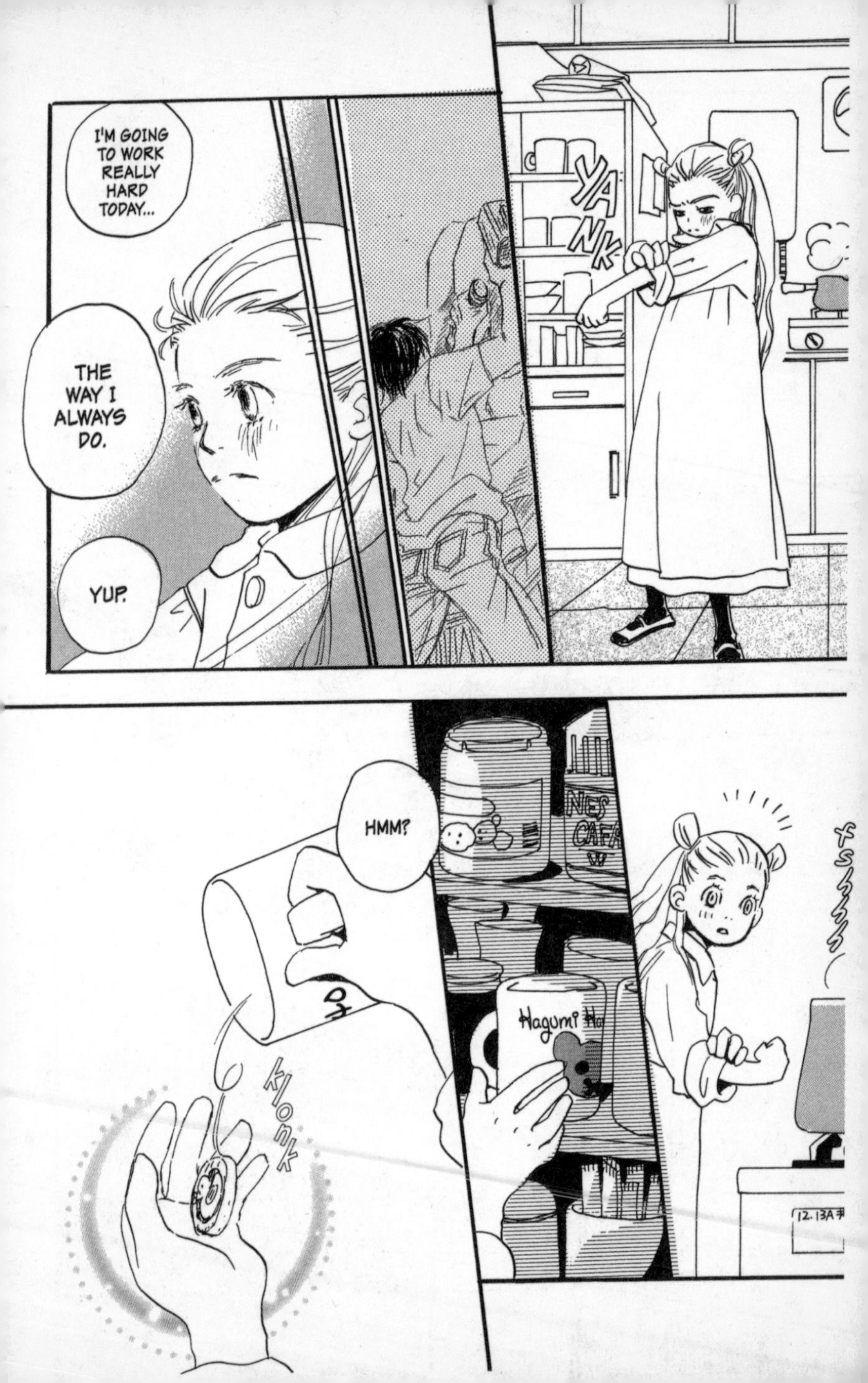
YANK
I'M GOING TO WORK REALLY HARD TODAY...
THE WAY I ALWAYS DO.
YUP.
HMM?
Hagumi
klonk

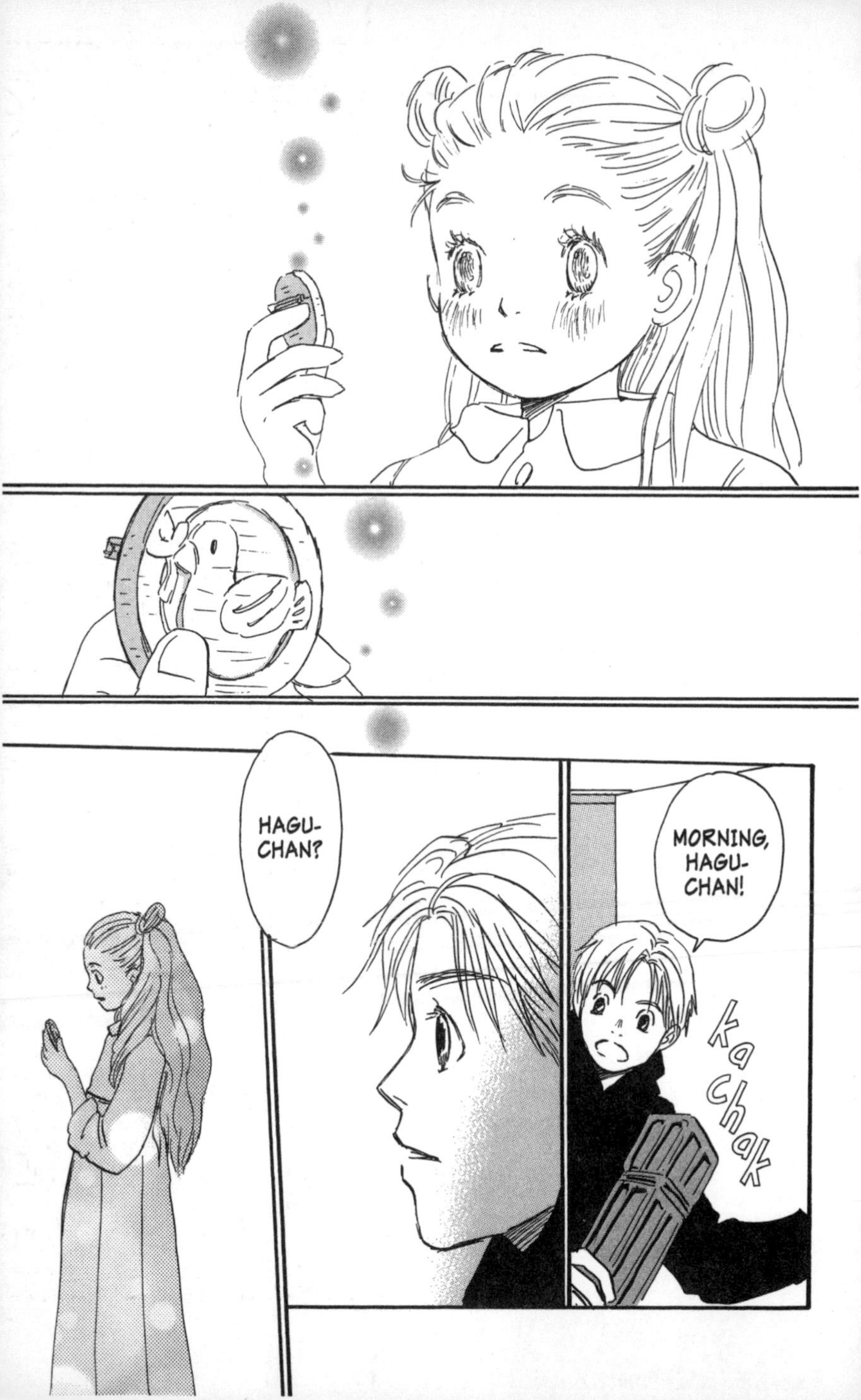
MORNING, HAGU-CHAN!
ka chak
HAGU-CHAN?

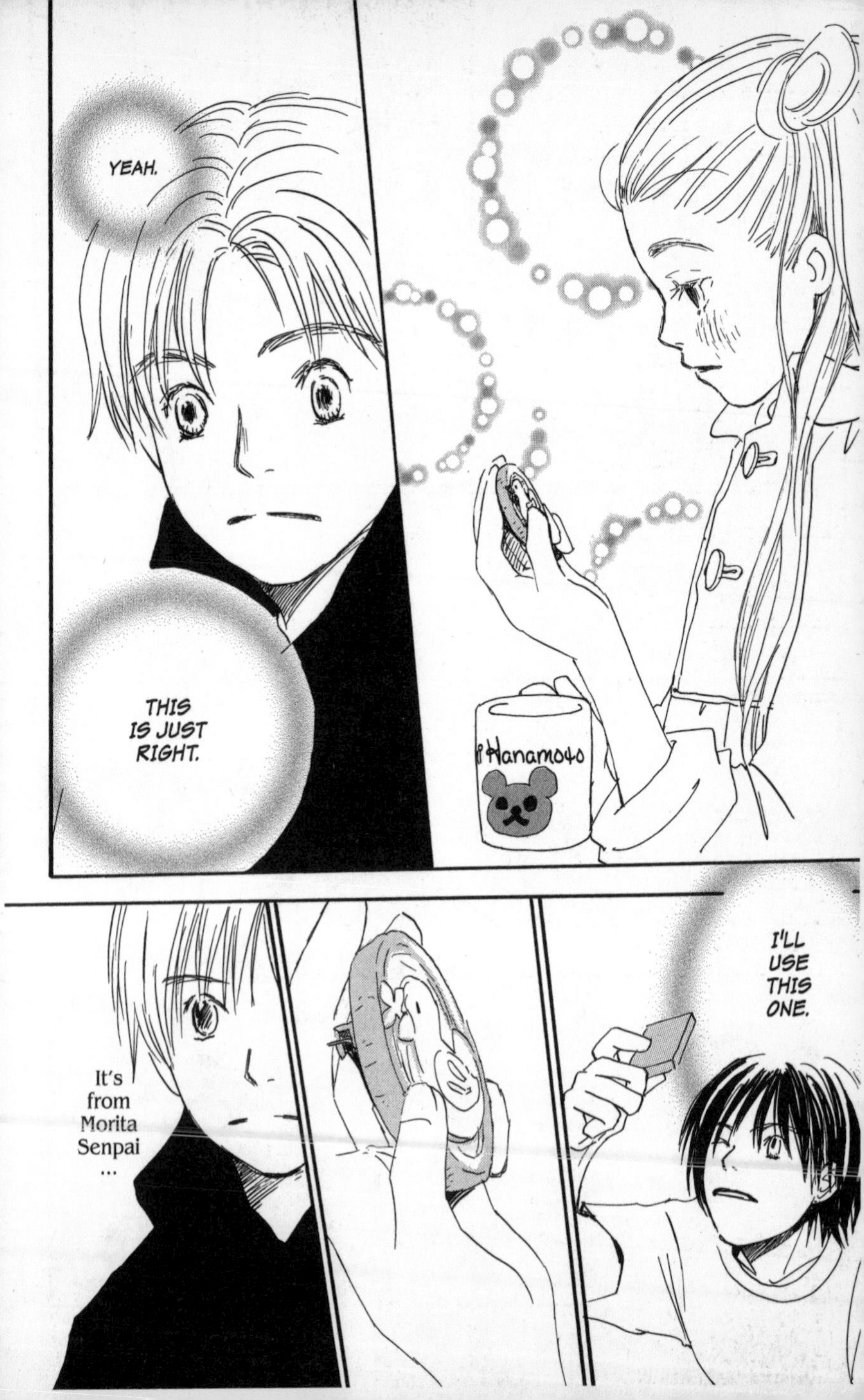
Hanamoto
YEAH.
THIS IS JUST RIGHT.
I'LL USE THIS ONE.
It's from Morita Senpai ...

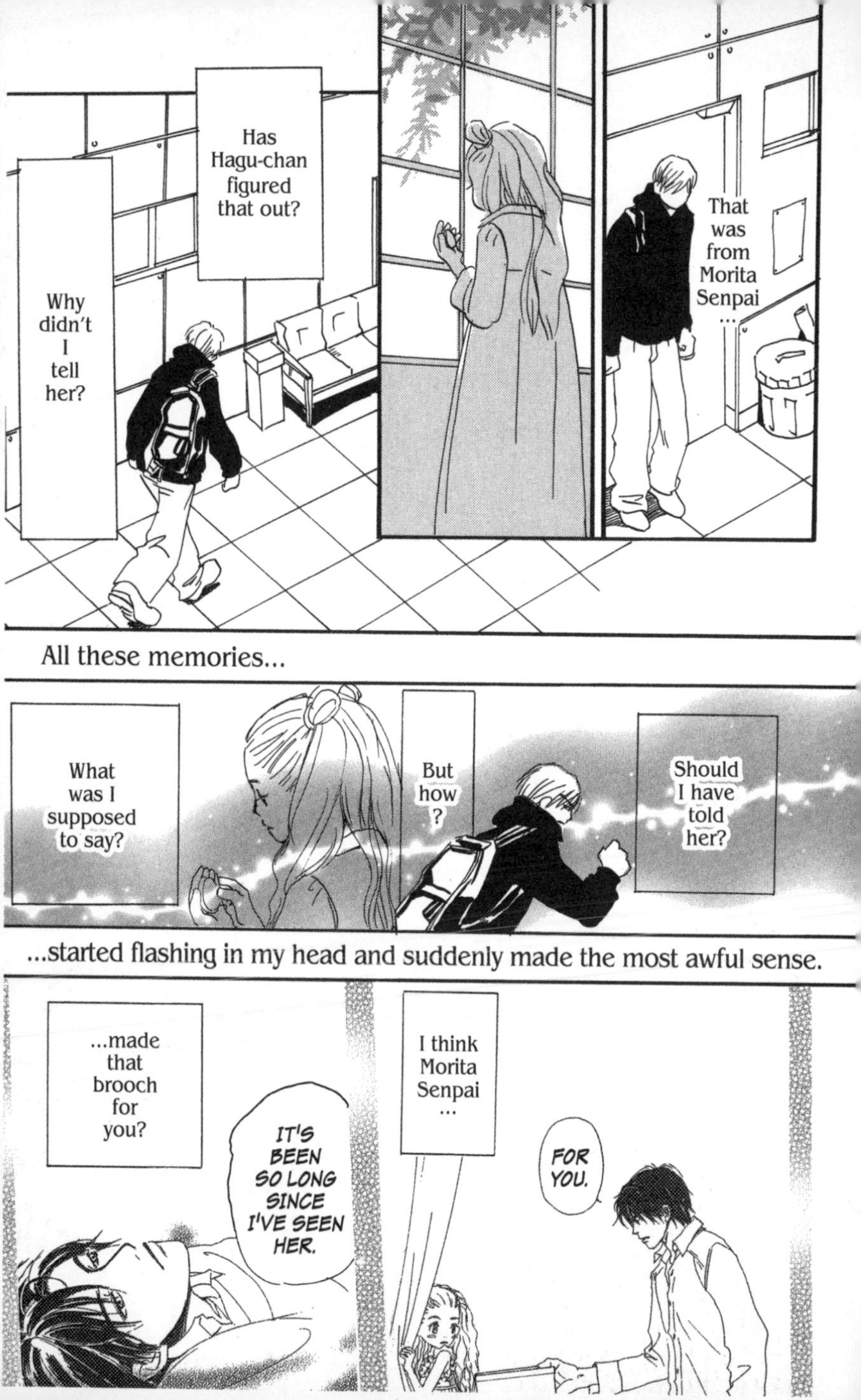
That was from Morita Senpai...
Has Hagu-chan figured that out?
Why didn't I tell her?
All these memories...
Should I have told her?
But how?
What was I supposed to say?
...started flashing in my head and suddenly made the most awful sense.
I think Morita Senpai...
FOR YOU.
...made that brooch for you?
IT'S BEEN SO LONG SINCE I'VE SEEN HER.

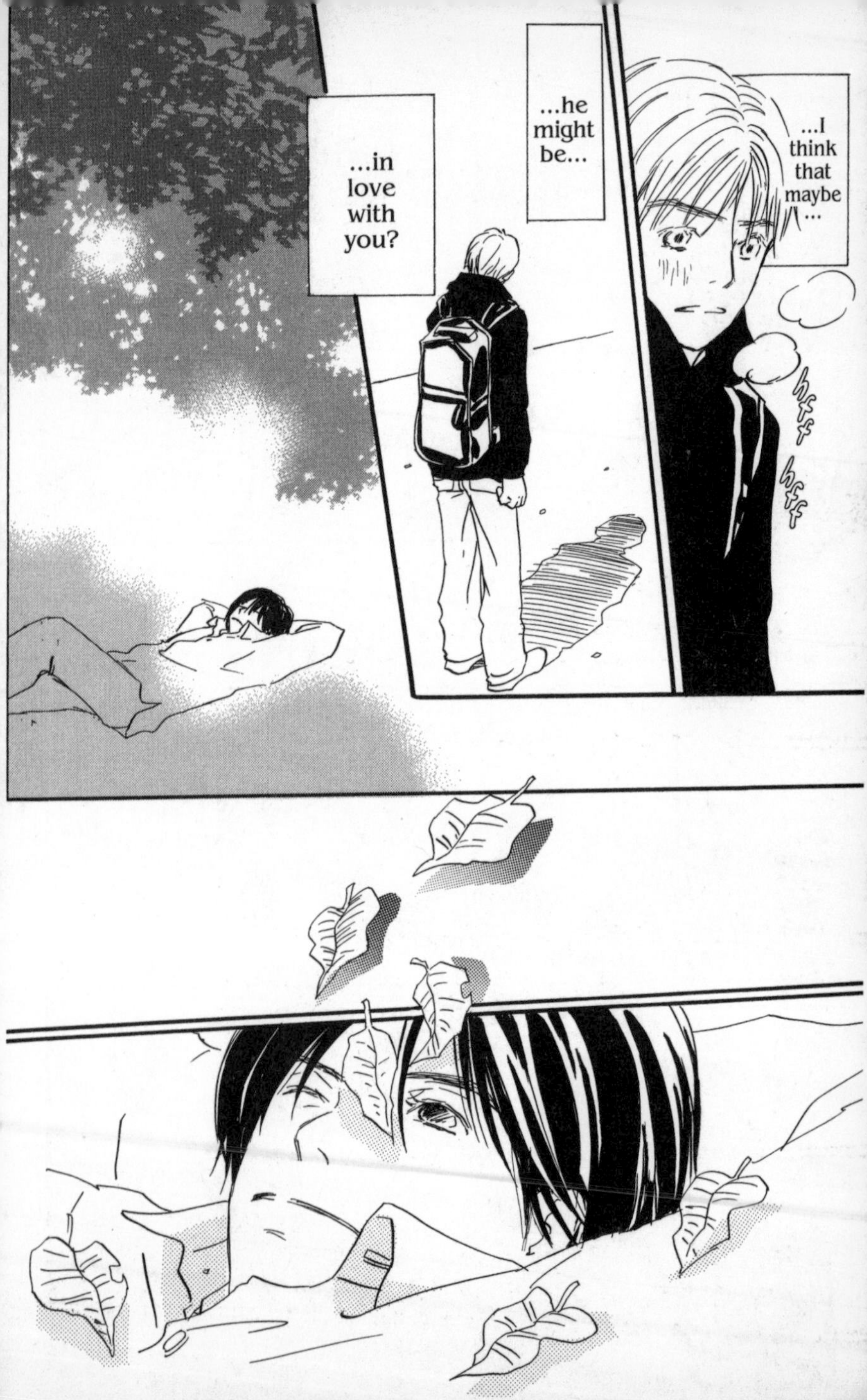
...I think that maybe...
hff hff
...he might be...
...in love with you?

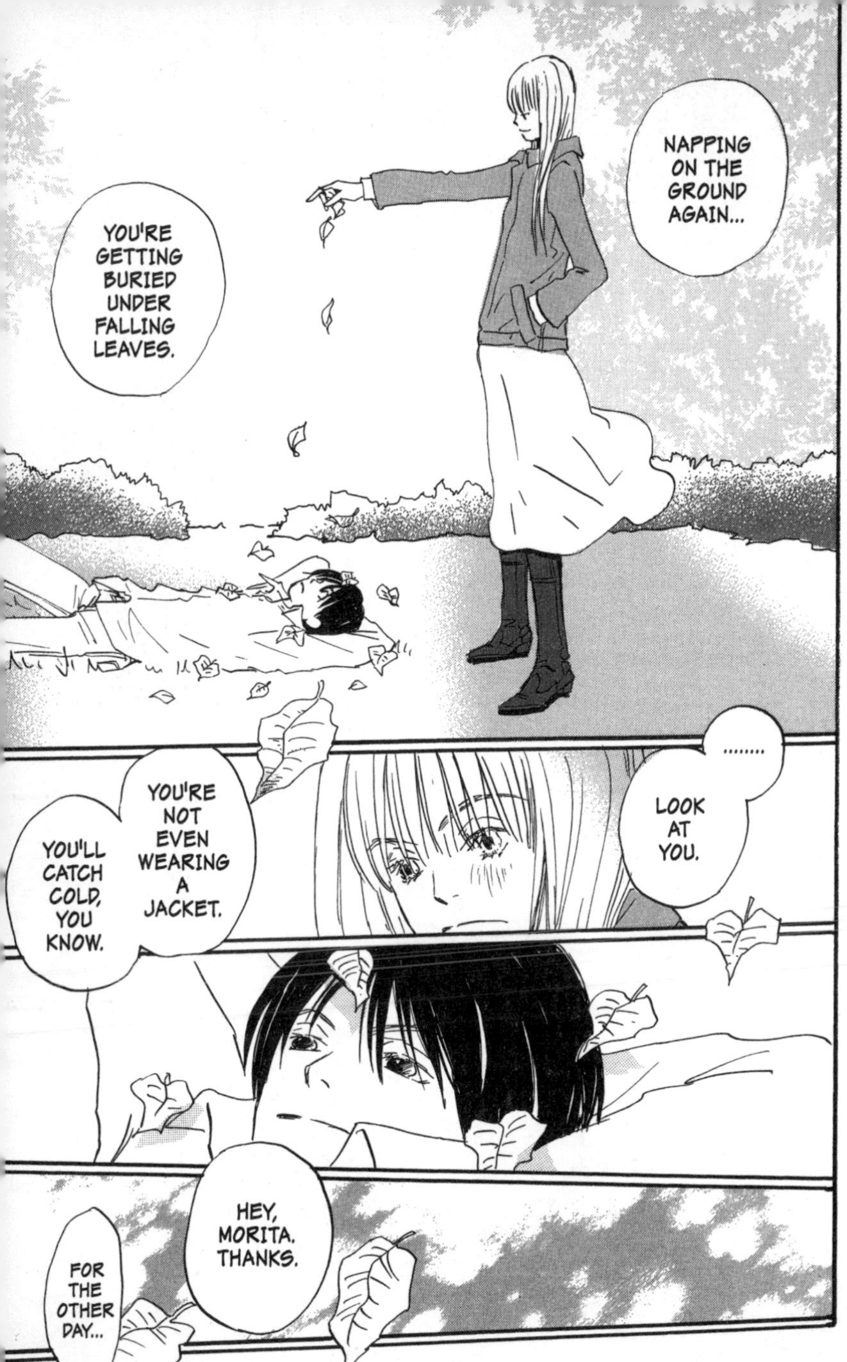
NAPPING ON THE GROUND AGAIN...
YOU'RE GETTING BURIED UNDER FALLING LEAVES.
....
LOOK AT YOU.
YOU'RE NOT EVEN WEARING A JACKET.
YOU'LL CATCH COLD, YOU KNOW.
HEY, MORITA. THANKS.
FOR THE OTHER DAY...

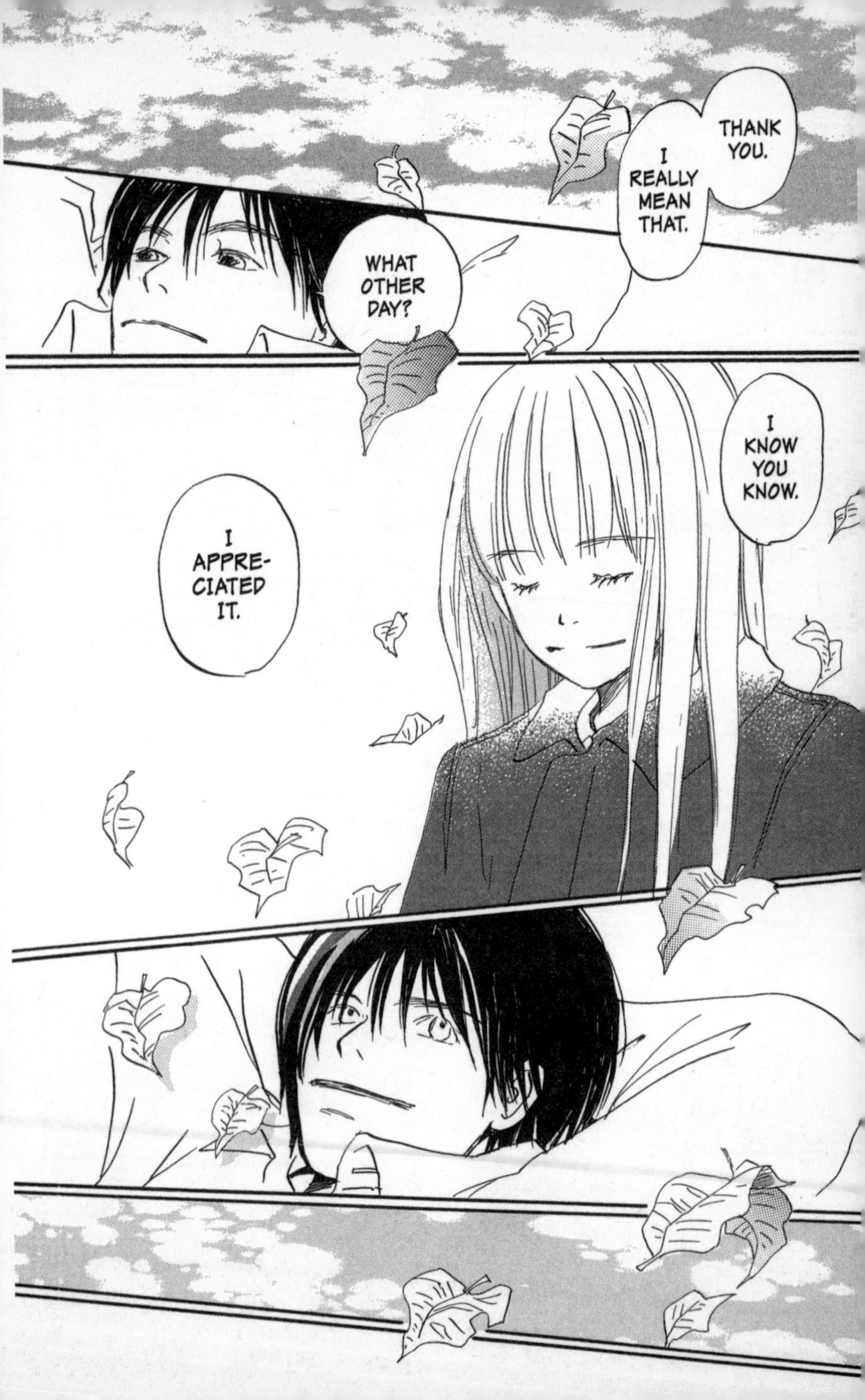
THANK YOU.
I REALLY MEAN THAT.
WHAT OTHER DAY?
I KNOW YOU KNOW.
I APPRECIATED IT.

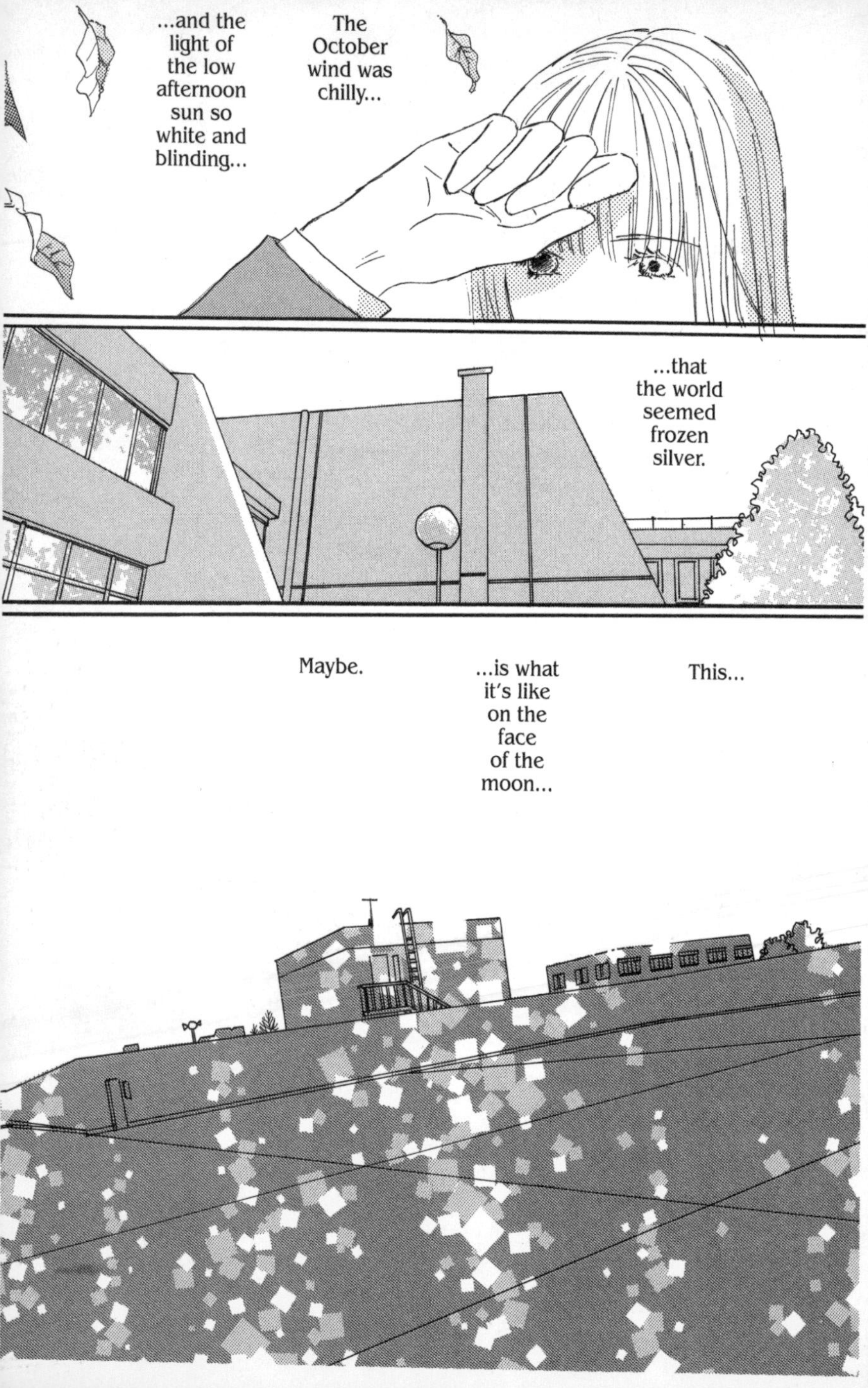
The October wind was chilly...
...and the light of the low afternoon sun so white and blinding...
...that the world seemed frozen silver.
This...
...is what it's like on the face of the moon...
Maybe.

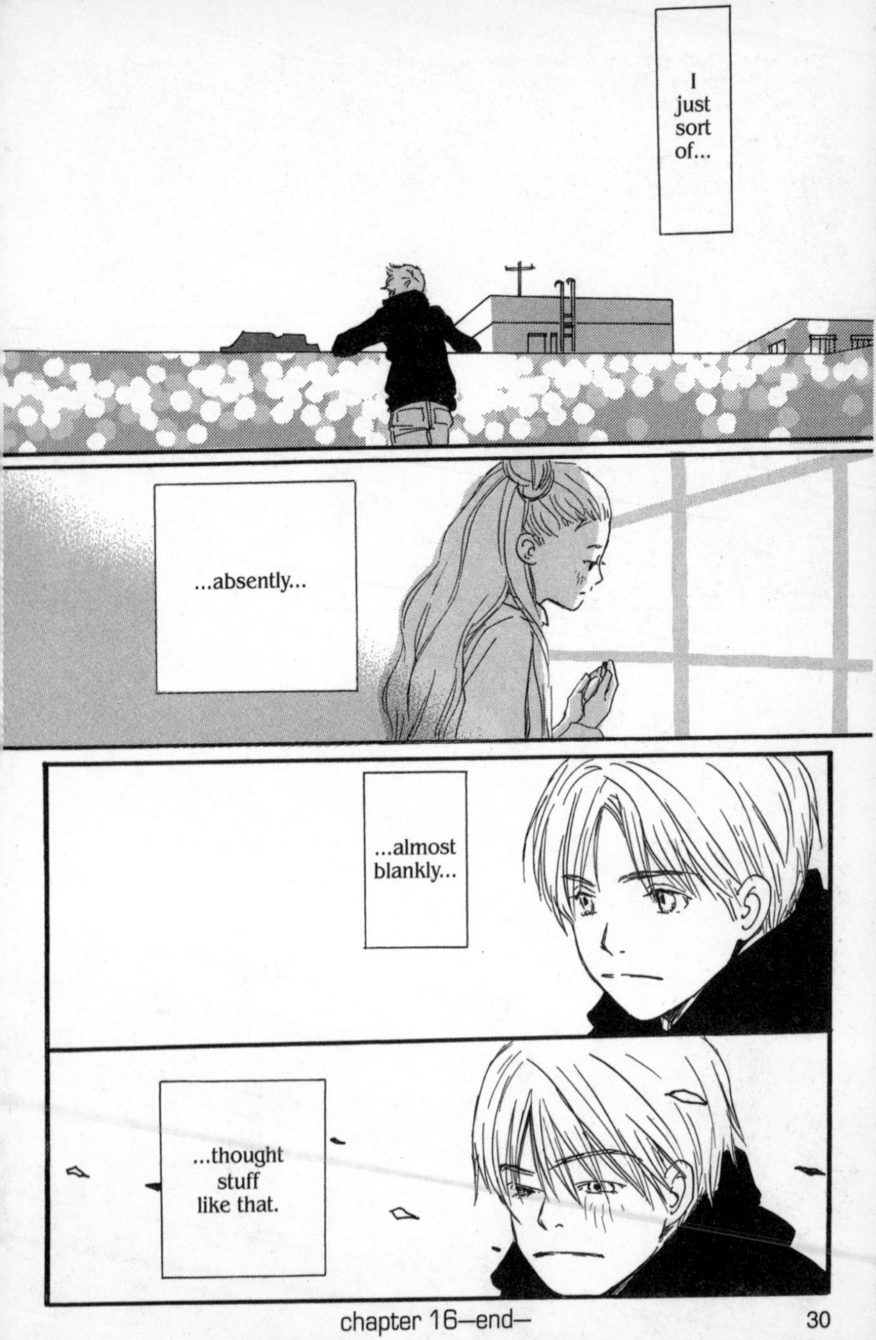
I just sort of...
...absently...
...almost blankly...
...thought stuff like that.

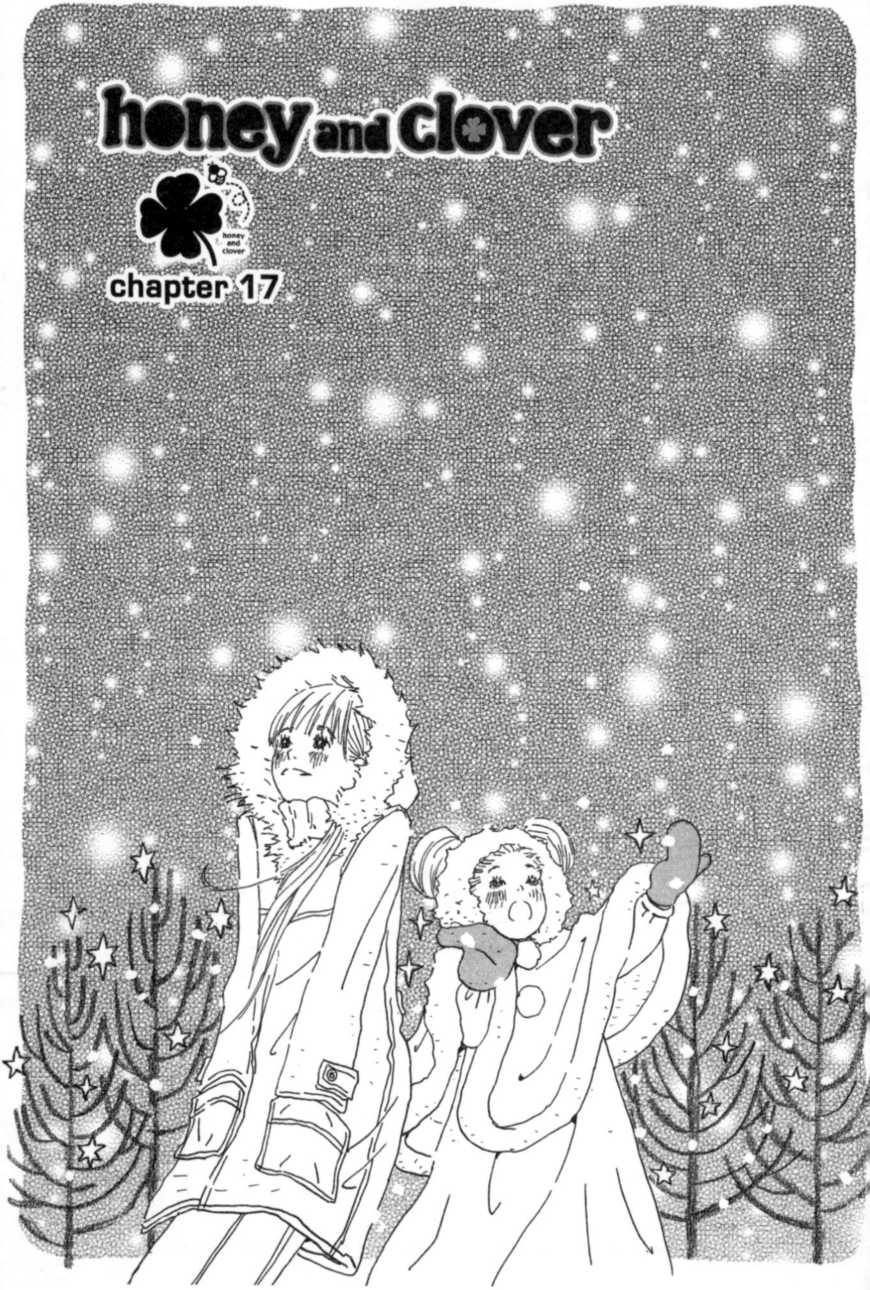
honey and clover
honey and clover
chapter 17

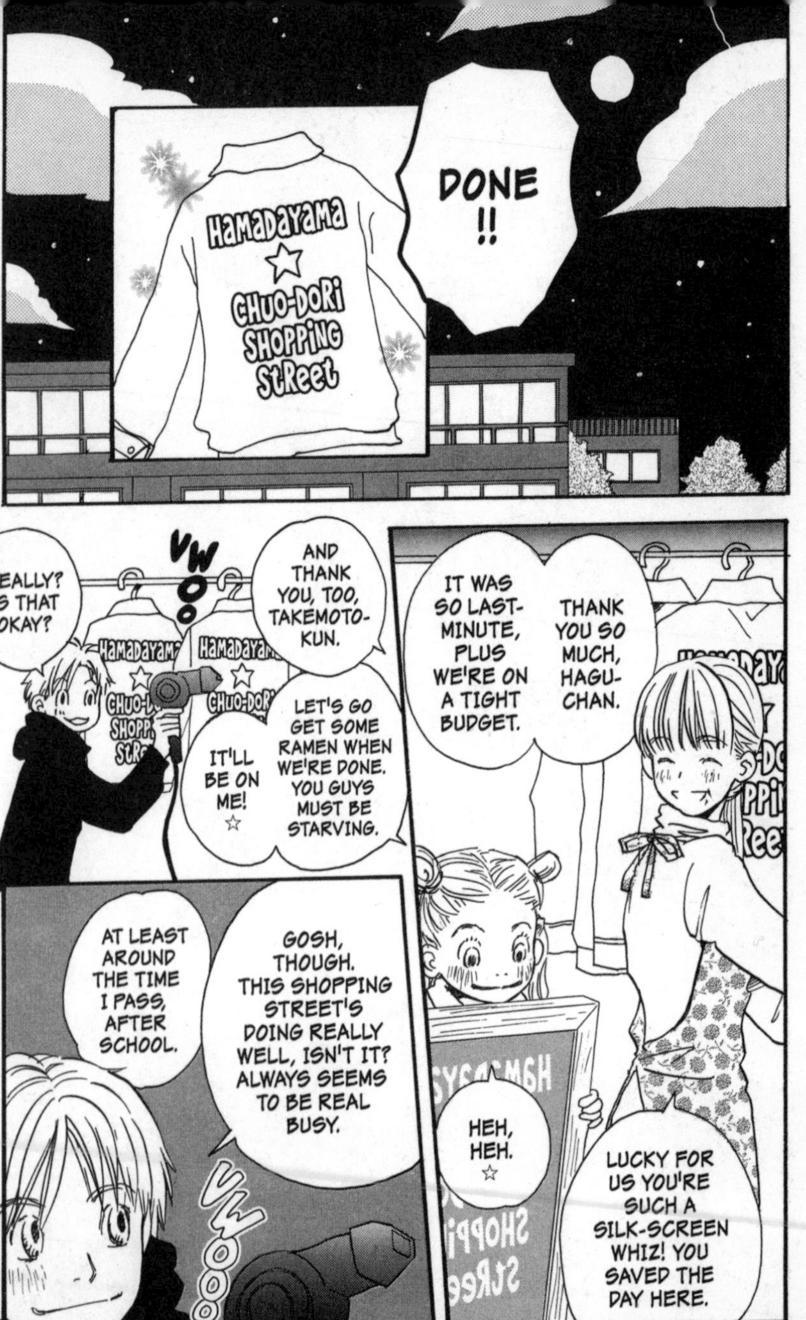
HAMADAYAMA ☆ CHUO-DORI SHOPPING STREET
DONE !!
THANK YOU SO MUCH, HAGU-CHAN.
IT WAS SO LAST-MINUTE, PLUS WE'RE ON A TIGHT BUDGET.
HEH, HEH. ☆
LUCKY FOR US YOU'RE SUCH A SILK-SCREEN WHIZ! YOU SAVED THE DAY HERE.
AND THANK YOU, TOO, TAKEMOTO-KUN.
VWOOO
LET'S GO GET SOME RAMEN WHEN WE'RE DONE. YOU GUYS MUST BE STARVING.
IT'LL BE ON ME! ☆
REALLY? IS THAT OKAY?
GOSH, THOUGH. THIS SHOPPING STREET'S DOING REALLY WELL, ISN'T IT? ALWAYS SEEMS TO BE REAL BUSY.
AT LEAST AROUND THE TIME I PASS, AFTER SCHOOL.
VWOOO

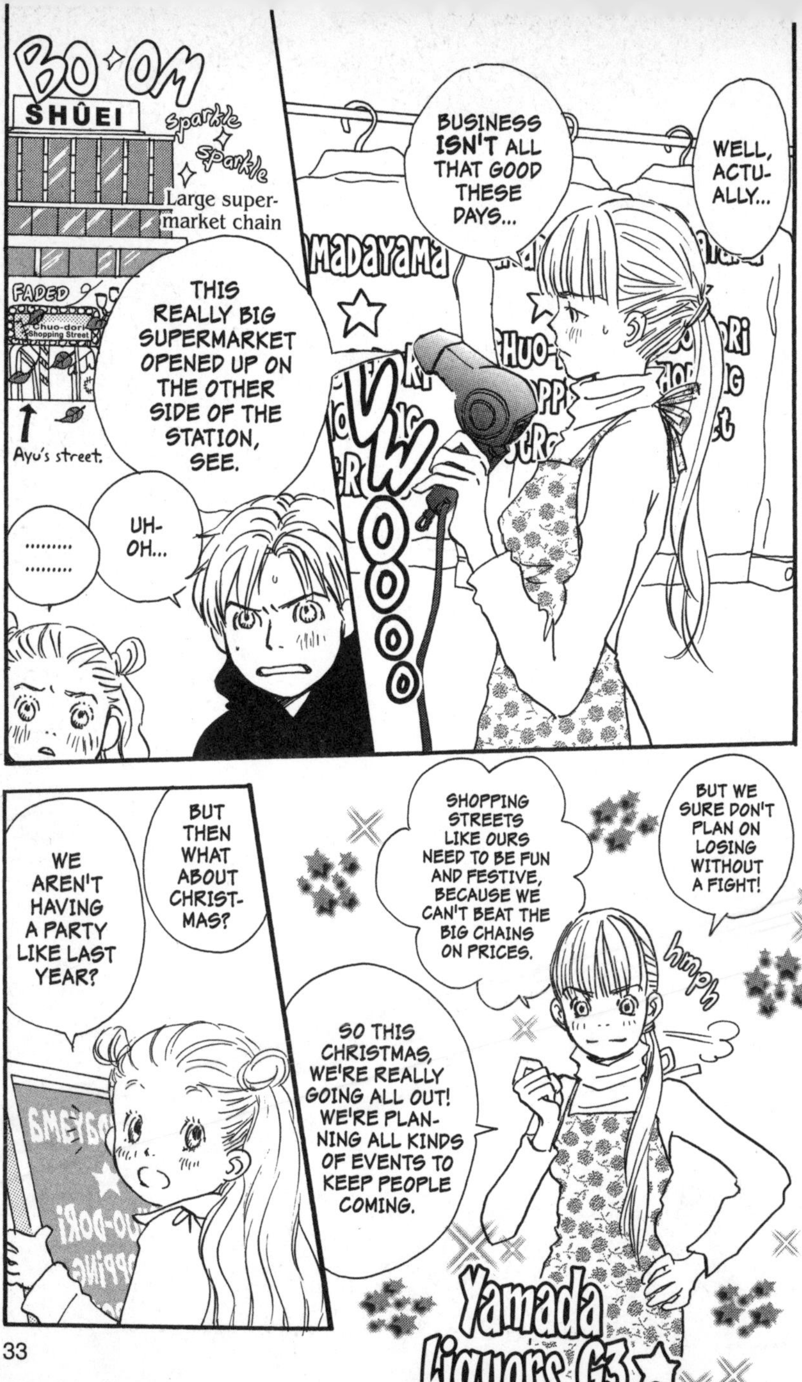
WELL, ACTU-ALLY...
BUSINESS ISN'T ALL THAT GOOD THESE DAYS...
YAMADAYAMA ★ CHUO-DORI SHOPPING STREET
VWOOOOOO
BO✧OM
SHÛEI
sparkle ✧ sparkle
Large super-market chain
FADED
Chuo-dori Shopping Street
Ayu's street.
THIS REALLY BIG SUPERMARKET OPENED UP ON THE OTHER SIDE OF THE STATION, SEE.
UH-OH...
....
....
BUT WE SURE DON'T PLAN ON LOSING WITHOUT A FIGHT!
SHOPPING STREETS LIKE OURS NEED TO BE FUN AND FESTIVE, BECAUSE WE CAN'T BEAT THE BIG CHAINS ON PRICES.
hmph
BUT THEN WHAT ABOUT CHRISTMAS?
WE AREN'T HAVING A PARTY LIKE LAST YEAR?
SO THIS CHRISTMAS, WE'RE REALLY GOING ALL OUT! WE'RE PLAN-NING ALL KINDS OF EVENTS TO KEEP PEOPLE COMING.
Yamada Liquors G3★

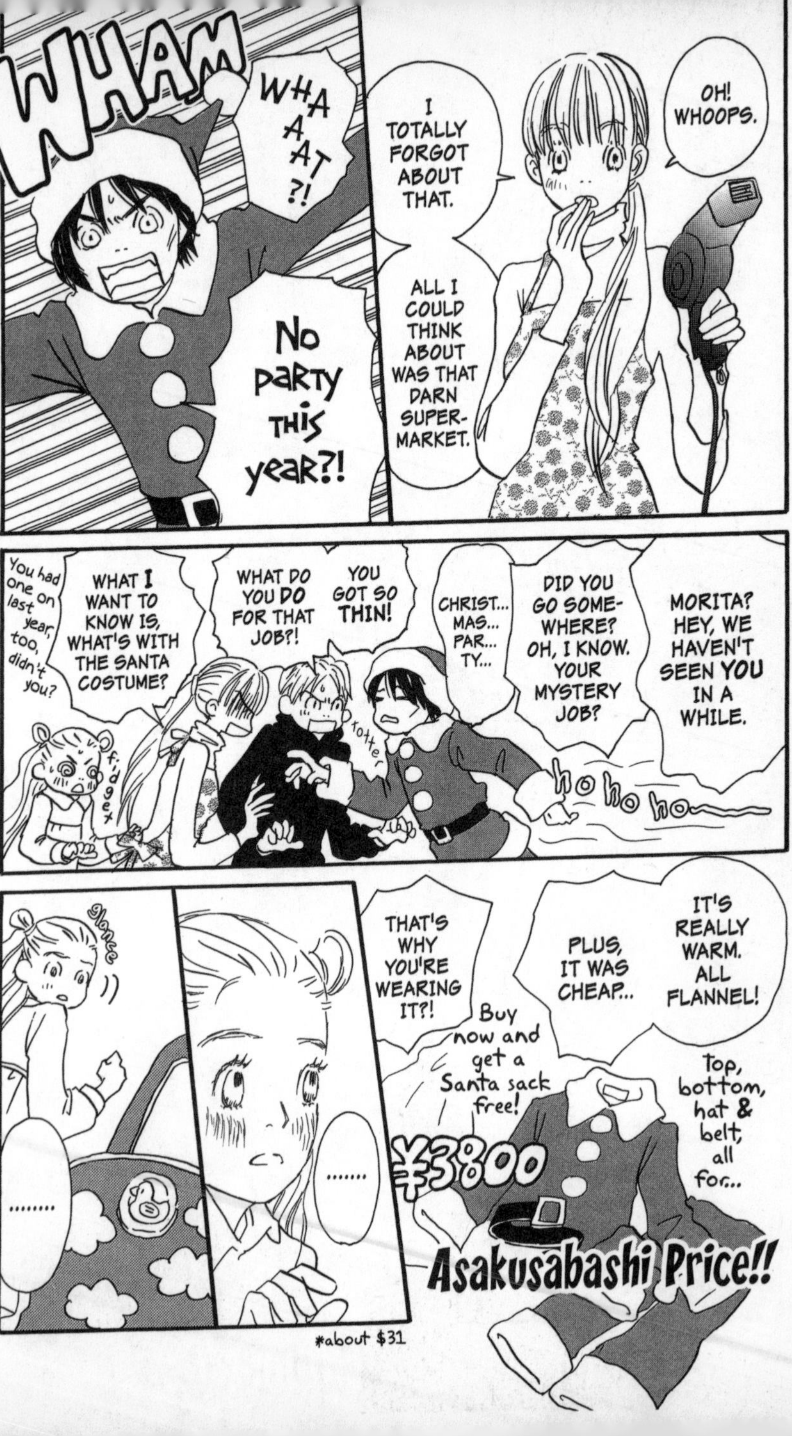
OH! WHOOPS.
I TOTALLY FORGOT ABOUT THAT.
ALL I COULD THINK ABOUT WAS THAT DARN SUPER-MARKET.
WHAM
WHA A AT?!
No party this year?!
ho ho ho——
MORITA? HEY, WE HAVEN'T SEEN YOU IN A WHILE.
DID YOU GO SOME-WHERE? OH, I KNOW. YOUR MYSTERY JOB?
CHRIST... MAS... PAR... TY...
totter
YOU GOT SO THIN!
WHAT DO YOU DO FOR THAT JOB?!
WHAT I WANT TO KNOW IS, WHAT'S WITH THE SANTA COSTUME?
You had one on last year, too, didn't you?
fidget
IT'S REALLY WARM. ALL FLANNEL!
PLUS, IT WAS CHEAP...
THAT'S WHY YOU'RE WEARING IT?!
Buy now and get a Santa sack free!
top, bottom, hat & belt, all for...
¥3800
Asakusabashi Price!!
......
glance
......

*about $31

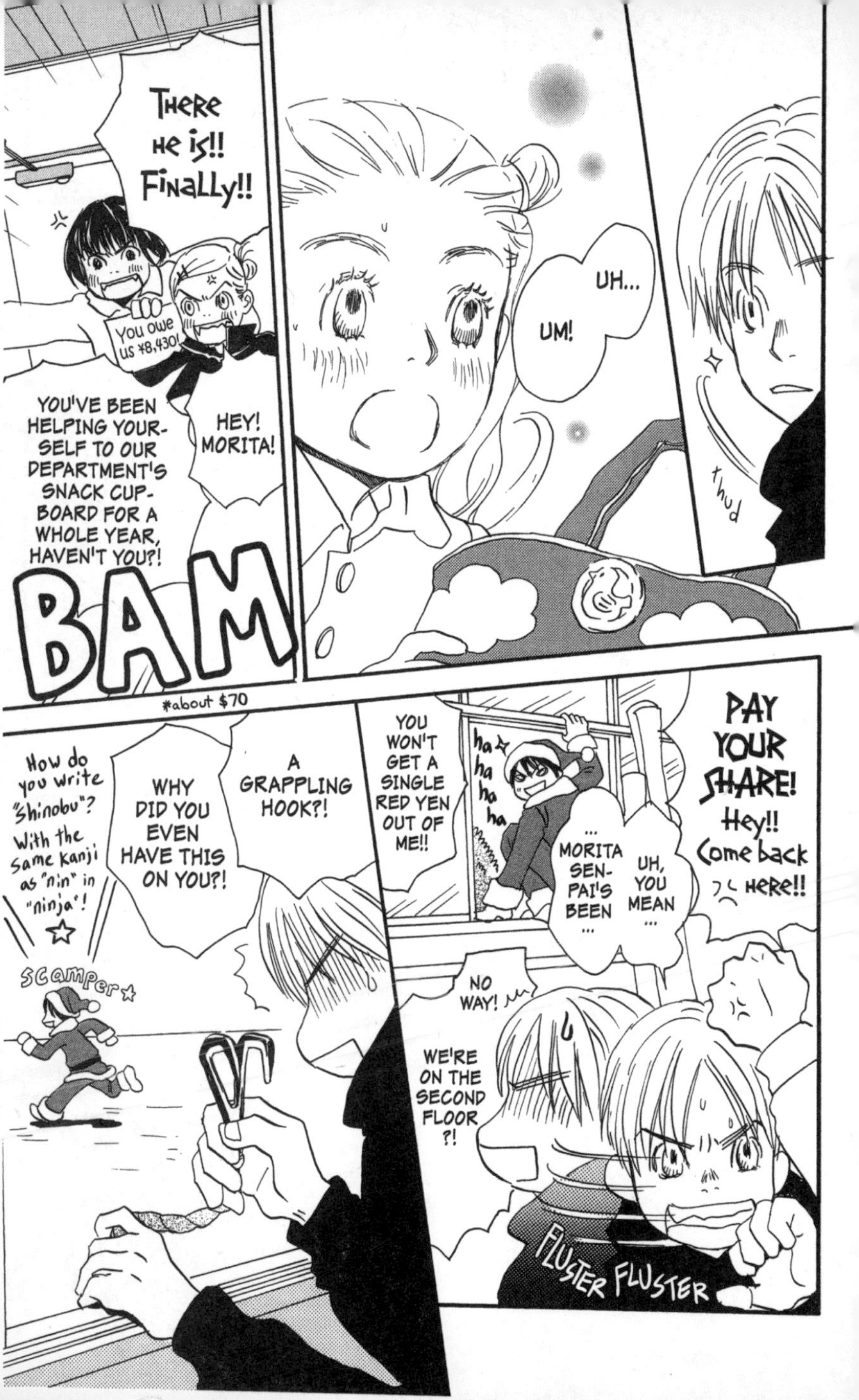
thud
UH...
UM!
There he is!! Finally!!
HEY! MORITA!
YOU'VE BEEN HELPING YOUR-SELF TO OUR DEPARTMENT'S SNACK CUP-BOARD FOR A WHOLE YEAR, HAVEN'T YOU?!
You owe us ¥8,430!
BAM
*about $70
PAY YOUR SHARE! Hey!! Come back here!!
YOU WON'T GET A SINGLE RED YEN OUT OF ME!!
ha ha ha ha
UH, YOU MEAN ...
... MORITA SEN-PAI'S BEEN ...
NO WAY!
WE'RE ON THE SECOND FLOOR ?!
FLUSTER FLUSTER
A GRAPPLING HOOK?!
WHY DID YOU EVEN HAVE THIS ON YOU?!
How do you write "Shinobu"? With the same kanji as "nin" in "ninja"! ☆
scamper

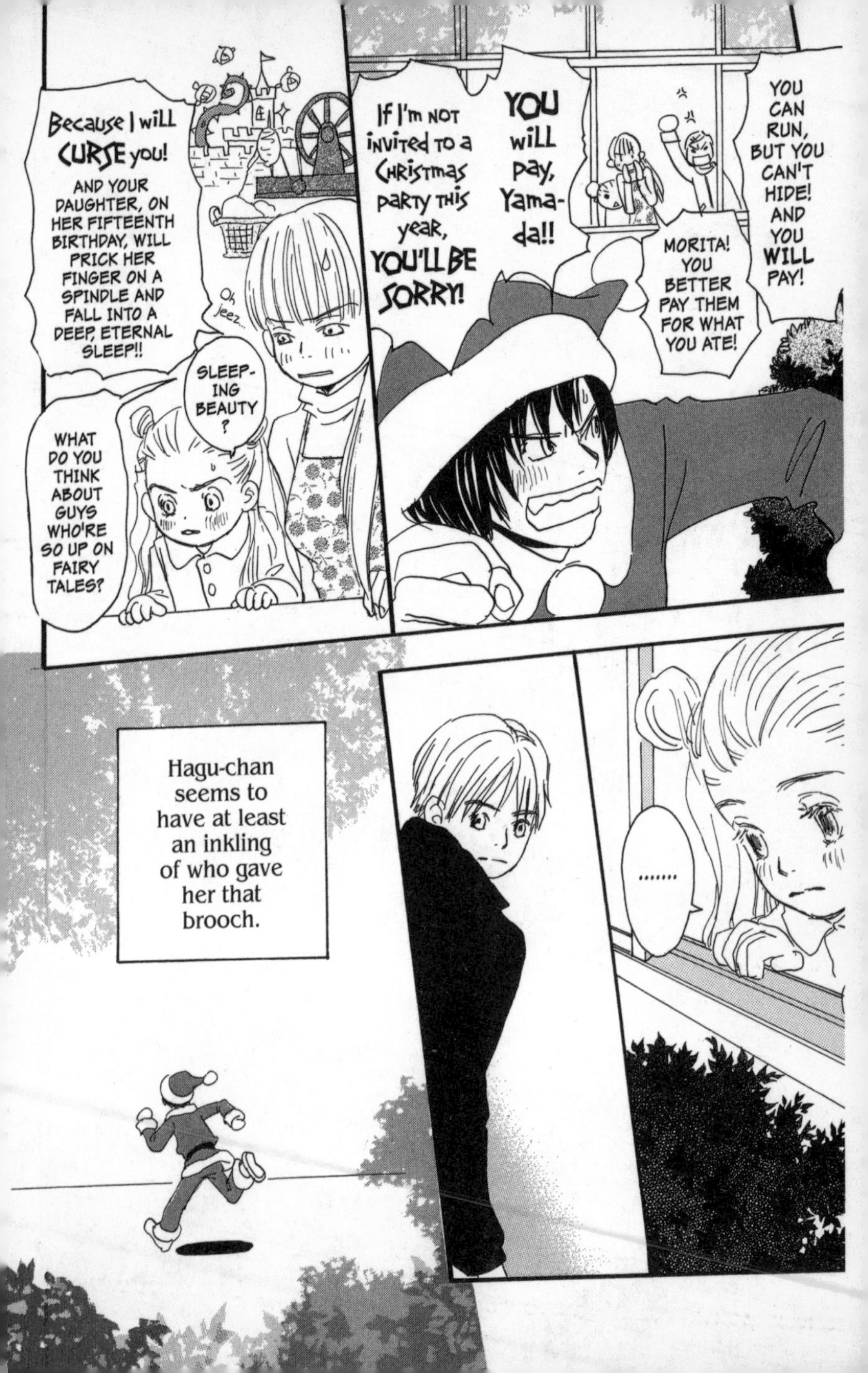
YOU CAN RUN, BUT YOU CAN'T HIDE! AND YOU WILL PAY!
MORITA! YOU BETTER PAY THEM FOR WHAT YOU ATE!
YOU will pay, Yamada!!
If I'm NOT invited to a CHRISTMAS party this year, YOU'LL BE SORRY!
Because I will CURSE you! AND YOUR DAUGHTER, ON HER FIFTEENTH BIRTHDAY, WILL PRICK HER FINGER ON A SPINDLE AND FALL INTO A DEEP, ETERNAL SLEEP!!
Oh jeez...
SLEEPING BEAUTY?
WHAT DO YOU THINK ABOUT GUYS WHO'RE SO UP ON FAIRY TALES?
....
Hagu-chan seems to have at least an inkling of who gave her that brooch.

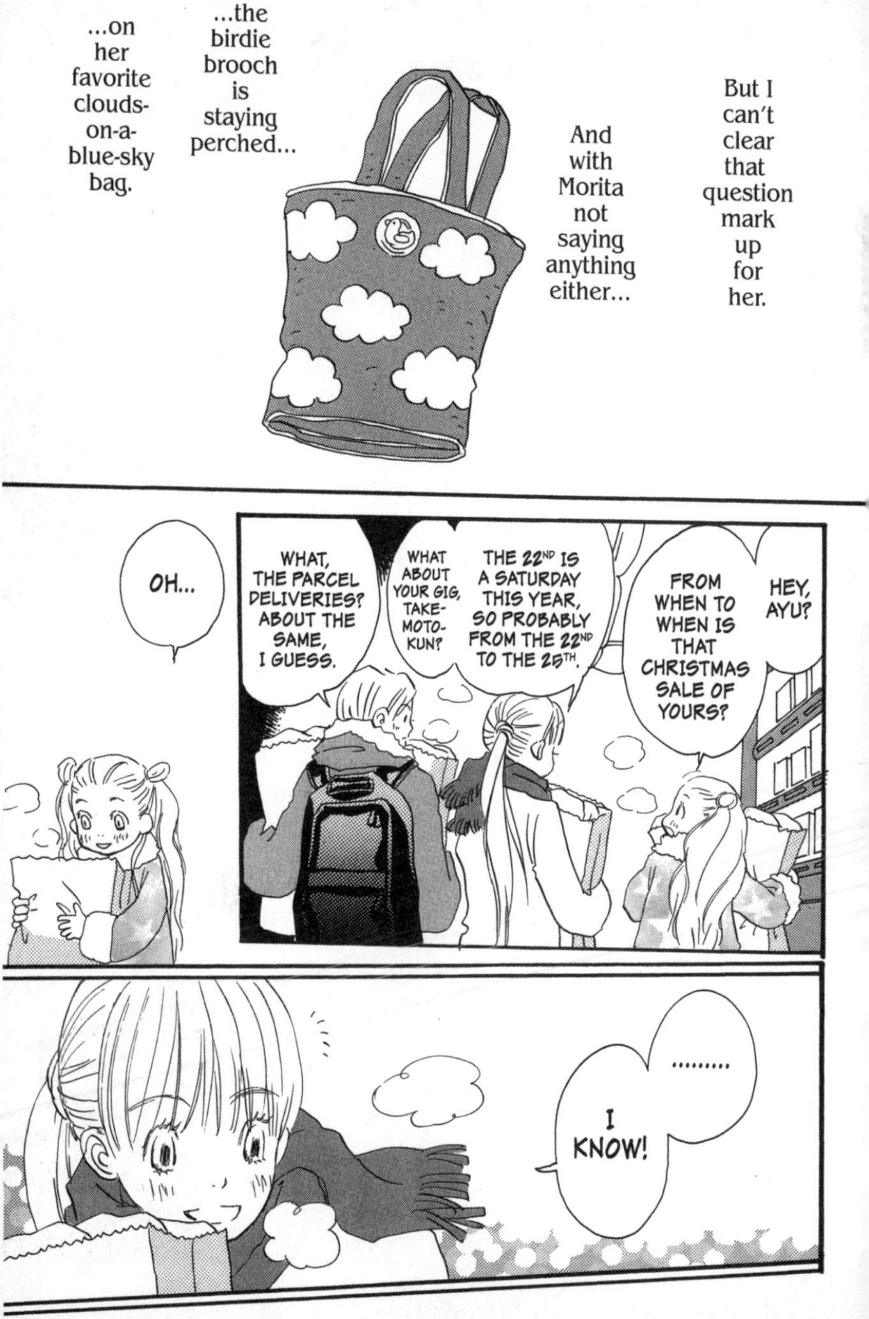

But I can't clear that question mark up for her.
And with Morita not saying anything either...
...the birdie brooch is staying perched...
...on her favorite clouds-on-a-blue-sky bag.
HEY, AYU?
FROM WHEN TO WHEN IS THAT CHRISTMAS SALE OF YOURS?
THE 22ND IS A SATURDAY THIS YEAR, SO PROBABLY FROM THE 22ND TO THE 25TH.
WHAT ABOUT YOUR GIG, TAKE-MOTO-KUN?
WHAT, THE PARCEL DELIVERIES? ABOUT THE SAME, I GUESS.
OH...
....
I KNOW!

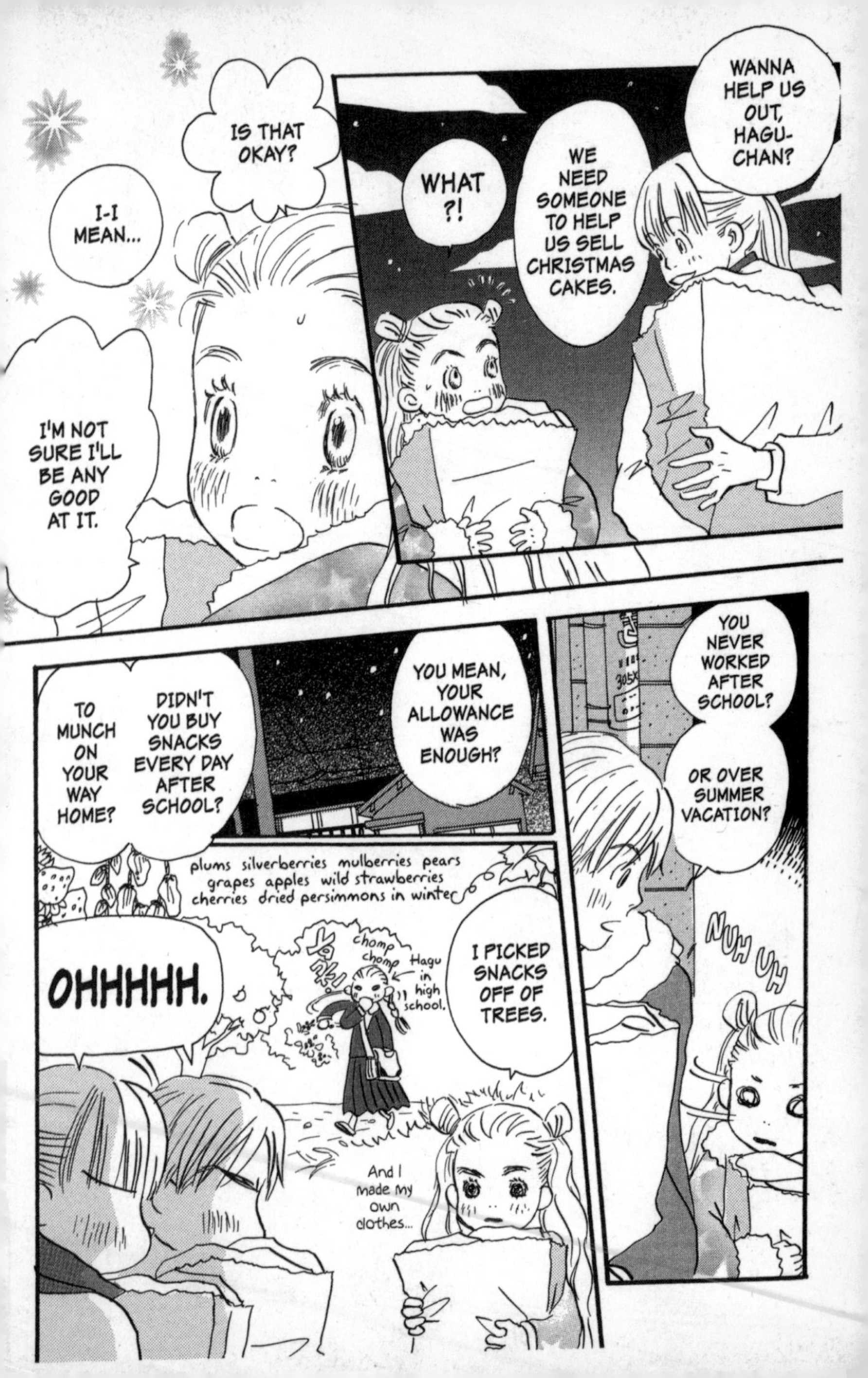
WANNA HELP US OUT, HAGU-CHAN?
WE NEED SOMEONE TO HELP US SELL CHRISTMAS CAKES.
WHAT ?!
IS THAT OKAY?
I-I MEAN...
I'M NOT SURE I'LL BE ANY GOOD AT IT.
YOU NEVER WORKED AFTER SCHOOL?
OR OVER SUMMER VACATION?
NUH UH
YOU MEAN, YOUR ALLOWANCE WAS ENOUGH?
DIDN'T YOU BUY SNACKS EVERY DAY AFTER SCHOOL?
TO MUNCH ON YOUR WAY HOME?
I PICKED SNACKS OFF OF TREES.
plums silverberries mulberries pears grapes apples wild strawberries cherries dried persimmons in winter
chomp chomp
Hagu in high school.
And I made my own clothes...
OHHHHH.

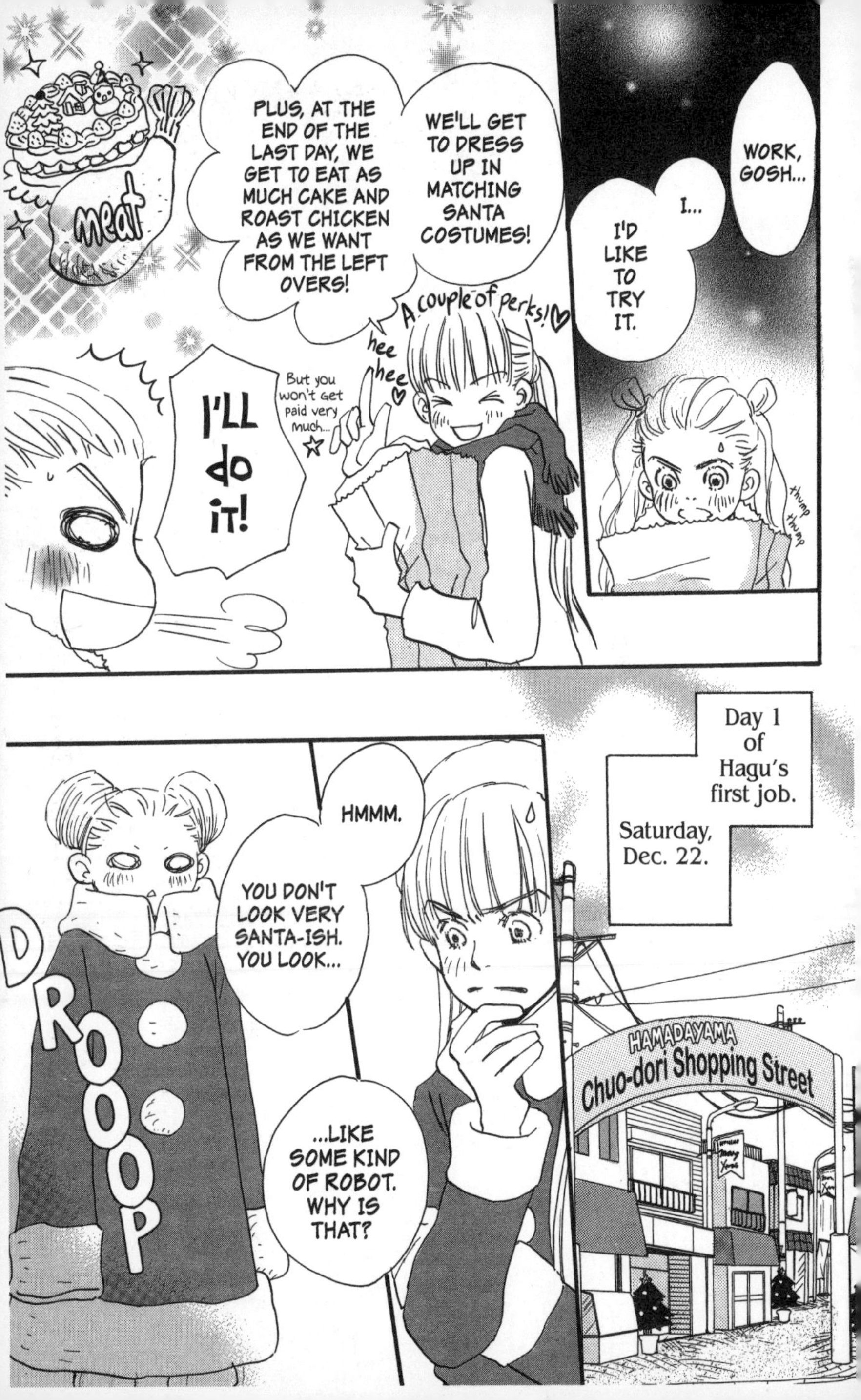
WORK, GOSH...
I...
I'D LIKE TO TRY IT.
thump thump
WE'LL GET TO DRESS UP IN MATCHING SANTA COSTUMES!
PLUS, AT THE END OF THE LAST DAY, WE GET TO EAT AS MUCH CAKE AND ROAST CHICKEN AS WE WANT FROM THE LEFT OVERS!
meat
A couple of perks!
hee hee
But you won't get paid very much...
I'LL do it!
Day 1 of Hagu's first job.
Saturday, Dec. 22.
HAMADAYAMA
Chuo-dori Shopping Street
HMMM.
YOU DON'T LOOK VERY SANTA-ISH. YOU LOOK...
...LIKE SOME KIND OF ROBOT. WHY IS THAT?
DROOOP

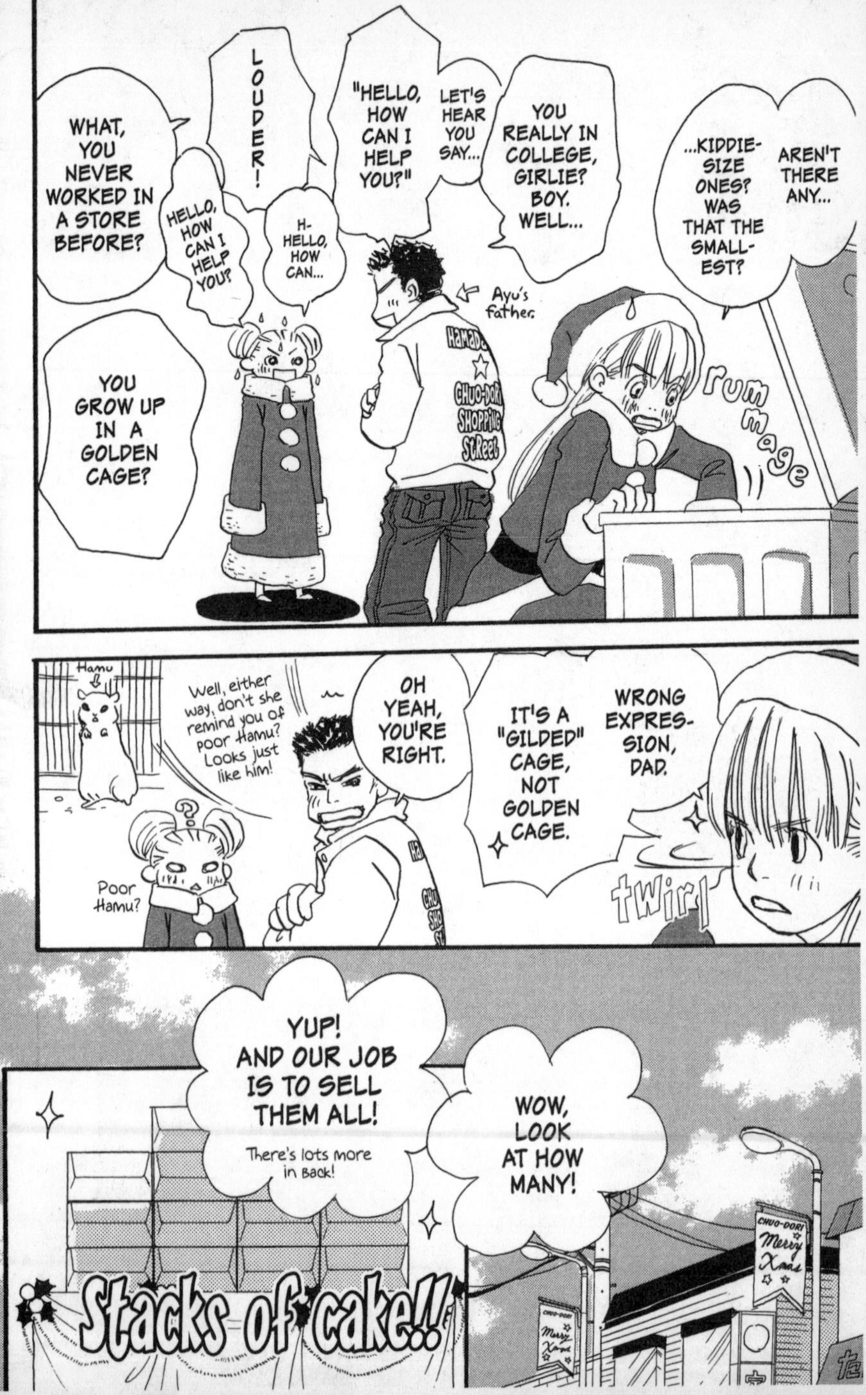
rummage
AREN'T THERE ANY...
...KIDDIE-SIZE ONES? WAS THAT THE SMALLEST?
YOU REALLY IN COLLEGE, GIRLIE? BOY. WELL...
LET'S HEAR YOU SAY...
"HELLO, HOW CAN I HELP YOU?"
Ayu's father.
HAMADA ☆ CHUO-DORI SHOPPING STREET
LOUDER!
H-HELLO, HOW CAN...
HELLO, HOW CAN I HELP YOU?
WHAT, YOU NEVER WORKED IN A STORE BEFORE?
YOU GROW UP IN A GOLDEN CAGE?
WRONG EXPRESSION, DAD.
twirl
IT'S A "GILDED" CAGE, NOT GOLDEN CAGE.
OH YEAH, YOU'RE RIGHT.
Well, either way, don't she remind you of poor Hamu? Looks just like him!
Hamu
Poor Hamu?
CHUO-DORI Merry Xmas
WOW, LOOK AT HOW MANY!
YUP! AND OUR JOB IS TO SELL THEM ALL!
There's lots more in back!
CHUO-DORI Merry Xmas
Stacks of cake!!

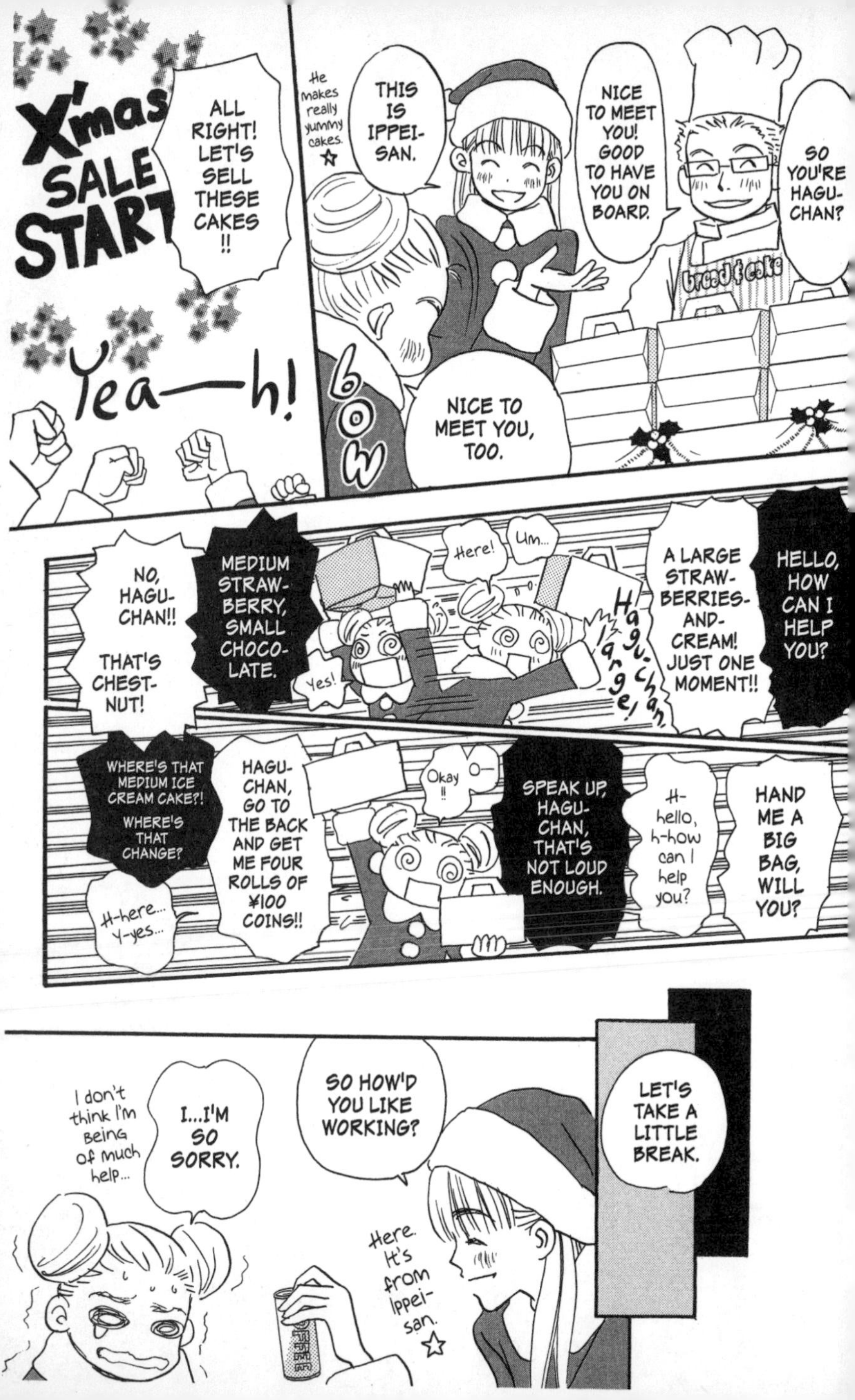
SO YOU'RE HAGU-CHAN?
NICE TO MEET YOU! GOOD TO HAVE YOU ON BOARD.
THIS IS IPPEI-SAN.
He makes really yummy cakes. ☆
NICE TO MEET YOU, TOO.
bow
ALL RIGHT! LET'S SELL THESE CAKES!!
X'mas SALE START
Yea—h!
HELLO, HOW CAN I HELP YOU?
A LARGE STRAW-BERRIES-AND-CREAM! JUST ONE MOMENT!!
Hagu-chan, large!
Um...
Here!
Yes!
MEDIUM STRAW-BERRY, SMALL CHOCO-LATE.
NO, HAGU-CHAN!! THAT'S CHEST-NUT!
HAND ME A BIG BAG, WILL YOU?
H-hello, h-how can I help you?
SPEAK UP, HAGU-CHAN, THAT'S NOT LOUD ENOUGH.
Okay!!
HAGU-CHAN, GO TO THE BACK AND GET ME FOUR ROLLS OF ¥100 COINS!!
WHERE'S THAT MEDIUM ICE CREAM CAKE?! WHERE'S THAT CHANGE?
H-here... Y-yes...
LET'S TAKE A LITTLE BREAK.
SO HOW'D YOU LIKE WORKING?
Here. It's from Ippei-san. ☆
I...I'M SO SORRY.
I don't think I'm being of much help...

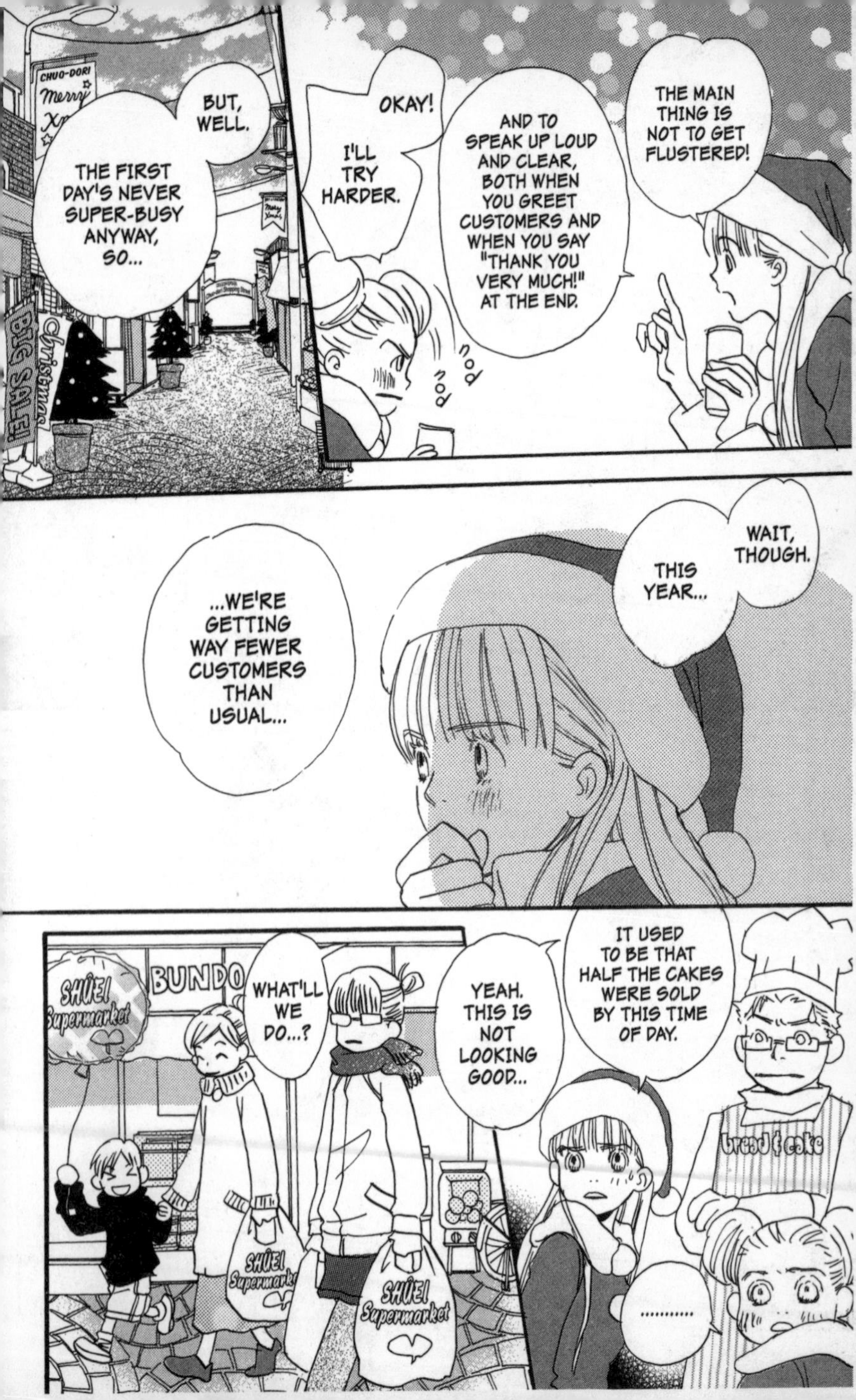
THE MAIN THING IS NOT TO GET FLUSTERED!
AND TO SPEAK UP LOUD AND CLEAR, BOTH WHEN YOU GREET CUSTOMERS AND WHEN YOU SAY "THANK YOU VERY MUCH!" AT THE END.
OKAY!
I'LL TRY HARDER.
nod nod
BUT, WELL.
THE FIRST DAY'S NEVER SUPER-BUSY ANYWAY, SO...
CHUO-DORI
Merry Xmas
Christmas
BIG SALE!
WAIT, THOUGH.
THIS YEAR...
...WE'RE GETTING WAY FEWER CUSTOMERS THAN USUAL...
IT USED TO BE THAT HALF THE CAKES WERE SOLD BY THIS TIME OF DAY.
bread & cake
....
YEAH. THIS IS NOT LOOKING GOOD...
WHAT'LL WE DO...?
BUNDO
SHÛEI Supermarket
SHÛEI Supermarket
SHÛEI Supermarket

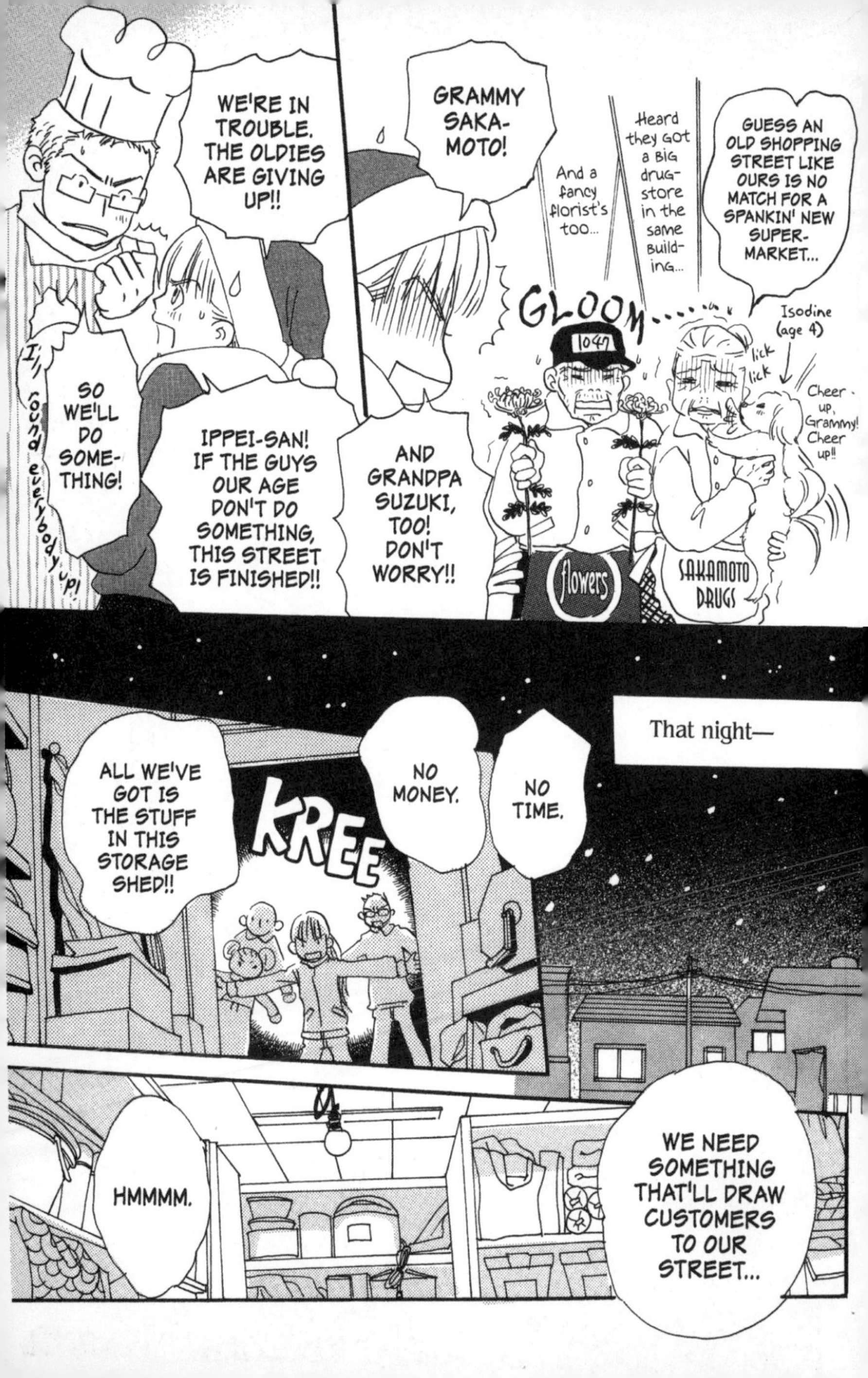
GUESS AN OLD SHOPPING STREET LIKE OURS IS NO MATCH FOR A SPANKIN' NEW SUPER-MARKET...
Heard they got a BIG drug-store in the same Build-ing...
And a fancy florist's too...
GRAMMY SAKA-MOTO!
GLOOM.....
1047
Isodine (age 4)
lick lick
Cheer up, Grammy! Cheer up!!
flowers
SAKAMOTO DRUGS
AND GRANDPA SUZUKI, TOO! DON'T WORRY!!
WE'RE IN TROUBLE. THE OLDIES ARE GIVING UP!!
IPPEI-SAN! IF THE GUYS OUR AGE DON'T DO SOMETHING, THIS STREET IS FINISHED!!
SO WE'LL DO SOME-THING!
I'll round everybody up!
That night—
NO TIME.
NO MONEY.
KREE
ALL WE'VE GOT IS THE STUFF IN THIS STORAGE SHED!!
WE NEED SOMETHING THAT'LL DRAW CUSTOMERS TO OUR STREET...
HMMMM.

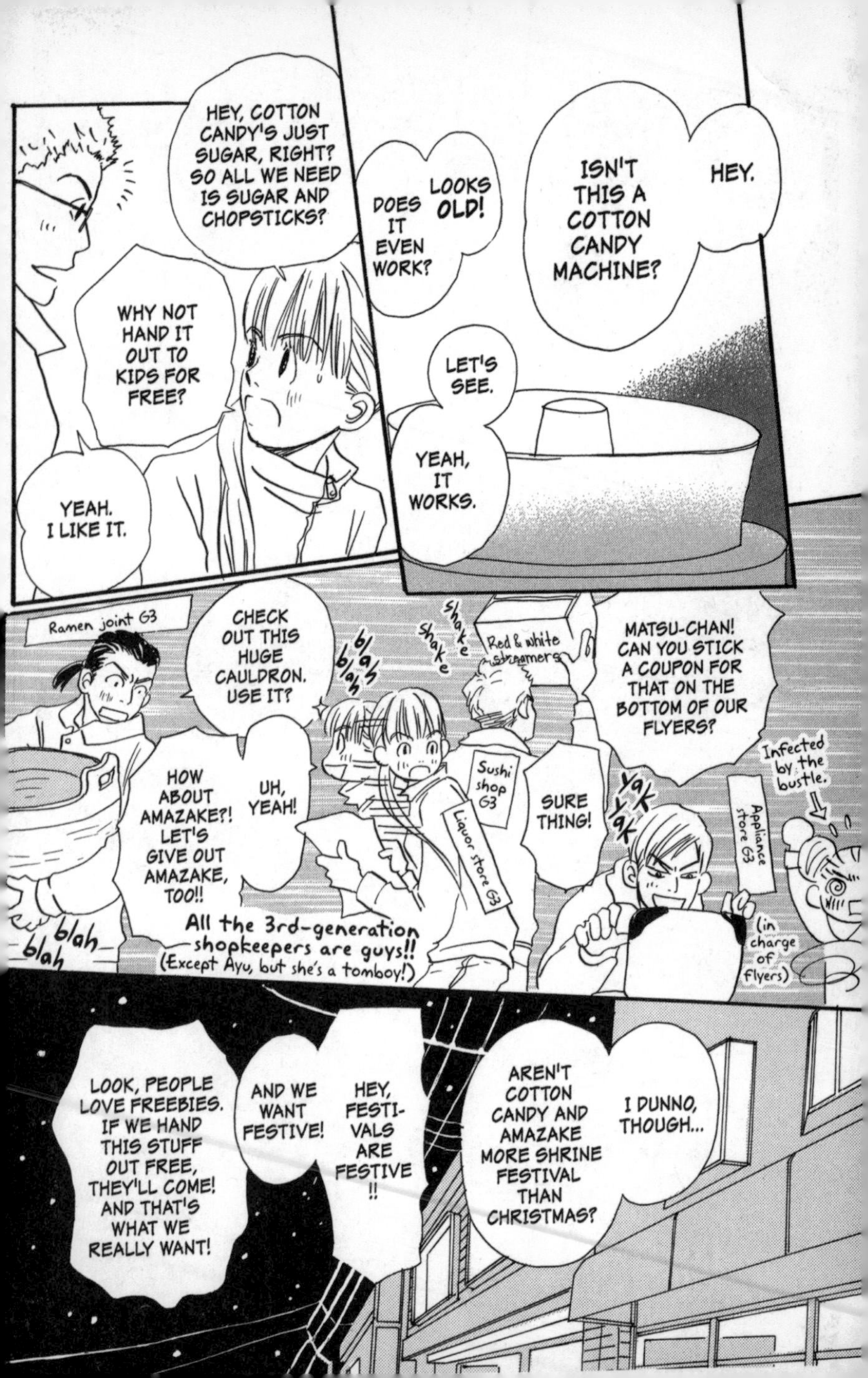
HEY.
ISN'T THIS A COTTON CANDY MACHINE?
LOOKS OLD!
DOES IT EVEN WORK?
LET'S SEE.
YEAH, IT WORKS.
HEY, COTTON CANDY'S JUST SUGAR, RIGHT? SO ALL WE NEED IS SUGAR AND CHOPSTICKS?
WHY NOT HAND IT OUT TO KIDS FOR FREE?
YEAH. I LIKE IT.
MATSU-CHAN! CAN YOU STICK A COUPON FOR THAT ON THE BOTTOM OF OUR FLYERS?
Infected by the bustle.
Appliance store G3
(in charge of flyers)
yak yak
SURE THING!
shake shake
Red & white streamers
Sushi shop G3
Liquor store G3
Ramen joint G3
CHECK OUT THIS HUGE CAULDRON. USE IT?
blah blah
UH, YEAH!
HOW ABOUT AMAZAKE?! LET'S GIVE OUT AMAZAKE, TOO!!
blah blah
All the 3rd-generation shopkeepers are guys!! (Except Ayu, but she's a tomboy!)
I DUNNO, THOUGH...
AREN'T COTTON CANDY AND AMAZAKE MORE SHRINE FESTIVAL THAN CHRISTMAS?
HEY, FESTIVALS ARE FESTIVE!!
AND WE WANT FESTIVE!
LOOK, PEOPLE LOVE FREEBIES. IF WE HAND THIS STUFF OUT FREE, THEY'LL COME! AND THAT'S WHAT WE REALLY WANT!

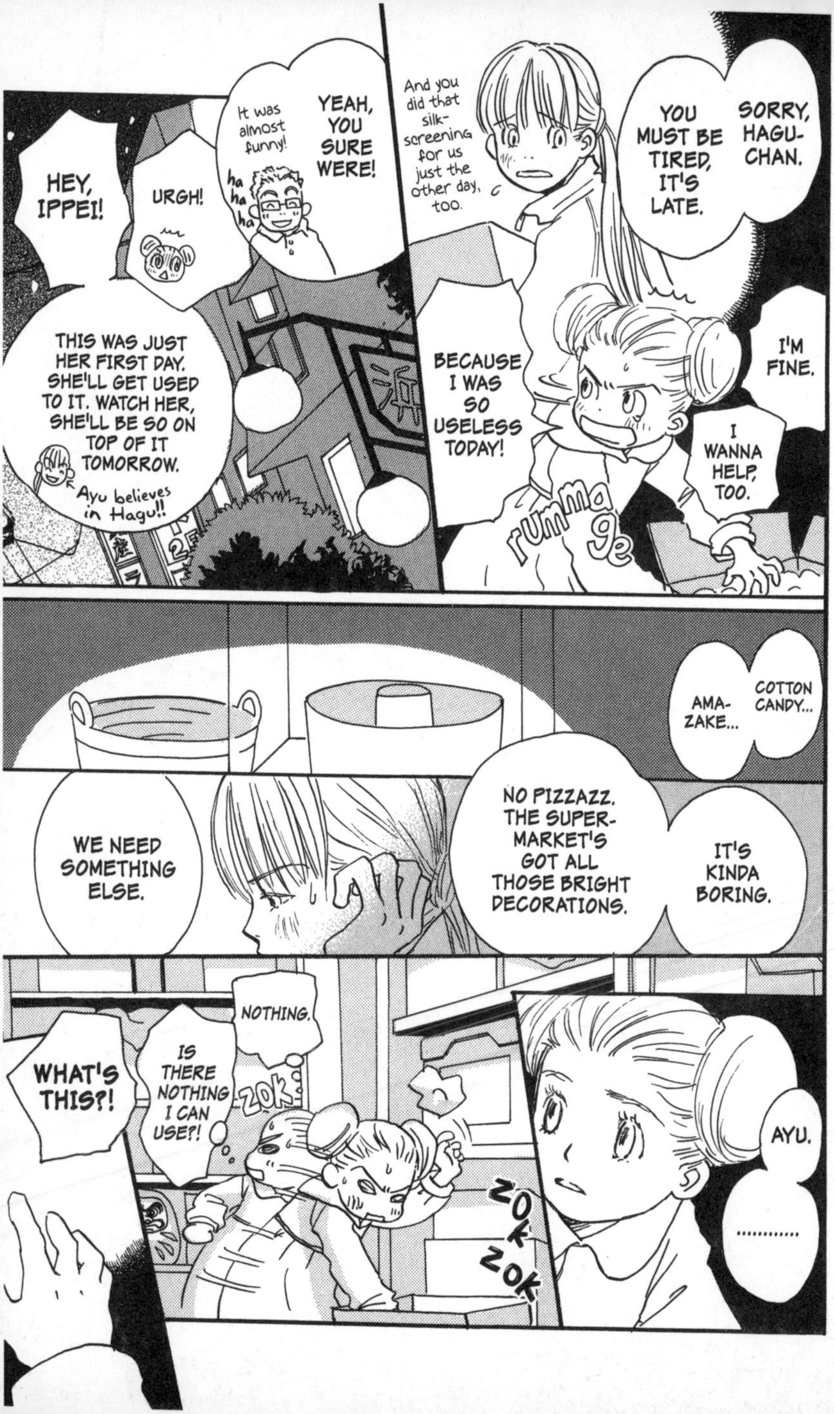
SORRY, HAGU-CHAN.
YOU MUST BE TIRED, IT'S LATE.
And you did that silk-screening for us just the other day, too.
I'M FINE.
I WANNA HELP, TOO.
BECAUSE I WAS SO USELESS TODAY!
rummage
YEAH, YOU SURE WERE!
It was almost funny!
ha ha ha
URGH!
HEY, IPPEI!
THIS WAS JUST HER FIRST DAY. SHE'LL GET USED TO IT. WATCH HER, SHE'LL BE SO ON TOP OF IT TOMORROW.
Ayu believes in Hagu!!
COTTON CANDY...
AMA-ZAKE...
IT'S KINDA BORING.
NO PIZZAZZ. THE SUPER-MARKET'S GOT ALL THOSE BRIGHT DECORATIONS.
WE NEED SOMETHING ELSE.
AYU.
....
ZOK ZOK
NOTHING.
IS THERE NOTHING I CAN USE?!
ZOK
WHAT'S THIS?!

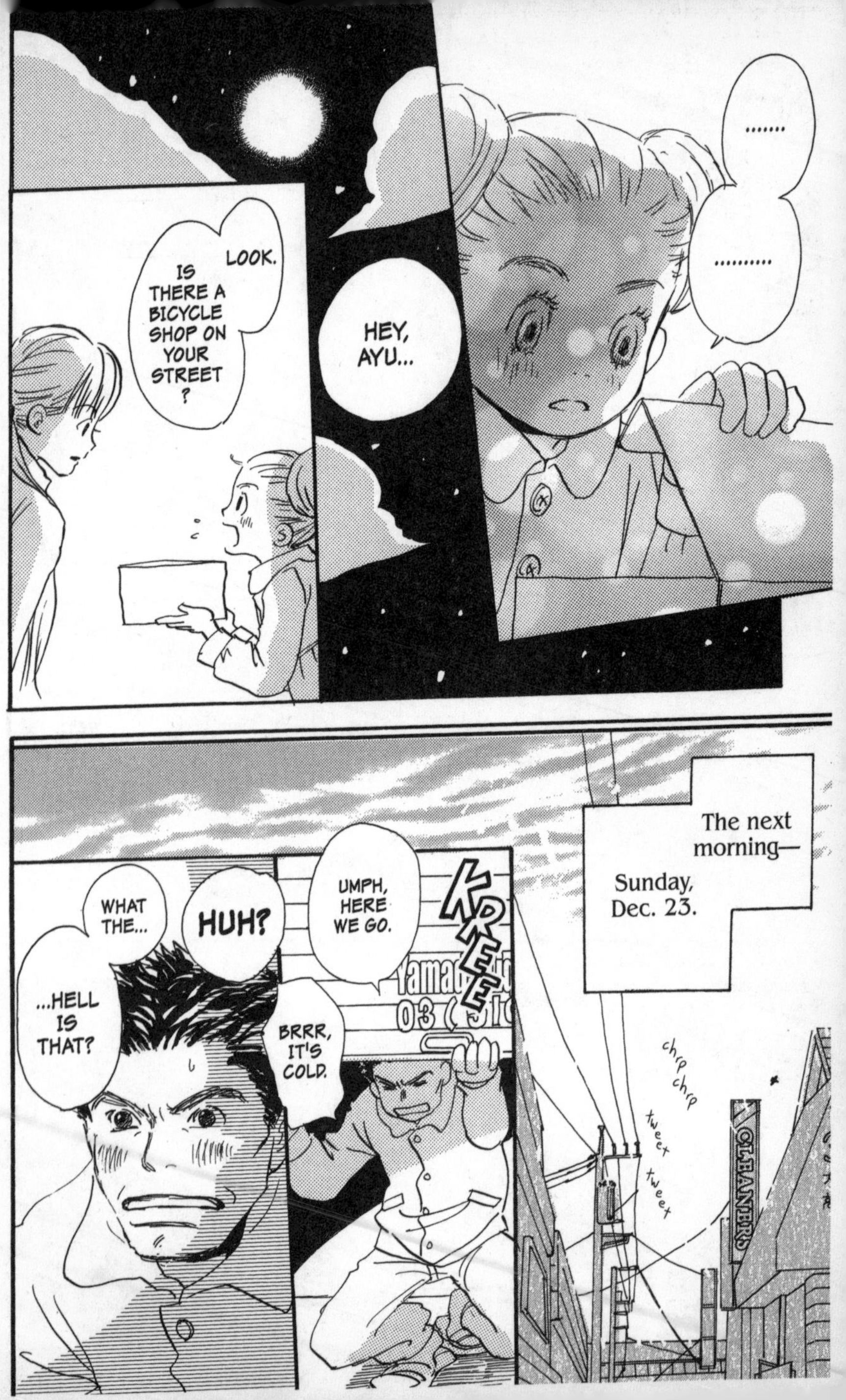
......
....
HEY, AYU...
LOOK.
IS THERE A BICYCLE SHOP ON YOUR STREET?
The next morning—
Sunday, Dec. 23.
chrp chrp
tweet tweet
CLEANERS
UMPH, HERE WE GO.
KREEE
BRRR, IT'S COLD.
HUH?
WHAT THE...
...HELL IS THAT?

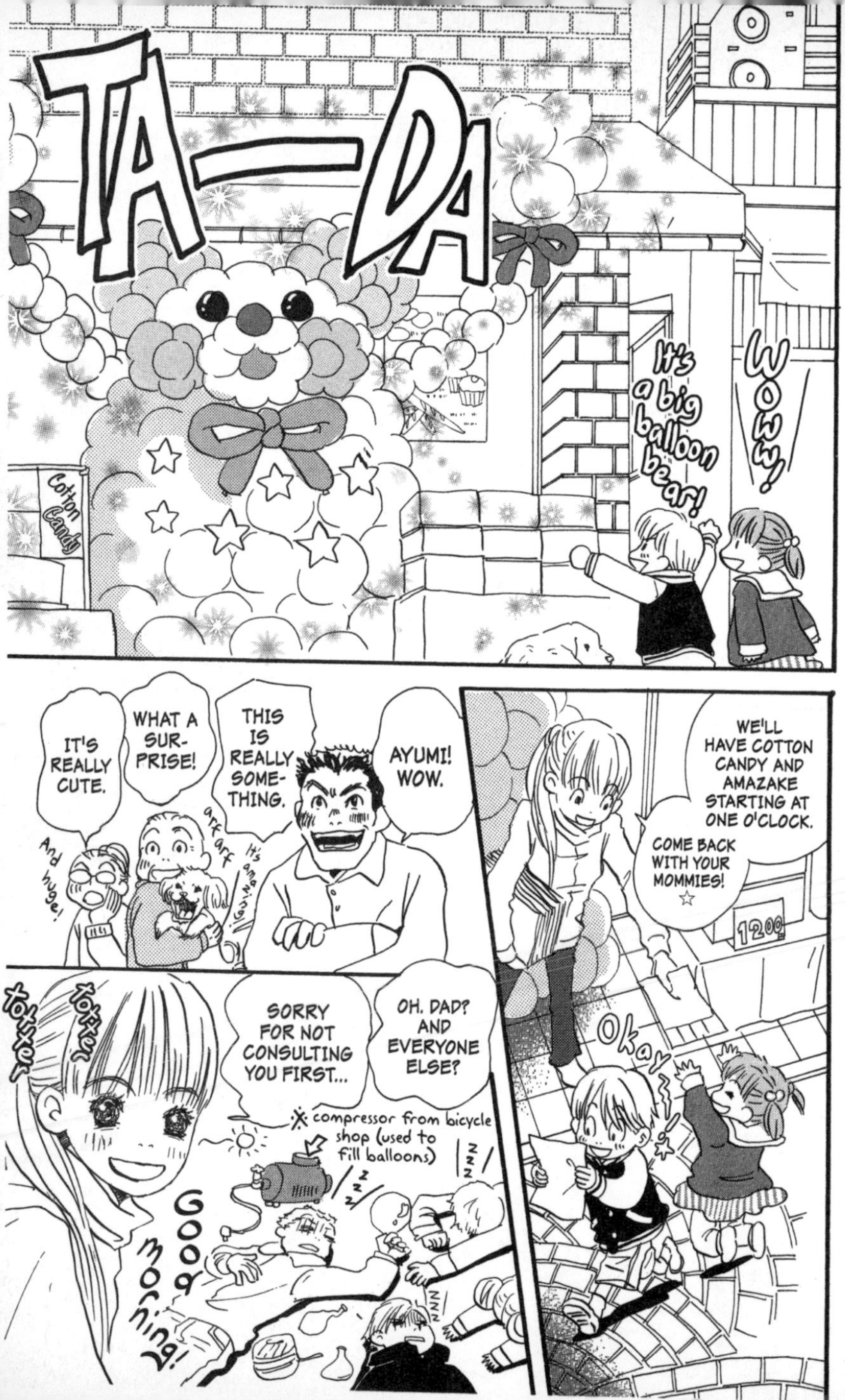
TA—DA
Woww!
It's a big balloon bear!
Cotton Candy
WE'LL HAVE COTTON CANDY AND AMAZAKE STARTING AT ONE O'CLOCK.
COME BACK WITH YOUR MOMMIES! ☆
1200
Okay~!
AYUMI! WOW.
THIS IS REALLY SOME-THING.
WHAT A SUR-PRISE!
IT'S REALLY CUTE.
It's amazing!
arf arf
And huge!
OH. DAD? AND EVERYONE ELSE?
SORRY FOR NOT CONSULTING YOU FIRST...
totter totter
※ compressor from bicycle shop (used to fill balloons)
Good morning!

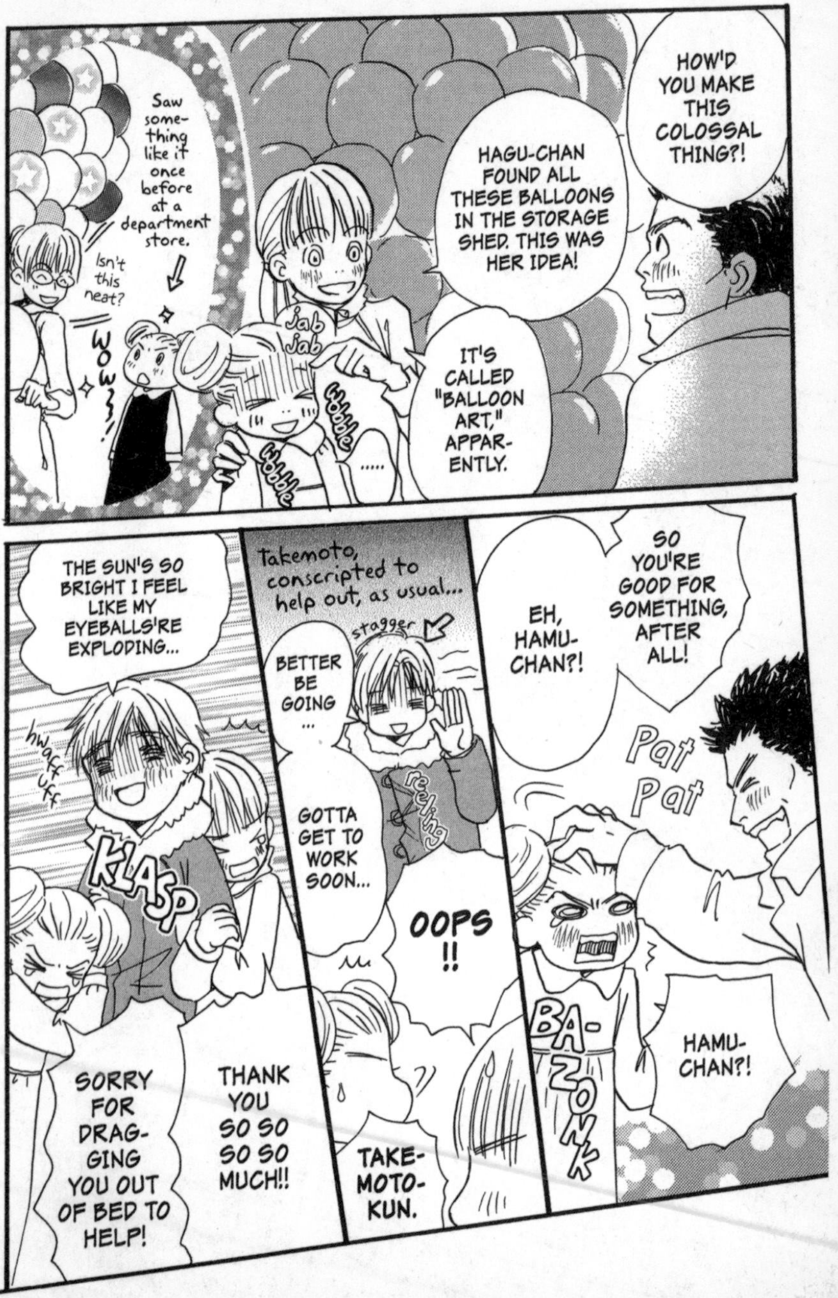
HOW'D YOU MAKE THIS COLOSSAL THING?!
HAGU-CHAN FOUND ALL THESE BALLOONS IN THE STORAGE SHED. THIS WAS HER IDEA!
IT'S CALLED "BALLOON ART," APPARENTLY.
jab jab
wobble wobble
.....
Saw something like it once before at a department store.
Isn't this neat?
WOW~!
SO YOU'RE GOOD FOR SOMETHING, AFTER ALL!
EH, HAMU-CHAN?!
Pat Pat
BA-ZONK
HAMU-CHAN?!
Takemoto, conscripted to help out, as usual...
stagger
BETTER BE GOING ...
reeling
GOTTA GET TO WORK SOON...
OOPS !!
TAKE-MOTO-KUN.
THE SUN'S SO BRIGHT I FEEL LIKE MY EYEBALLS'RE EXPLODING...
hwaff uff
KLASP
THANK YOU SO SO SO SO MUCH!!
SORRY FOR DRAGGING YOU OUT OF BED TO HELP!

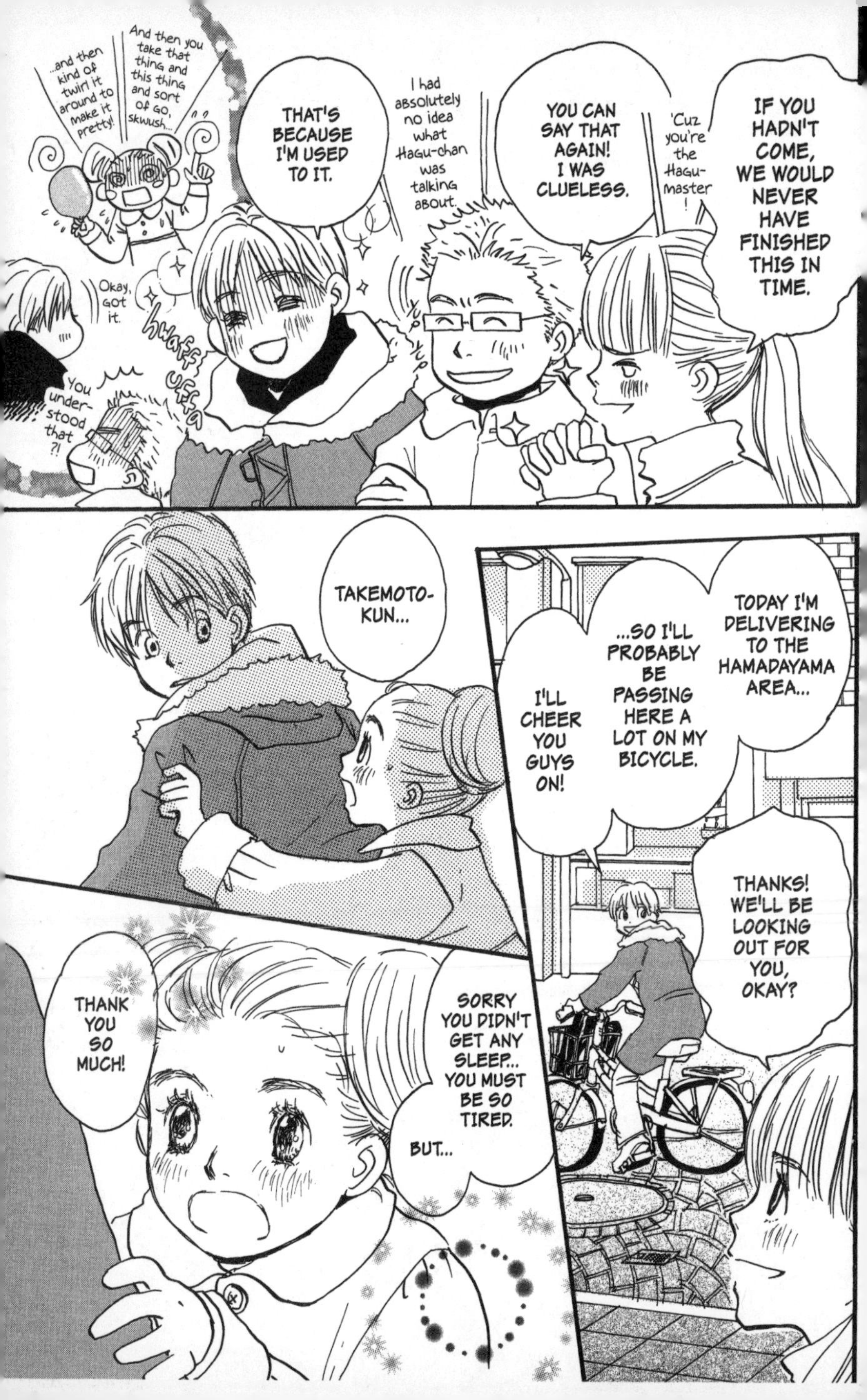
IF YOU HADN'T COME, WE WOULD NEVER HAVE FINISHED THIS IN TIME.
'Cuz you're the Hagu-master!
YOU CAN SAY THAT AGAIN! I WAS CLUELESS.
I had absolutely no idea what Hagu-chan was talking about.
THAT'S BECAUSE I'M USED TO IT.
And then you take that thing and this thing and sort of go, skwush...
...and then kind of twirl it around to make it pretty!
Okay, got it.
hwaff uffa
You under-stood that?!
TODAY I'M DELIVERING TO THE HAMADAYAMA AREA...
...SO I'LL PROBABLY BE PASSING HERE A LOT ON MY BICYCLE.
I'LL CHEER YOU GUYS ON!
THANKS! WE'LL BE LOOKING OUT FOR YOU, OKAY?
TAKEMOTO-KUN...
SORRY YOU DIDN'T GET ANY SLEEP... YOU MUST BE SO TIRED.
BUT...
THANK YOU SO MUCH!

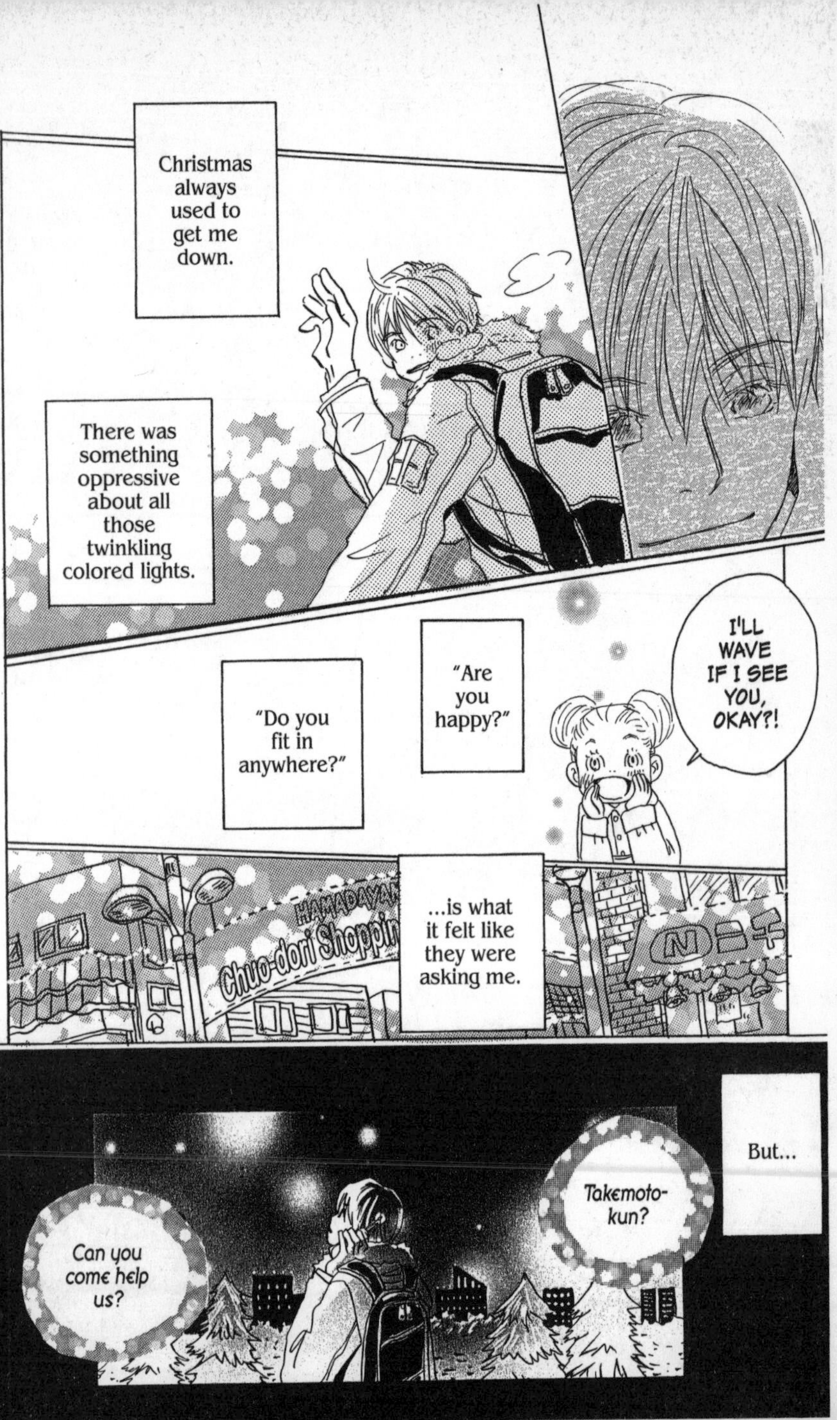
Christmas always used to get me down.
There was something oppressive about all those twinkling colored lights.
I'LL WAVE IF I SEE YOU, OKAY?!
"Are you happy?"
"Do you fit in anywhere?"
HAMADAYAN
Chuo-dori Shoppin
...is what it felt like they were asking me.
But...
Takemoto-kun?
Can you come help us?

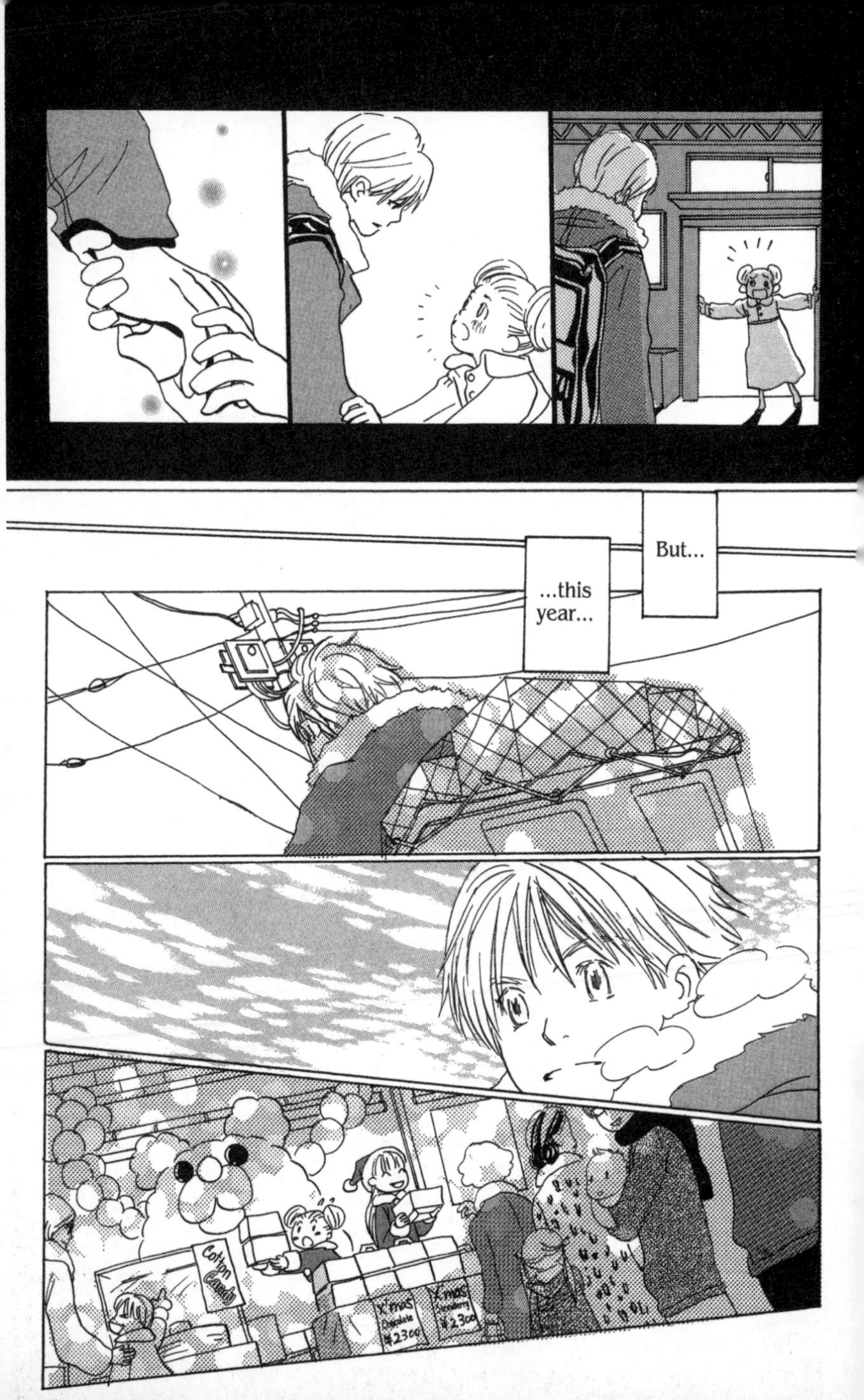
But...
...this year...
Cotton Candy
X'mas Strawberry ¥2300
X'mas Chocolate ¥2300

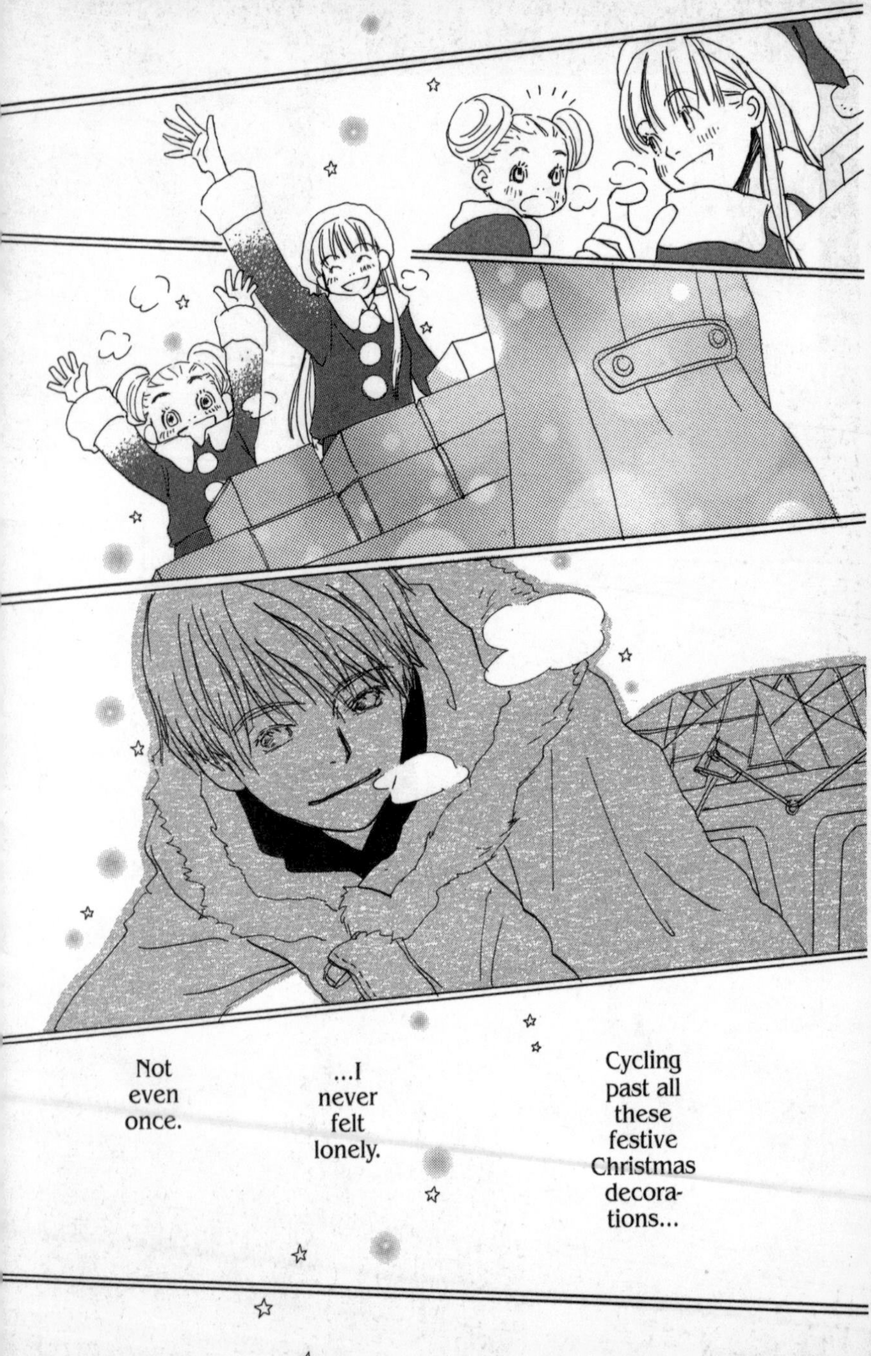
Cycling past all these festive Christmas decora-tions...
...I never felt lonely.
Not even once.

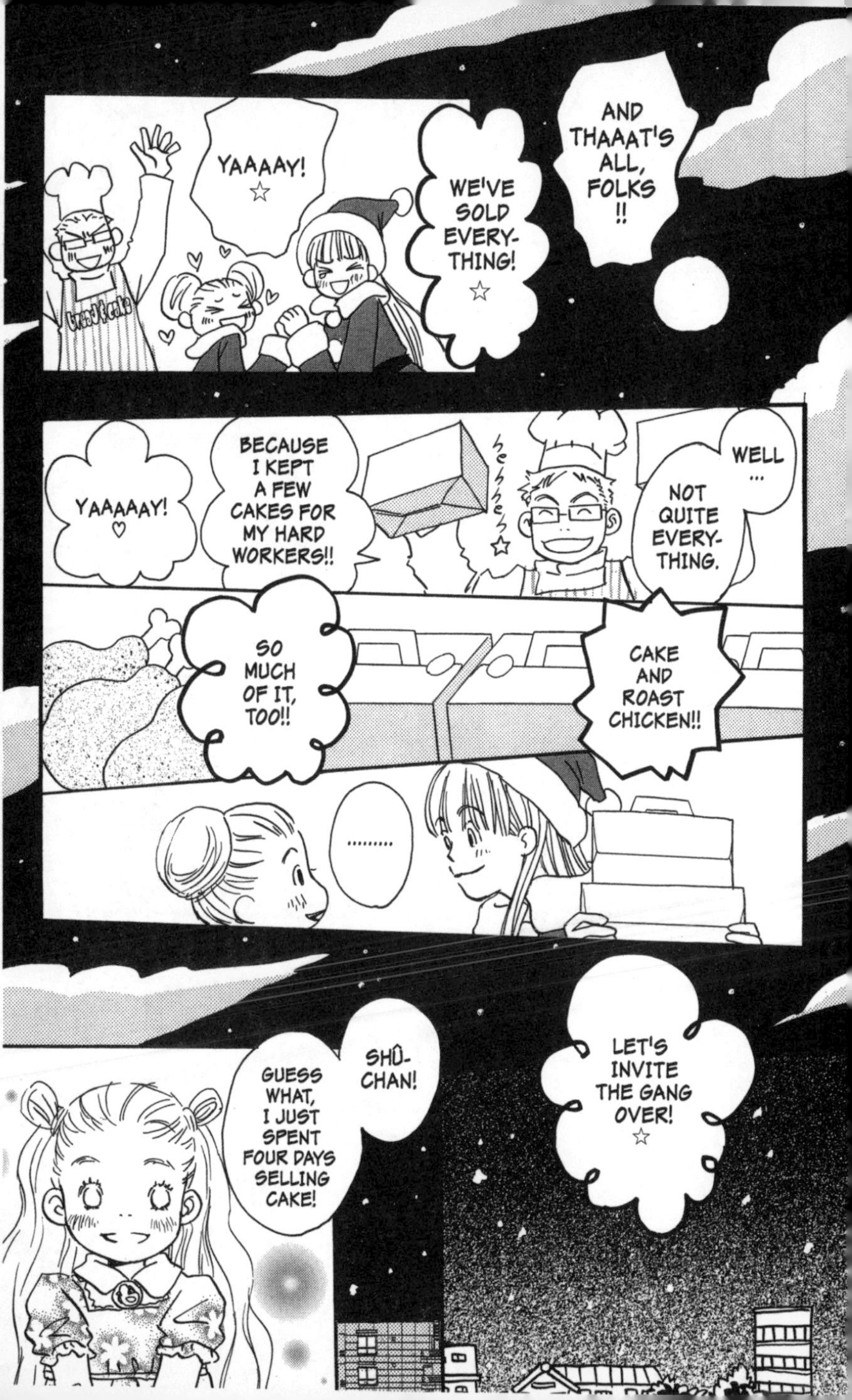
AND THAAAT'S ALL, FOLKS !!
WE'VE SOLD EVERY-THING! ☆
YAAAAY! ☆
WELL ... NOT QUITE EVERY-THING.
BECAUSE I KEPT A FEW CAKES FOR MY HARD WORKERS!!
YAAAAAY! ♡
CAKE AND ROAST CHICKEN!!
SO MUCH OF IT, TOO!!
....
LET'S INVITE THE GANG OVER! ☆
SHÔ-CHAN!
GUESS WHAT, I JUST SPENT FOUR DAYS SELLING CAKE!

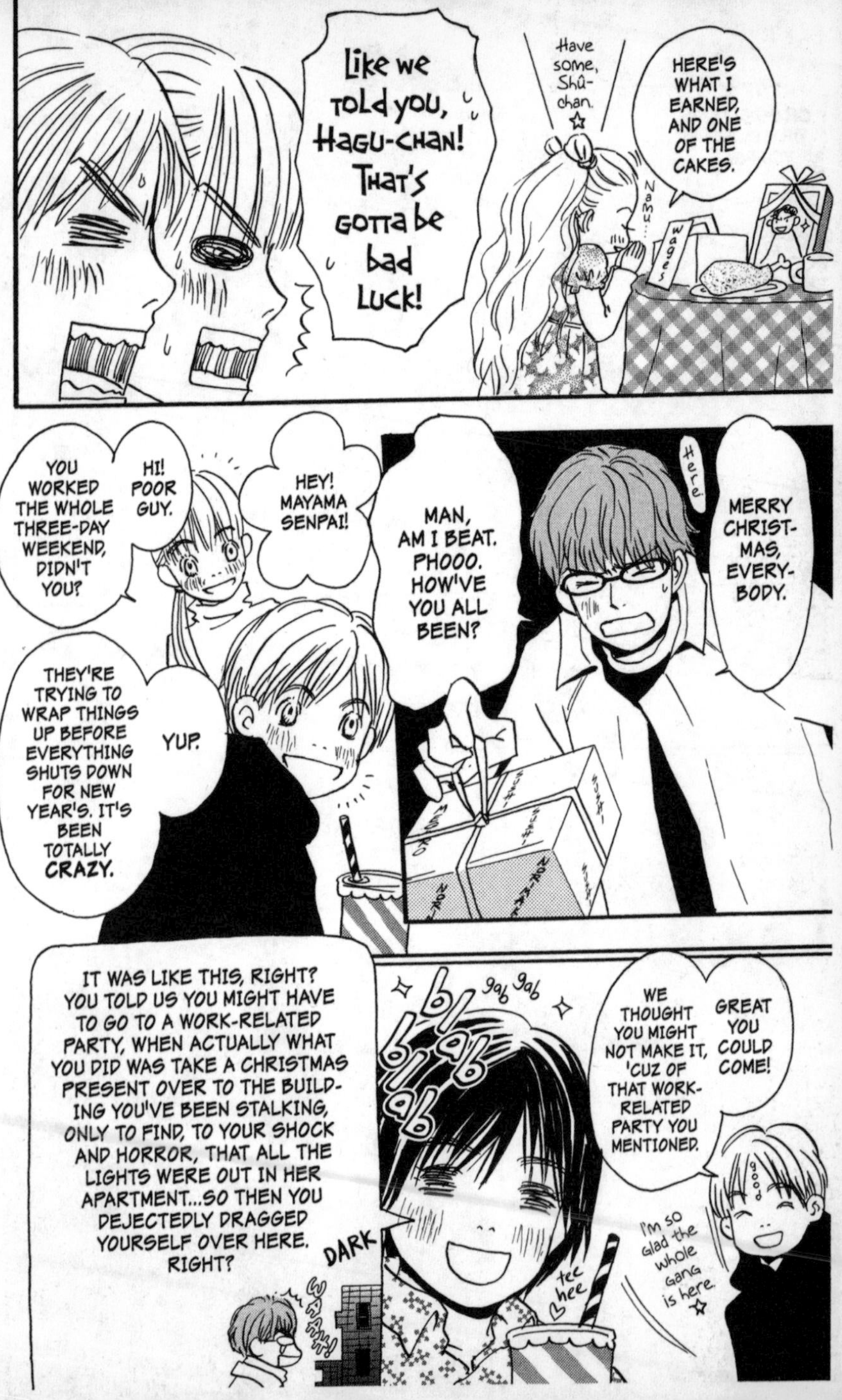
HERE'S WHAT I EARNED, AND ONE OF THE CAKES.
Have some, Shû-chan. ☆
Namu...
Wages
Like we told you, Hagu-chan! That's gotta be bad luck!
MERRY CHRISTMAS, EVERYBODY.
Here.
MAN, AM I BEAT. PHOOO. HOW'VE YOU ALL BEEN?
HEY! MAYAMA SENPAI!
HI! POOR GUY.
YOU WORKED THE WHOLE THREE-DAY WEEKEND, DIDN'T YOU?
YUP.
THEY'RE TRYING TO WRAP THINGS UP BEFORE EVERYTHING SHUTS DOWN FOR NEW YEAR'S. IT'S BEEN TOTALLY CRAZY.
GREAT YOU COULD COME!
WE THOUGHT YOU MIGHT NOT MAKE IT, 'CUZ OF THAT WORK-RELATED PARTY YOU MENTIONED.
good
I'm so glad the whole gang is here. ☆
gab gab
blab blab blab
tee hee
IT WAS LIKE THIS, RIGHT? YOU TOLD US YOU MIGHT HAVE TO GO TO A WORK-RELATED PARTY, WHEN ACTUALLY WHAT YOU DID WAS TAKE A CHRISTMAS PRESENT OVER TO THE BUILDING YOU'VE BEEN STALKING, ONLY TO FIND, TO YOUR SHOCK AND HORROR, THAT ALL THE LIGHTS WERE OUT IN HER APARTMENT...SO THEN YOU DEJECTEDLY DRAGGED YOURSELF OVER HERE. RIGHT?
DARK
WAAAH!

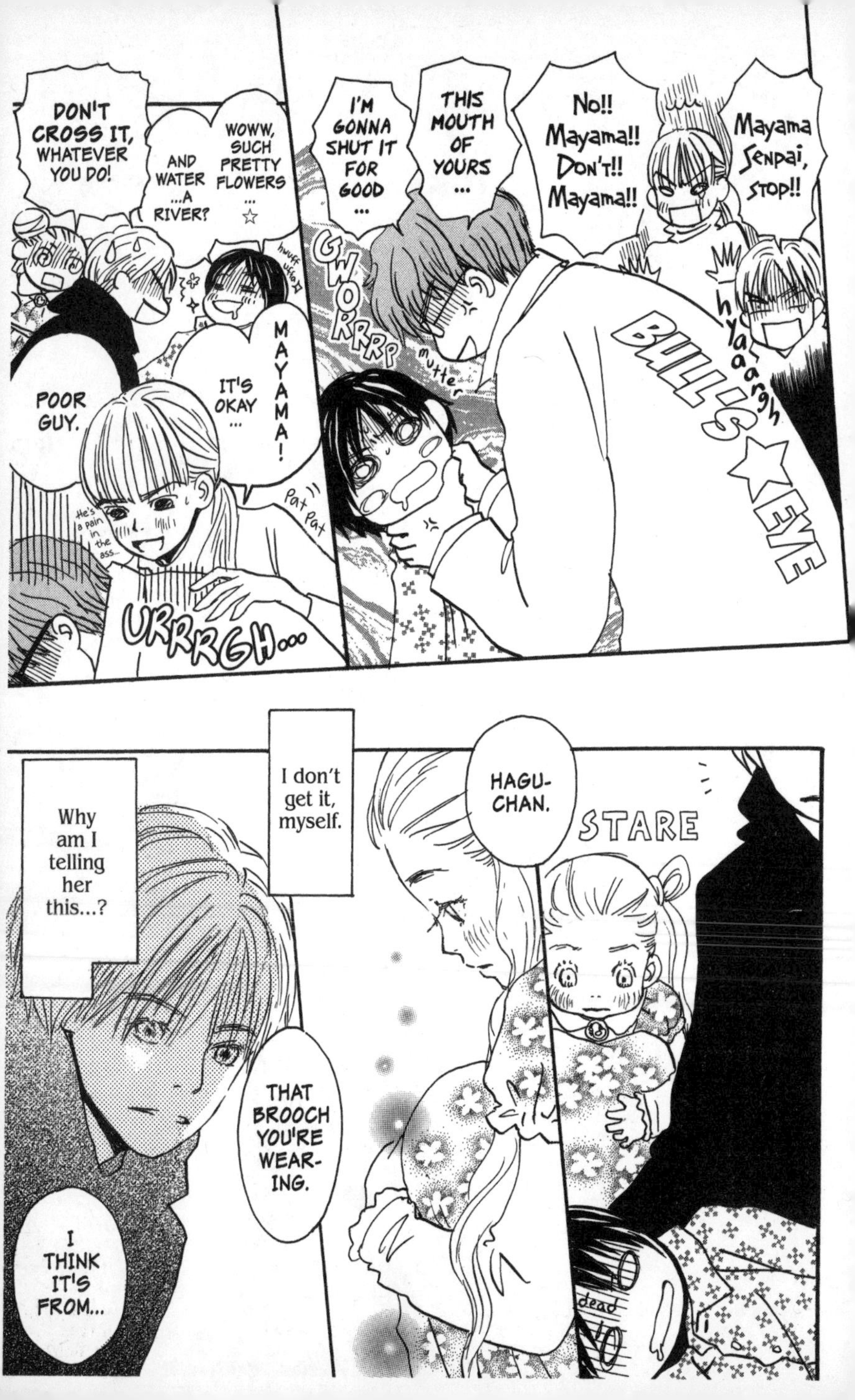
Mayama Senpai, stop!!
No!! Mayama!! Don't!! Mayama!!
THIS MOUTH OF YOURS ...
I'M GONNA SHUT IT FOR GOOD ...
hyaaargh
GWORRRP
mutter
BULL'S ★ EYE
WOWW, SUCH PRETTY FLOWERS ... ☆
AND WATER ...A RIVER?
DON'T CROSS IT, WHATEVER YOU DO!
hwuff uffo
MAYAMA!
IT'S OKAY ...
POOR GUY.
Pat pat
He's a pain in the ass...
URRRGH...
STARE
HAGU-CHAN.
dead
I don't get it, myself.
THAT BROOCH YOU'RE WEAR-ING.
Why am I telling her this...?
I THINK IT'S FROM...

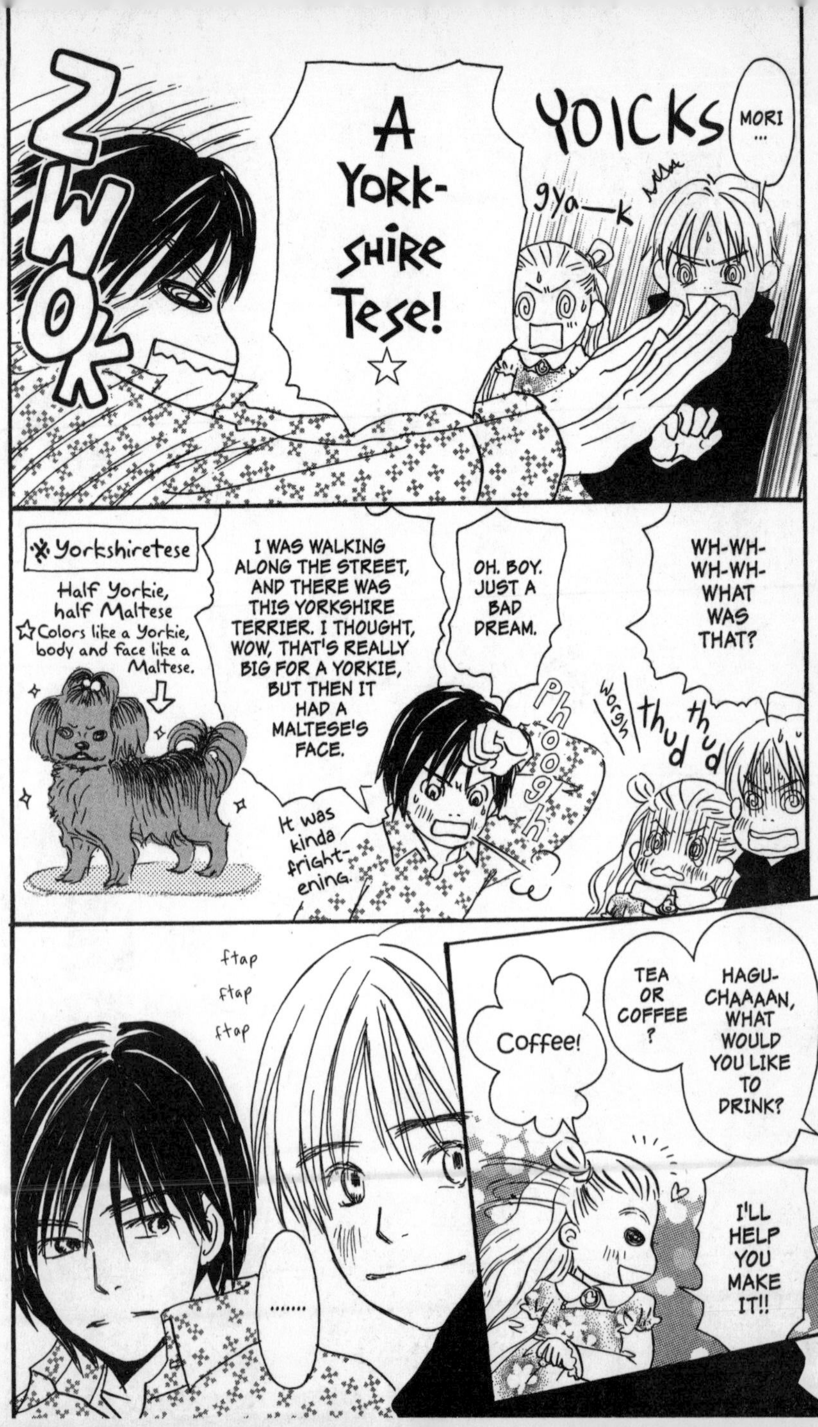
MORI ...
YOICKS
gya—k
A YORK-SHIRE TESE! ☆
ZWOK
WH-WH-WH-WH-WHAT WAS THAT?
thud thud
worgh
OH. BOY. JUST A BAD DREAM.
Phooogh
I WAS WALKING ALONG THE STREET, AND THERE WAS THIS YORKSHIRE TERRIER. I THOUGHT, WOW, THAT'S REALLY BIG FOR A YORKIE, BUT THEN IT HAD A MALTESE'S FACE.
It was kinda fright-ening.
※Yorkshiretese
Half Yorkie, half Maltese ☆Colors like a Yorkie, body and face like a Maltese.
HAGU-CHAAAAN, WHAT WOULD YOU LIKE TO DRINK?
TEA OR COFFEE?
Coffee!
I'LL HELP YOU MAKE IT!!
ftap ftap ftap
....

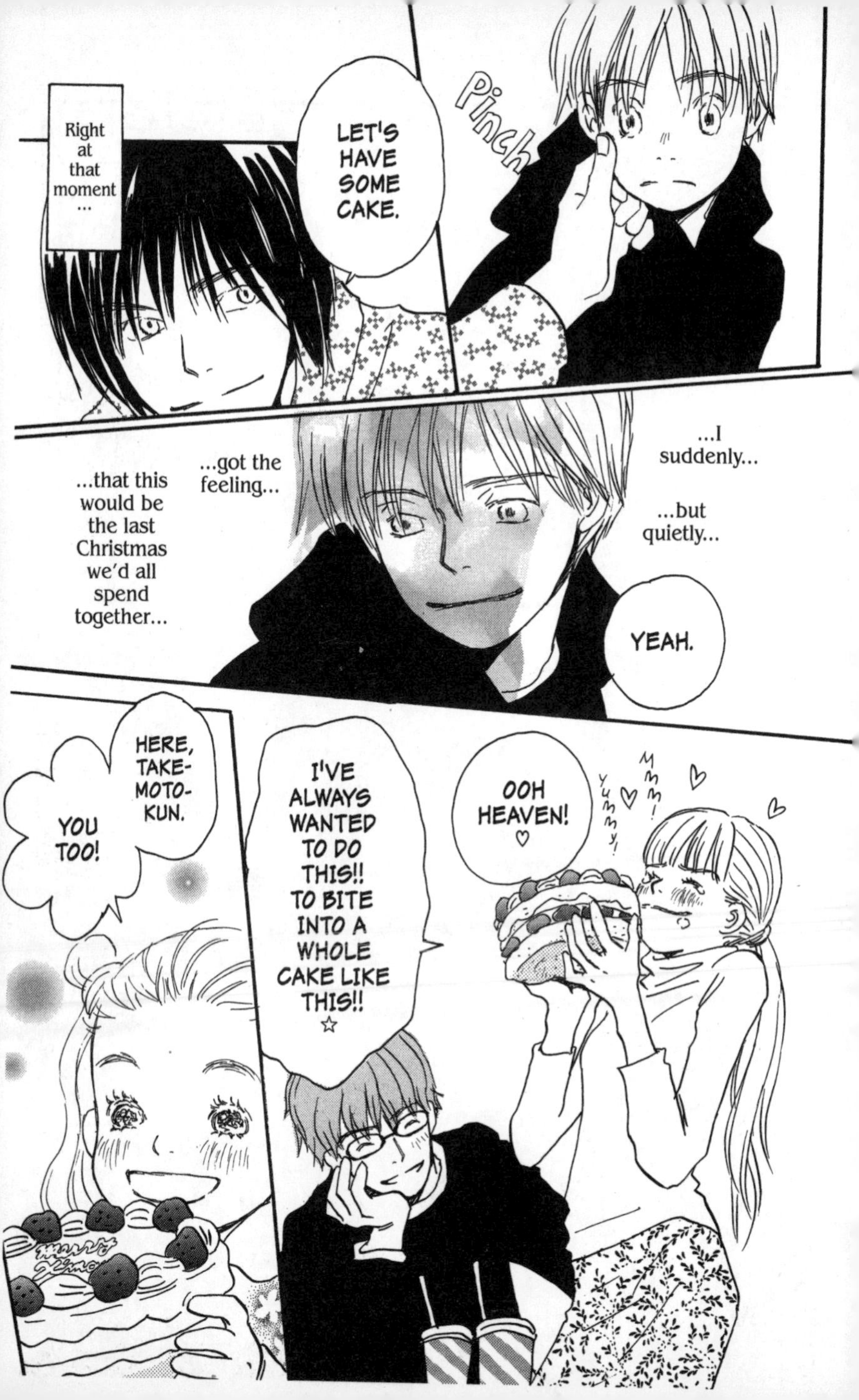
Pinch
LET'S HAVE SOME CAKE.
Right at that moment...
...I suddenly...
...but quietly...
YEAH.
...got the feeling...
...that this would be the last Christmas we'd all spend together...
OOH HEAVEN! ♡
Mmm!
Yummy!
I'VE ALWAYS WANTED TO DO THIS!! TO BITE INTO A WHOLE CAKE LIKE THIS!! ☆
HERE, TAKE-MOTO-KUN.
YOU TOO!

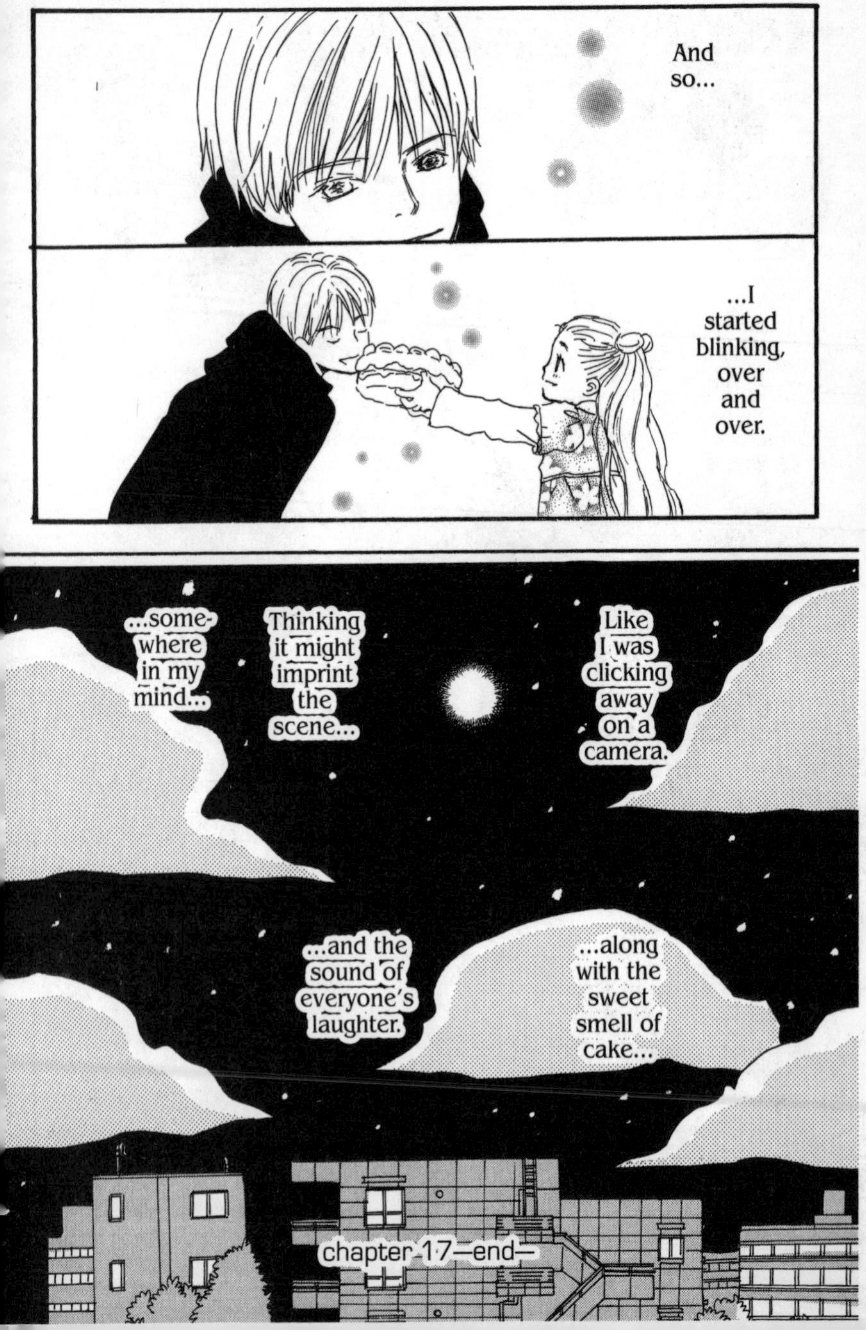
And so...
...I started blinking, over and over.
Like I was clicking away on a camera.
Thinking it might imprint the scene...
...somewhere in my mind...
...along with the sweet smell of cake...
...and the sound of everyone's laughter.
chapter 17—end—

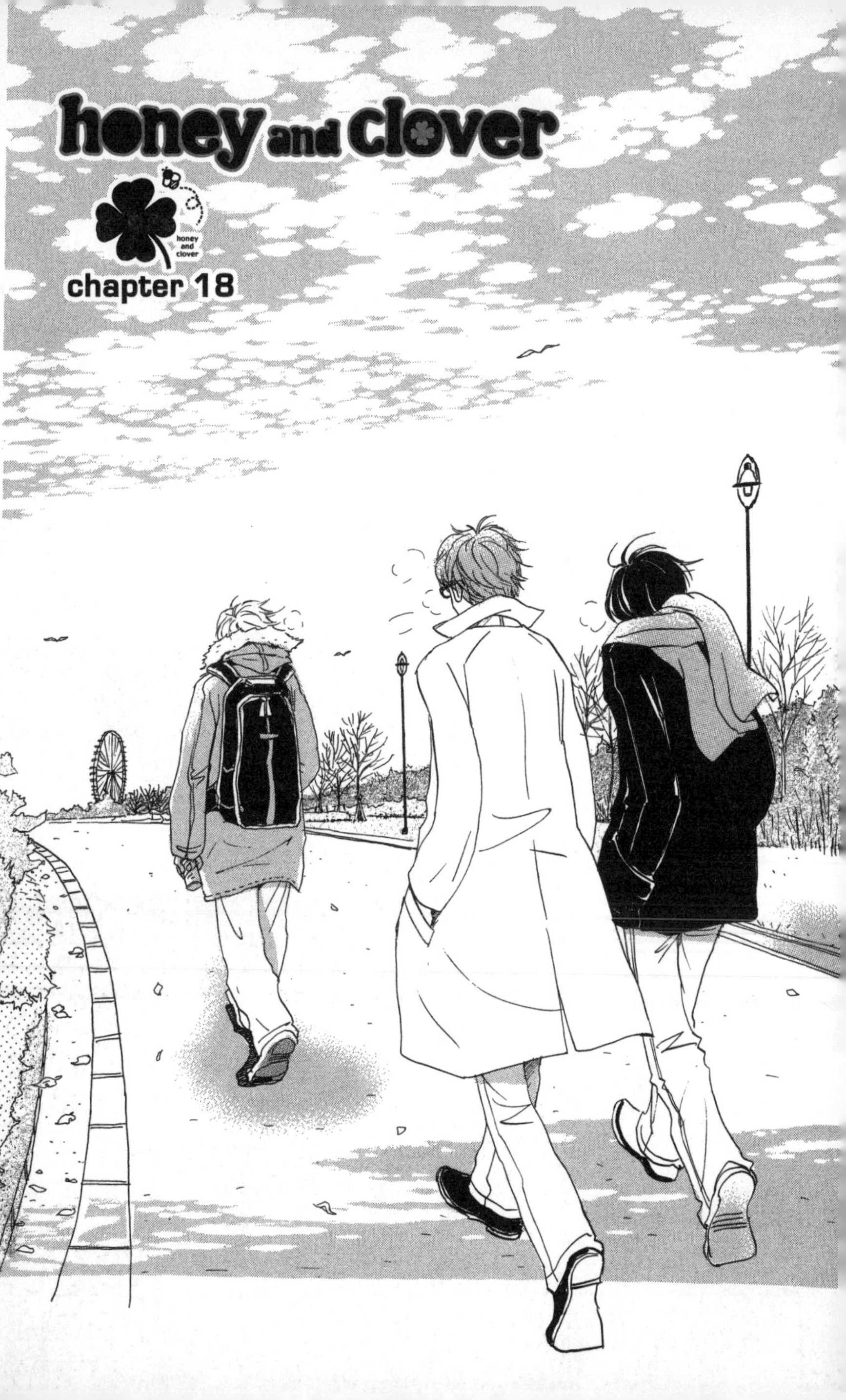
honey and clover
honey and clover
chapter 18

On the 29th of December...

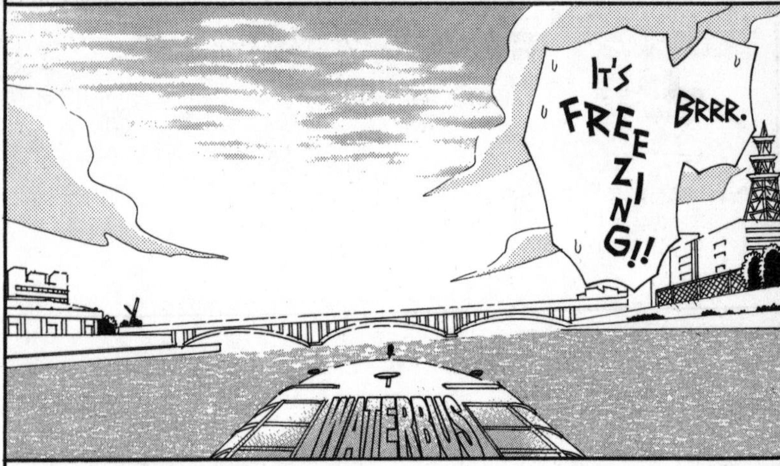
BRRR.
IT'S FREEZING!!
WATERBUS

...we boarded a waterbus and went for a mini-cruise.

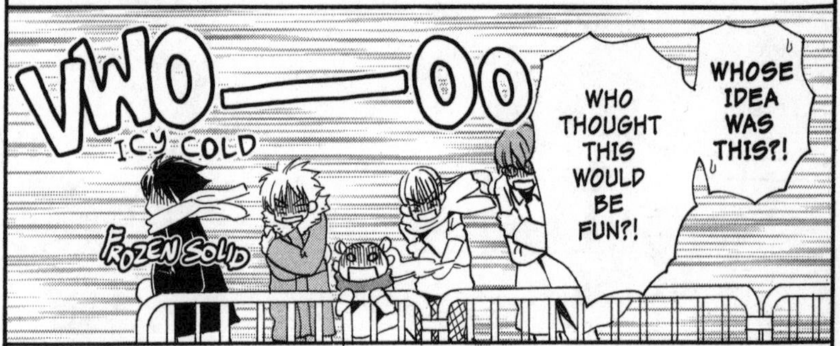
WHOSE IDEA WAS THIS?!
WHO THOUGHT THIS WOULD BE FUN?!
VWO——OO
ICY COLD
FROZEN SOLID

The student art exhibition, finals, projects to turn in, Christmas jobs...

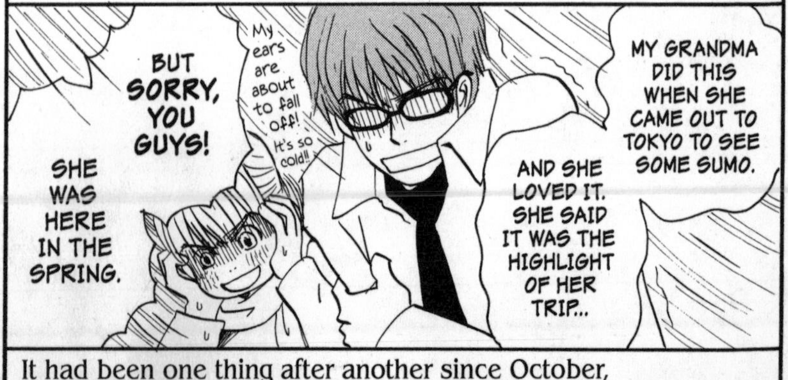
MY GRANDMA DID THIS WHEN SHE CAME OUT TO TOKYO TO SEE SOME SUMO.
AND SHE LOVED IT. SHE SAID IT WAS THE HIGHLIGHT OF HER TRIP...
My ears are about to fall off!
It's so cold!!
BUT SORRY, YOU GUYS!
SHE WAS HERE IN THE SPRING.

It had been one thing after another since October, and when it was all over...

...we all wanted to go somewhere huge and wide open.

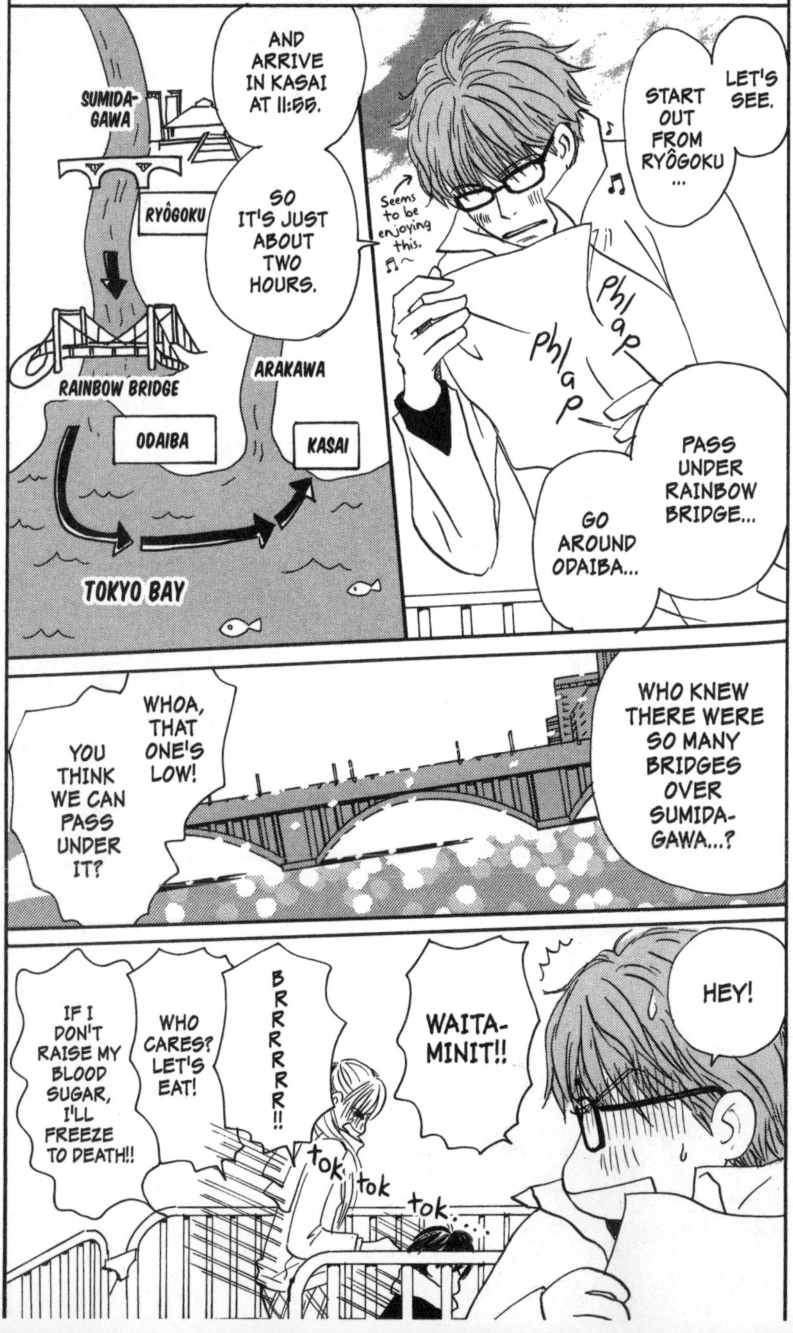
LET'S SEE.
START OUT FROM RYÔGOKU...
PASS UNDER RAINBOW BRIDGE...
GO AROUND ODAIBA...
Seems to be enjoying this.
phlap
phlap
AND ARRIVE IN KASAI AT 11:55.
SO IT'S JUST ABOUT TWO HOURS.
SUMIDA-GAWA
RYÔGOKU
RAINBOW BRIDGE
ARAKAWA
ODAIBA
KASAI
TOKYO BAY
WHO KNEW THERE WERE SO MANY BRIDGES OVER SUMIDA-GAWA...?
WHOA, THAT ONE'S LOW!
YOU THINK WE CAN PASS UNDER IT?
HEY!
WAITA-MINIT!!
BRRRRRR!!
WHO CARES? LET'S EAT!
IF I DON'T RAISE MY BLOOD SUGAR, I'LL FREEZE TO DEATH!!
tok
tok
tok

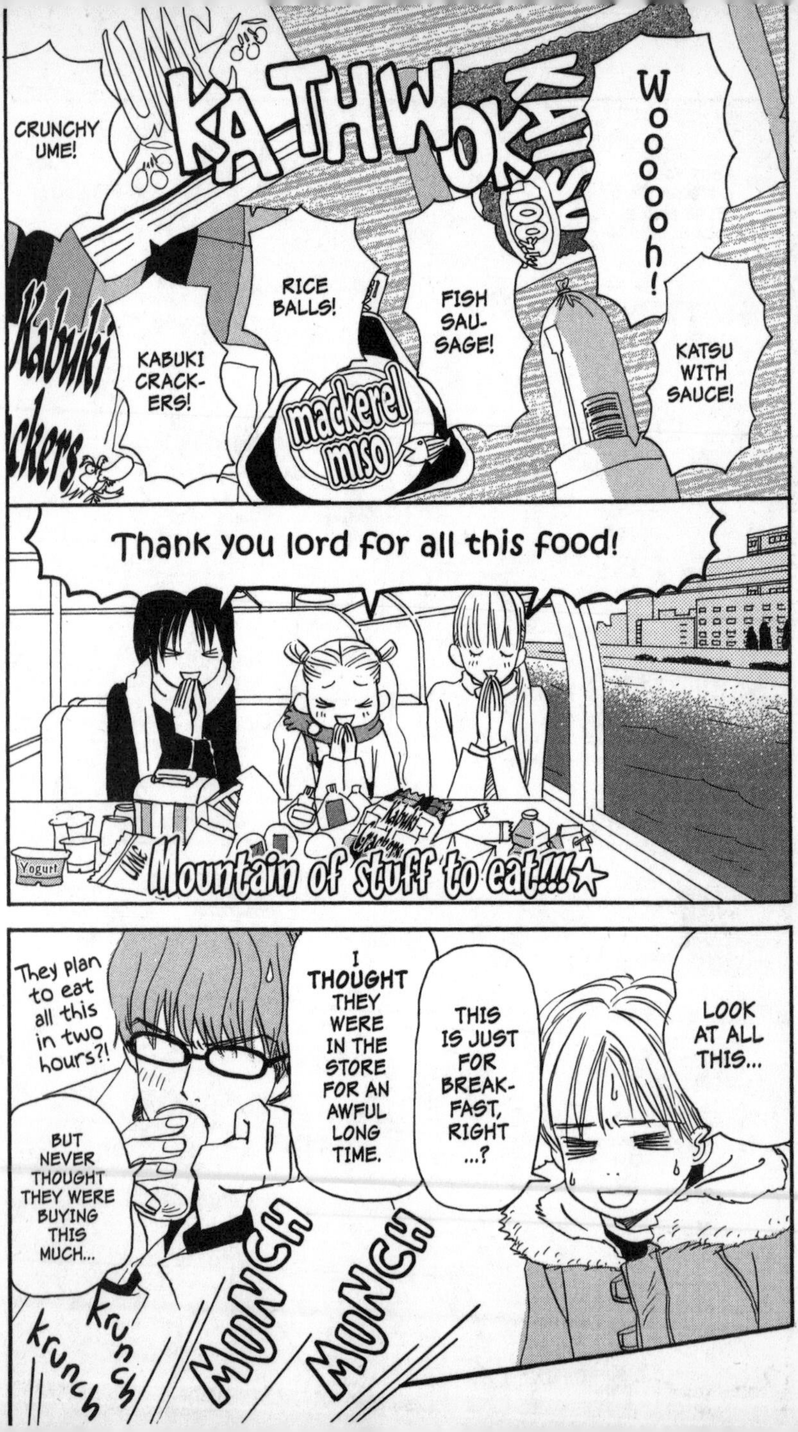

Wooooh!
KATSU WITH SAUCE!
KATSU
100%
KA-THWOK
FISH SAU-SAGE!
RICE BALLS!
mackerel miso
KABUKI CRACK-ERS!
Kabuki Crackers
CRUNCHY UME!
UME
Thank you lord for all this food!
Mountain of stuff to eat!!!★
Yogurt
LOOK AT ALL THIS...
THIS IS JUST FOR BREAK-FAST, RIGHT ...?
I THOUGHT THEY WERE IN THE STORE FOR AN AWFUL LONG TIME.
They plan to eat all this in two hours?!
BUT NEVER THOUGHT THEY WERE BUYING THIS MUCH...
MUNCH
MUNCH
krunch
krunch

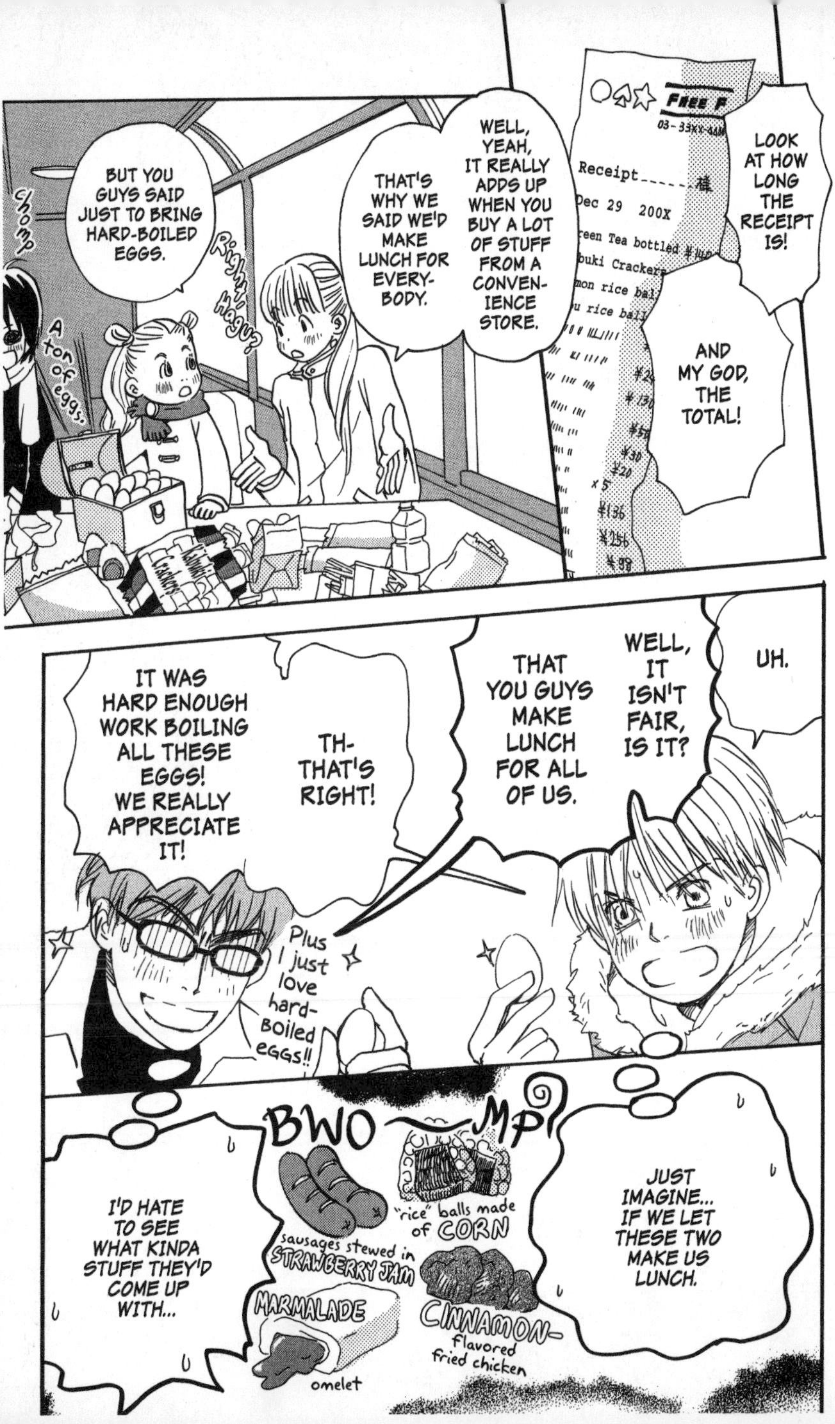
Free F
03-33XX-44
Receipt
Dec 29 200X
LOOK AT HOW LONG THE RECEIPT IS!
AND MY GOD, THE TOTAL!
WELL, YEAH, IT REALLY ADDS UP WHEN YOU BUY A LOT OF STUFF FROM A CONVEN-IENCE STORE.
THAT'S WHY WE SAID WE'D MAKE LUNCH FOR EVERY-BODY.
Right, Hagu?
BUT YOU GUYS SAID JUST TO BRING HARD-BOILED EGGS.
chomp
A ton of eggs.
UH.
WELL, IT ISN'T FAIR, IS IT?
THAT YOU GUYS MAKE LUNCH FOR ALL OF US.
TH-THAT'S RIGHT!
IT WAS HARD ENOUGH WORK BOILING ALL THESE EGGS! WE REALLY APPRECIATE IT!
Plus I just love hard-boiled eggs!!
JUST IMAGINE... IF WE LET THESE TWO MAKE US LUNCH.
BWO—MP
"rice" balls made of CORN
sausages stewed in STRAWBERRY JAM
CINNAMON-flavored fried chicken
MARMALADE omelet
I'D HATE TO SEE WHAT KINDA STUFF THEY'D COME UP WITH...

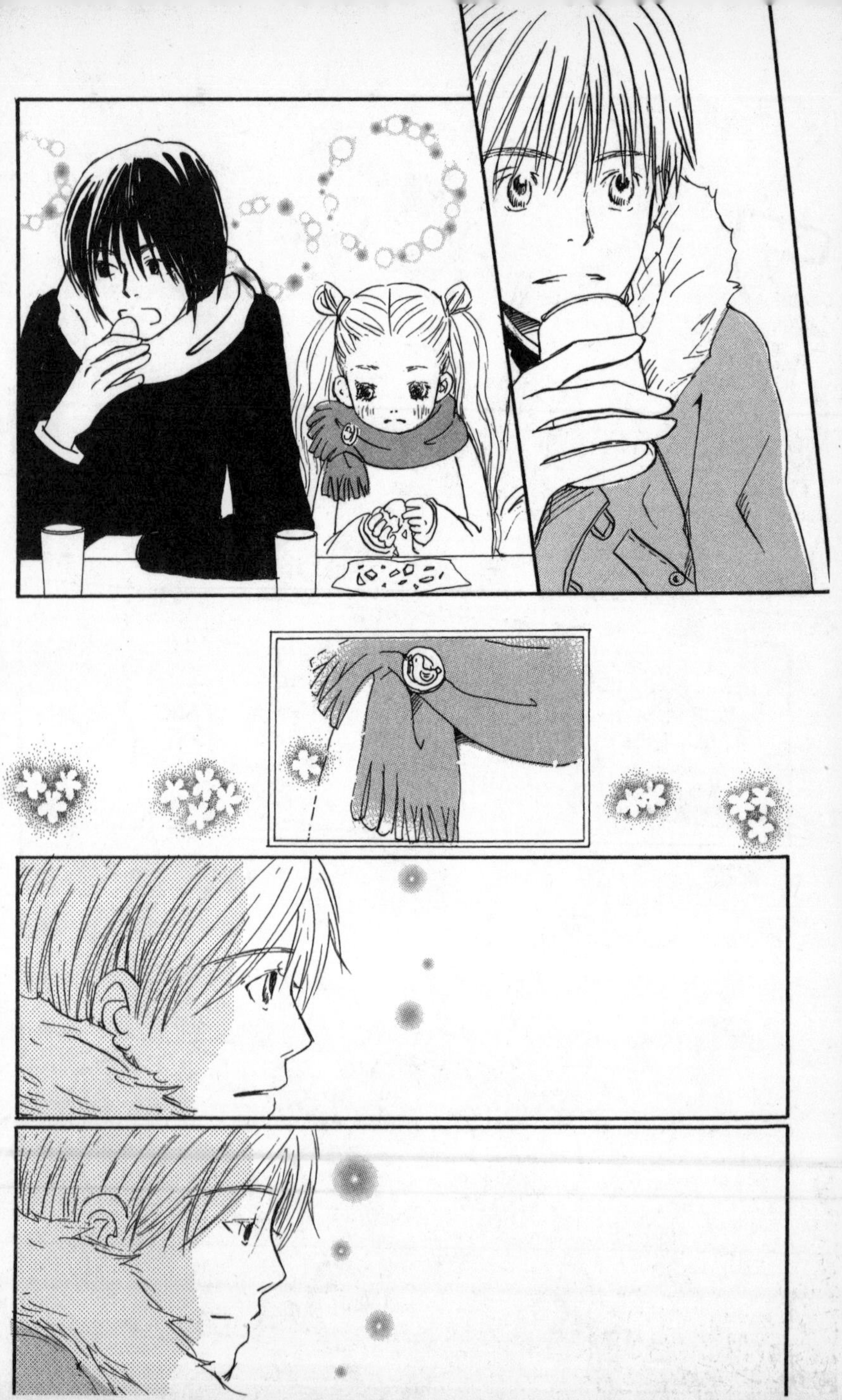

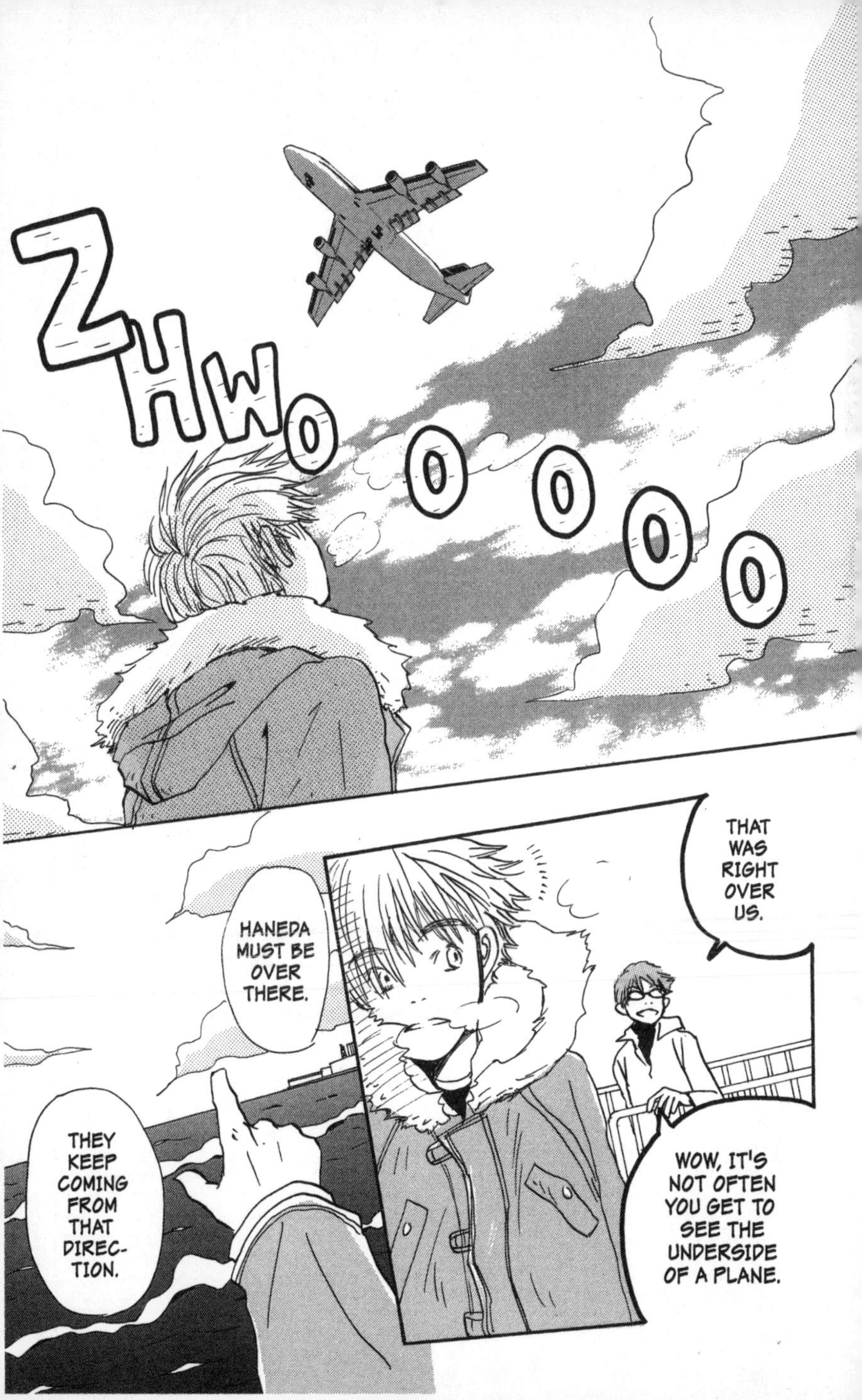
ZHWOOOOO
THAT WAS RIGHT OVER US.
WOW, IT'S NOT OFTEN YOU GET TO SEE THE UNDERSIDE OF A PLANE.
HANEDA MUST BE OVER THERE.
THEY KEEP COMING FROM THAT DIREC-TION.

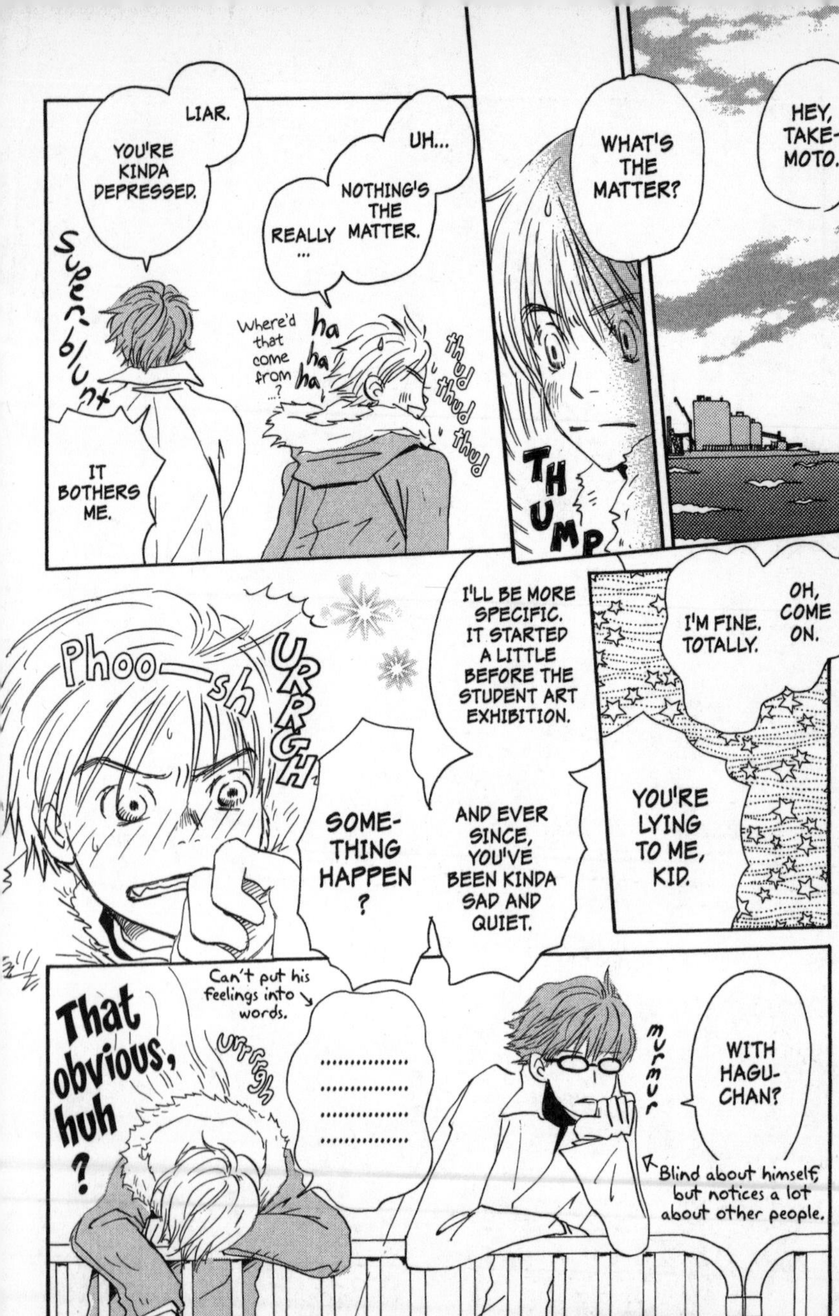
HEY, TAKE-MOTO.
WHAT'S THE MATTER?
THUMP
UH...
NOTHING'S THE MATTER.
REALLY...
ha ha ha,
Where'd that come from...?
thud thud thud
LIAR.
YOU'RE KINDA DEPRESSED.
Super-blunt
IT BOTHERS ME.
OH, COME ON.
I'M FINE. TOTALLY.
YOU'RE LYING TO ME, KID.
I'LL BE MORE SPECIFIC. IT STARTED A LITTLE BEFORE THE STUDENT ART EXHIBITION.
AND EVER SINCE, YOU'VE BEEN KINDA SAD AND QUIET.
SOME-THING HAPPEN?
URRGH
Phoo—sh
WITH HAGU-CHAN?
murmur
Blind about himself, but notices a lot about other people.
....
....
....
....
Can't put his feelings into words.
urrgh
That obvious, huh?

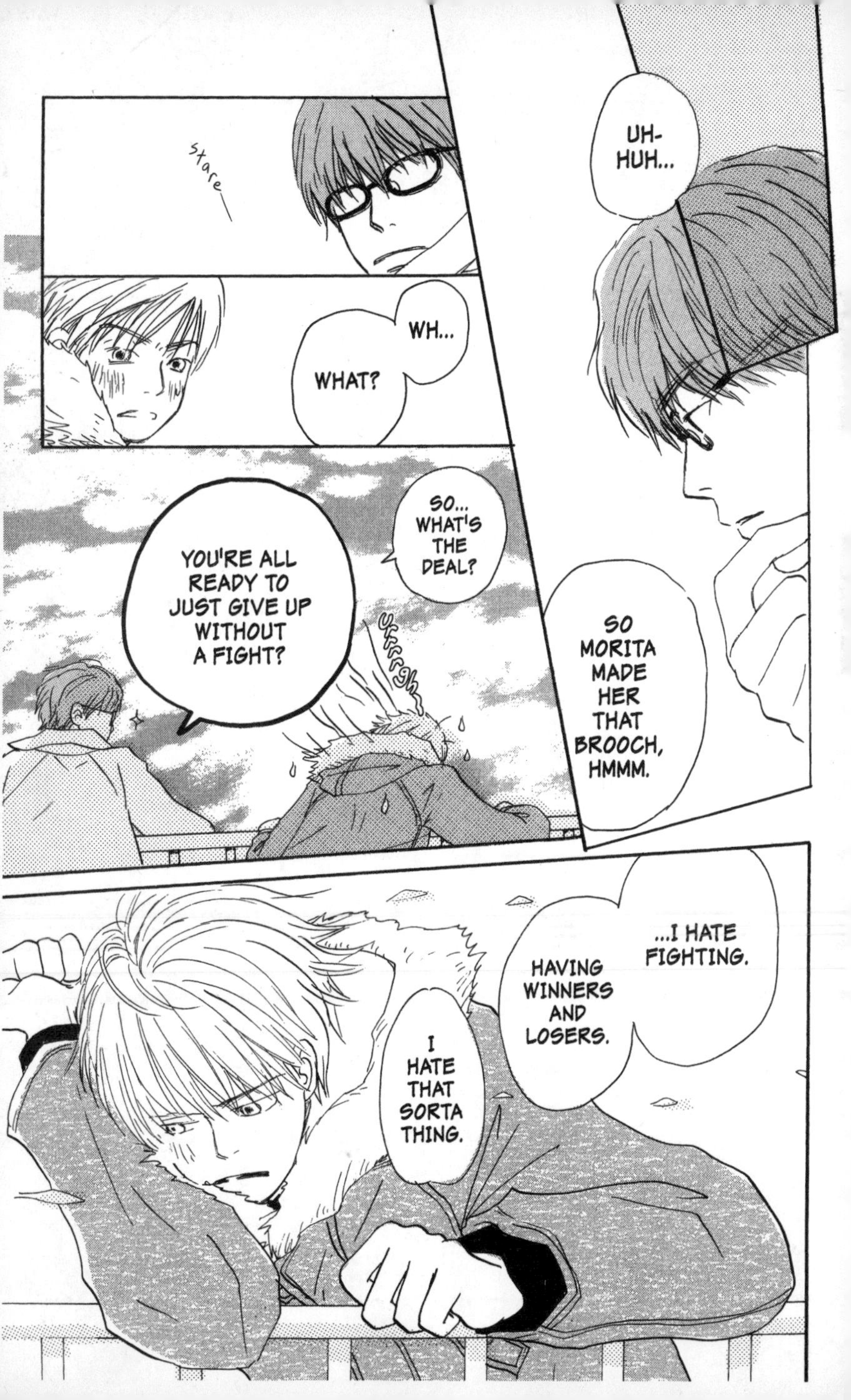
UH-HUH...
SO MORITA MADE HER THAT BROOCH, HMMM.
stare
WH...
WHAT?
SO... WHAT'S THE DEAL?
YOU'RE ALL READY TO JUST GIVE UP WITHOUT A FIGHT?
Urrrgh
...I HATE FIGHTING.
HAVING WINNERS AND LOSERS.
I HATE THAT SORTA THING.

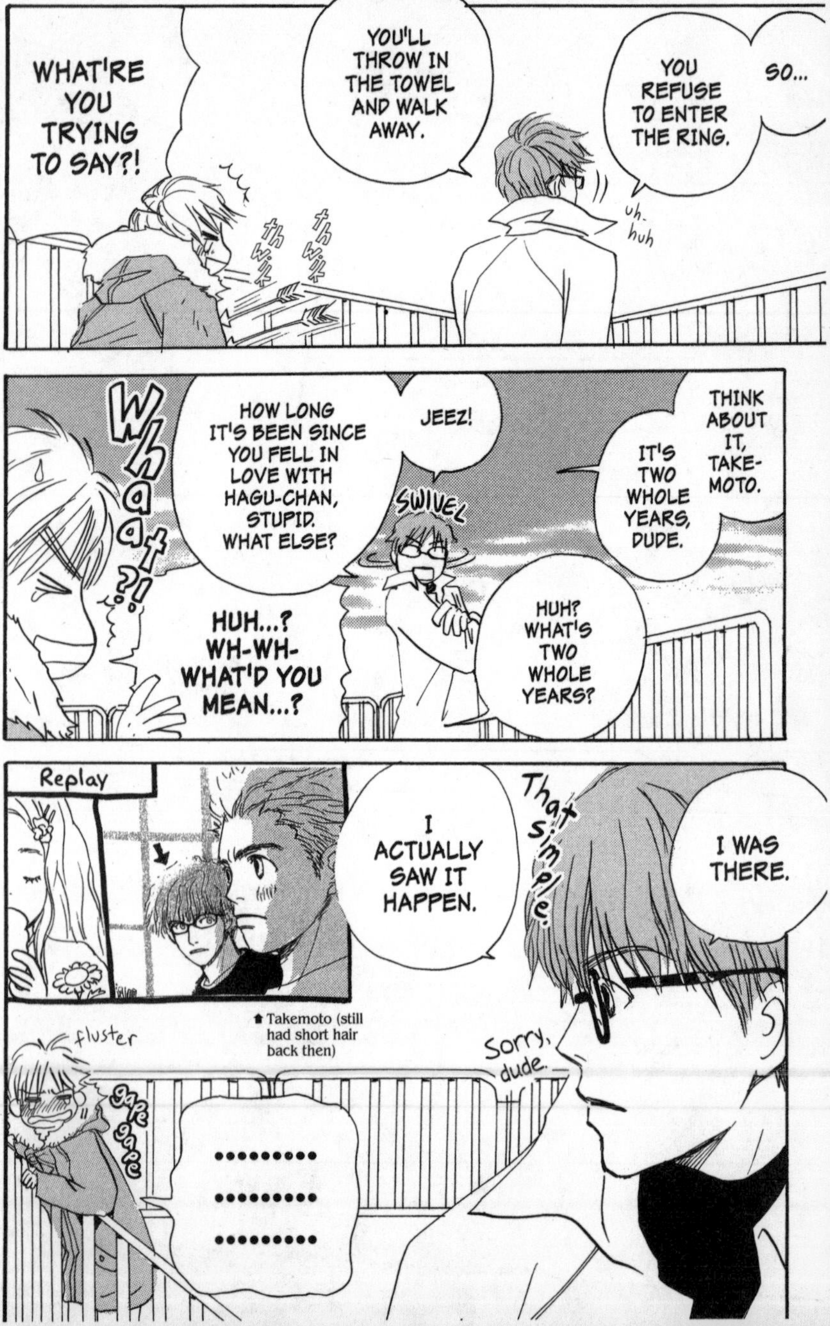
SO...
YOU REFUSE TO ENTER THE RING.
uh-huh
YOU'LL THROW IN THE TOWEL AND WALK AWAY.
WHAT'RE YOU TRYING TO SAY?!
thwik thwik
THINK ABOUT IT, TAKE-MOTO.
IT'S TWO WHOLE YEARS, DUDE.
HUH? WHAT'S TWO WHOLE YEARS?
JEEZ!
SWIVEL
HOW LONG IT'S BEEN SINCE YOU FELL IN LOVE WITH HAGU-CHAN, STUPID. WHAT ELSE?
HUH...? WH-WH-WHAT'D YOU MEAN...?
Whaat?!
I WAS THERE.
That simple.
Sorry, dude.
I ACTUALLY SAW IT HAPPEN.
Replay
Takemoto (still had short hair back then)
fluster
gape gape
....
....
....

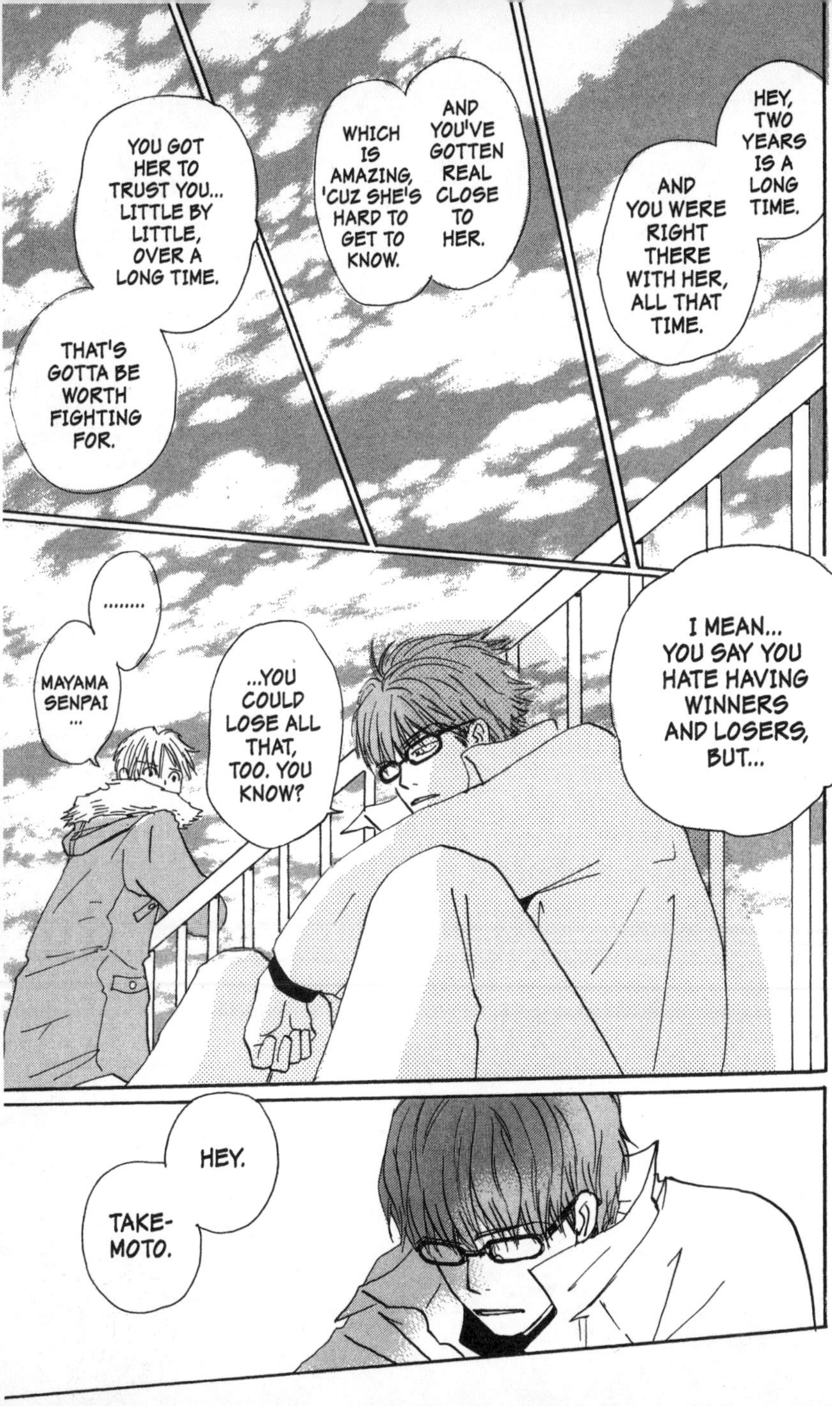
HEY, TWO YEARS IS A LONG TIME.
AND YOU WERE RIGHT THERE WITH HER, ALL THAT TIME.
AND YOU'VE GOTTEN REAL CLOSE TO HER.
WHICH IS AMAZING, 'CUZ SHE'S HARD TO GET TO KNOW.
YOU GOT HER TO TRUST YOU... LITTLE BY LITTLE, OVER A LONG TIME.
THAT'S GOTTA BE WORTH FIGHTING FOR.
I MEAN... YOU SAY YOU HATE HAVING WINNERS AND LOSERS, BUT...
...YOU COULD LOSE ALL THAT, TOO. YOU KNOW?
....
MAYAMA SENPAI ...
HEY.
TAKE-MOTO.

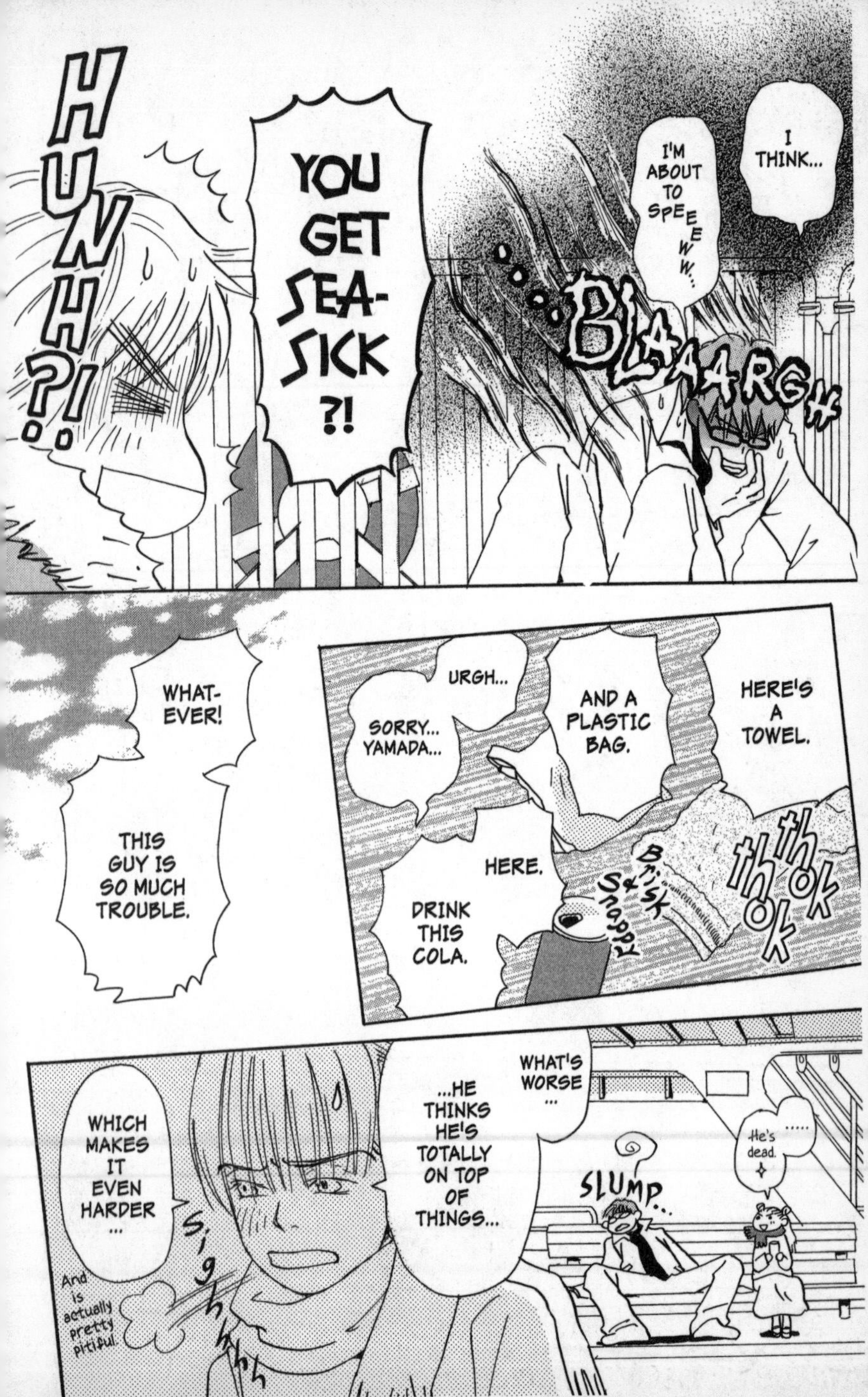
I THINK...
I'M ABOUT TO SPEEEWW...
...BLAARGH
YOU GET SEA-SICK?!
HUNH?!
HERE'S A TOWEL.
AND A PLASTIC BAG.
thok thok
URGH...
SORRY... YAMADA...
HERE.
DRINK THIS COLA.
Brisk & Snappy
WHAT-EVER!
THIS GUY IS SO MUCH TROUBLE.
......
He's dead.
SLUMP...
WHAT'S WORSE...
...HE THINKS HE'S TOTALLY ON TOP OF THINGS...
WHICH MAKES IT EVEN HARDER...
Sighhhh
And is actually pretty pitiful.

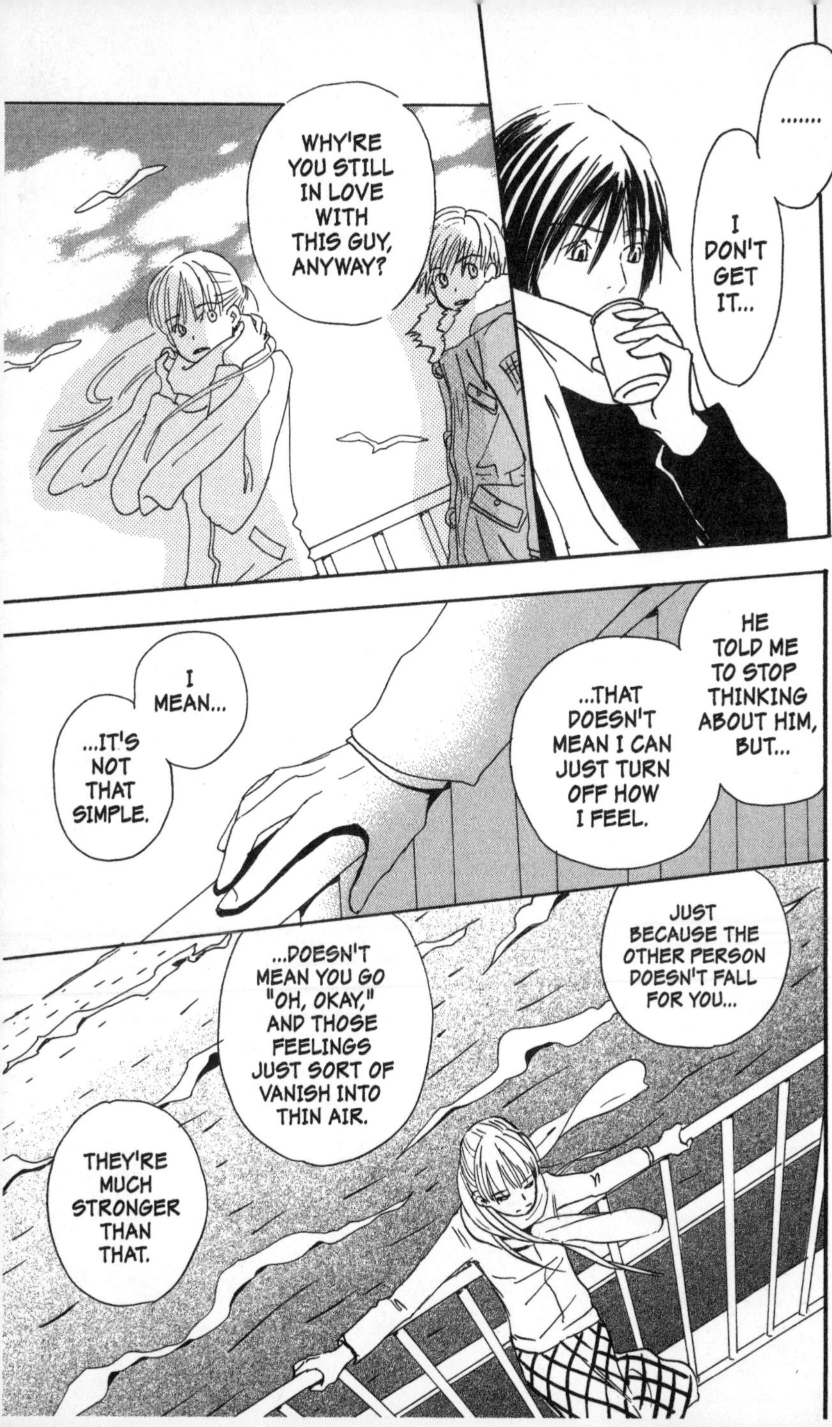

....
I DON'T GET IT...
WHY'RE YOU STILL IN LOVE WITH THIS GUY, ANYWAY?
HE TOLD ME TO STOP THINKING ABOUT HIM, BUT...
...THAT DOESN'T MEAN I CAN JUST TURN OFF HOW I FEEL.
I MEAN...
...IT'S NOT THAT SIMPLE.
JUST BECAUSE THE OTHER PERSON DOESN'T FALL FOR YOU...
...DOESN'T MEAN YOU GO "OH, OKAY," AND THOSE FEELINGS JUST SORT OF VANISH INTO THIN AIR.
THEY'RE MUCH STRONGER THAN THAT.

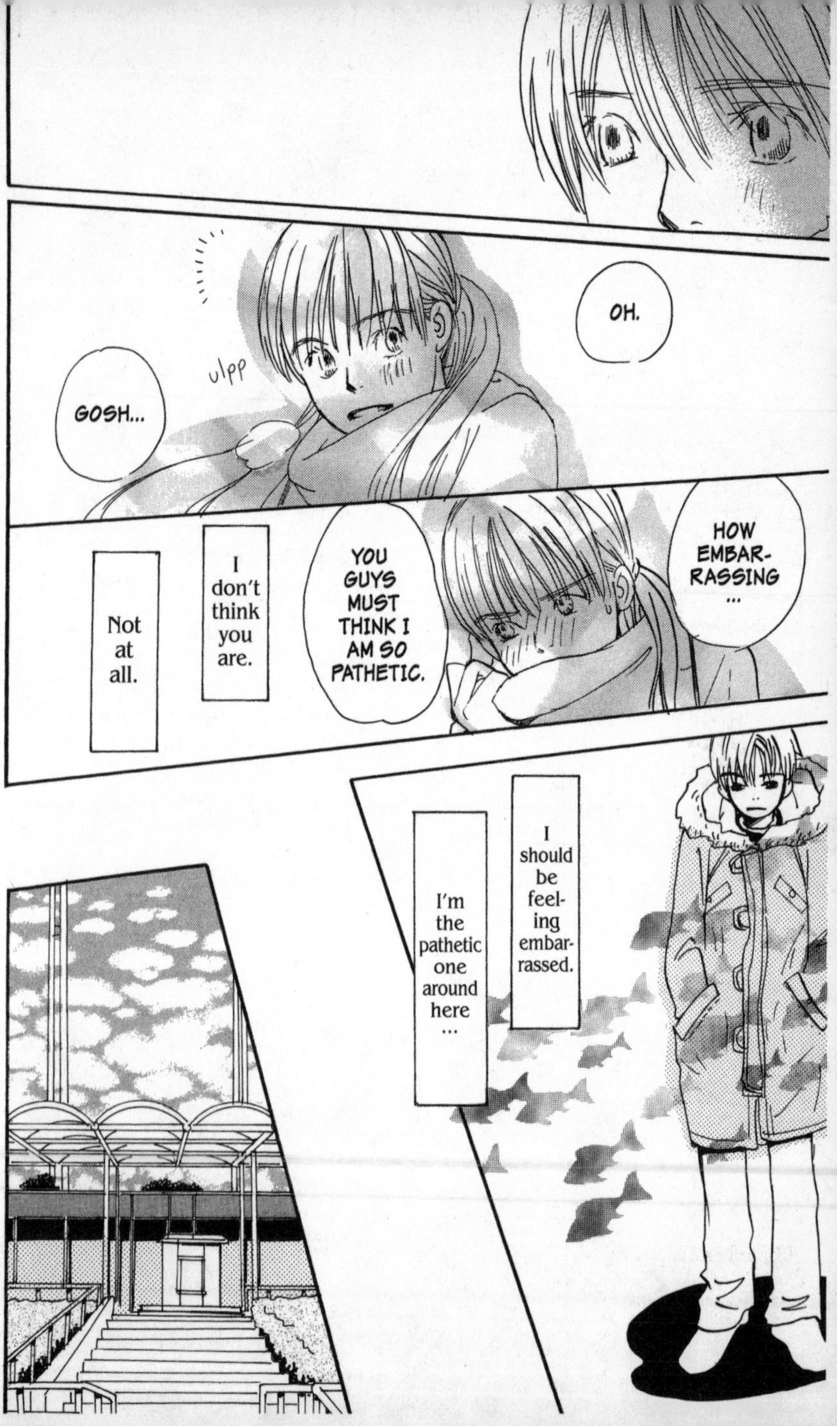
OH.
ulpp
GOSH...
HOW EMBARRASSING...
YOU GUYS MUST THINK I AM SO PATHETIC.
I don't think you are.
Not at all.
I should be feeling embarrassed.
I'm the pathetic one around here...

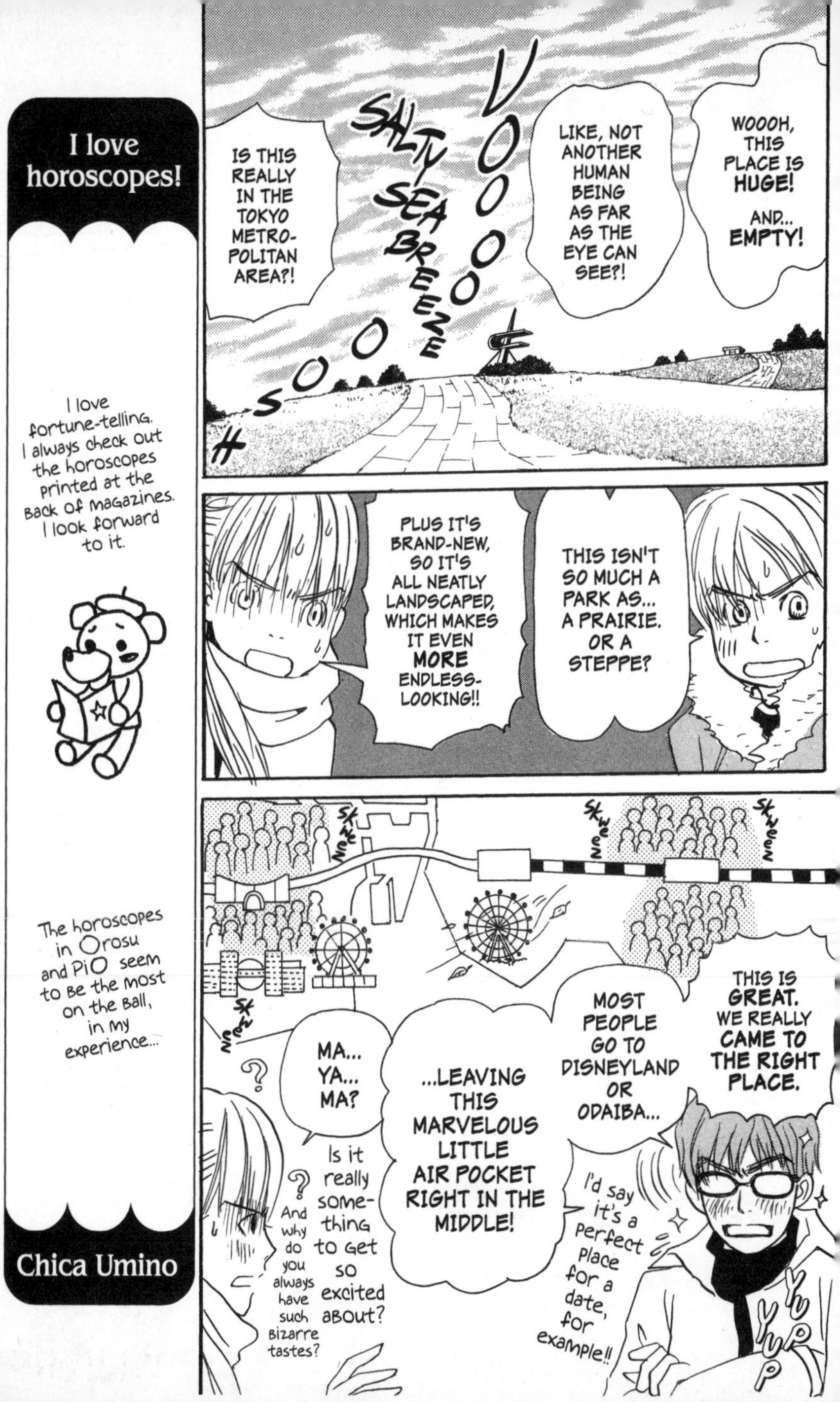
WOOOH, THIS PLACE IS HUGE!
AND... EMPTY!
LIKE, NOT ANOTHER HUMAN BEING AS FAR AS THE EYE CAN SEE?!
VOOOOOOSH
SALTY SEA BREEZE
IS THIS REALLY IN THE TOKYO METRO-POLITAN AREA?!
THIS ISN'T SO MUCH A PARK AS... A PRAIRIE. OR A STEPPE?
PLUS IT'S BRAND-NEW, SO IT'S ALL NEATLY LANDSCAPED, WHICH MAKES IT EVEN MORE ENDLESS-LOOKING!!
SKWEEN
SKWEEN
SKWEEN
SKWEEN
THIS IS GREAT. WE REALLY CAME TO THE RIGHT PLACE.
MOST PEOPLE GO TO DISNEYLAND OR ODAIBA...
...LEAVING THIS MARVELOUS LITTLE AIR POCKET RIGHT IN THE MIDDLE!
I'd say it's a perfect place for a date, for example!!
YUP YUP
MA... YA... MA?
Is it really something to get so excited about?
And why do you always have such bizarre tastes?

I love horoscopes!

I love fortune-telling. I always check out the horoscopes printed at the back of magazines. I look forward to it.

The horoscopes in Orosu and PiO seem to be the most on the ball, in my experience...

Chica Umino

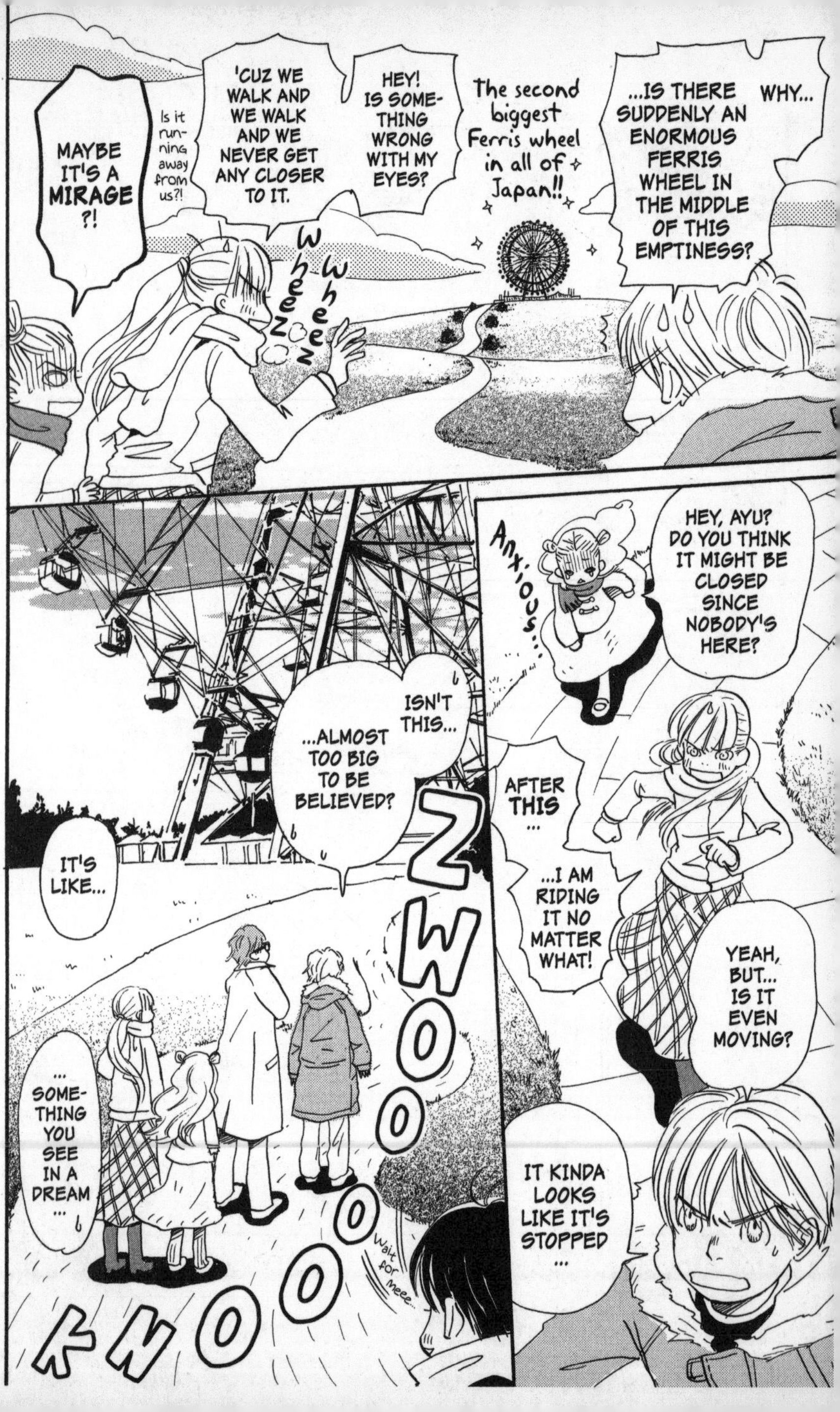
WHY...
...IS THERE SUDDENLY AN ENORMOUS FERRIS WHEEL IN THE MIDDLE OF THIS EMPTINESS?
The second biggest Ferris wheel in all of Japan!!
HEY! IS SOMETHING WRONG WITH MY EYES?
'CUZ WE WALK AND WE WALK AND WE NEVER GET ANY CLOSER TO IT.
Is it running away from us?!
MAYBE IT'S A MIRAGE?!
Wheeze wheeze
HEY, AYU? DO YOU THINK IT MIGHT BE CLOSED SINCE NOBODY'S HERE?
Anxious...
AFTER THIS...
...I AM RIDING IT NO MATTER WHAT!
YEAH, BUT... IS IT EVEN MOVING?
IT KINDA LOOKS LIKE IT'S STOPPED...
ISN'T THIS...
...ALMOST TOO BIG TO BE BELIEVED?
IT'S LIKE...
...SOMETHING YOU SEE IN A DREAM...
ZWOOOOOOONK
Wait for meee...

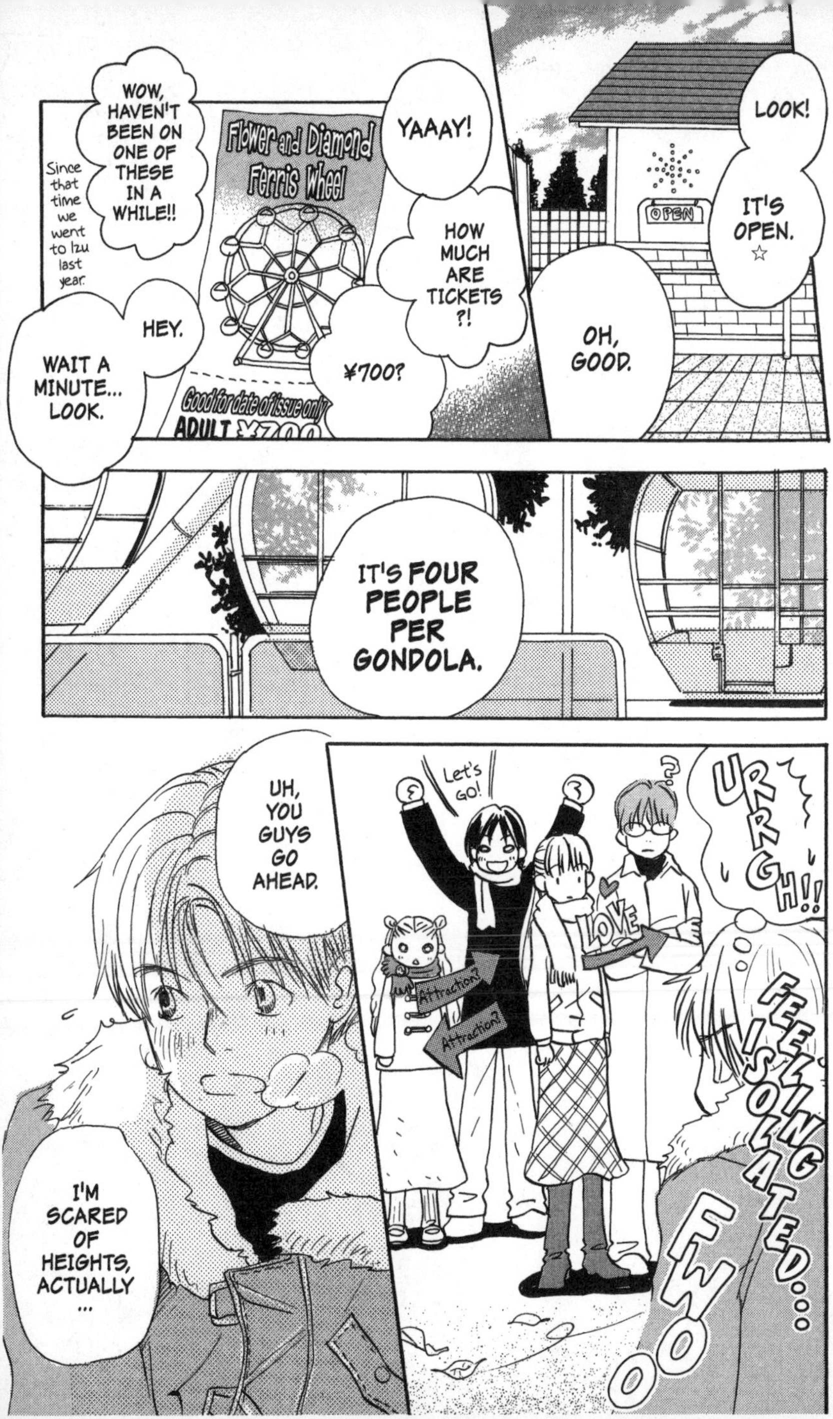
LOOK!
IT'S OPEN. ☆
OPEN
OH, GOOD.
YAAAY!
HOW MUCH ARE TICKETS ?!
¥700?
Flower and Diamond Ferris Wheel
Good for date of issue only
ADULT
WOW, HAVEN'T BEEN ON ONE OF THESE IN A WHILE!!
Since that time we went to Izu last year.
HEY.
WAIT A MINUTE... LOOK.
IT'S FOUR PEOPLE PER GONDOLA.
URRGH!!
FEELING ISOLATED...
FWOOO
Let's GO!
LOVE
Attraction?
Attraction?
UH, YOU GUYS GO AHEAD.
I'M SCARED OF HEIGHTS, ACTUALLY...

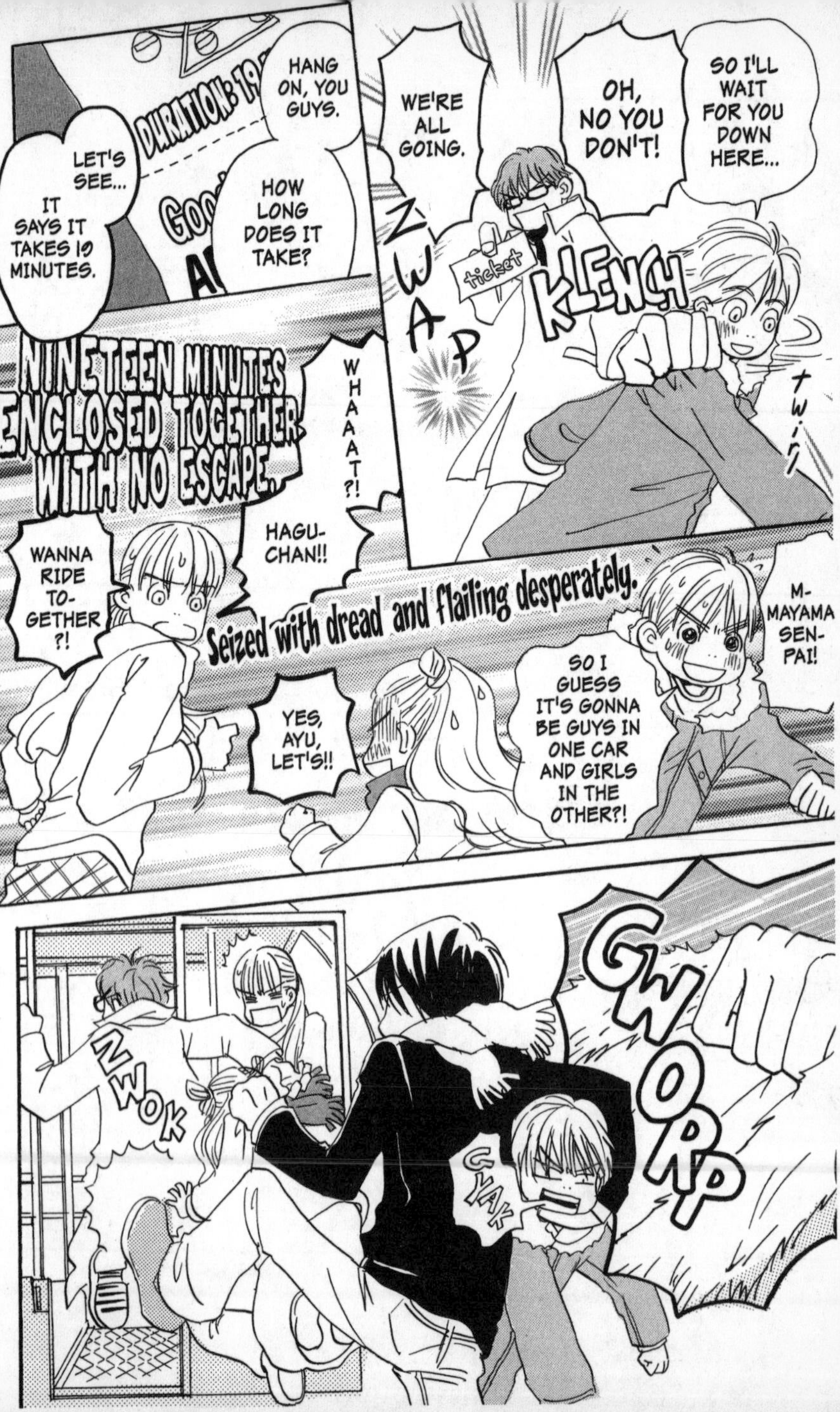
SO I'LL WAIT FOR YOU DOWN HERE...
OH, NO YOU DON'T!
WE'RE ALL GOING.
ZWAP
ticket
KLENCH
TWIRL
DURATION: 19
HANG ON, YOU GUYS.
HOW LONG DOES IT TAKE?
LET'S SEE...
IT SAYS IT TAKES 19 MINUTES.
M-MAYAMA SEN-PAI!
SO I GUESS IT'S GONNA BE GUYS IN ONE CAR AND GIRLS IN THE OTHER?!
Seized with dread and flailing desperately.
YES, AYU, LET'S!!
WHAAAAT?!
HAGU-CHAN!!
WANNA RIDE TO-GETHER?!
NINETEEN MINUTES ENCLOSED TOGETHER WITH NO ESCAPE.
GWORP
GYAK
NWOK

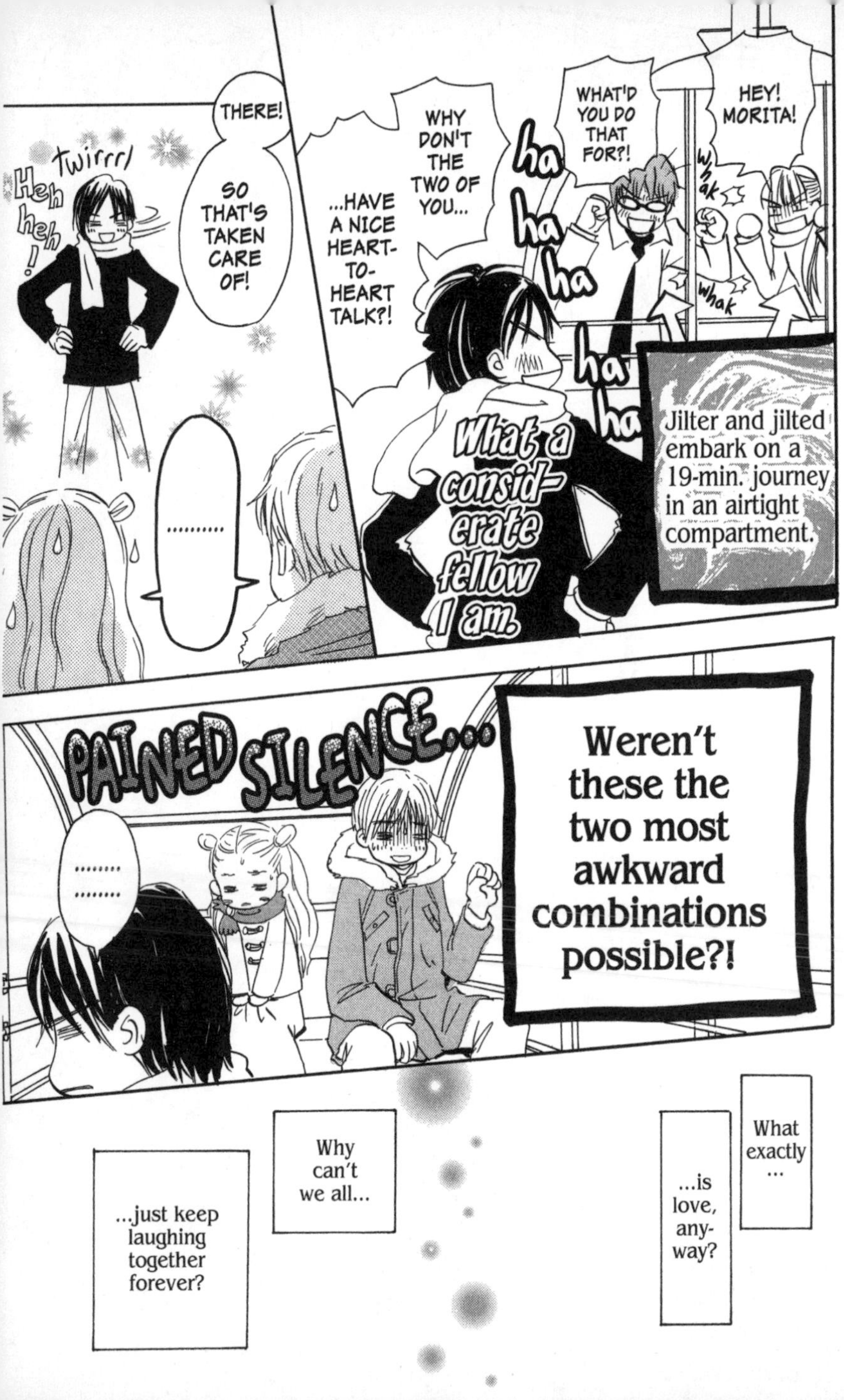
HEY! MORITA!
WHAT'D YOU DO THAT FOR?!
Whak
whak
ha ha ha ha ha ha
WHY DON'T THE TWO OF YOU...
...HAVE A NICE HEART-TO-HEART TALK?!
What a consid-erate fellow I am.
Jilter and jilted embark on a 19-min. journey in an airtight compartment.
THERE!
SO THAT'S TAKEN CARE OF!
Twirrrl
Heh heh!
....
Weren't these the two most awkward combinations possible?!
PAINED SILENCE...
....
....
What exactly ...
...is love, any-way?
Why can't we all...
...just keep laughing together forever?

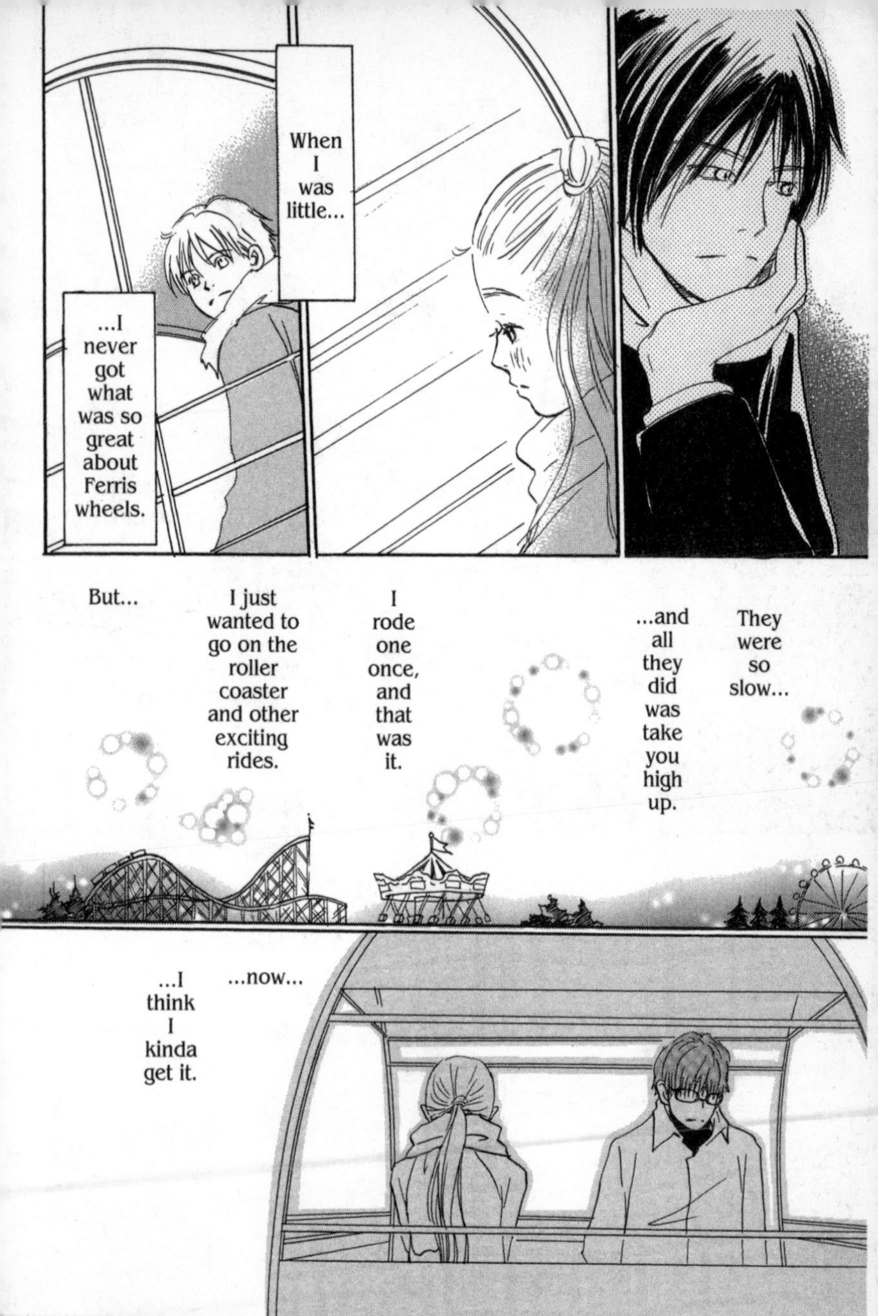
When I was little...
...I never got what was so great about Ferris wheels.
They were so slow...
...and all they did was take you high up.
I rode one once, and that was it.
I just wanted to go on the roller coaster and other exciting rides.
But...
...now...
...I think I kinda get it.

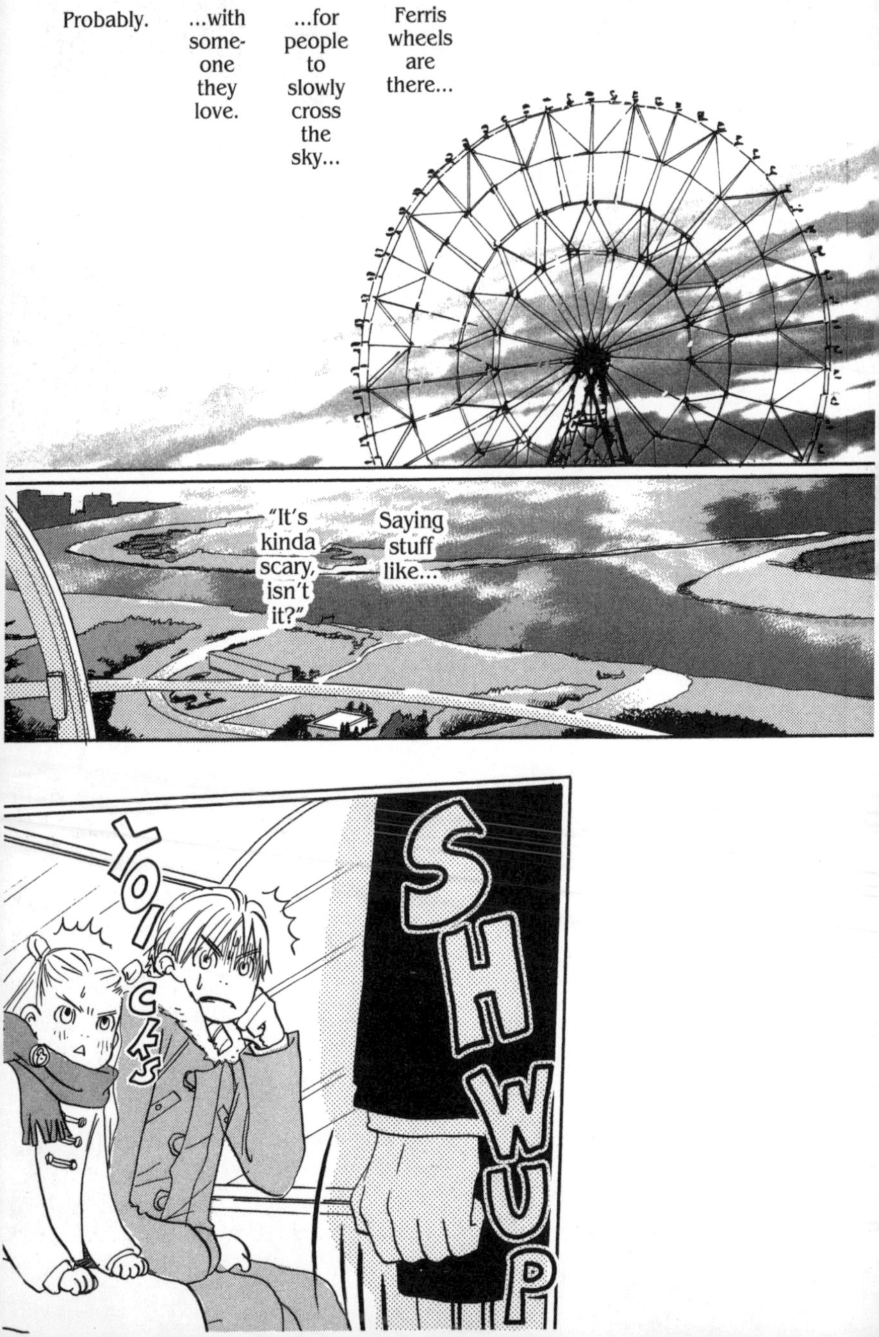
Ferris wheels are there...
...for people to slowly cross the sky...
...with someone they love.
Probably.
Saying stuff like...
"It's kinda scary, isn't it?"
SHWUP
YOICKS

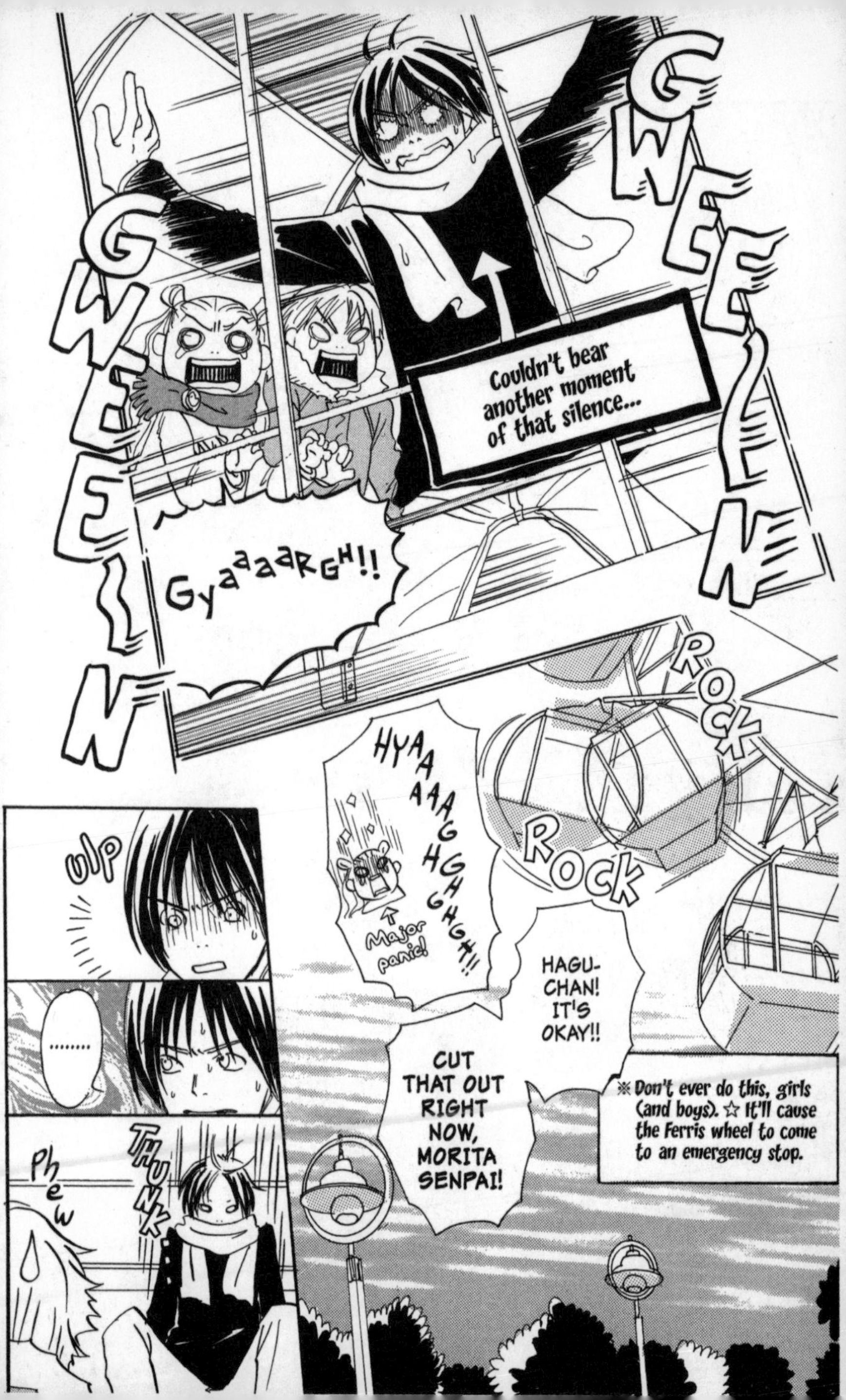
GWEEEN
Couldn't bear another moment of that silence...
GWEEE~N
GyaaaaRGH!!
ROCK
ROCK
HYAAAAAAGHGHGHGH!!
Major panic!
HAGU-CHAN! IT'S OKAY!!
CUT THAT OUT RIGHT NOW, MORITA SENPAI!
※Don't ever do this, girls (and boys). ☆ It'll cause the Ferris wheel to come to an emergency stop.
ulp
....
THUNK
Phew

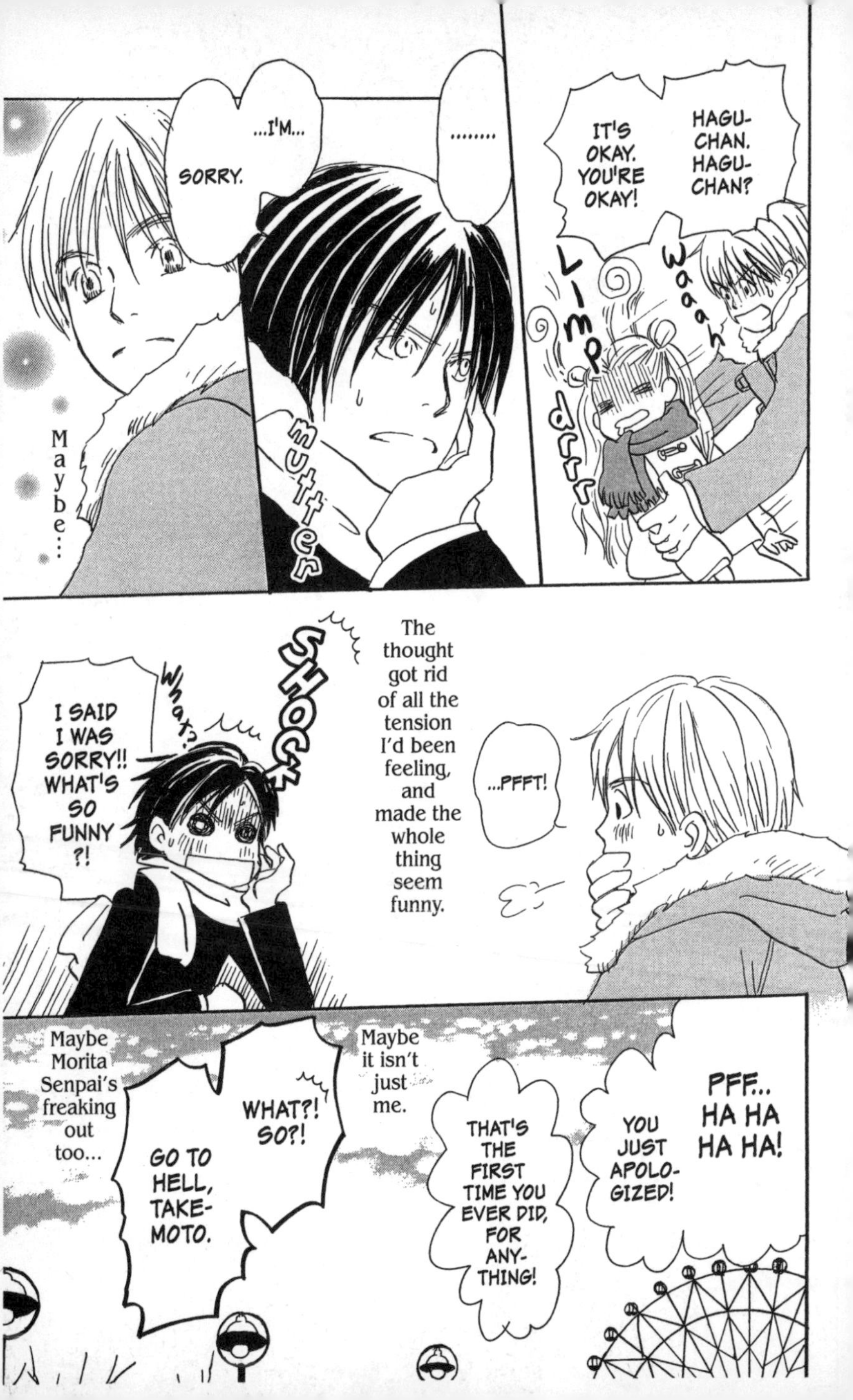
HAGU-CHAN. HAGU-CHAN?
IT'S OKAY. YOU'RE OKAY!
Waaah
Limp
drrr
....
mutter
...I'M... SORRY.
Maybe...
...PFFT!
The thought got rid of all the tension I'd been feeling, and made the whole thing seem funny.
SHOCK
What?!
I SAID I WAS SORRY!! WHAT'S SO FUNNY?!
PFF... HA HA HA HA!
YOU JUST APOLOGIZED!
THAT'S THE FIRST TIME YOU EVER DID, FOR ANYTHING!
Maybe it isn't just me.
WHAT?! SO?!
GO TO HELL, TAKE-MOTO.
Maybe Morita Senpai's freaking out too...

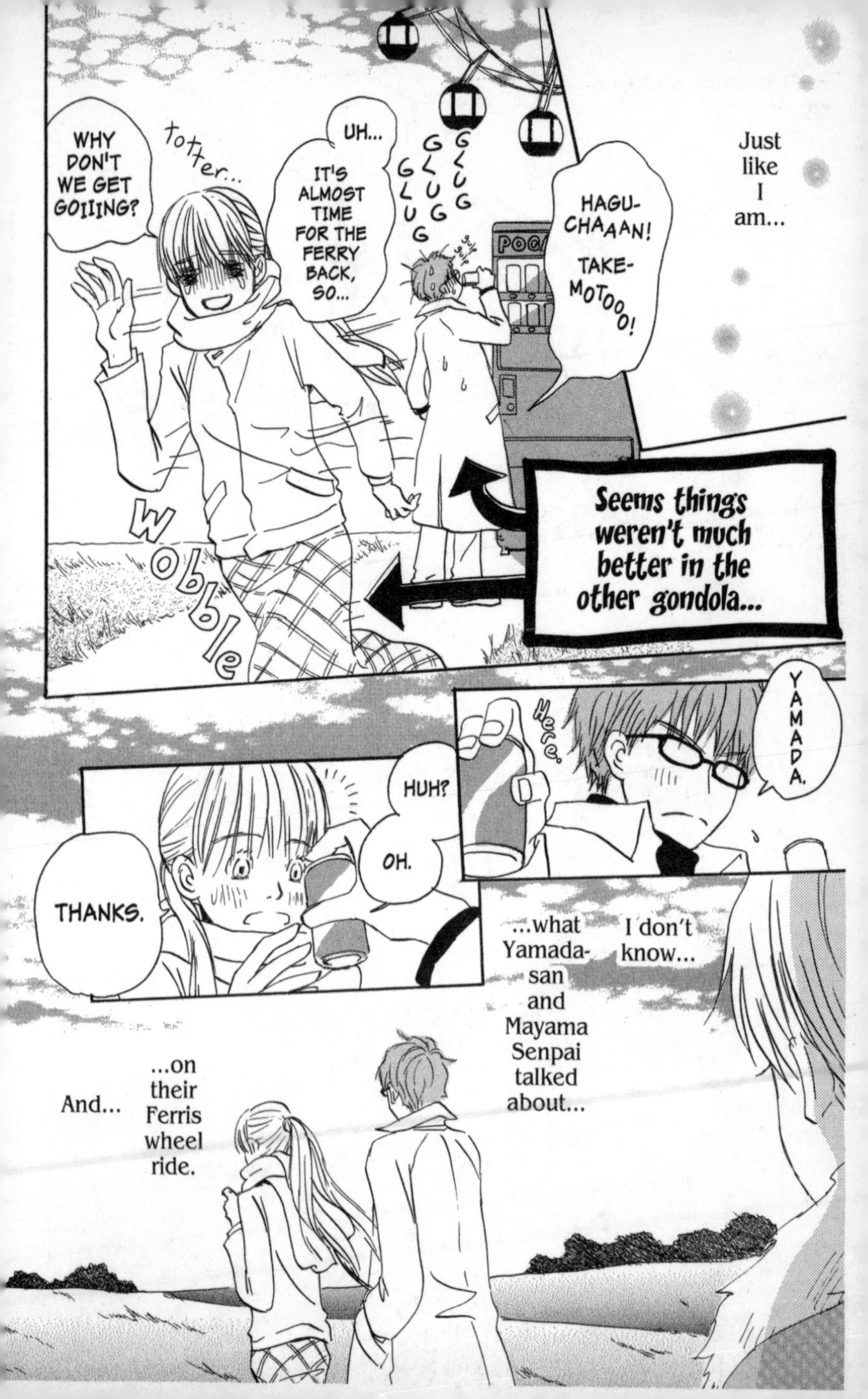
Just like I am...
HAGU-CHAAAN! TAKE-MOTOOO!
GLUG GLUG GLUG GLUG
gulp gulp
UH... IT'S ALMOST TIME FOR THE FERRY BACK, SO...
totter...
WHY DON'T WE GET GOIIING?
Seems things weren't much better in the other gondola...
wobble
YAMADA.
Here.
HUH?
OH.
THANKS.
I don't know...
...what Yamada-san and Mayama Senpai talked about...
...on their Ferris wheel ride.
And...

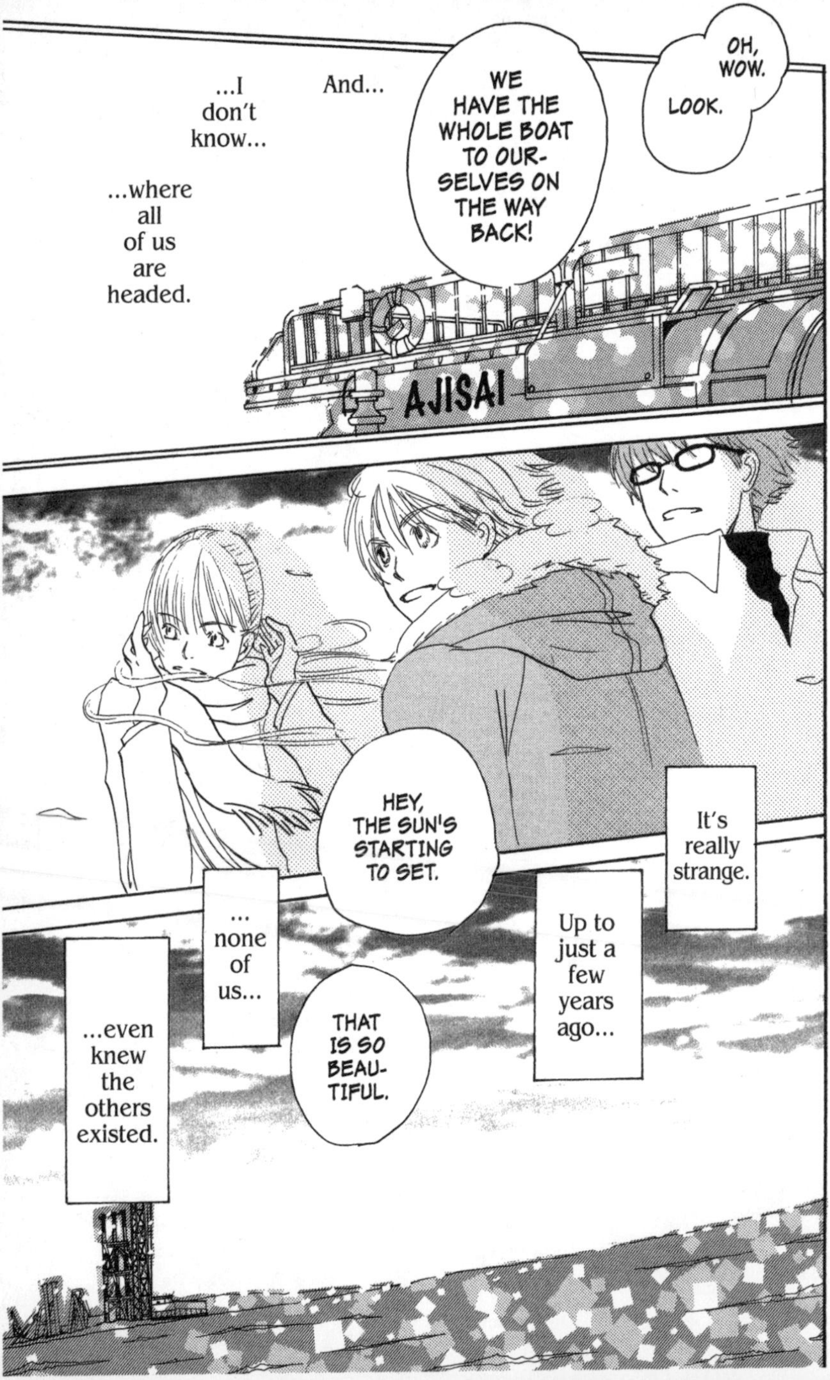

OH, WOW.
LOOK.
WE HAVE THE WHOLE BOAT TO OURSELVES ON THE WAY BACK!
And...
...I don't know...
...where all of us are headed.
AJISAI
It's really strange.
HEY, THE SUN'S STARTING TO SET.
Up to just a few years ago...
...none of us...
THAT IS SO BEAUTIFUL.
...even knew the others existed.

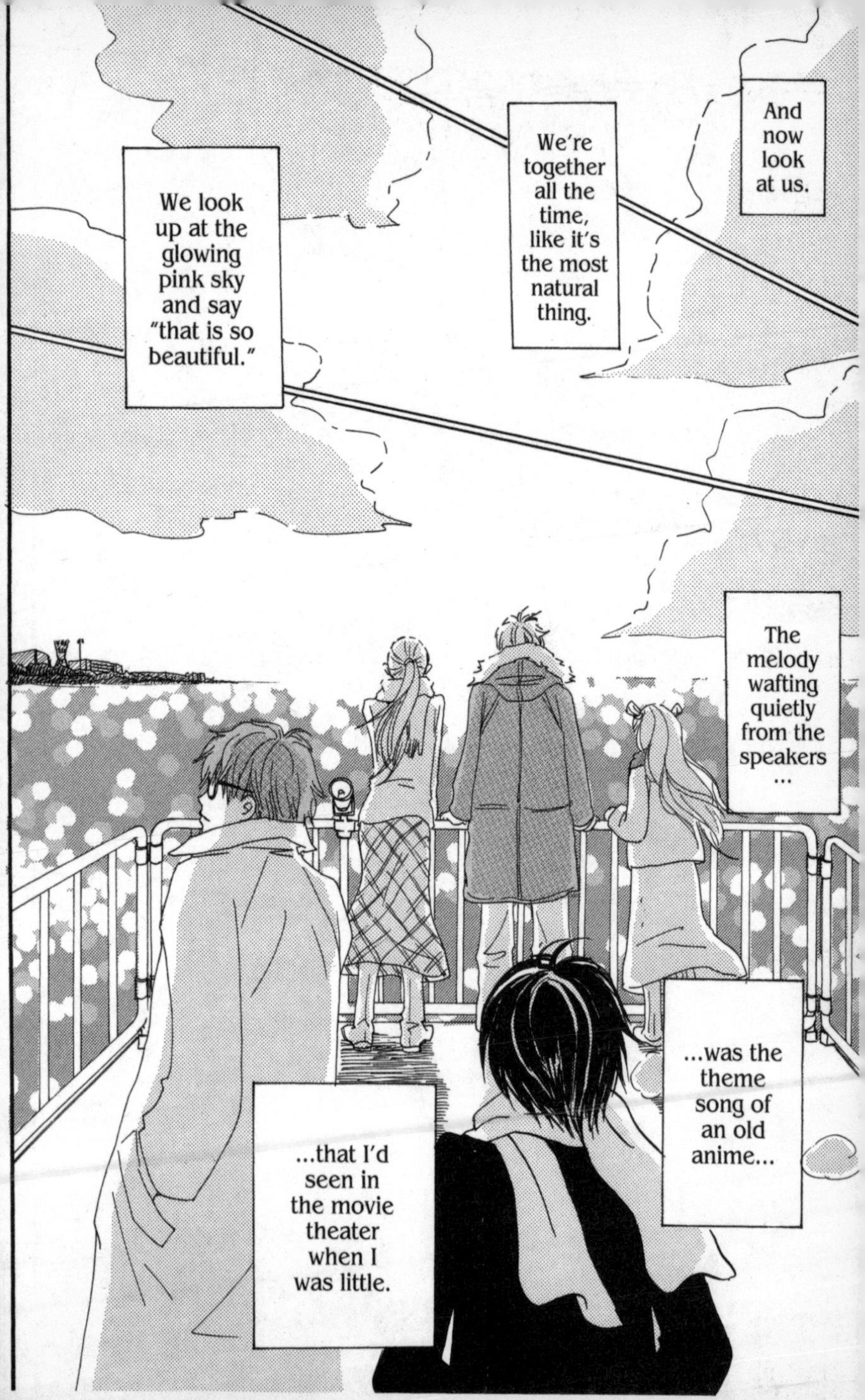
And now look at us.
We're together all the time, like it's the most natural thing.
We look up at the glowing pink sky and say "that is so beautiful."
The melody wafting quietly from the speakers ...
...was the theme song of an old anime...
...that I'd seen in the movie theater when I was little.

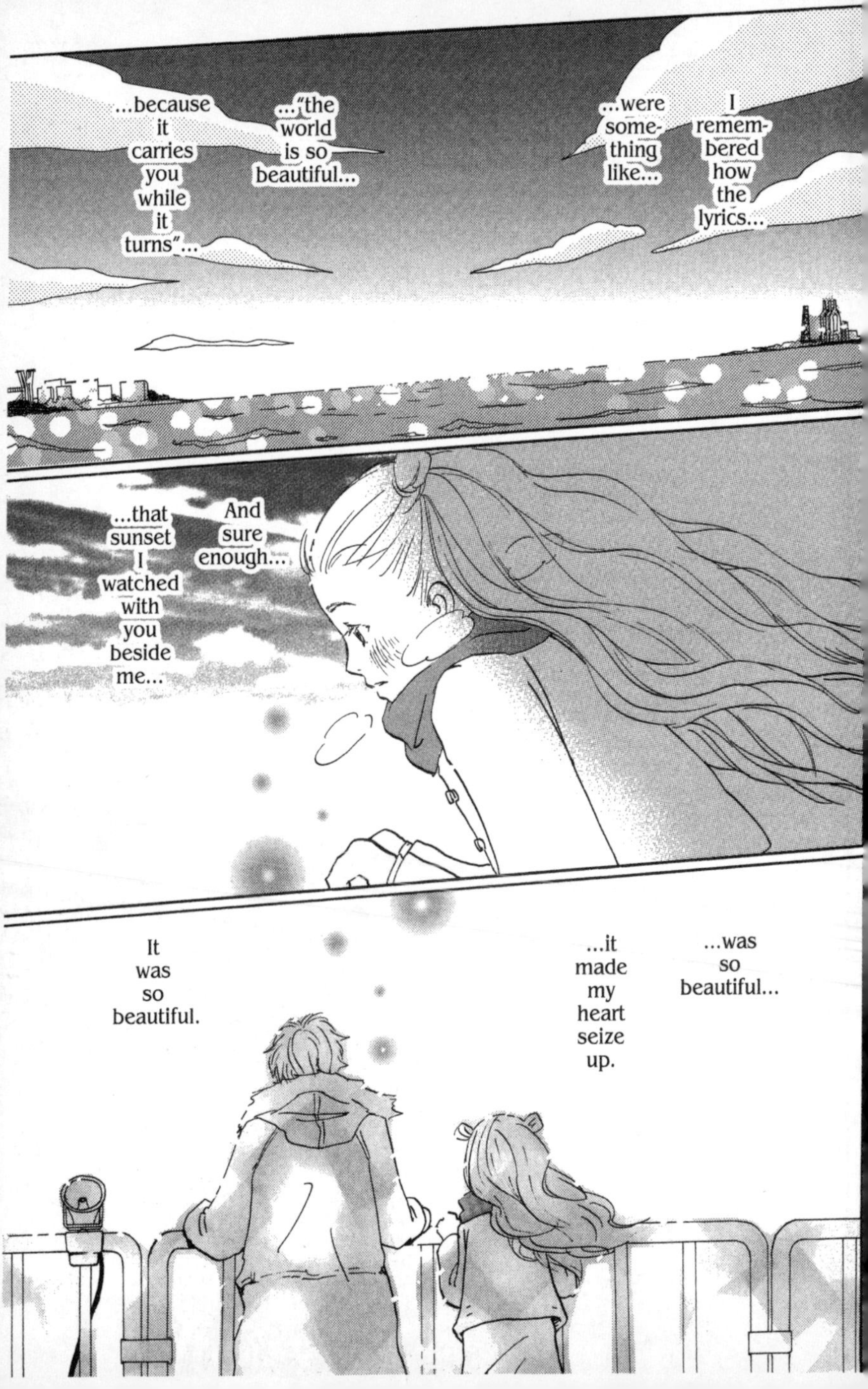
I remembered how the lyrics...
...were something like...
..."the world is so beautiful...
...because it carries you while it turns"...
And sure enough...
...that sunset I watched with you beside me...
...was so beautiful...
...it made my heart seize up.
It was so beautiful.

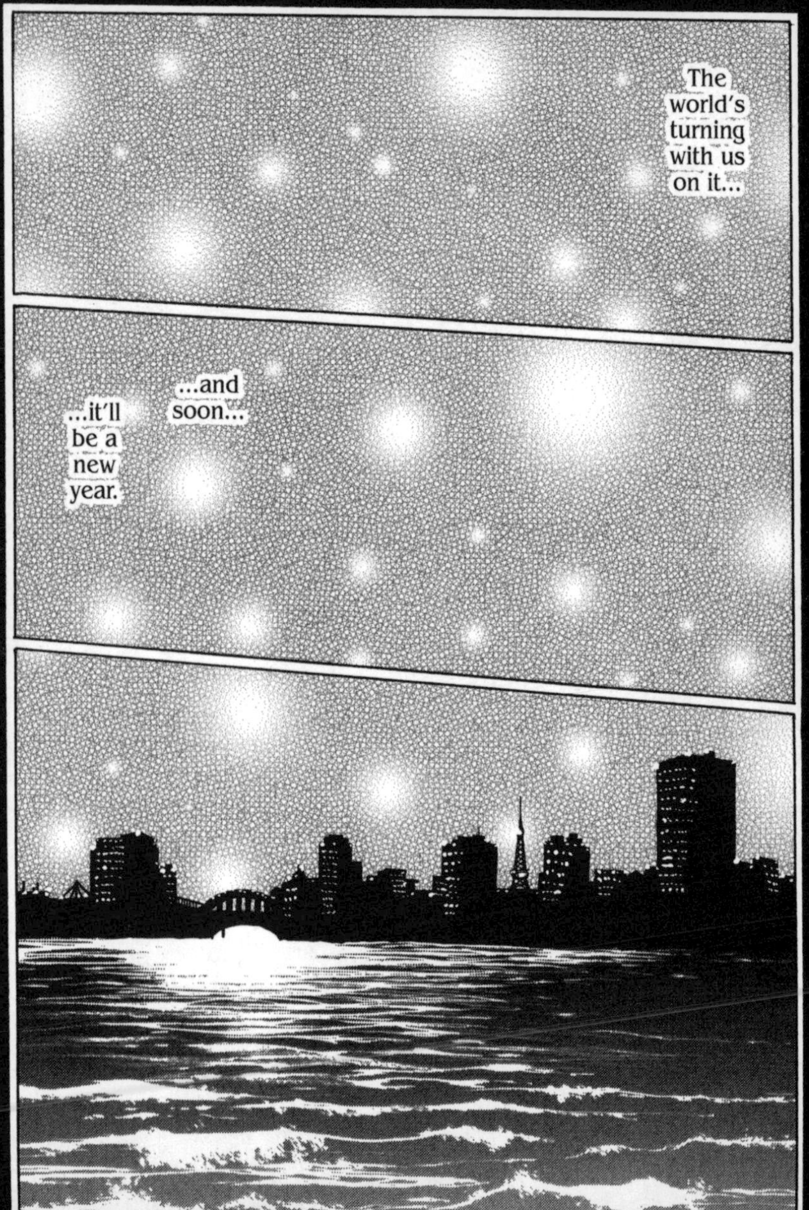
The world's turning with us on it...
...and soon...
...it'll be a new year.

chapter 18—end—

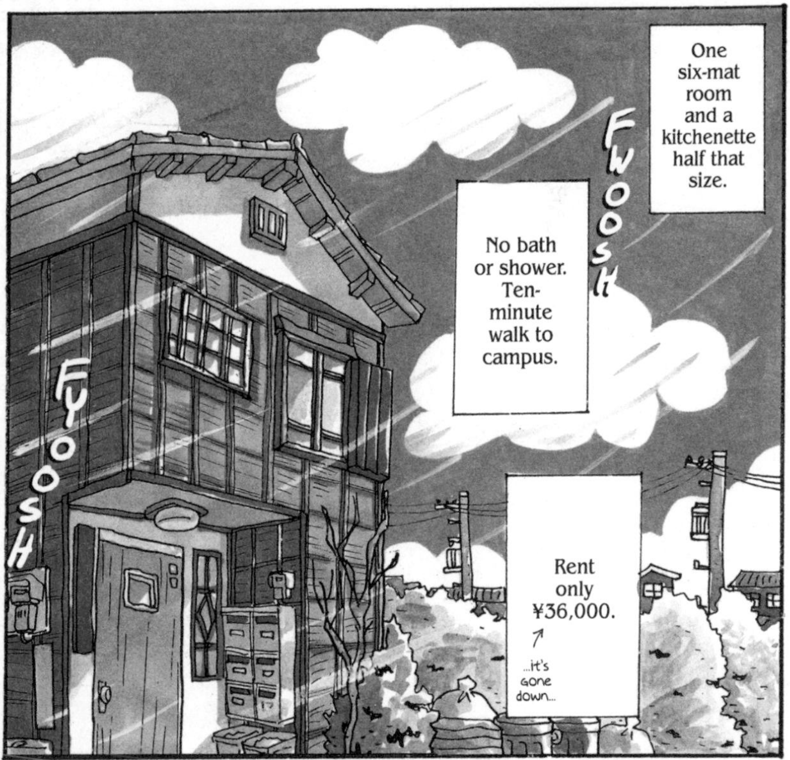
One six-mat room and a kitchenette half that size.
FWOOSH
No bath or shower. Ten-minute walk to campus.
Rent only ¥36,000.
...it's gone down...
FYOOOSH

*about $290

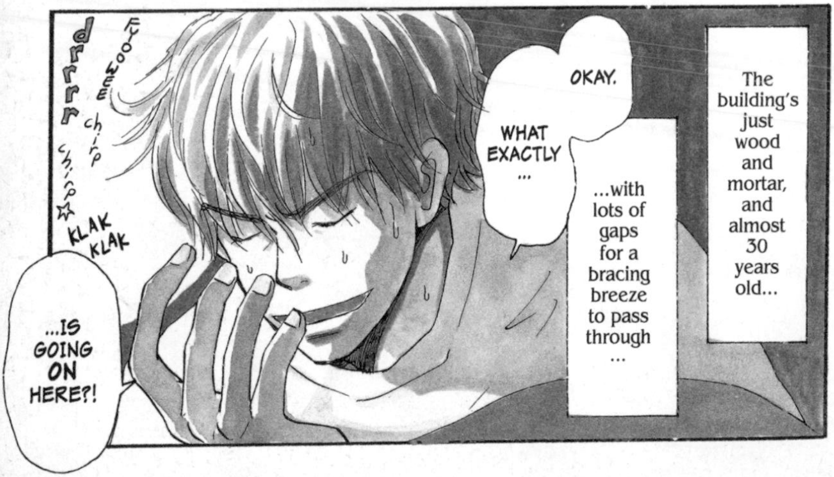
The building's just wood and mortar, and almost 30 years old...
...with lots of gaps for a bracing breeze to pass through...
OKAY.
WHAT EXACTLY...
FYOOWEE
chirp
drrrr
chirp☆
KLAK KLAK
...IS GOING ON HERE?!

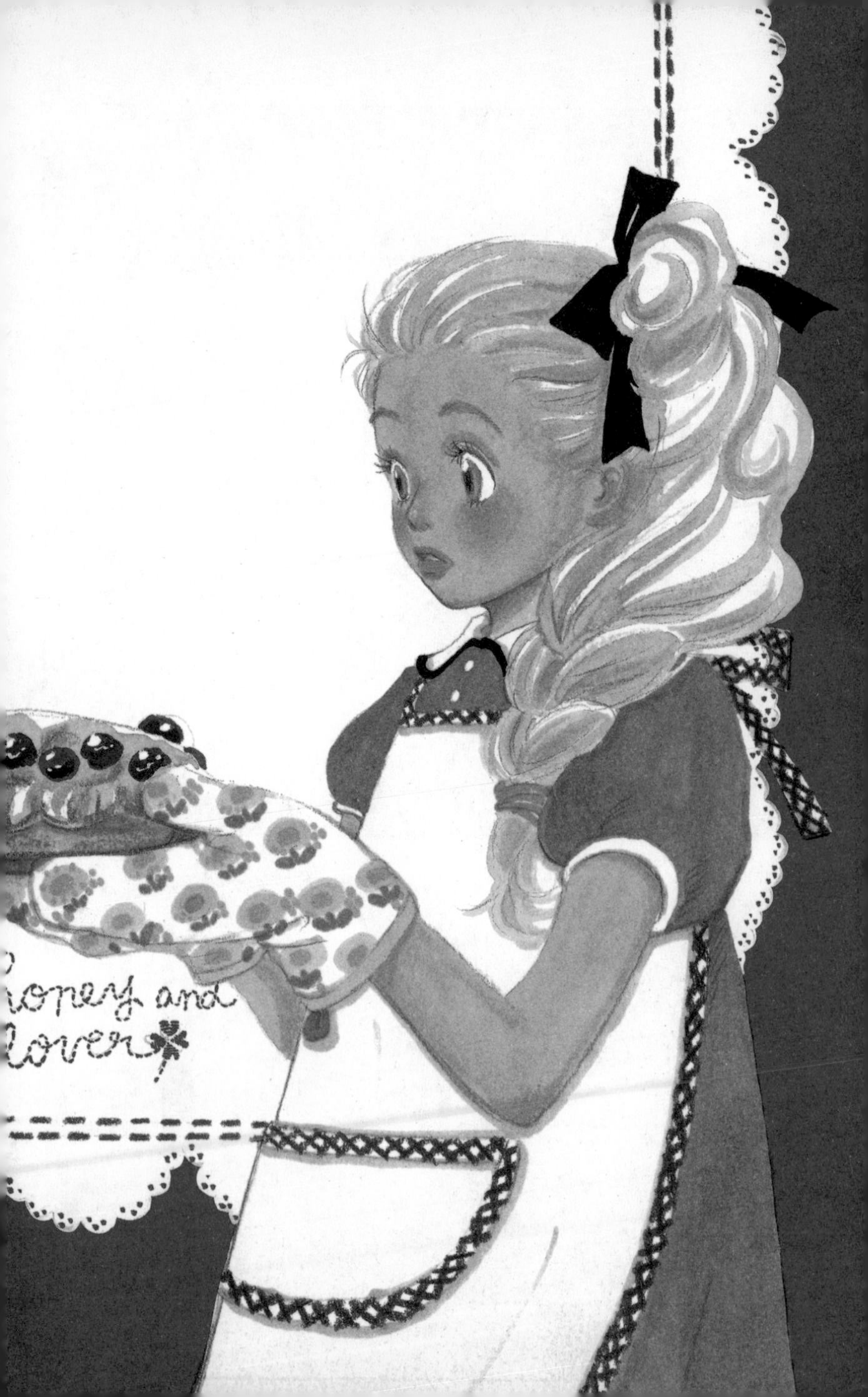
oney and
lover

honey and clover

chapter 19

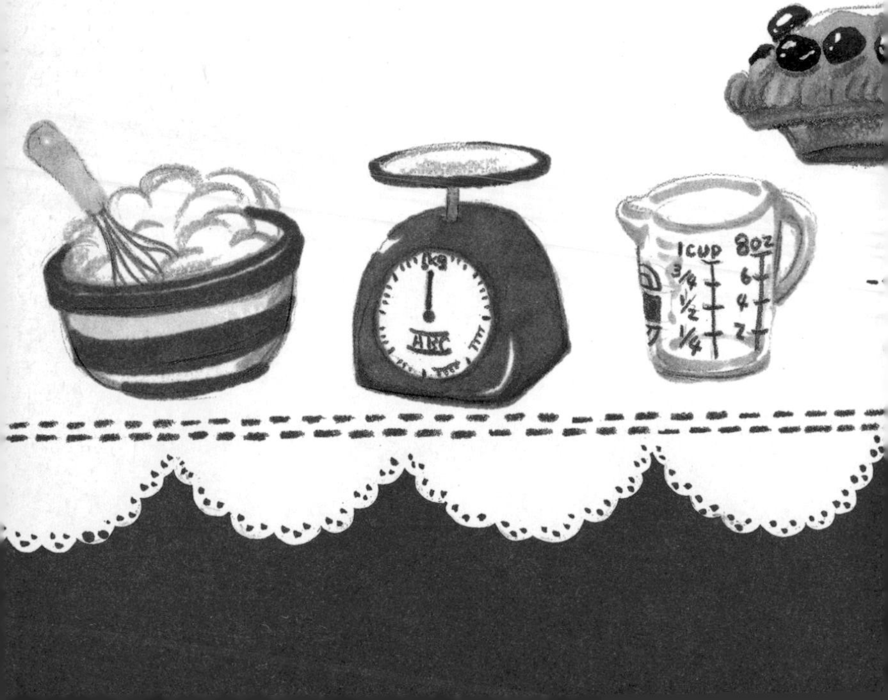
1kg
ABC
1CUP
8oz
3/4
1/2
1/4
6
4
2

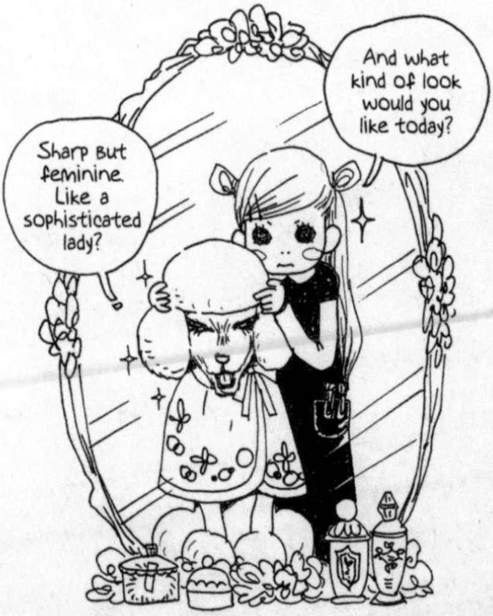
And what kind of look would you like today?
Sharp but feminine. Like a sophisticated lady?

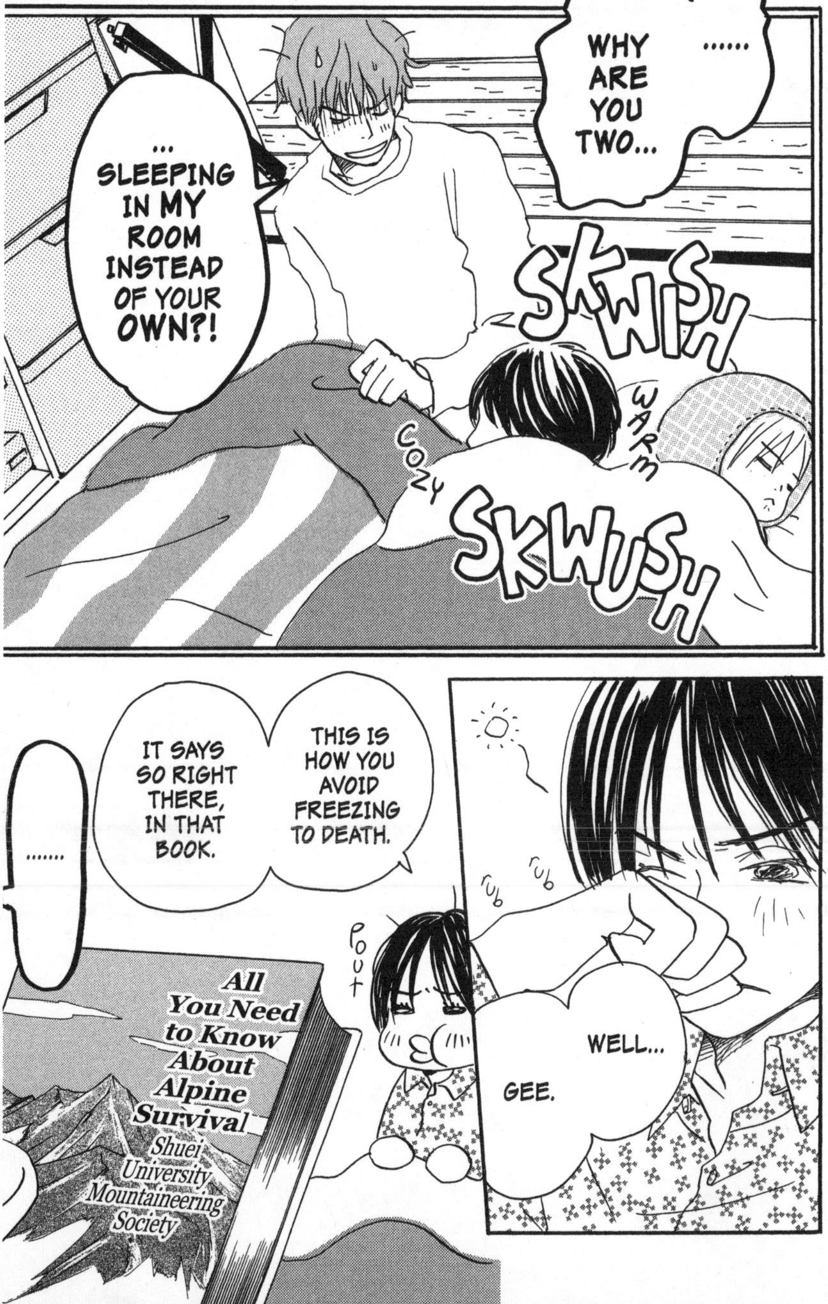
......
WHY ARE YOU TWO...
... SLEEPING IN MY ROOM INSTEAD OF YOUR OWN?!
SKWISH
WARM
COZY
SKWUSH
rub rub
WELL...
GEE.
THIS IS HOW YOU AVOID FREEZING TO DEATH.
IT SAYS SO RIGHT THERE, IN THAT BOOK.
POUT
......
All You Need to Know About Alpine Survival
Shuei University Mountaineering Society

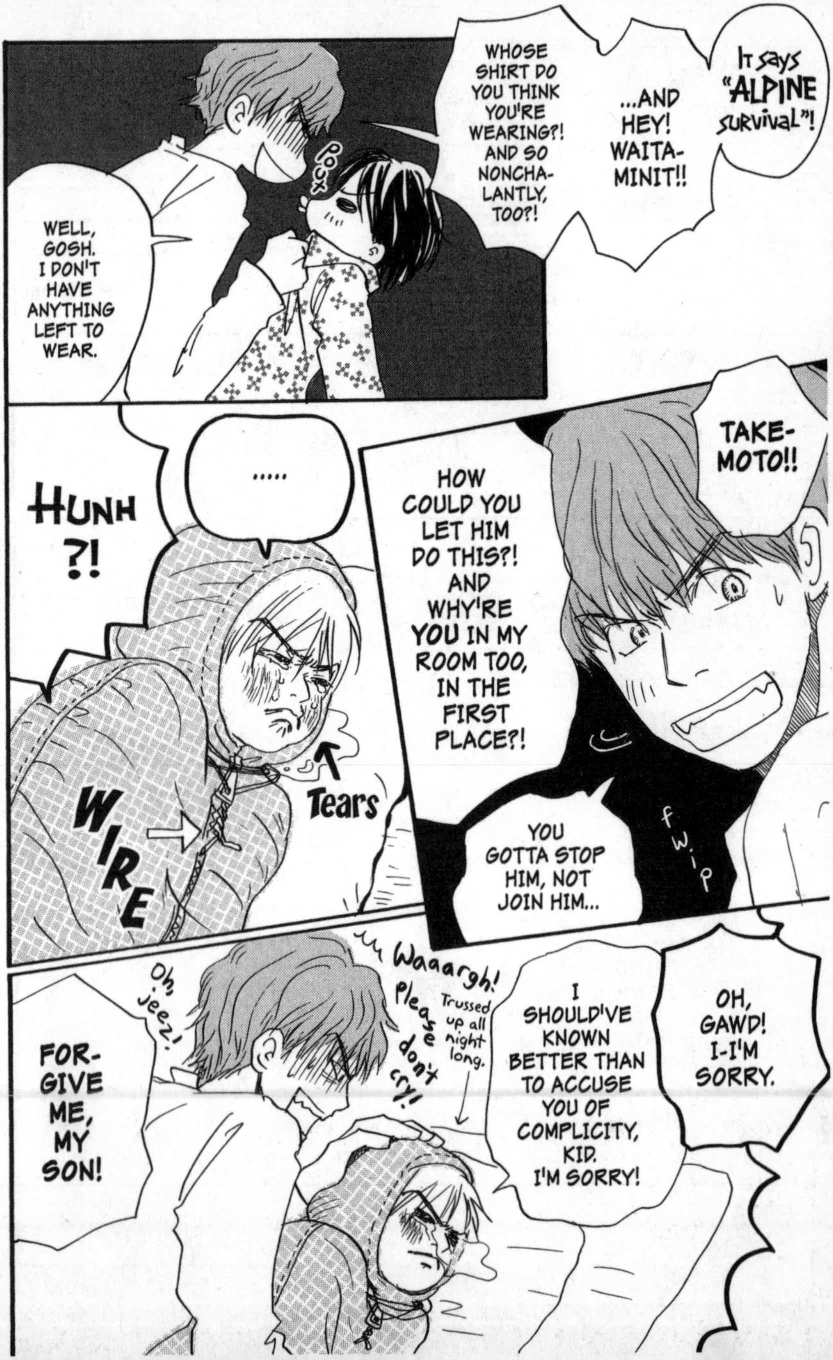
It says "ALPINE survival"!
...AND HEY! WAITA-MINIT!!
WHOSE SHIRT DO YOU THINK YOU'RE WEARING?! AND SO NONCHA-LANTLY, TOO?!
POUT
WELL, GOSH. I DON'T HAVE ANYTHING LEFT TO WEAR.
TAKE-MOTO!!
HOW COULD YOU LET HIM DO THIS?! AND WHY'RE YOU IN MY ROOM TOO, IN THE FIRST PLACE?!
fwip
YOU GOTTA STOP HIM, NOT JOIN HIM...
.....
HUNH ?!
Tears
WIRE
OH, GAWD! I-I'M SORRY.
I SHOULD'VE KNOWN BETTER THAN TO ACCUSE YOU OF COMPLICITY, KID. I'M SORRY!
Waaargh!
Trussed up all night long.
Please don't cry!
Oh, jeez!
FOR-GIVE ME, MY SON!

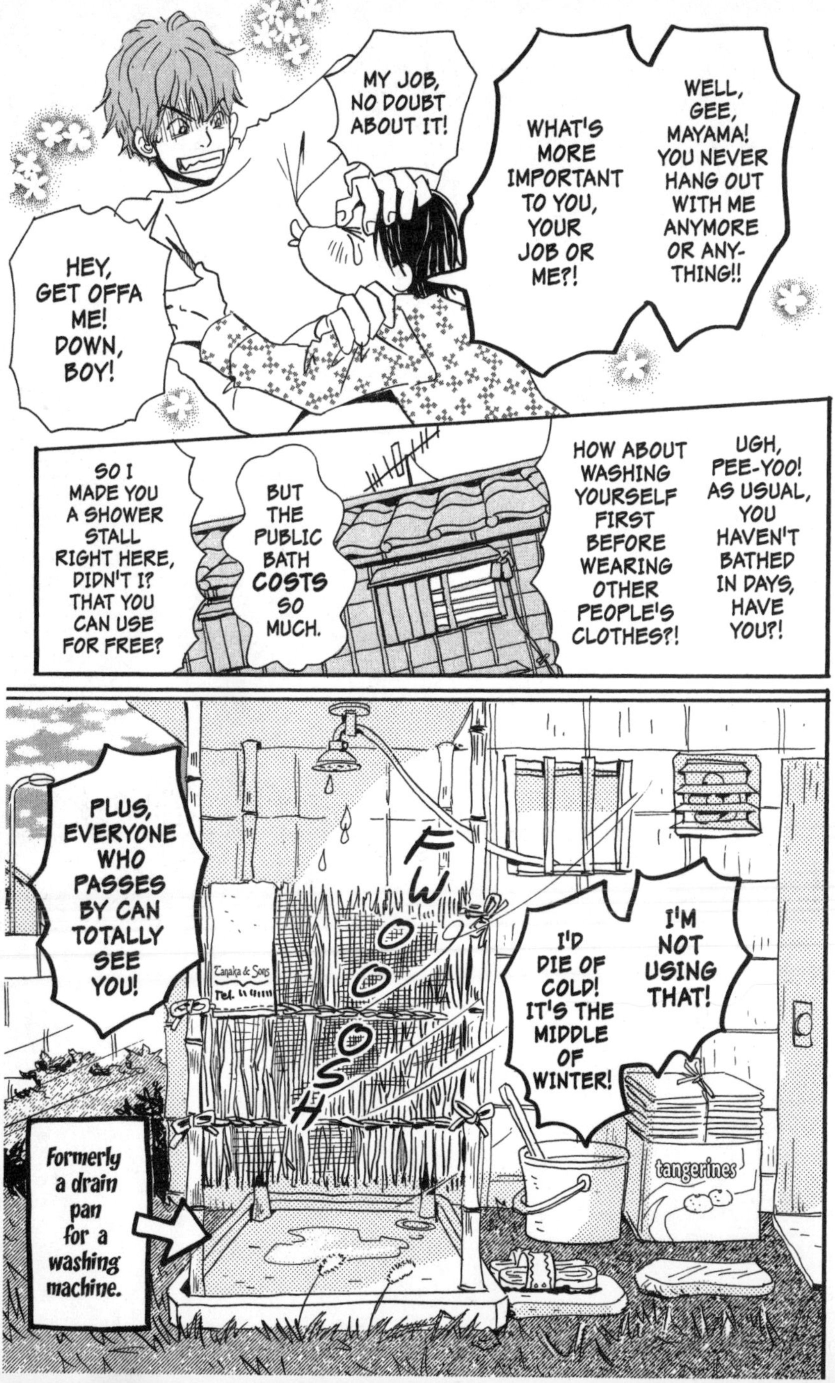
WELL, GEE, MAYAMA! YOU NEVER HANG OUT WITH ME ANYMORE OR ANYTHING!!
WHAT'S MORE IMPORTANT TO YOU, YOUR JOB OR ME?!
MY JOB, NO DOUBT ABOUT IT!
HEY, GET OFFA ME! DOWN, BOY!
UGH, PEE-YOO! AS USUAL, YOU HAVEN'T BATHED IN DAYS, HAVE YOU?!
HOW ABOUT WASHING YOURSELF FIRST BEFORE WEARING OTHER PEOPLE'S CLOTHES?!
BUT THE PUBLIC BATH COSTS SO MUCH.
SO I MADE YOU A SHOWER STALL RIGHT HERE, DIDN'T I? THAT YOU CAN USE FOR FREE?
I'M NOT USING THAT!
I'D DIE OF COLD! IT'S THE MIDDLE OF WINTER!
FWOOOOSH
PLUS, EVERYONE WHO PASSES BY CAN TOTALLY SEE YOU!
Tanaka & Sons
tangerines
Formerly a drain pan for a washing machine.

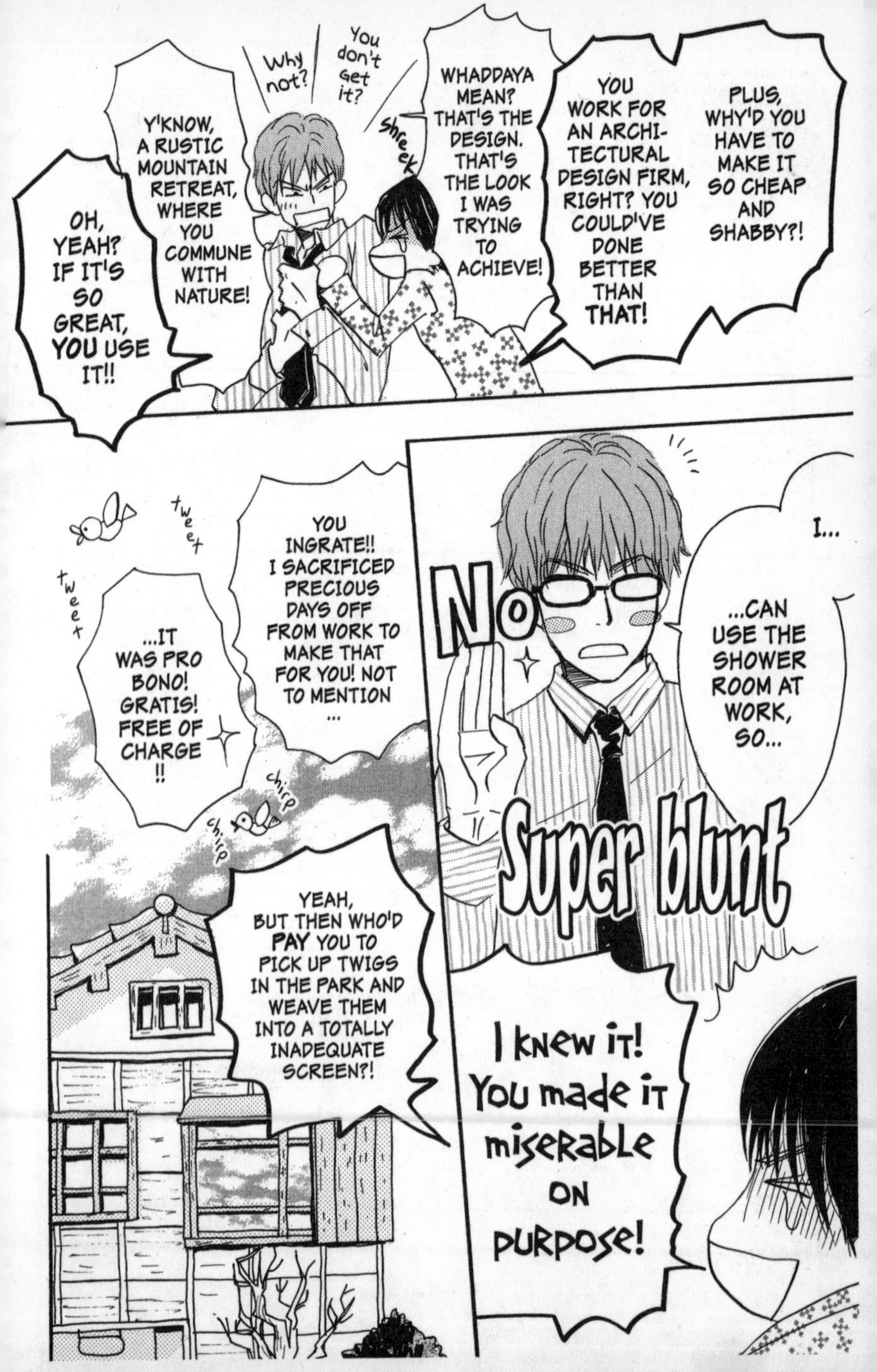
PLUS, WHY'D YOU HAVE TO MAKE IT SO CHEAP AND SHABBY?!
YOU WORK FOR AN ARCHITECTURAL DESIGN FIRM, RIGHT? YOU COULD'VE DONE BETTER THAN THAT!
WHADDAYA MEAN? THAT'S THE DESIGN. THAT'S THE LOOK I WAS TRYING TO ACHIEVE!
Shreek
You don't get it?
Why not?
Y'KNOW, A RUSTIC MOUNTAIN RETREAT, WHERE YOU COMMUNE WITH NATURE!
OH, YEAH? IF IT'S SO GREAT, YOU USE IT!!
I...
...CAN USE THE SHOWER ROOM AT WORK, SO...
No
Super blunt
I knew it! You made it miserable on purpose!
YOU INGRATE!! I SACRIFICED PRECIOUS DAYS OFF FROM WORK TO MAKE THAT FOR YOU! NOT TO MENTION ...
tweet
tweet
...IT WAS PRO BONO! GRATIS! FREE OF CHARGE !!
chirp
chirp
YEAH, BUT THEN WHO'D PAY YOU TO PICK UP TWIGS IN THE PARK AND WEAVE THEM INTO A TOTALLY INADEQUATE SCREEN?!

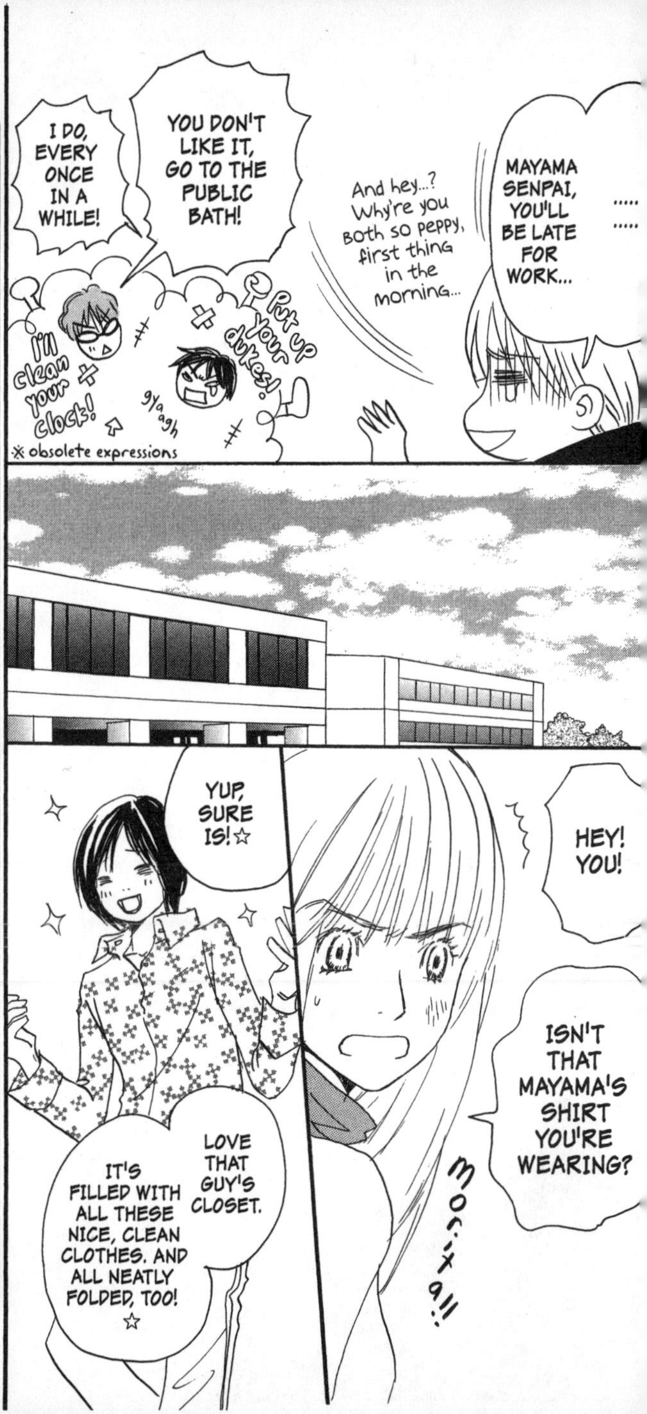
.....
.....
MAYAMA SENPAI, YOU'LL BE LATE FOR WORK...
And hey...? Why're you both so peppy, first thing in the morning...
YOU DON'T LIKE IT, GO TO THE PUBLIC BATH!
I DO, EVERY ONCE IN A WHILE!
Put up your dukes!
gyaagh
I'll clean your clock!
※obsolete expressions
HEY! YOU!
ISN'T THAT MAYAMA'S SHIRT YOU'RE WEARING?
Morita!!
YUP, SURE IS!☆
LOVE THAT GUY'S CLOSET.
IT'S FILLED WITH ALL THESE NICE, CLEAN CLOTHES. AND ALL NEATLY FOLDED, TOO! ☆

I love flowers!

A flower I have growing on my veranda.

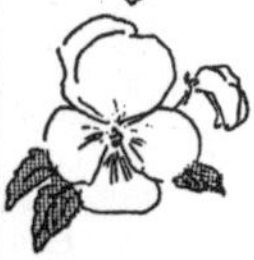

I love flowers that grow on trees.

- ★ Sweet osmanthus ← I get antsy with anticipation whenever October rolls around.
- Sakura
- Daphne

Philadelphia Fleabane

Really like this a lot.

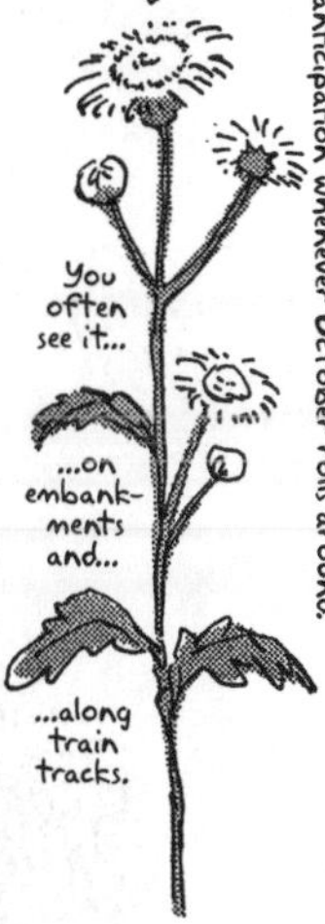
You often see it...
...on embankments and...
...along train tracks.

Chica Umino

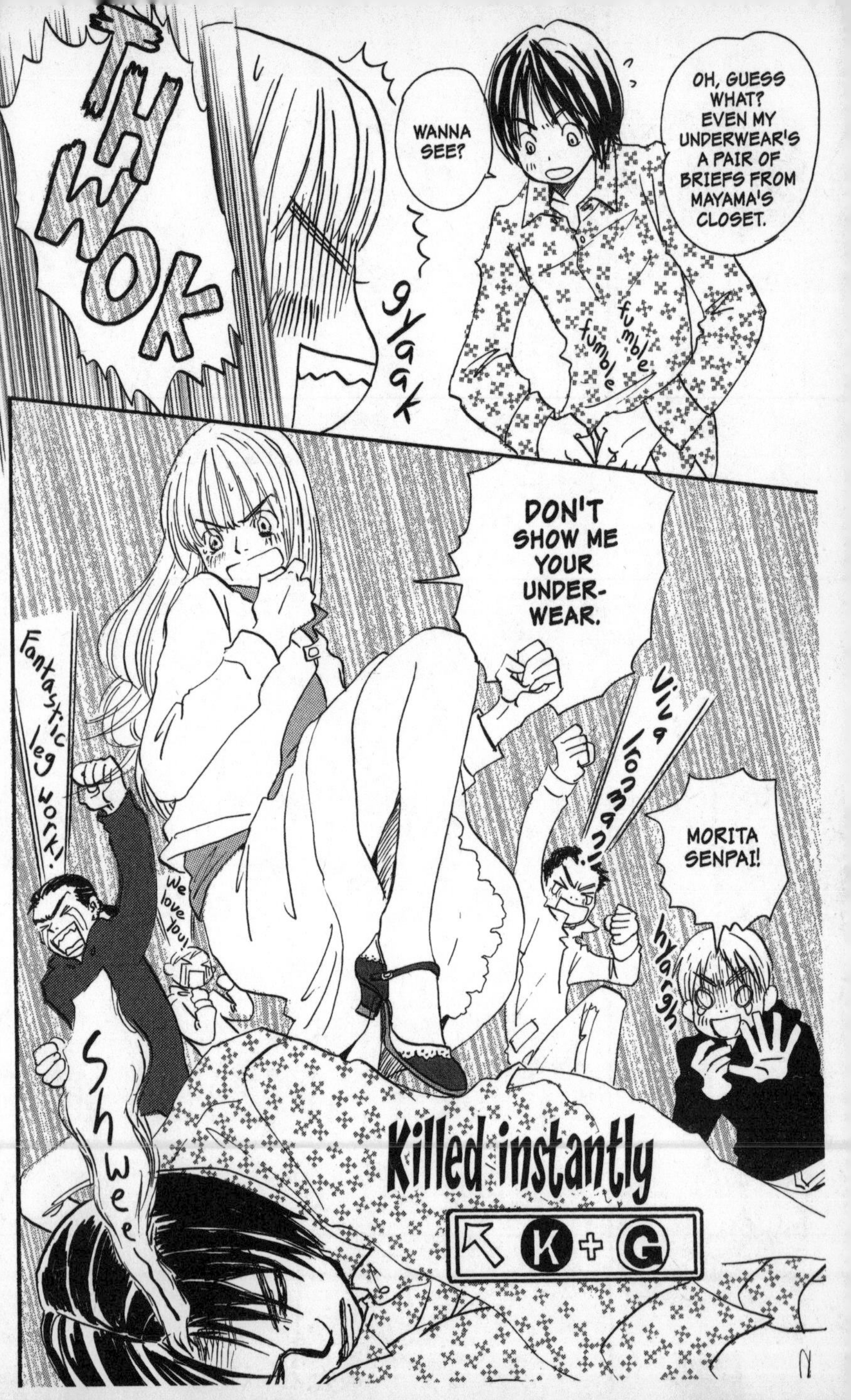
OH, GUESS WHAT? EVEN MY UNDERWEAR'S A PAIR OF BRIEFS FROM MAYAMA'S CLOSET.
fumble fumble
WANNA SEE?
gyaak
THWOK
DON'T SHOW ME YOUR UNDER-WEAR.
MORITA SENPAI!
hyargh
Viva Ironman!
Fantastic leg work!
We love you!
Shwee
Killed instantly
K + G

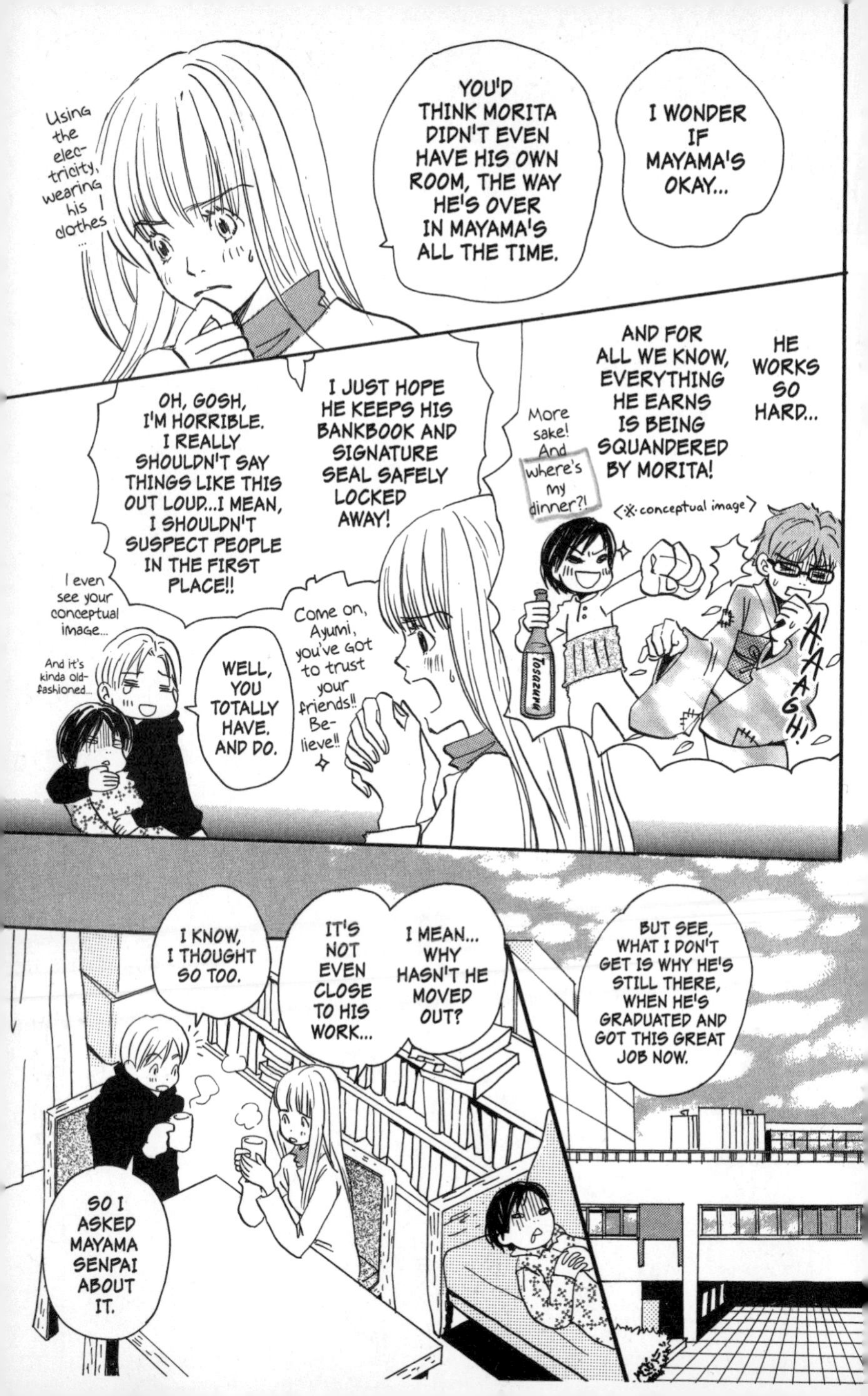

I WONDER IF MAYAMA'S OKAY...
YOU'D THINK MORITA DIDN'T EVEN HAVE HIS OWN ROOM, THE WAY HE'S OVER IN MAYAMA'S ALL THE TIME.
Using the electricity, wearing his clothes...
HE WORKS SO HARD...
AND FOR ALL WE KNOW, EVERYTHING HE EARNS IS BEING SQUANDERED BY MORITA!
<※ conceptual image>
More sake! And where's my dinner?!
AAAGH!
Tosazuru
I JUST HOPE HE KEEPS HIS BANKBOOK AND SIGNATURE SEAL SAFELY LOCKED AWAY!
OH, GOSH, I'M HORRIBLE. I REALLY SHOULDN'T SAY THINGS LIKE THIS OUT LOUD...I MEAN, I SHOULDN'T SUSPECT PEOPLE IN THE FIRST PLACE!!
Come on, Ayumi, you've got to trust your friends!! Believe!!
WELL, YOU TOTALLY HAVE. AND DO.
I even see your conceptual image...
And it's kinda old-fashioned...
BUT SEE, WHAT I DON'T GET IS WHY HE'S STILL THERE, WHEN HE'S GRADUATED AND GOT THIS GREAT JOB NOW.
I MEAN... WHY HASN'T HE MOVED OUT?
IT'S NOT EVEN CLOSE TO HIS WORK...
I KNOW, I THOUGHT SO TOO.
SO I ASKED MAYAMA SENPAI ABOUT IT.

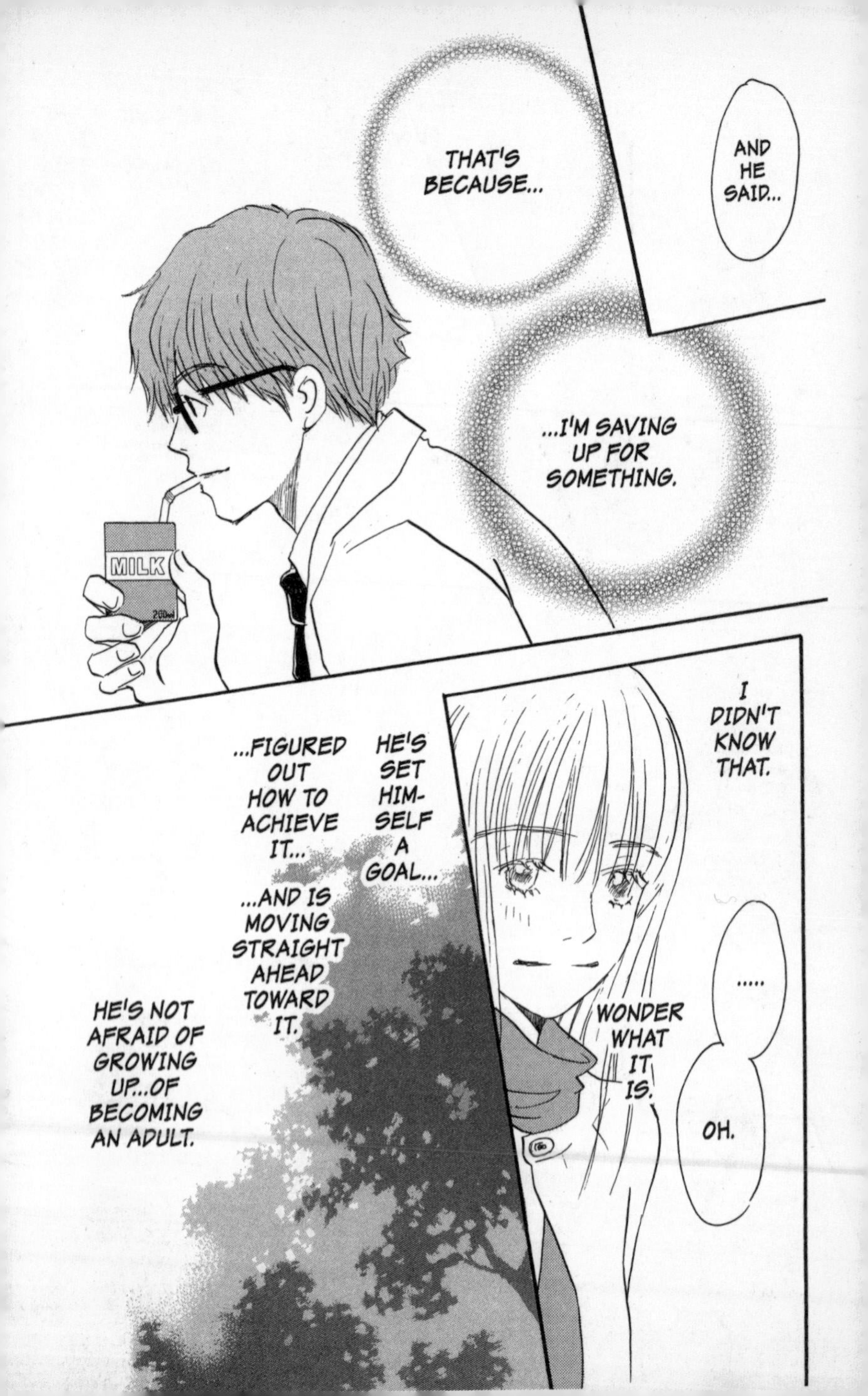
AND HE SAID...
THAT'S BECAUSE...
...I'M SAVING UP FOR SOMETHING.
MILK
I DIDN'T KNOW THAT.
.....
OH.
WONDER WHAT IT IS.
HE'S SET HIM-SELF A GOAL...
...FIGURED OUT HOW TO ACHIEVE IT...
...AND IS MOVING STRAIGHT AHEAD TOWARD IT.
HE'S NOT AFRAID OF GROWING UP...OF BECOMING AN ADULT.

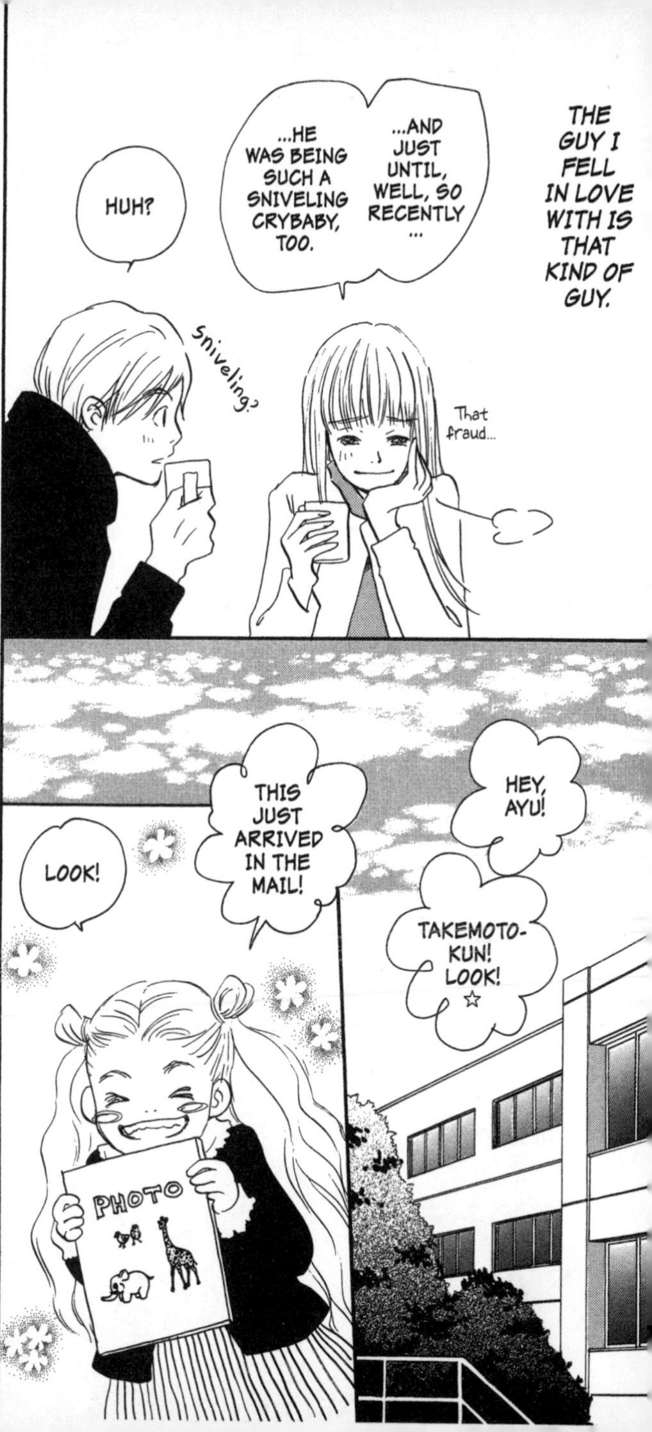
THE GUY I FELL IN LOVE WITH IS THAT KIND OF GUY.
...AND JUST UNTIL, WELL, SO RECENTLY...
...HE WAS BEING SUCH A SNIVELING CRYBABY, TOO.
HUH?
That fraud...
Sniveling?
HEY, AYU!
TAKEMOTO-KUN! LOOK!
THIS JUST ARRIVED IN THE MAIL!
LOOK!
PHOTO

Thank you so much for reading Honey and Clover. I'll keep working hard at it, so please watch over me and my efforts! ☆

I'm keeping a diary on the Internet. It would make me happy if you checked it out now and then.

http://www2.diary.ne.jp/user/162279/

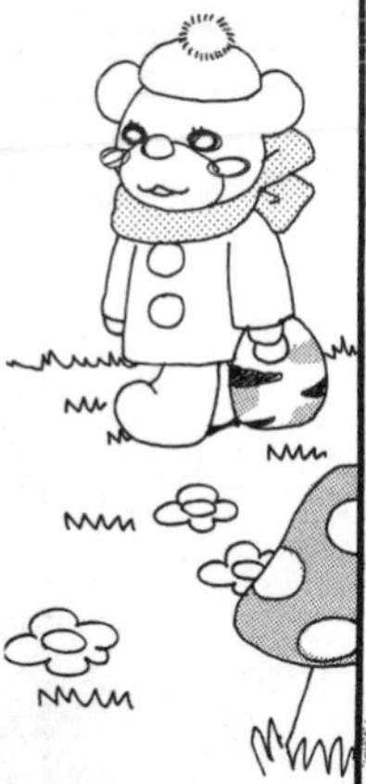

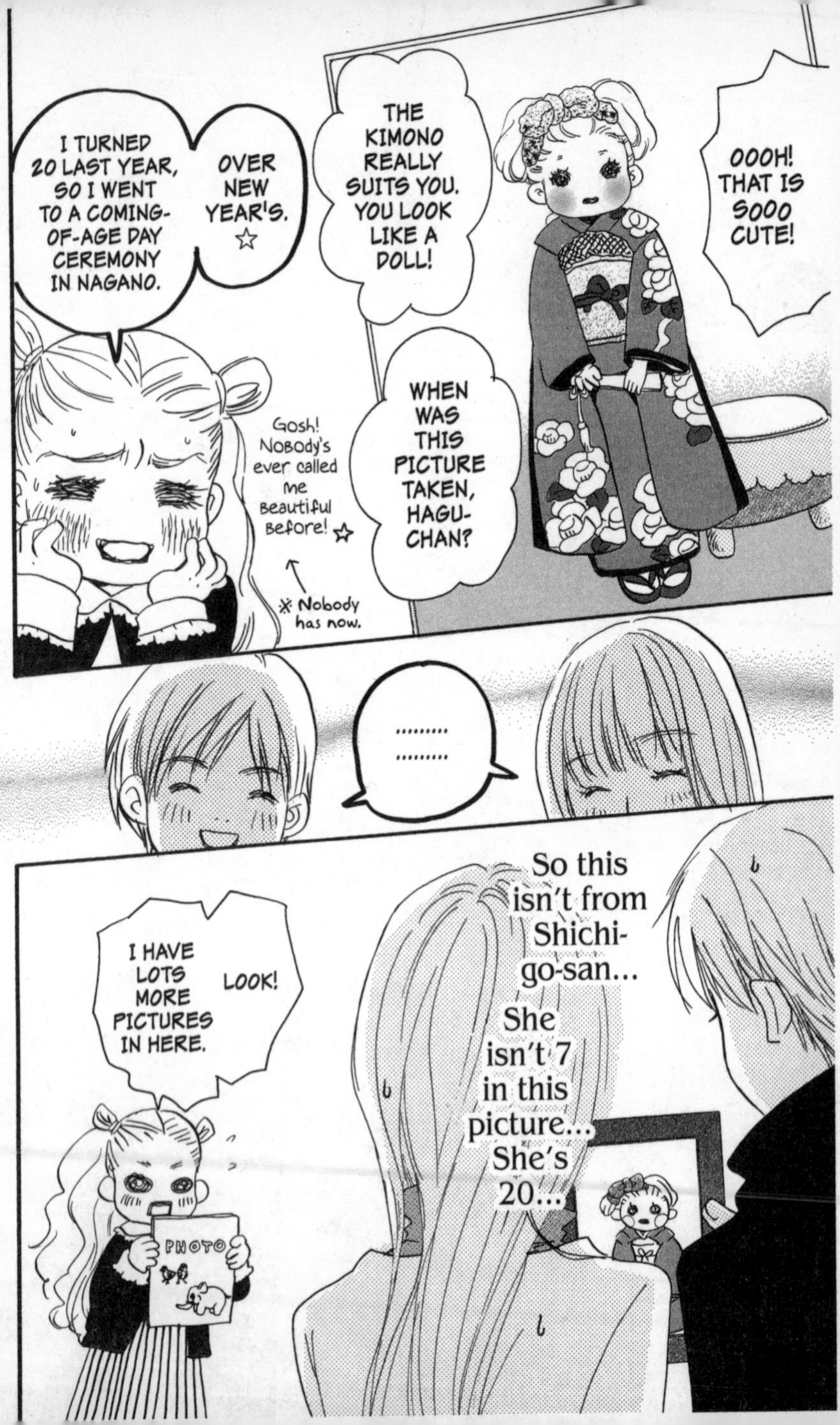
OOOH! THAT IS SOOO CUTE!
THE KIMONO REALLY SUITS YOU. YOU LOOK LIKE A DOLL!
WHEN WAS THIS PICTURE TAKEN, HAGU-CHAN?
OVER NEW YEAR'S. ☆
I TURNED 20 LAST YEAR, SO I WENT TO A COMING-OF-AGE DAY CEREMONY IN NAGANO.
Gosh! Nobody's ever called me beautiful before! ☆
※ Nobody has now.
....
....
So this isn't from Shichi-go-san...
She isn't 7 in this picture... She's 20...
LOOK!
I HAVE LOTS MORE PICTURES IN HERE.
PHOTO

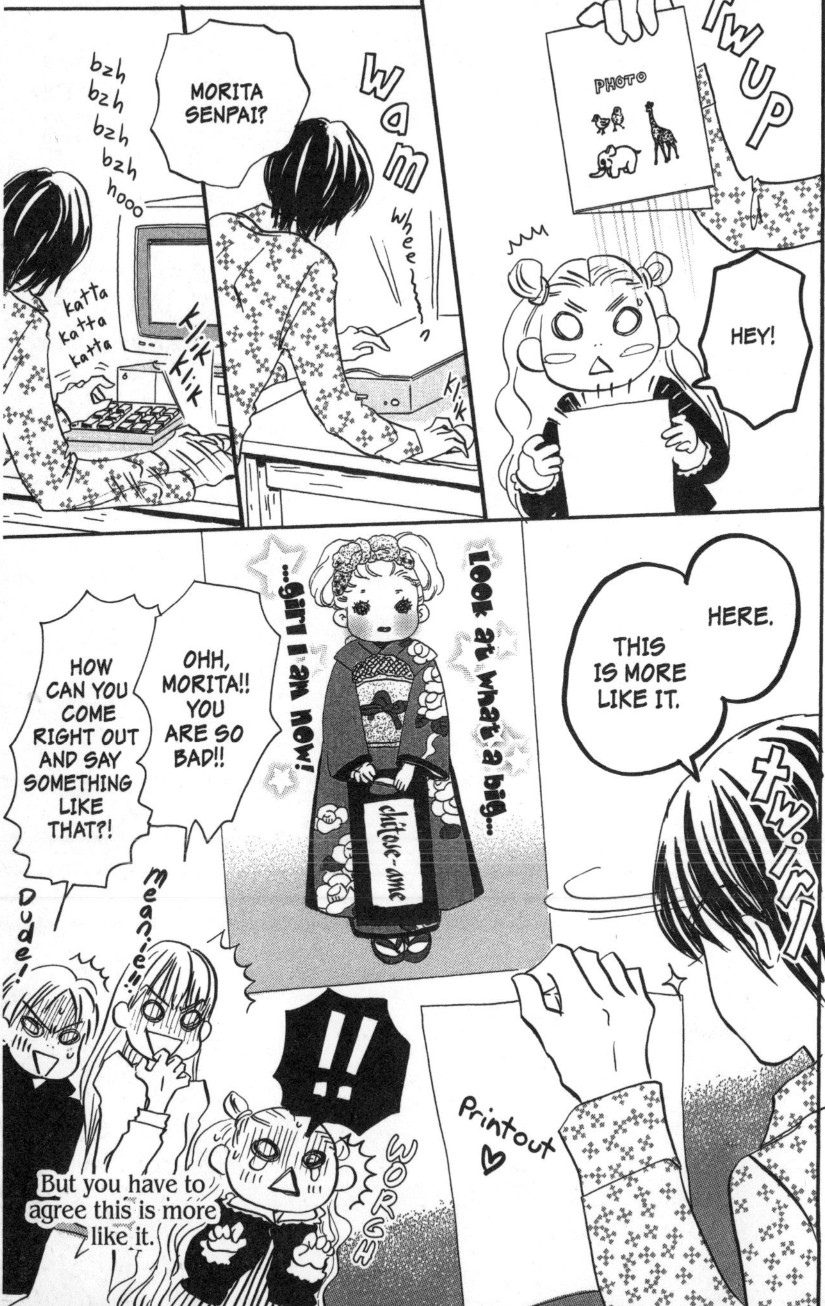
fwUP
PHOTO
HEY!
MORITA SENPAI?
wam
whee
klik
bzh bzh bzh bzh hooo
katta katta katta
klik klik
HERE. THIS IS MORE LIKE IT.
twirl
Printout
Look at what a big... ...girl I am now!
chitose-ame
OHH, MORITA!! YOU ARE SO BAD!!
HOW CAN YOU COME RIGHT OUT AND SAY SOMETHING LIKE THAT?!
meanie!!
Dude!
!!
WORGH
But you have to agree this is more like it.

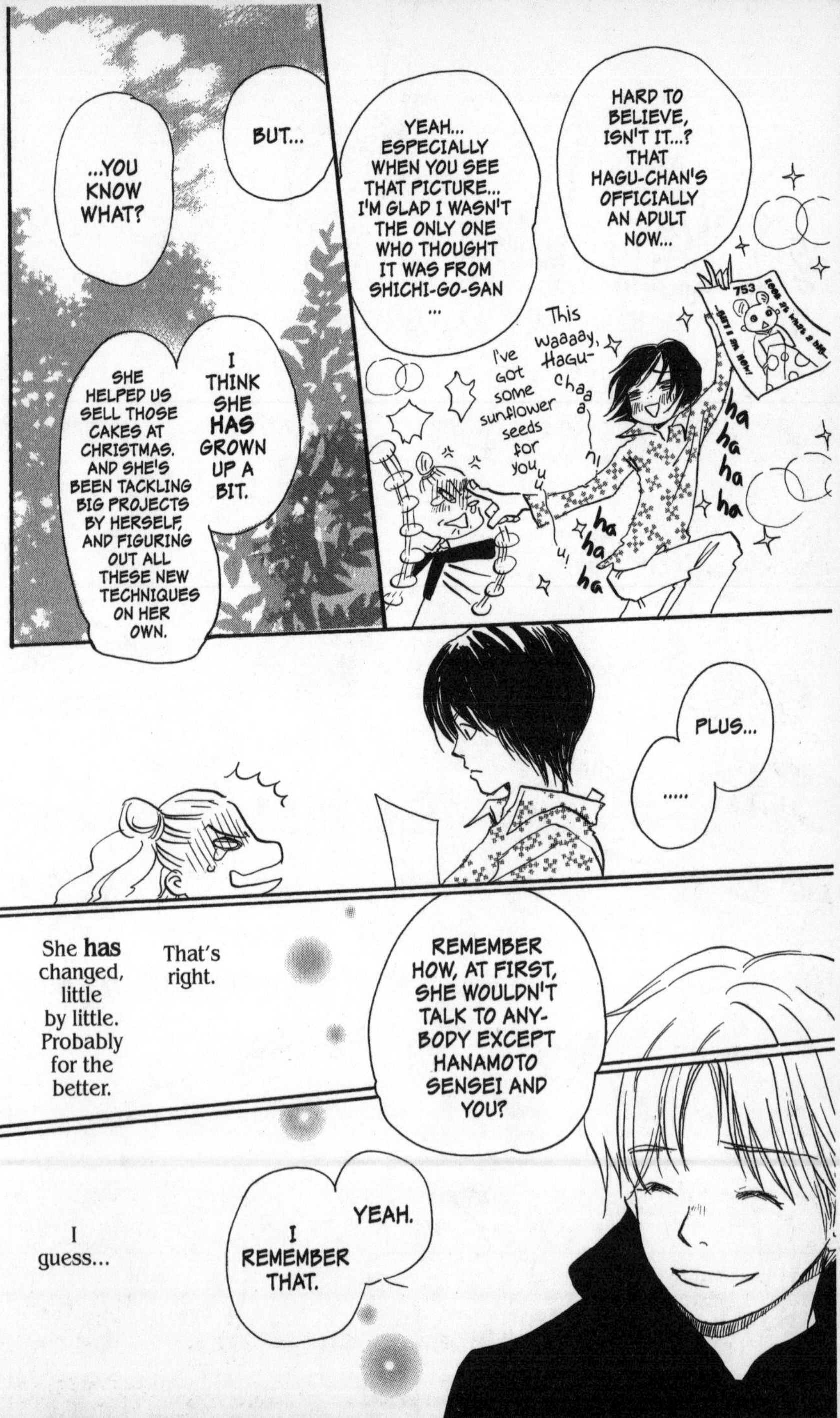
HARD TO BELIEVE, ISN'T IT...? THAT HAGU-CHAN'S OFFICIALLY AN ADULT NOW...
YEAH... ESPECIALLY WHEN YOU SEE THAT PICTURE... I'M GLAD I WASN'T THE ONLY ONE WHO THOUGHT IT WAS FROM SHICHI-GO-SAN ...
753
This waaaay, Hagu-chaaan!
I've got some sunflower seeds for youuu!
ha ha ha ha
ha ha ha
BUT...
...YOU KNOW WHAT?
I THINK SHE HAS GROWN UP A BIT.
SHE HELPED US SELL THOSE CAKES AT CHRISTMAS. AND SHE'S BEEN TACKLING BIG PROJECTS BY HERSELF, AND FIGURING OUT ALL THESE NEW TECHNIQUES ON HER OWN.
PLUS...
.....
REMEMBER HOW, AT FIRST, SHE WOULDN'T TALK TO ANY-BODY EXCEPT HANAMOTO SENSEI AND YOU?
That's right.
She **has** changed, little by little. Probably for the better.
YEAH.
I REMEMBER THAT.
I guess...

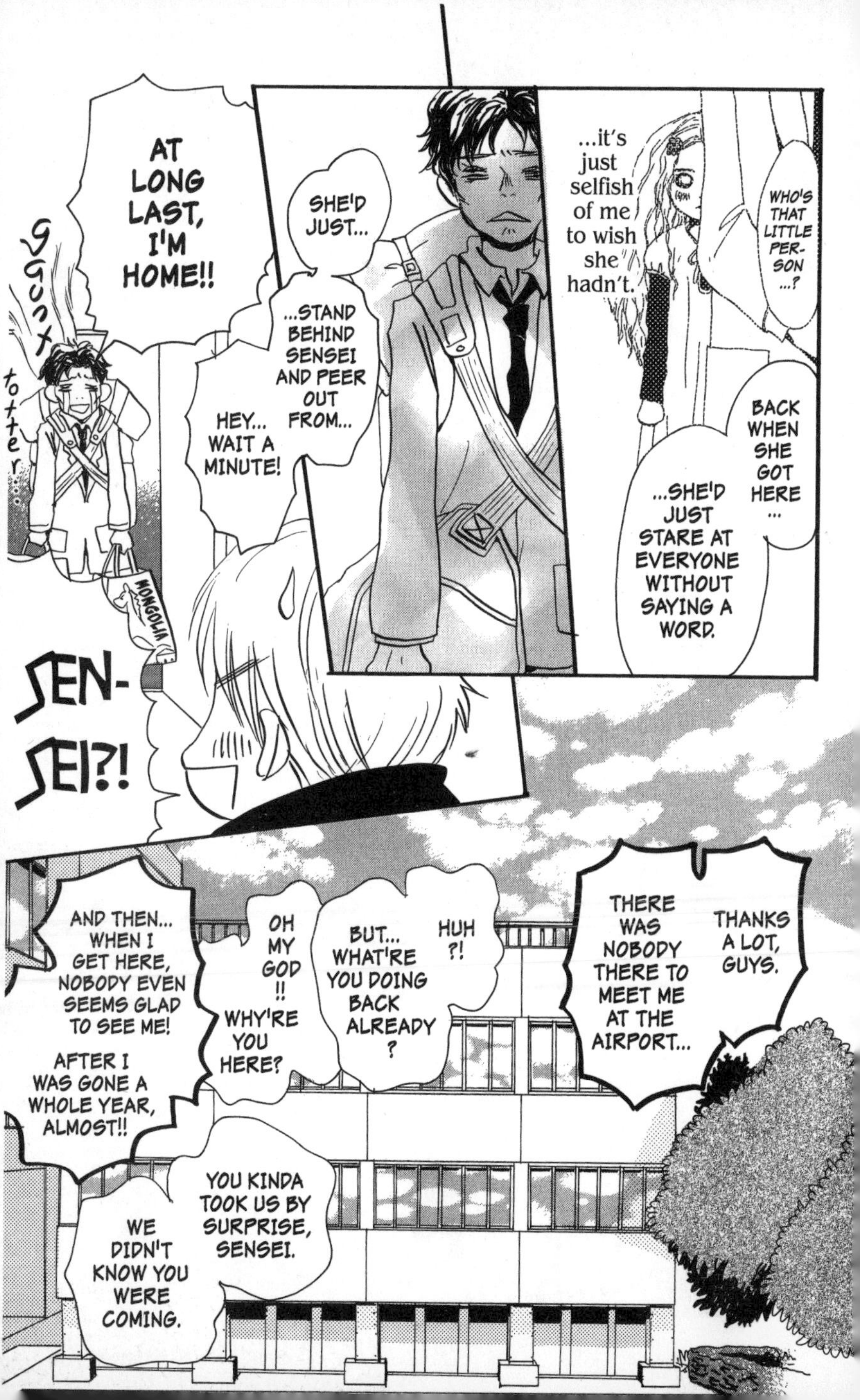
WHO'S THAT LITTLE PERSON ...?
...it's just selfish of me to wish she hadn't.
BACK WHEN SHE GOT HERE ...
...SHE'D JUST STARE AT EVERYONE WITHOUT SAYING A WORD.
SHE'D JUST...
...STAND BEHIND SENSEI AND PEER OUT FROM...
HEY... WAIT A MINUTE!
AT LONG LAST, I'M HOME!!
totter...
MONGOLIA
SEN-SEI?!
THANKS A LOT, GUYS.
THERE WAS NOBODY THERE TO MEET ME AT THE AIRPORT...
HUH ?!
BUT... WHAT'RE YOU DOING BACK ALREADY ?
OH MY GOD !!
WHY'RE YOU HERE?
AND THEN... WHEN I GET HERE, NOBODY EVEN SEEMS GLAD TO SEE ME!
AFTER I WAS GONE A WHOLE YEAR, ALMOST!!
YOU KINDA TOOK US BY SURPRISE, SENSEI.
WE DIDN'T KNOW YOU WERE COMING.

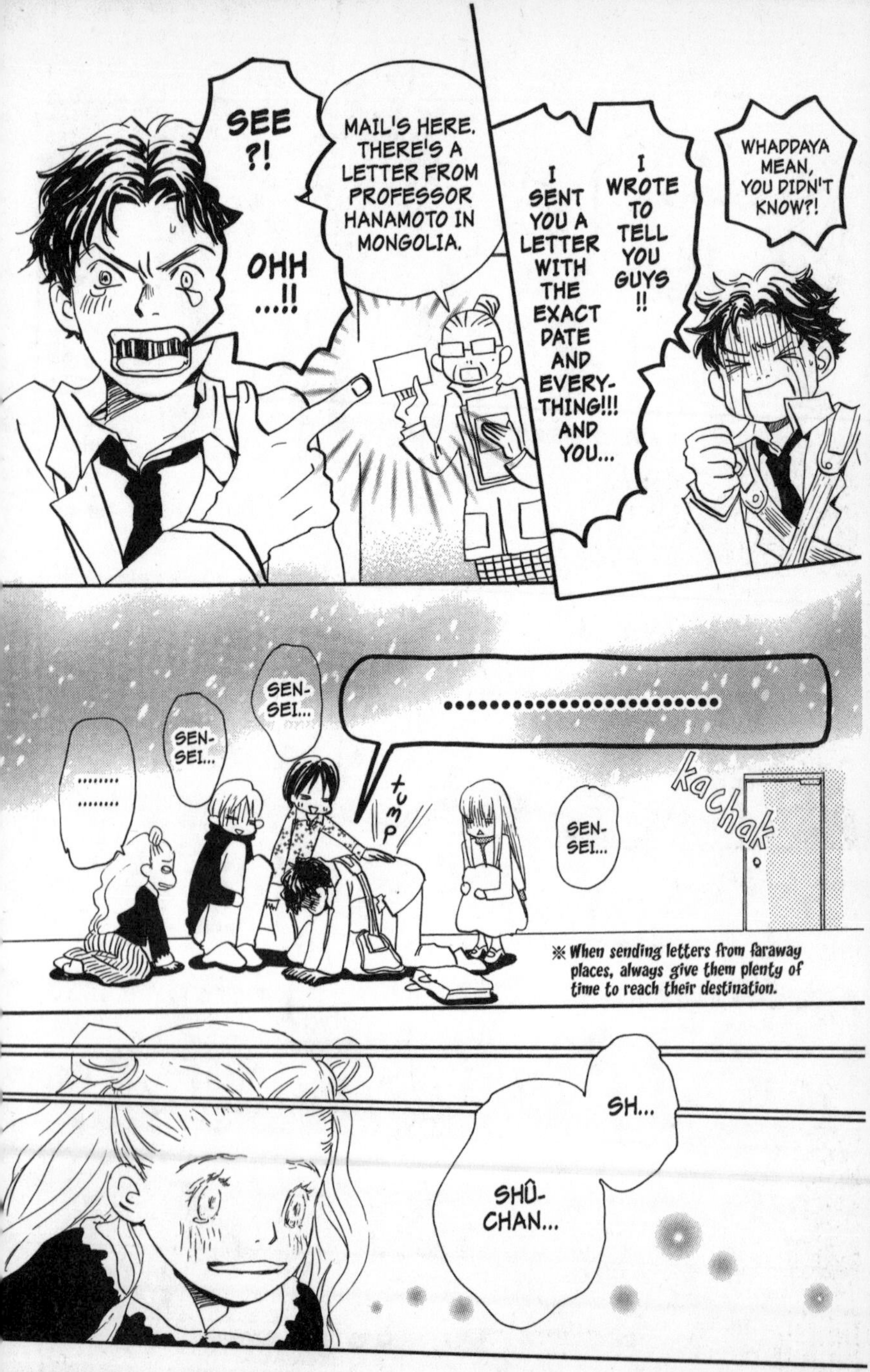
WHADDAYA MEAN, YOU DIDN'T KNOW?!
I WROTE TO TELL YOU GUYS !!
I SENT YOU A LETTER WITH THE EXACT DATE AND EVERY-THING!!! AND YOU...
MAIL'S HERE. THERE'S A LETTER FROM PROFESSOR HANAMOTO IN MONGOLIA.
SEE ?!
OHH ...!!
....
kachak
SEN-SEI...
TUMP
SEN-SEI...
SEN-SEI...
....
※ When sending letters from faraway places, always give them plenty of time to reach their destination.
SH...
SHÛ-CHAN...

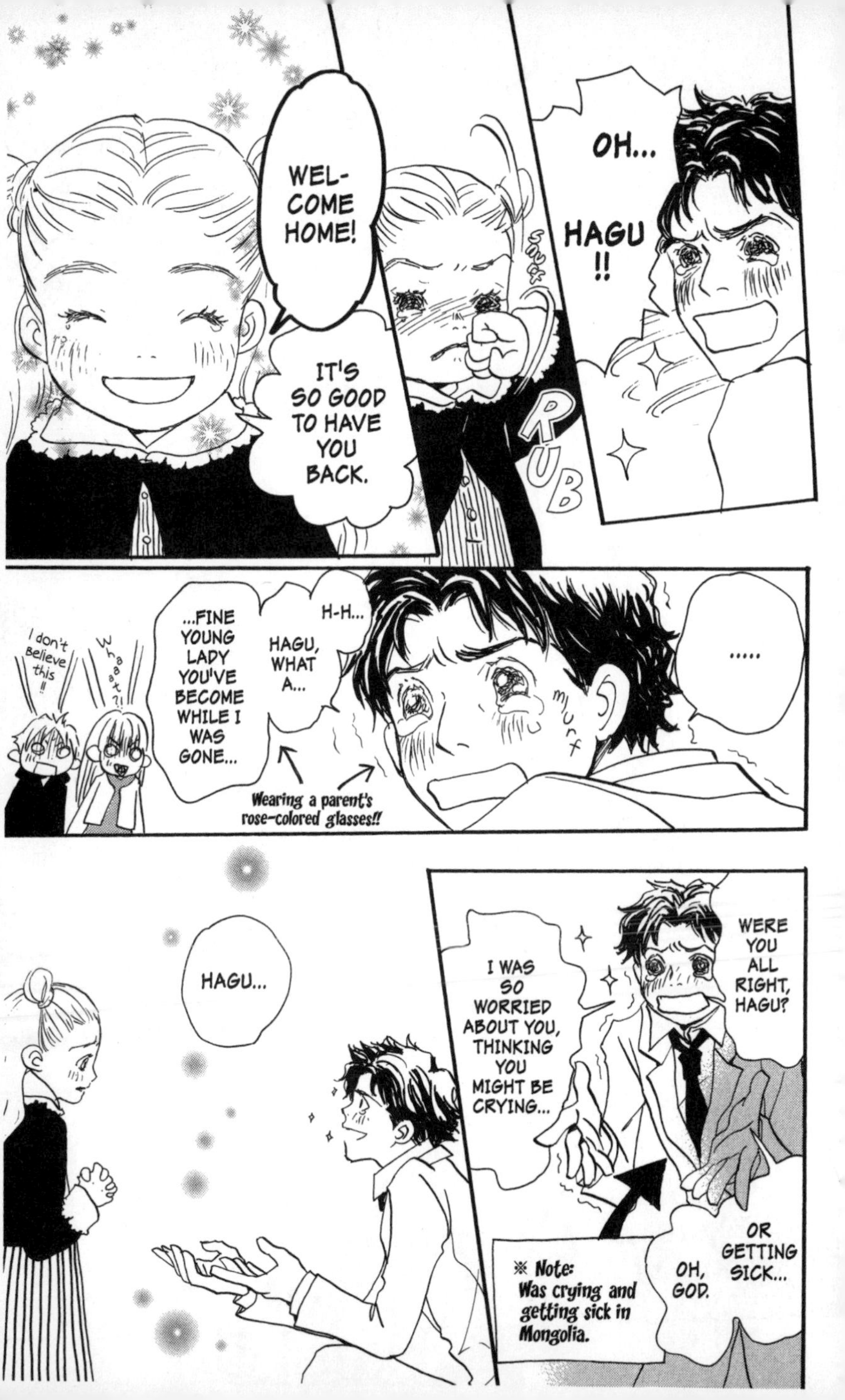

OH...
HAGU !!
RUB
WEL-COME HOME!
IT'S SO GOOD TO HAVE YOU BACK.
.....
H-H...
HAGU, WHAT A...
...FINE YOUNG LADY YOU'VE BECOME WHILE I WAS GONE...
Wearing a parent's rose-colored glasses!!
Whaaat?!
I don't Believe this !!
WERE YOU ALL RIGHT, HAGU?
I WAS SO WORRIED ABOUT YOU, THINKING YOU MIGHT BE CRYING...
OR GETTING SICK...
OH, GOD.
※ Note: Was crying and getting sick in Mongolia.
HAGU...

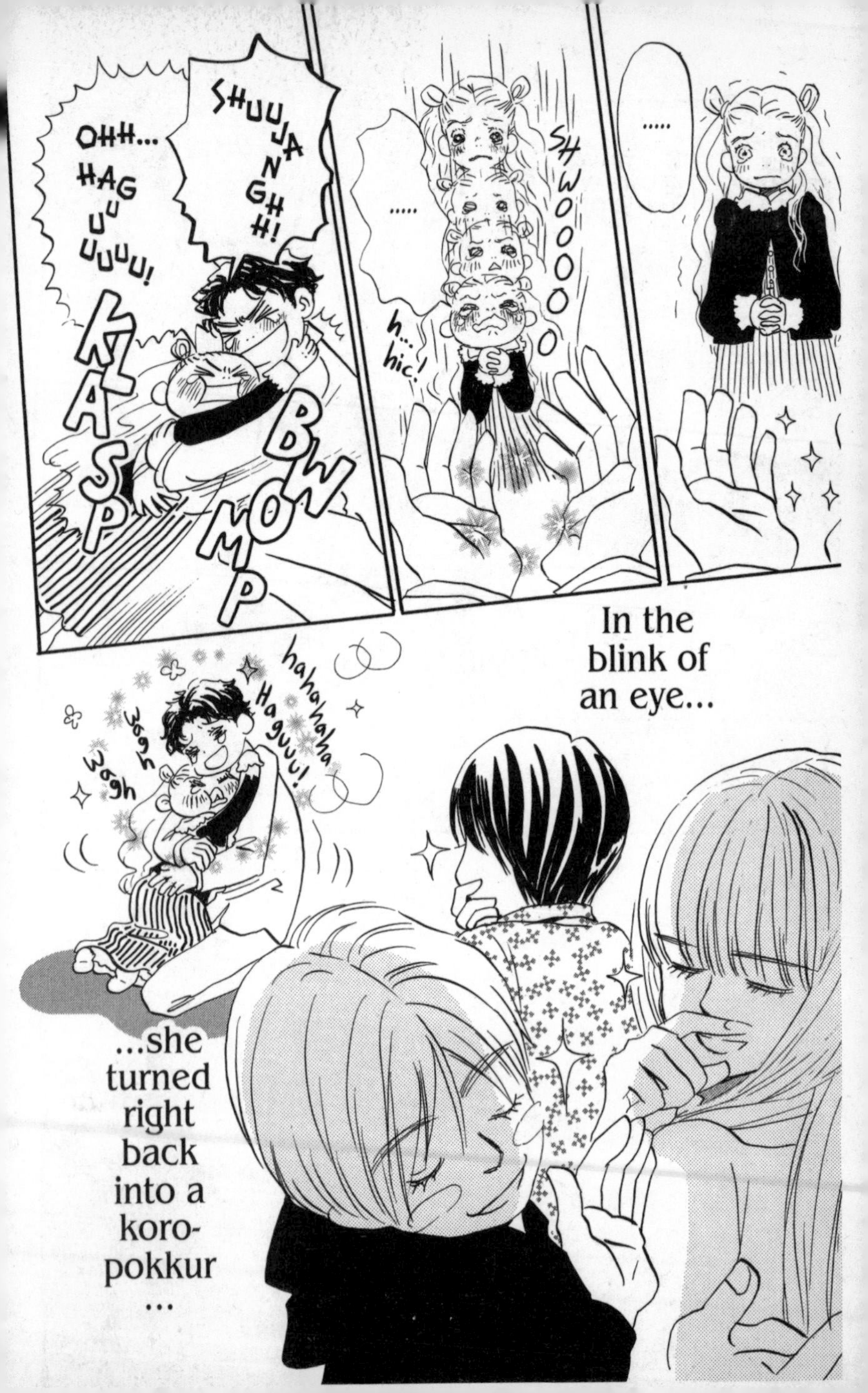
.....
.....
SHWOOOOOO
h... hic!
SHUUJANGHH!
OHH... HAGUUUUUUU!
KLASP
BWOMOMP
In the blink of an eye...
hahahaha
Haguuu!
Wagh
Wagh
...she turned right back into a koro-pokkur...

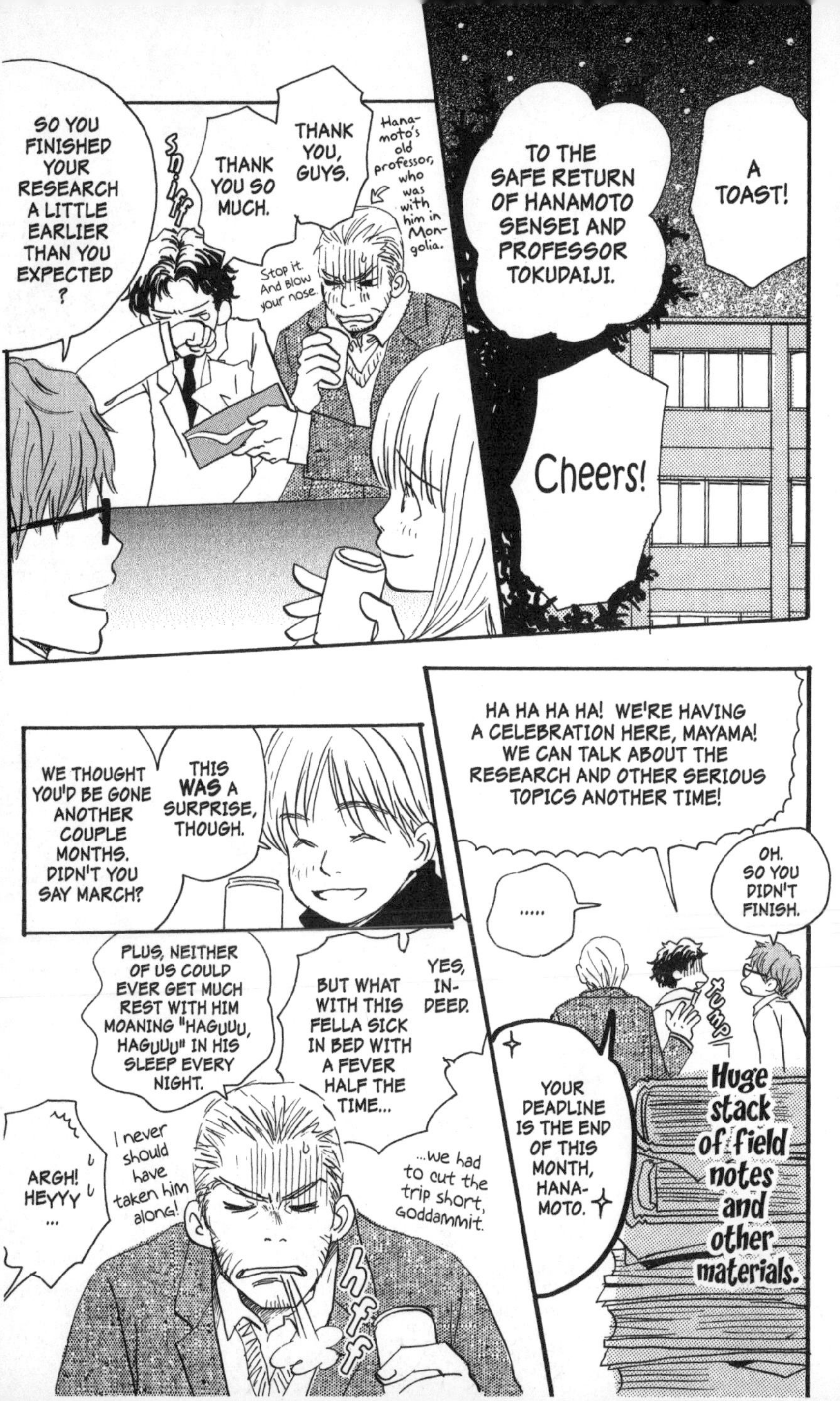
A TOAST!
TO THE SAFE RETURN OF HANAMOTO SENSEI AND PROFESSOR TOKUDAIJI.
Cheers!
THANK YOU, GUYS.
Hanamoto's old professor, who was with him in Mongolia.
THANK YOU SO MUCH.
sniff
Stop it. And blow your nose.
SO YOU FINISHED YOUR RESEARCH A LITTLE EARLIER THAN YOU EXPECTED?
HA HA HA HA! WE'RE HAVING A CELEBRATION HERE, MAYAMA! WE CAN TALK ABOUT THE RESEARCH AND OTHER SERIOUS TOPICS ANOTHER TIME!
OH. SO YOU DIDN'T FINISH.
.....
tump
YOUR DEADLINE IS THE END OF THIS MONTH, HANAMOTO.
Huge stack of field notes and other materials.
THIS WAS A SURPRISE, THOUGH.
WE THOUGHT YOU'D BE GONE ANOTHER COUPLE MONTHS. DIDN'T YOU SAY MARCH?
YES, INDEED.
BUT WHAT WITH THIS FELLA SICK IN BED WITH A FEVER HALF THE TIME...
PLUS, NEITHER OF US COULD EVER GET MUCH REST WITH HIM MOANING "HAGUUU, HAGUUU" IN HIS SLEEP EVERY NIGHT.
...we had to cut the trip short, Goddammit.
hff
I never should have taken him along!
ARGH! HEYYY ...

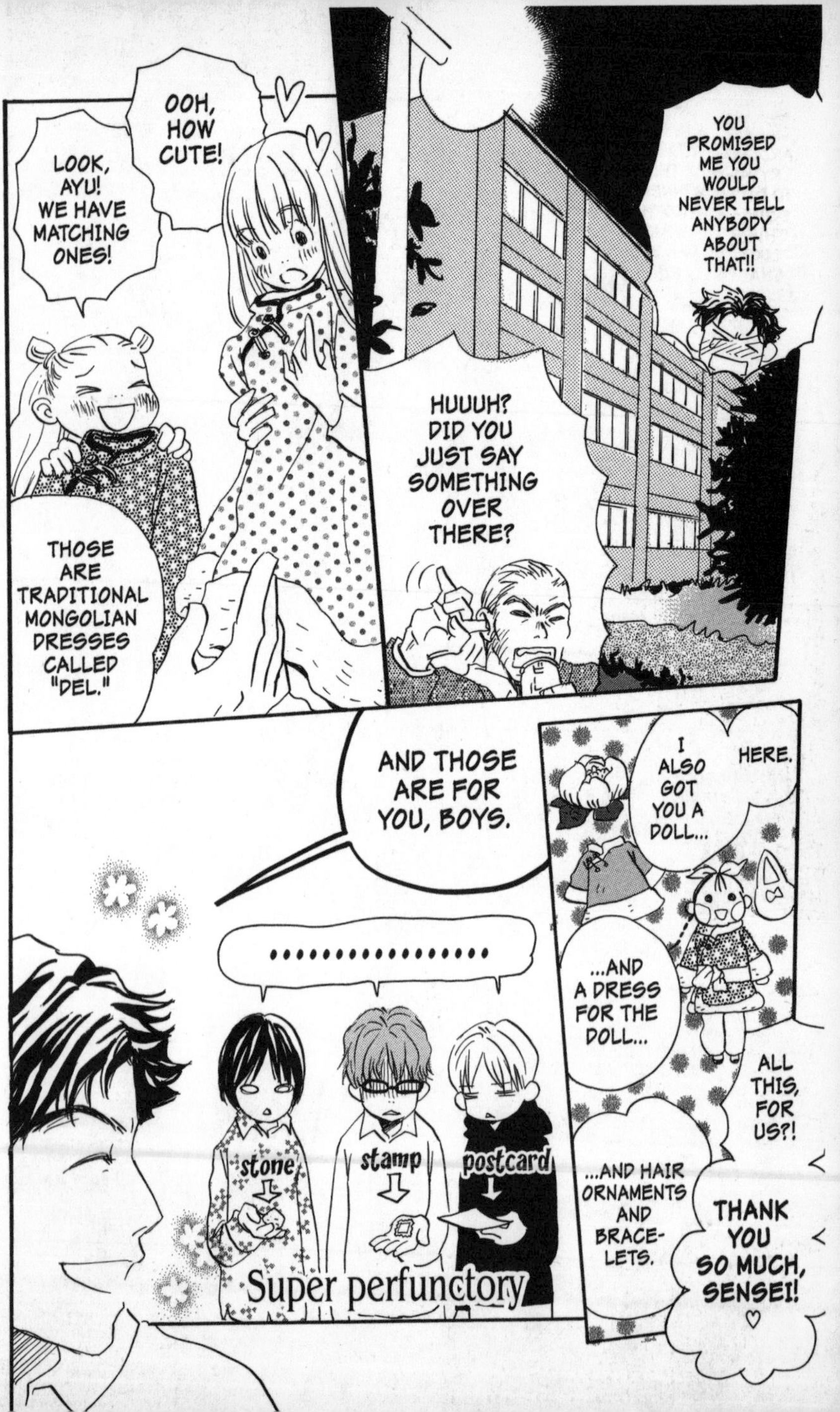
YOU PROMISED ME YOU WOULD NEVER TELL ANYBODY ABOUT THAT!!
HUUUH? DID YOU JUST SAY SOMETHING OVER THERE?
OOH, HOW CUTE!
LOOK, AYU! WE HAVE MATCHING ONES!
THOSE ARE TRADITIONAL MONGOLIAN DRESSES CALLED "DEL."
HERE.
I ALSO GOT YOU A DOLL...
...AND A DRESS FOR THE DOLL...
ALL THIS, FOR US?!
...AND HAIR ORNAMENTS AND BRACELETS.
THANK YOU SO MUCH, SENSEI! ♡
AND THOSE ARE FOR YOU, BOYS.
....
postcard
stamp
stone
Super perfunctory

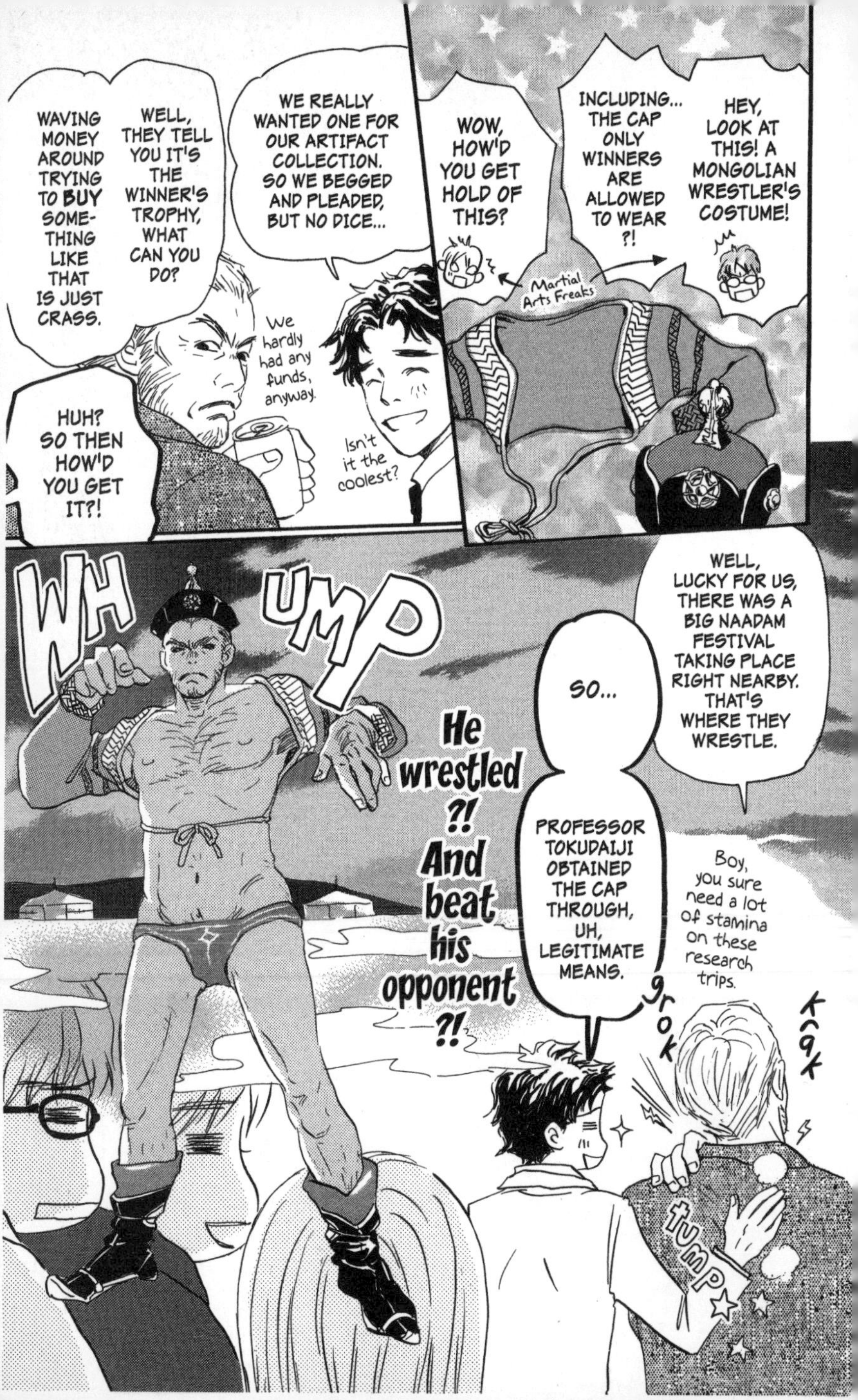
HEY, LOOK AT THIS! A MONGOLIAN WRESTLER'S COSTUME!
INCLUDING... THE CAP ONLY WINNERS ARE ALLOWED TO WEAR?!
WOW, HOW'D YOU GET HOLD OF THIS?
Martial Arts Freaks
WE REALLY WANTED ONE FOR OUR ARTIFACT COLLECTION. SO WE BEGGED AND PLEADED, BUT NO DICE...
WELL, THEY TELL YOU IT'S THE WINNER'S TROPHY, WHAT CAN YOU DO?
WAVING MONEY AROUND TRYING TO BUY SOMETHING LIKE THAT IS JUST CRASS.
We hardly had any funds, anyway.
Isn't it the coolest?
HUH? SO THEN HOW'D YOU GET IT?!
WELL, LUCKY FOR US, THERE WAS A BIG NAADAM FESTIVAL TAKING PLACE RIGHT NEARBY. THAT'S WHERE THEY WRESTLE.
SO... PROFESSOR TOKUDAIJI OBTAINED THE CAP THROUGH, UH, LEGITIMATE MEANS.
Boy, you sure need a lot of stamina on these research trips.
krak
grok
tump
WHUMP
He wrestled?! And beat his opponent?!

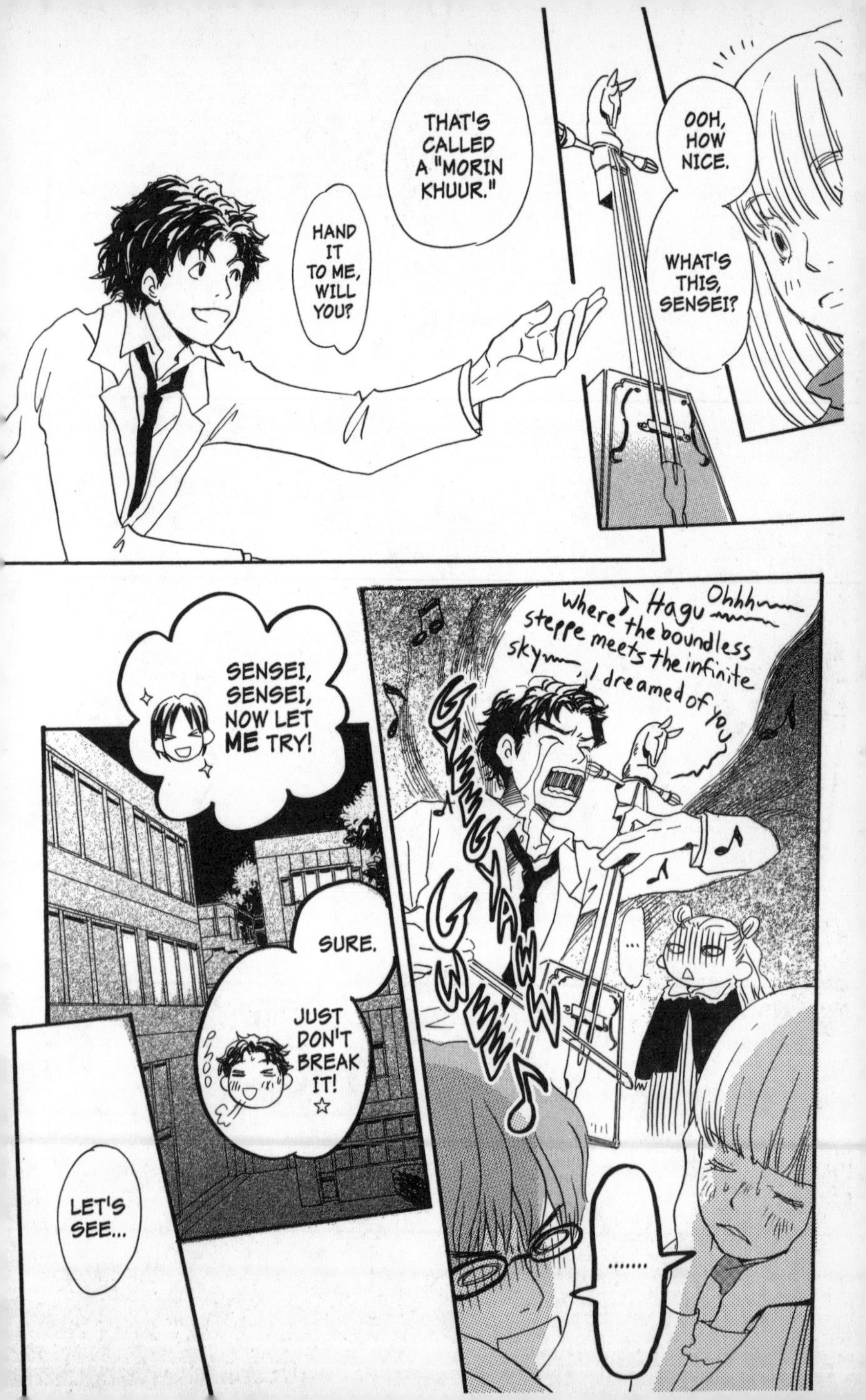
OOH, HOW NICE.
WHAT'S THIS, SENSEI?
THAT'S CALLED A "MORIN KHUUR."
HAND IT TO ME, WILL YOU?
Ohhh
Hagu where the boundless steppe meets the infinite sky, I dreamed of you
...
....
SENSEI, SENSEI, NOW LET ME TRY!
SURE.
JUST DON'T BREAK IT! ☆
Phoo
LET'S SEE...

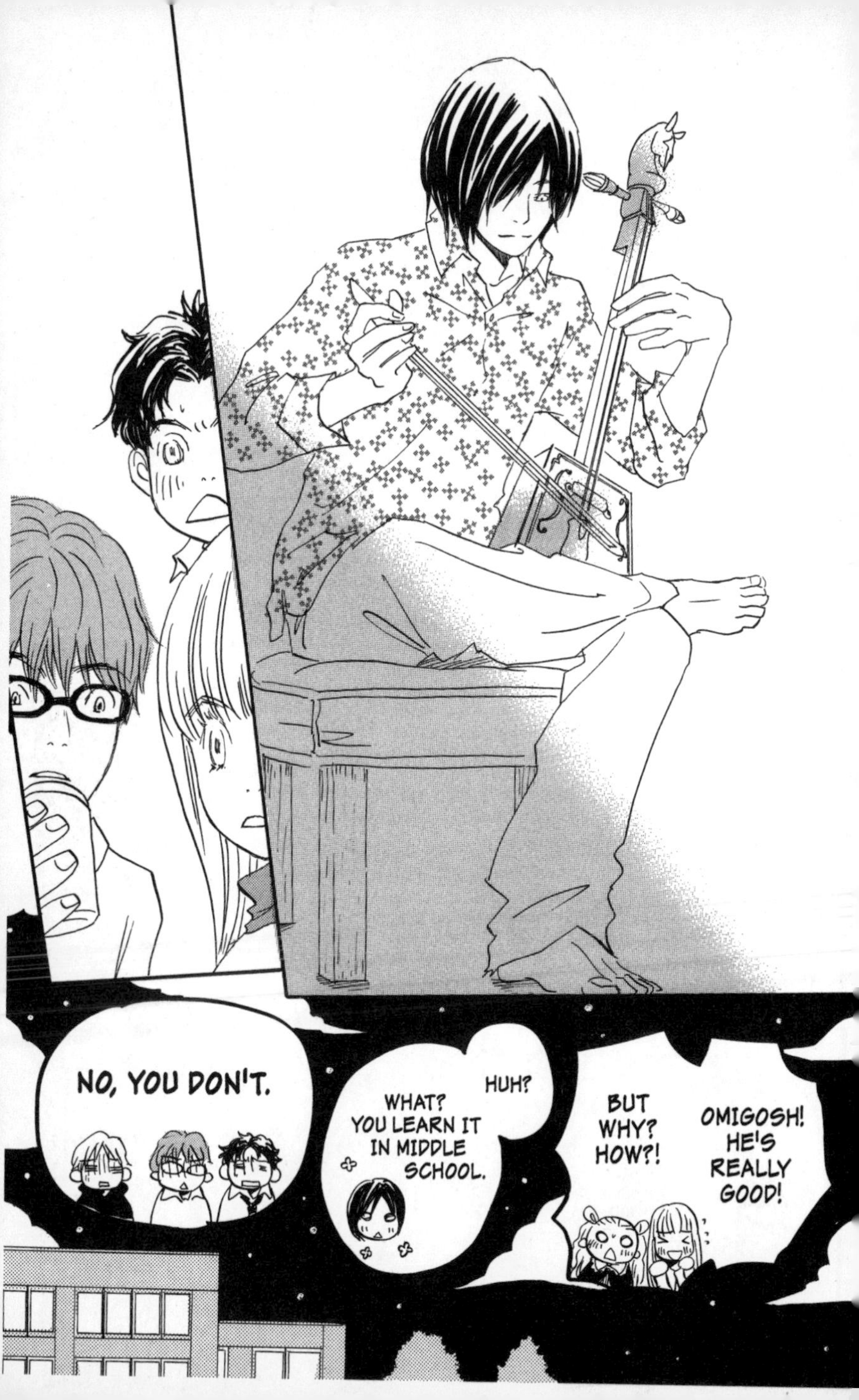

OMIGOSH! HE'S REALLY GOOD!
BUT WHY? HOW?!
HUH?
WHAT? YOU LEARN IT IN MIDDLE SCHOOL.
NO, YOU DON'T.

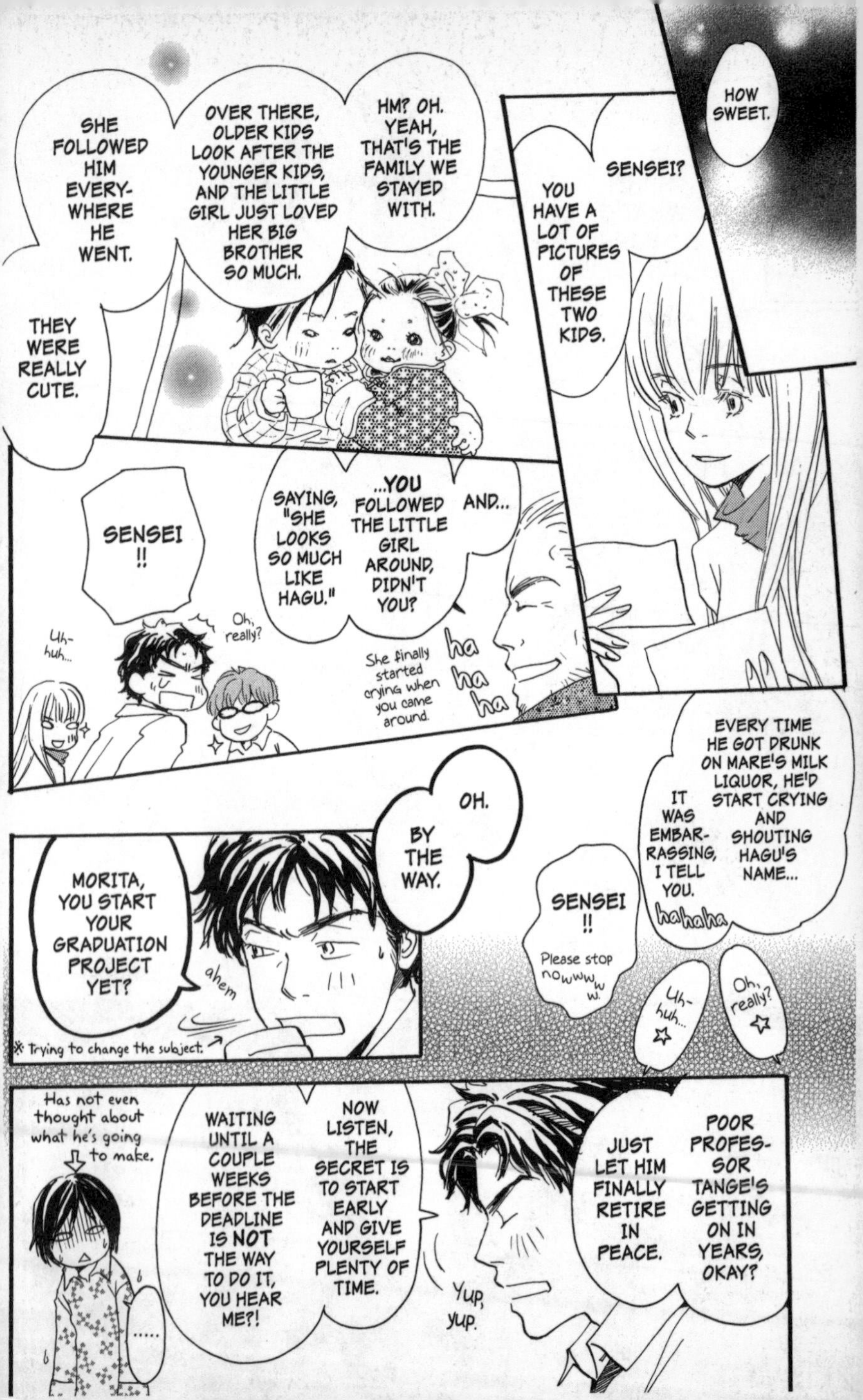
SENSEI?
YOU HAVE A LOT OF PICTURES OF THESE TWO KIDS.
HM? OH. YEAH, THAT'S THE FAMILY WE STAYED WITH.
OVER THERE, OLDER KIDS LOOK AFTER THE YOUNGER KIDS, AND THE LITTLE GIRL JUST LOVED HER BIG BROTHER SO MUCH.
SHE FOLLOWED HIM EVERY-WHERE HE WENT.
THEY WERE REALLY CUTE.
HOW SWEET.
AND...
...YOU FOLLOWED THE LITTLE GIRL AROUND, DIDN'T YOU?
SAYING, "SHE LOOKS SO MUCH LIKE HAGU."
ha ha ha
She finally started crying when you came around.
SENSEI !!
Oh, really?
Uh-huh...
EVERY TIME HE GOT DRUNK ON MARE'S MILK LIQUOR, HE'D START CRYING AND SHOUTING HAGU'S NAME...
IT WAS EMBAR-RASSING, I TELL YOU.
hahaha
SENSEI !!
Please stop nowwwww.
Oh, really?
Uh-huh...
OH.
BY THE WAY.
MORITA, YOU START YOUR GRADUATION PROJECT YET?
ahem
※ Trying to change the subject.
POOR PROFES-SOR TANGE'S GETTING ON IN YEARS, OKAY?
JUST LET HIM FINALLY RETIRE IN PEACE.
Yup, yup.
NOW LISTEN, THE SECRET IS TO START EARLY AND GIVE YOURSELF PLENTY OF TIME.
WAITING UNTIL A COUPLE WEEKS BEFORE THE DEADLINE IS NOT THE WAY TO DO IT, YOU HEAR ME?!
Has not even thought about what he's going to make.
.....

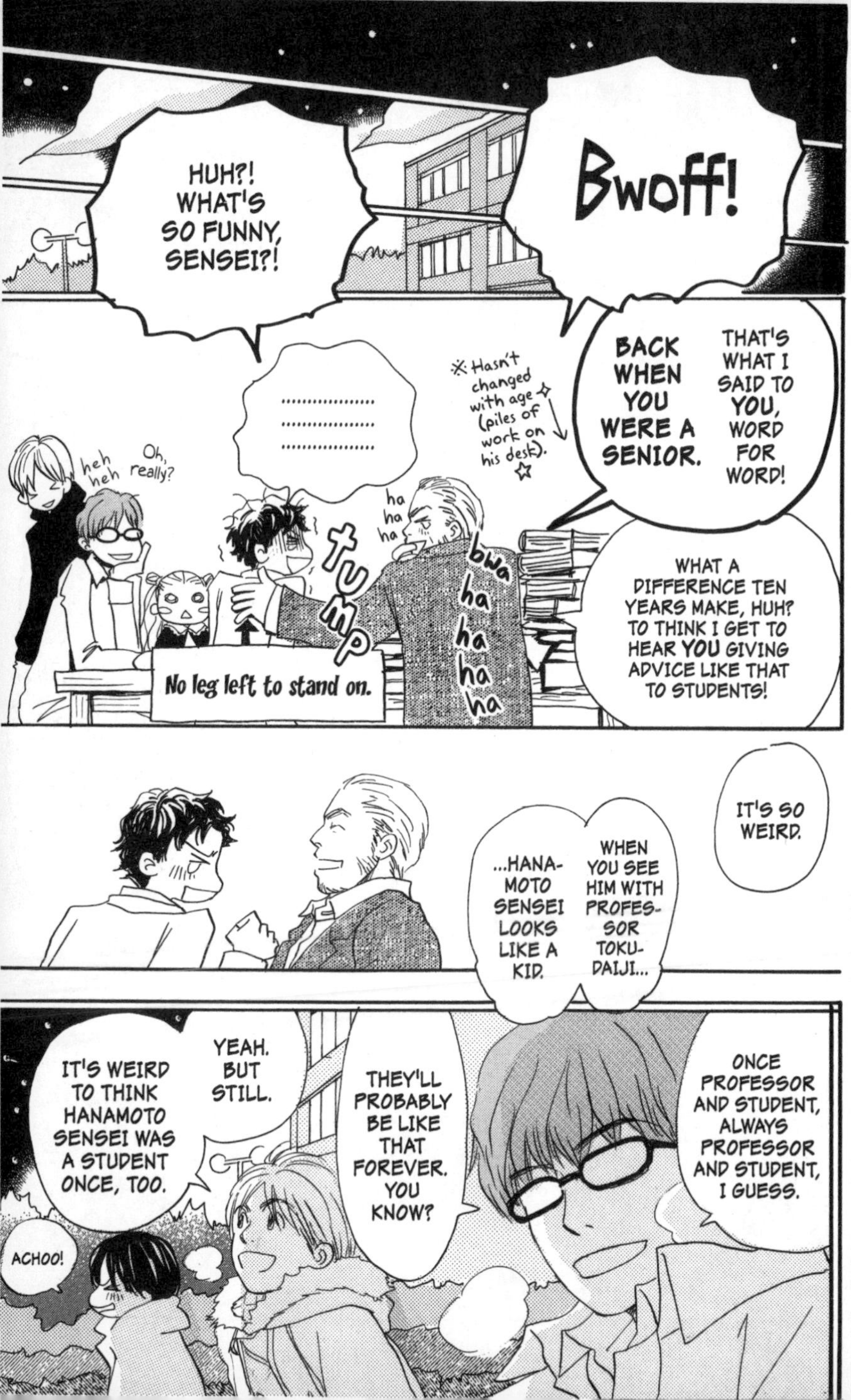
Bwoff!
HUH?! WHAT'S SO FUNNY, SENSEI?!
THAT'S WHAT I SAID TO YOU, WORD FOR WORD!
BACK WHEN YOU WERE A SENIOR.
WHAT A DIFFERENCE TEN YEARS MAKE, HUH? TO THINK I GET TO HEAR YOU GIVING ADVICE LIKE THAT TO STUDENTS!
※ Hasn't changed with age ✧ (piles of work on his desk). ☆
ha ha ha
bwa ha ha ha ha
TUMP
....
....
....
Oh, really?
heh heh
No leg left to stand on.
IT'S SO WEIRD.
WHEN YOU SEE HIM WITH PROFES-SOR TOKU-DAIJI...
...HANA-MOTO SENSEI LOOKS LIKE A KID.
ONCE PROFESSOR AND STUDENT, ALWAYS PROFESSOR AND STUDENT, I GUESS.
THEY'LL PROBABLY BE LIKE THAT FOREVER. YOU KNOW?
YEAH. BUT STILL.
IT'S WEIRD TO THINK HANAMOTO SENSEI WAS A STUDENT ONCE, TOO.
ACHOO!

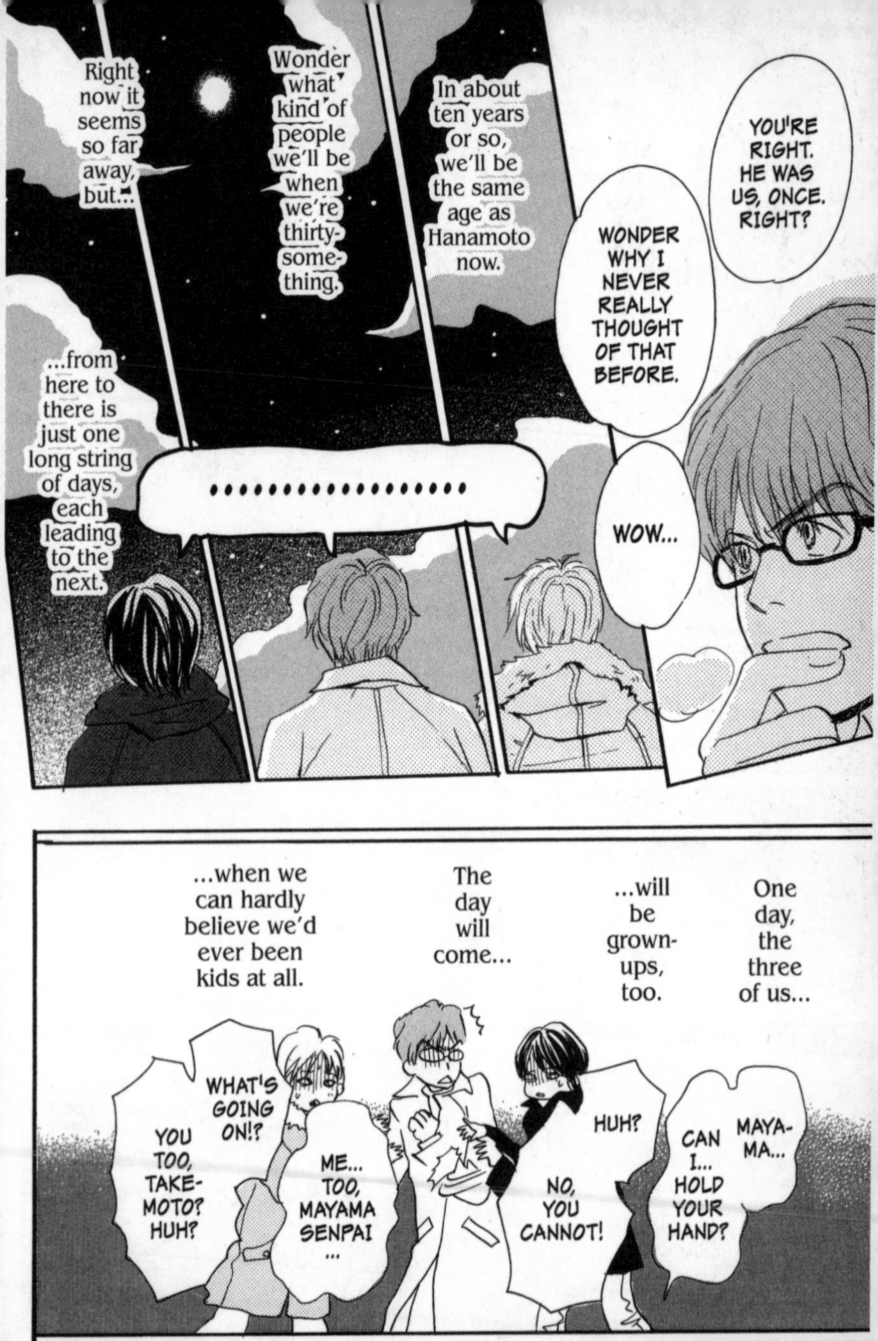
YOU'RE RIGHT. HE WAS US, ONCE. RIGHT?
WONDER WHY I NEVER REALLY THOUGHT OF THAT BEFORE.
WOW...
In about ten years or so, we'll be the same age as Hanamoto now.
Wonder what kind of people we'll be when we're thirty-something.
....
Right now it seems so far away, but...
...from here to there is just one long string of days, each leading to the next.
One day, the three of us...
...will be grown-ups, too.
The day will come...
...when we can hardly believe we'd ever been kids at all.
MAYA-MA...
CAN I... HOLD YOUR HAND?
HUH?
NO, YOU CANNOT!
ME... TOO, MAYAMA SENPAI ...
WHAT'S GOING ON!?
YOU TOO, TAKE-MOTO? HUH?

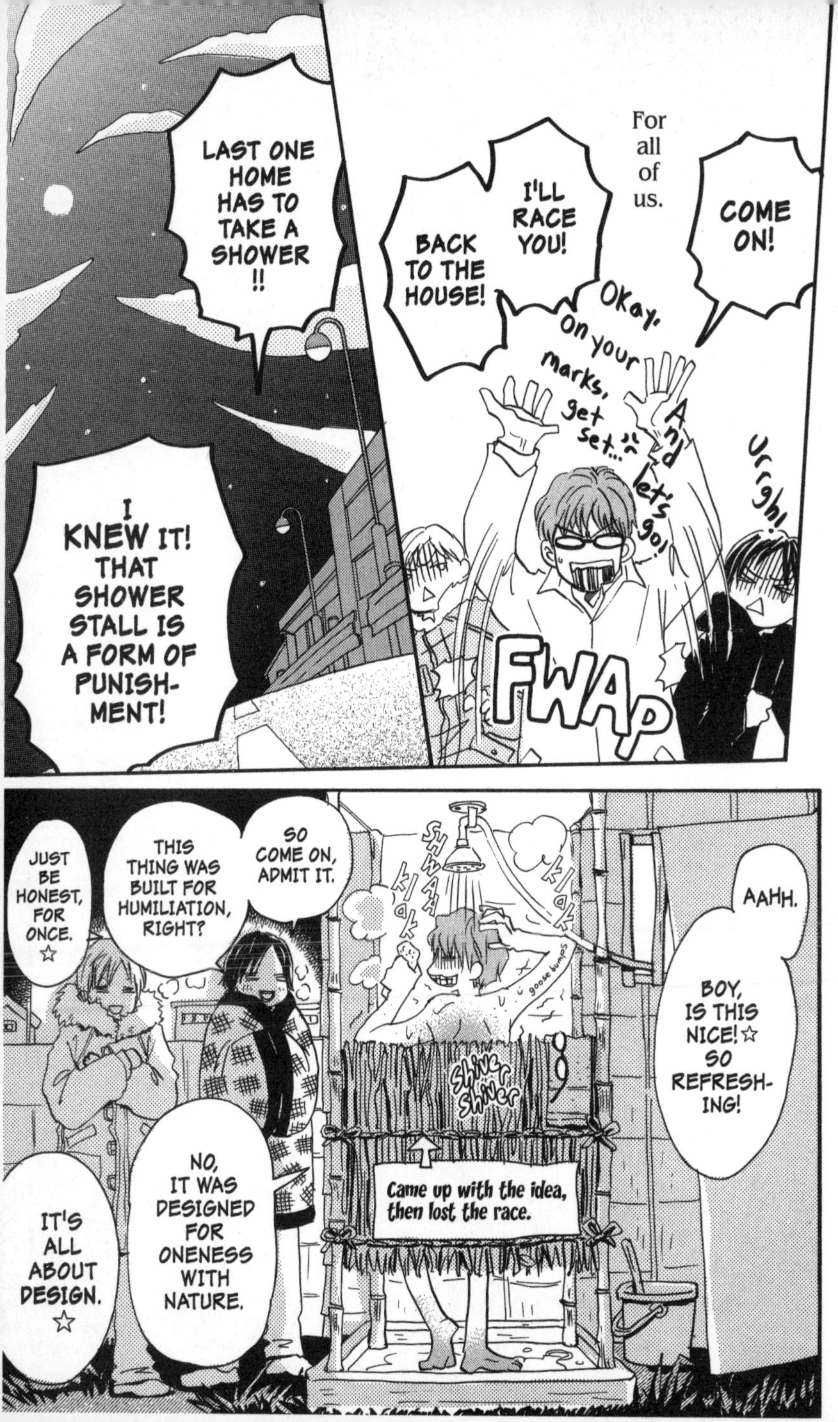
COME ON!
For all of us.
I'LL RACE YOU!
BACK TO THE HOUSE!
Okay. On your marks, get set...
And let's go!
Urrgh!
FWAP
LAST ONE HOME HAS TO TAKE A SHOWER !!
I KNEW IT! THAT SHOWER STALL IS A FORM OF PUNISHMENT!
AAHH.
BOY, IS THIS NICE!☆ SO REFRESHING!
klak
SHWAA
klak
goose bumps
Shiver shiver
Came up with the idea, then lost the race.
SO COME ON, ADMIT IT.
THIS THING WAS BUILT FOR HUMILIATION, RIGHT?
JUST BE HONEST, FOR ONCE. ☆
NO, IT WAS DESIGNED FOR ONENESS WITH NATURE.
IT'S ALL ABOUT DESIGN. ☆

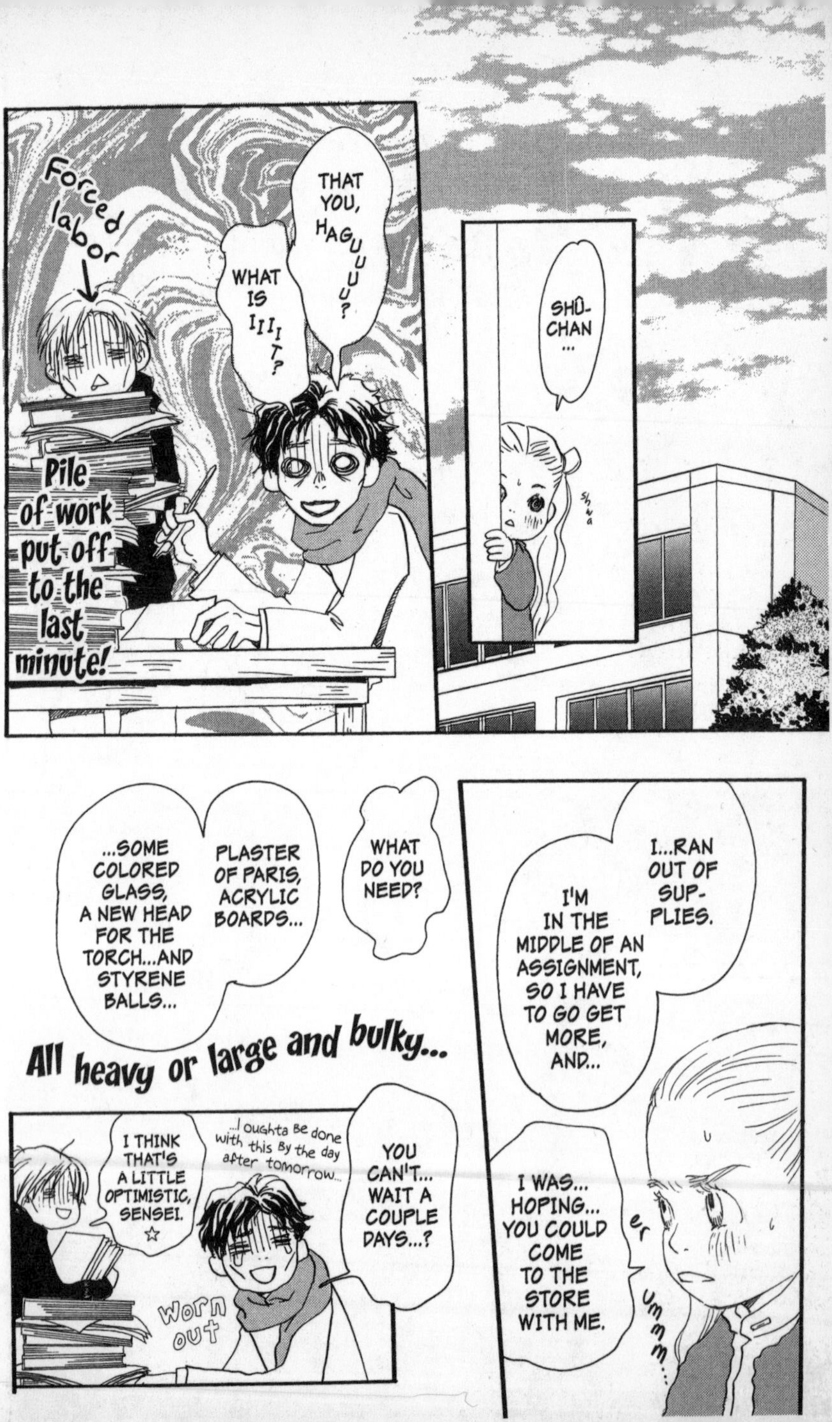
SHÛ-CHAN...
THAT YOU, HAGUUUU?
WHAT IS IIIT?
Forced labor
Pile of work put off to the last minute!
I...RAN OUT OF SUPPLIES.
I'M IN THE MIDDLE OF AN ASSIGNMENT, SO I HAVE TO GO GET MORE, AND...
I WAS... HOPING... YOU COULD COME TO THE STORE WITH ME.
er
Ummm...
WHAT DO YOU NEED?
PLASTER OF PARIS, ACRYLIC BOARDS...
...SOME COLORED GLASS, A NEW HEAD FOR THE TORCH...AND STYRENE BALLS...
All heavy or large and bulky...
YOU CAN'T... WAIT A COUPLE DAYS...?
...I oughta be done with this by the day after tomorrow...
I THINK THAT'S A LITTLE OPTIMISTIC, SENSEI. ☆
Worn out

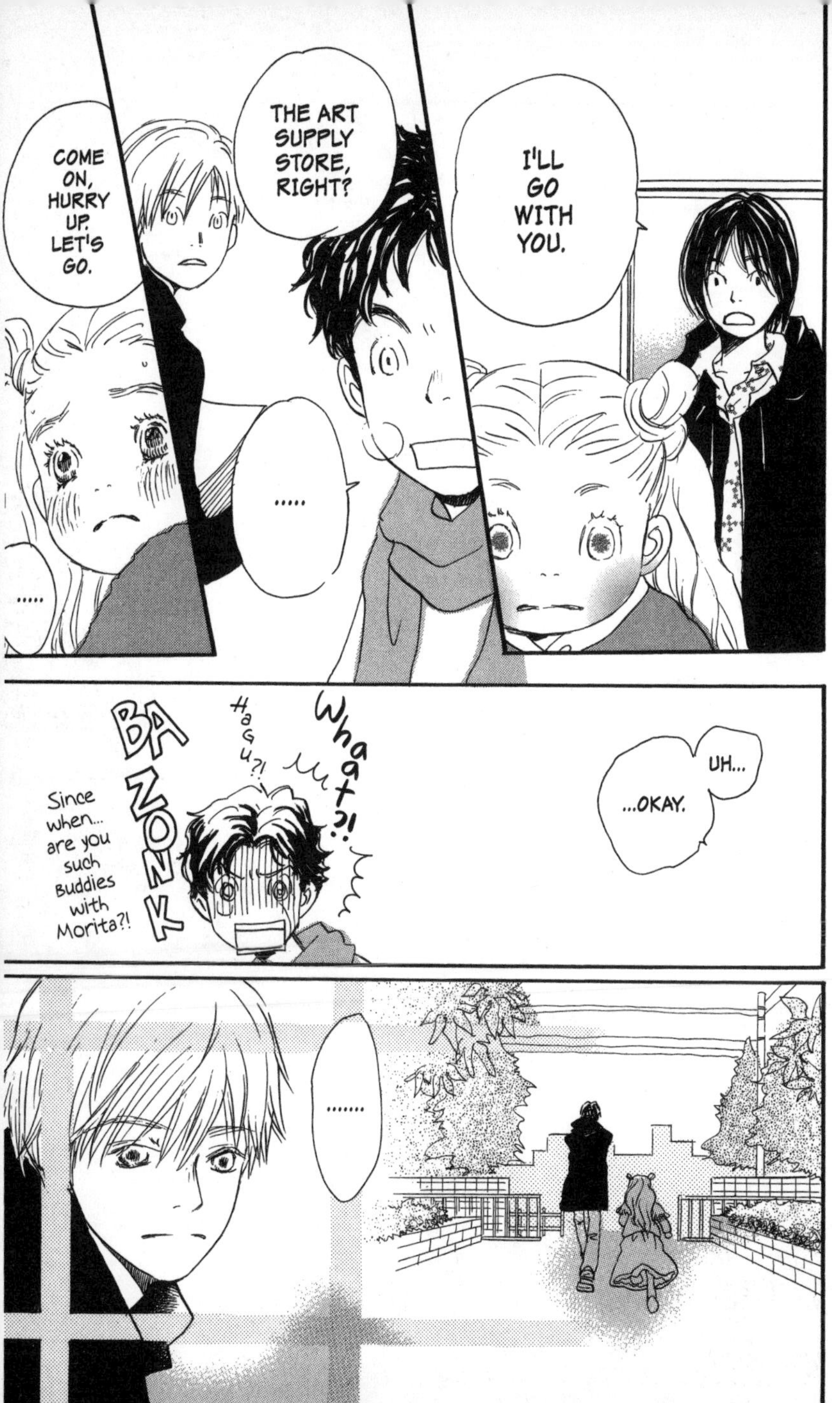
I'LL GO WITH YOU.
THE ART SUPPLY STORE, RIGHT?
.....
COME ON, HURRY UP. LET'S GO.
.....
UH...
...OKAY.
Whaaat?!
Hagu?!
BA ZONK
Since when... are you such buddies with Morita?!
....

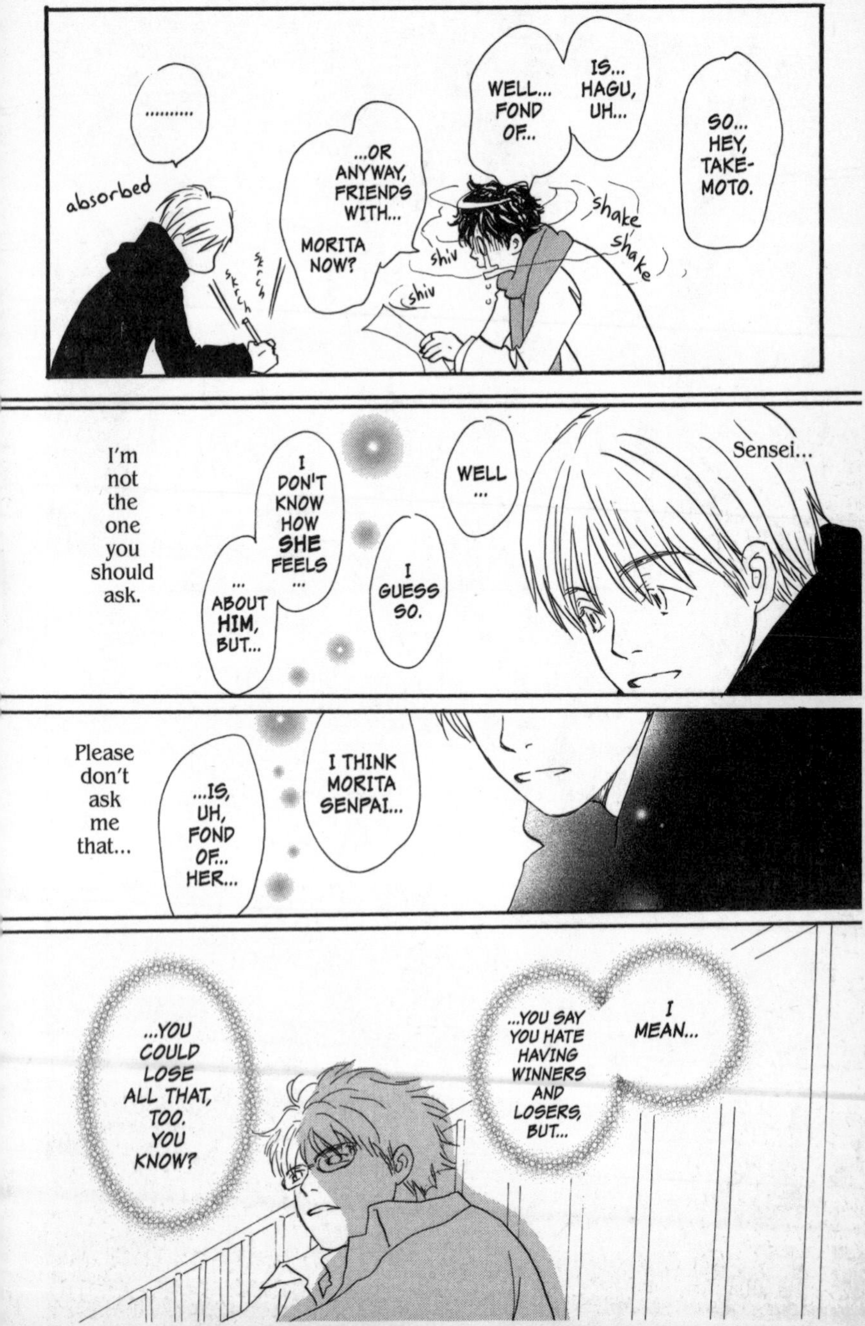
SO... HEY, TAKE-MOTO.
IS... HAGU, UH...
WELL... FOND OF...
shake shake
...OR ANYWAY, FRIENDS WITH...
MORITA NOW?
shiv
shiv
skrch skrch
absorbed
....
Sensei...
WELL ...
I GUESS SO.
I DON'T KNOW HOW SHE FEELS ...
... ABOUT HIM, BUT...
I'm not the one you should ask.
I THINK MORITA SENPAI...
...IS, UH, FOND OF.. HER...
Please don't ask me that...
I MEAN...
...YOU SAY YOU HATE HAVING WINNERS AND LOSERS, BUT...
...YOU COULD LOSE ALL THAT, TOO. YOU KNOW?

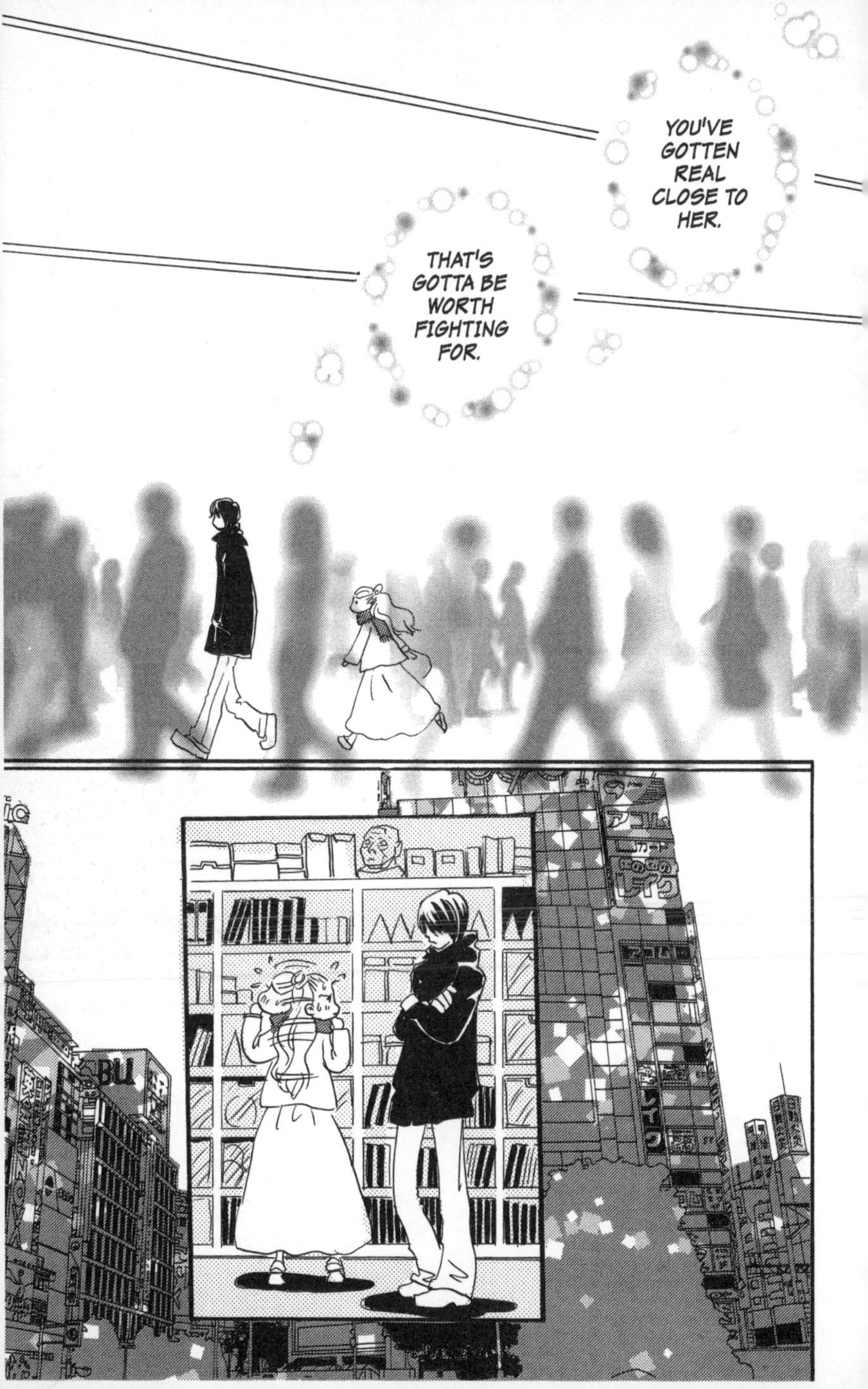
YOU'VE GOTTEN REAL CLOSE TO HER.
THAT'S GOTTA BE WORTH FIGHTING FOR.

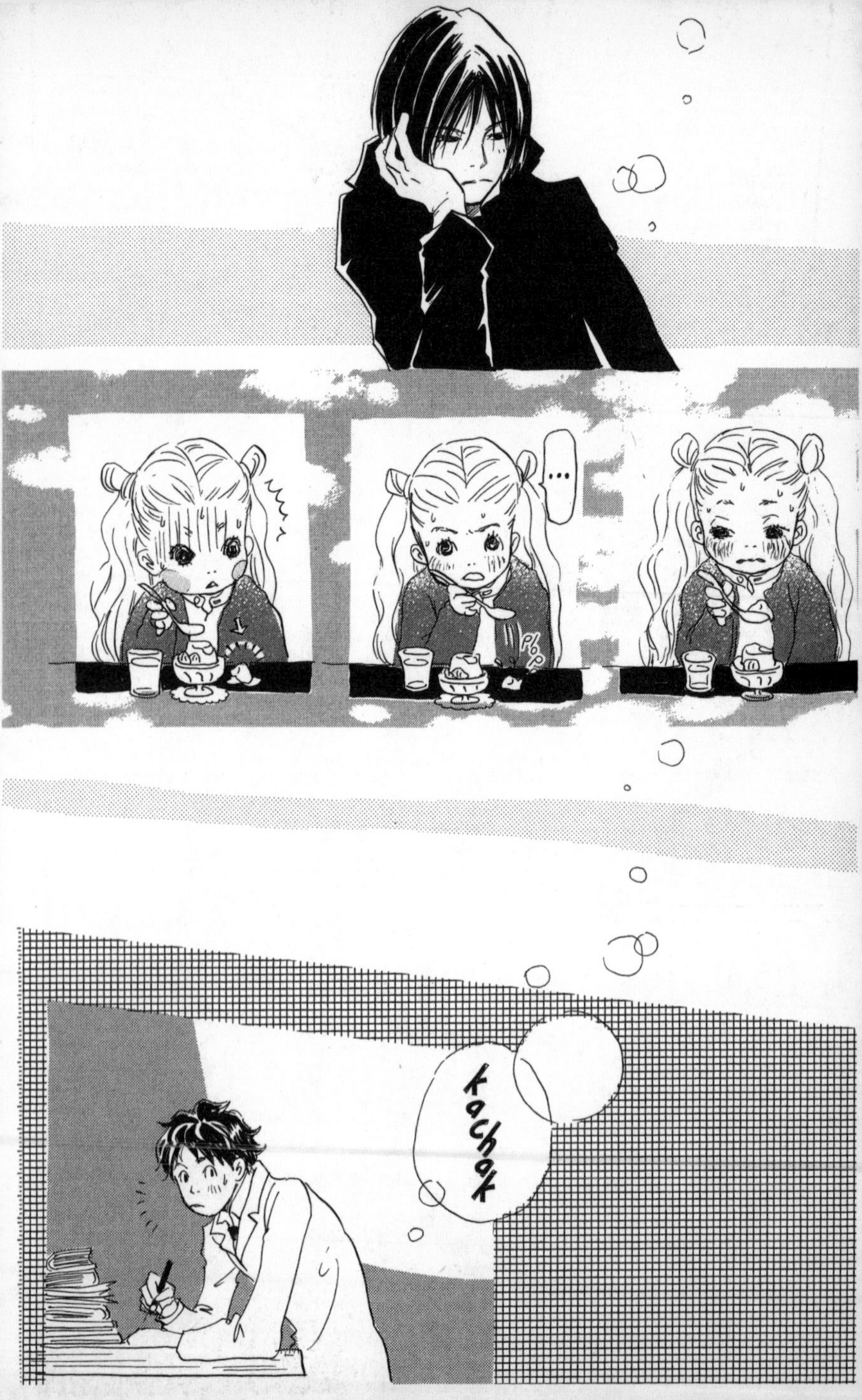
...
Plop
kachak

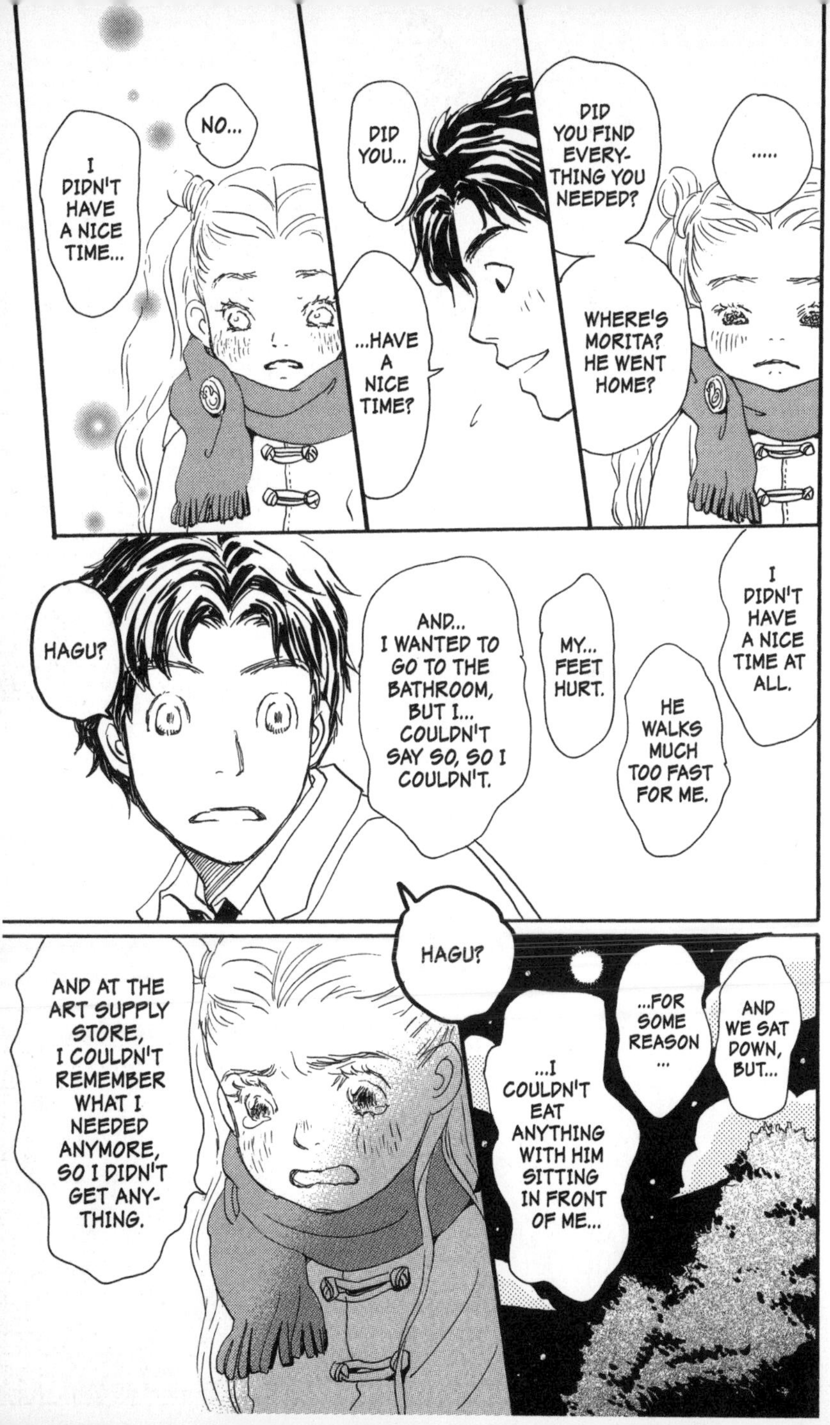
DID YOU FIND EVERY-THING YOU NEEDED?
.....
WHERE'S MORITA? HE WENT HOME?
DID YOU...
...HAVE A NICE TIME?
NO...
I DIDN'T HAVE A NICE TIME...
I DIDN'T HAVE A NICE TIME AT ALL.
HE WALKS MUCH TOO FAST FOR ME.
MY... FEET HURT.
AND... I WANTED TO GO TO THE BATHROOM, BUT I... COULDN'T SAY SO, SO I COULDN'T.
HAGU?
AND WE SAT DOWN, BUT...
...FOR SOME REASON ...
HAGU?
...I COULDN'T EAT ANYTHING WITH HIM SITTING IN FRONT OF ME...
AND AT THE ART SUPPLY STORE, I COULDN'T REMEMBER WHAT I NEEDED ANYMORE, SO I DIDN'T GET ANY-THING.

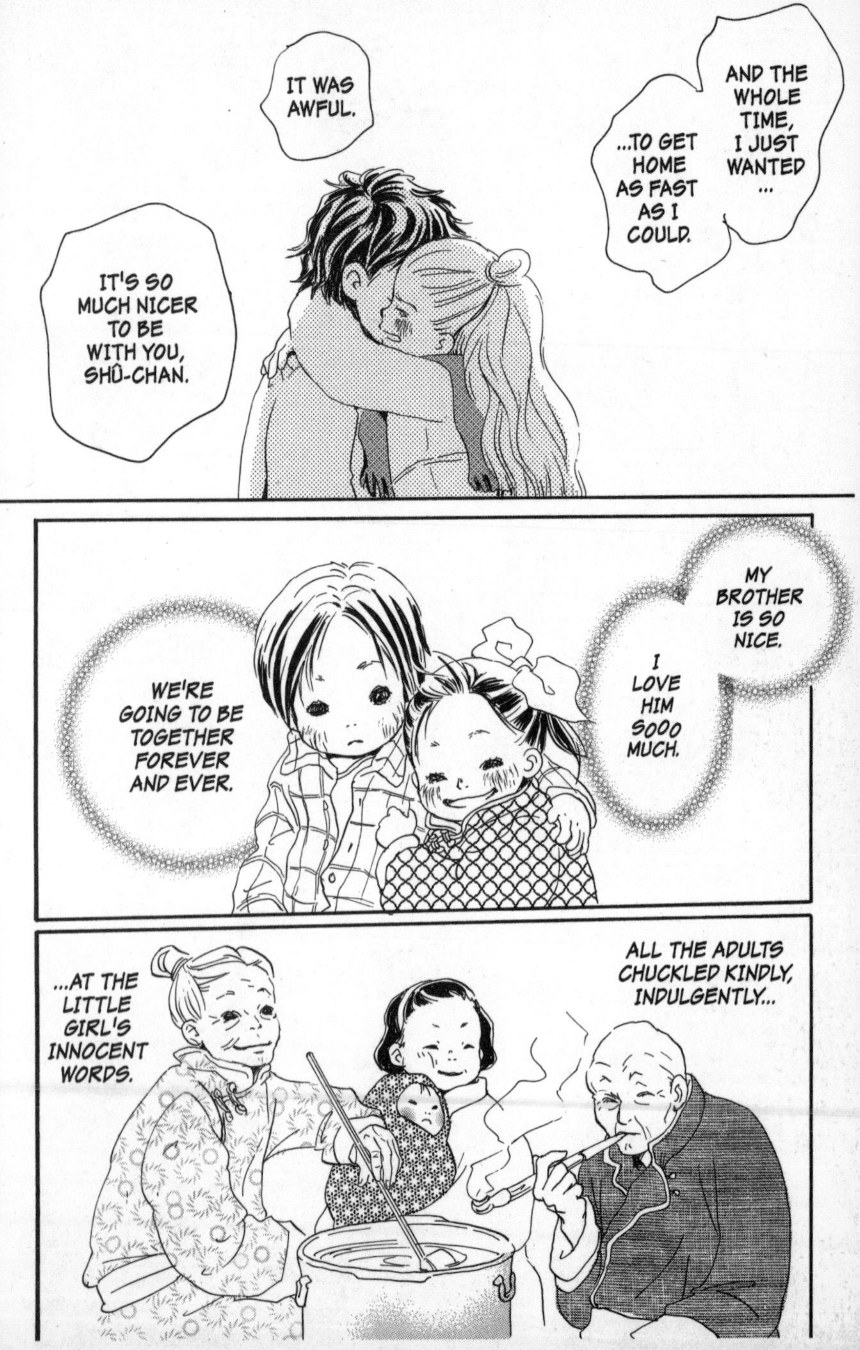
AND THE WHOLE TIME, I JUST WANTED ...
...TO GET HOME AS FAST AS I COULD.
IT WAS AWFUL.
IT'S SO MUCH NICER TO BE WITH YOU, SHÛ-CHAN.
MY BROTHER IS SO NICE.
I LOVE HIM SOOO MUCH.
WE'RE GOING TO BE TOGETHER FOREVER AND EVER.
ALL THE ADULTS CHUCKLED KINDLY, INDULGENTLY...
...AT THE LITTLE GIRL'S INNOCENT WORDS.

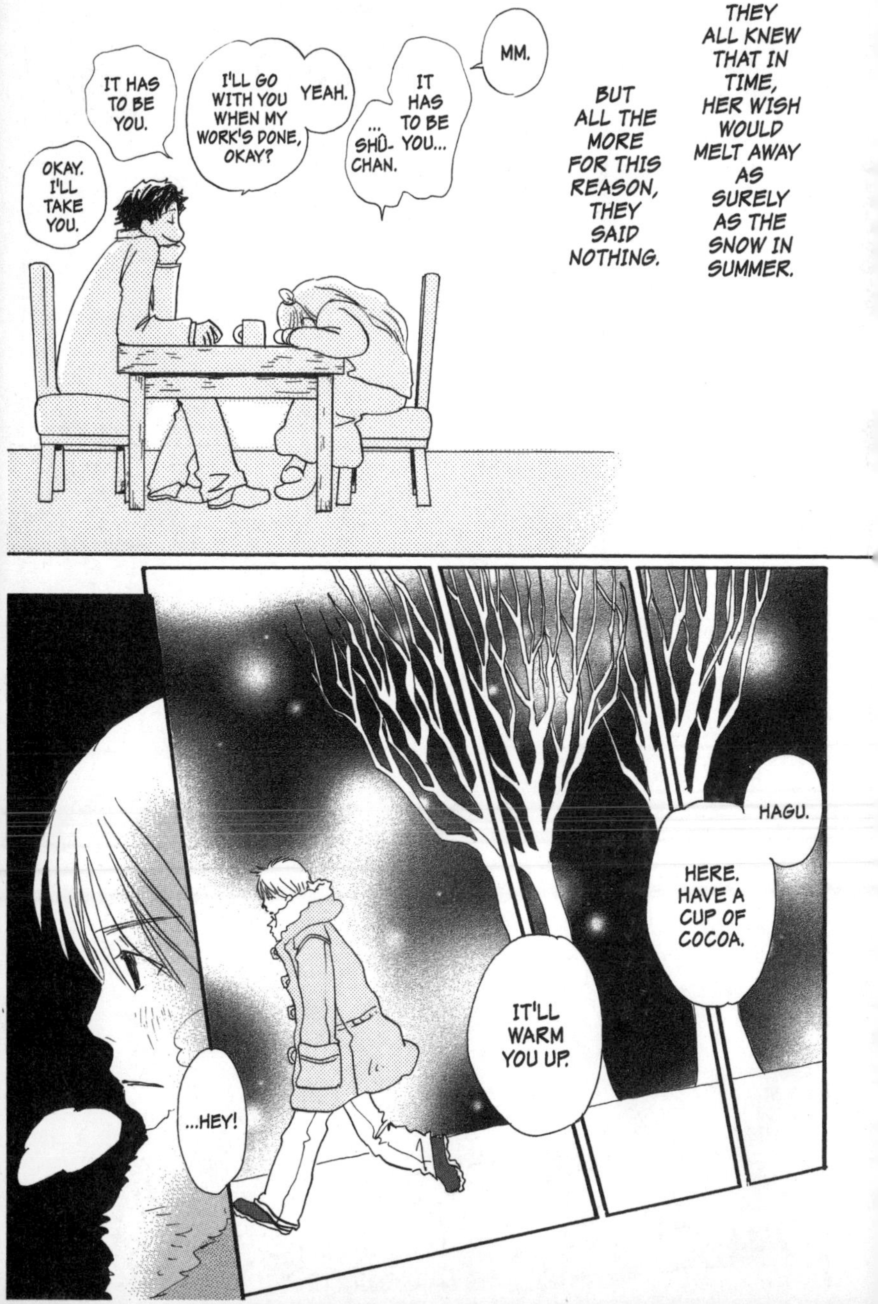
THEY ALL KNEW THAT IN TIME, HER WISH WOULD MELT AWAY AS SURELY AS THE SNOW IN SUMMER.
BUT ALL THE MORE FOR THIS REASON, THEY SAID NOTHING.
MM.
IT HAS TO BE YOU... ...SHÛ-CHAN.
YEAH.
I'LL GO WITH YOU WHEN MY WORK'S DONE, OKAY?
IT HAS TO BE YOU.
OKAY. I'LL TAKE YOU.
HAGU.
HERE. HAVE A CUP OF COCOA.
IT'LL WARM YOU UP.
...HEY!

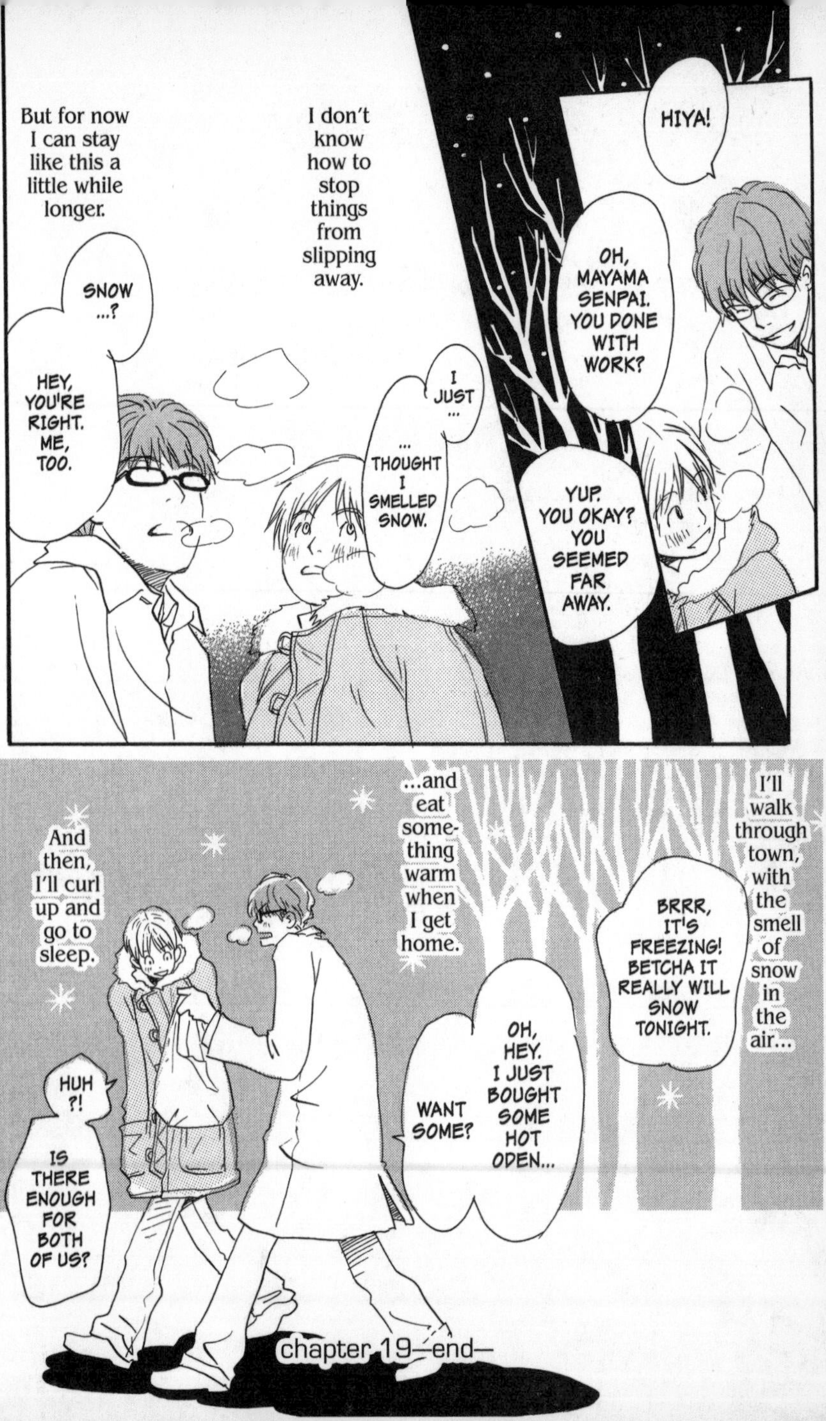
HIYA!
OH, MAYAMA SENPAI. YOU DONE WITH WORK?
YUP. YOU OKAY? YOU SEEMED FAR AWAY.
I don't know how to stop things from slipping away.
But for now I can stay like this a little while longer.
I JUST...
...THOUGHT I SMELLED SNOW.
SNOW...?
HEY, YOU'RE RIGHT. ME, TOO.
I'll walk through town, with the smell of snow in the air...
BRRR, IT'S FREEZING! BETCHA IT REALLY WILL SNOW TONIGHT.
...and eat something warm when I get home.
OH, HEY. I JUST BOUGHT SOME HOT ODEN...
WANT SOME?
And then, I'll curl up and go to sleep.
HUH?!
IS THERE ENOUGH FOR BOTH OF US?
chapter 19—end—

honey and clover

chapter 20

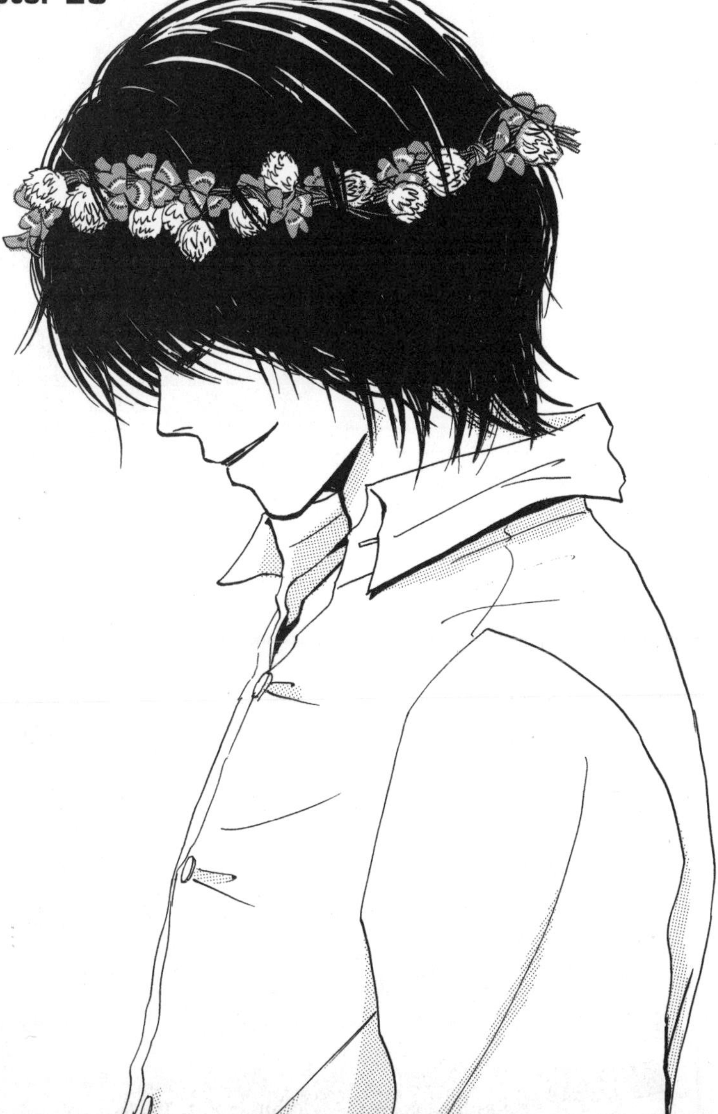

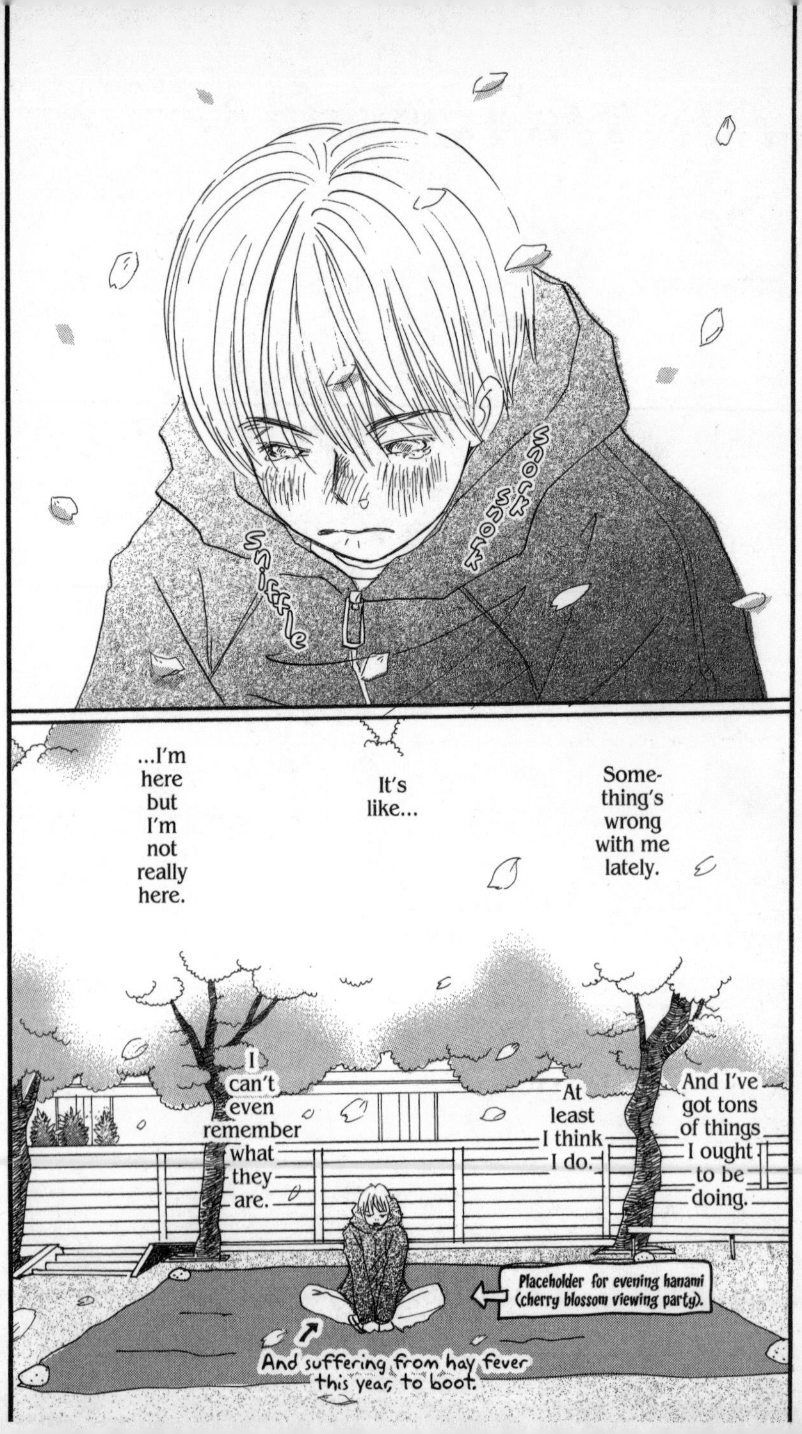
snork snork
sniffle
Some-thing's wrong with me lately.
It's like...
...I'm here but I'm not really here.
And I've got tons of things I ought to be doing.
At least I think I do.
I can't even remember what they are.
Placeholder for evening hanami (cherry blossom viewing party).
And suffering from hay fever this year, to boot.

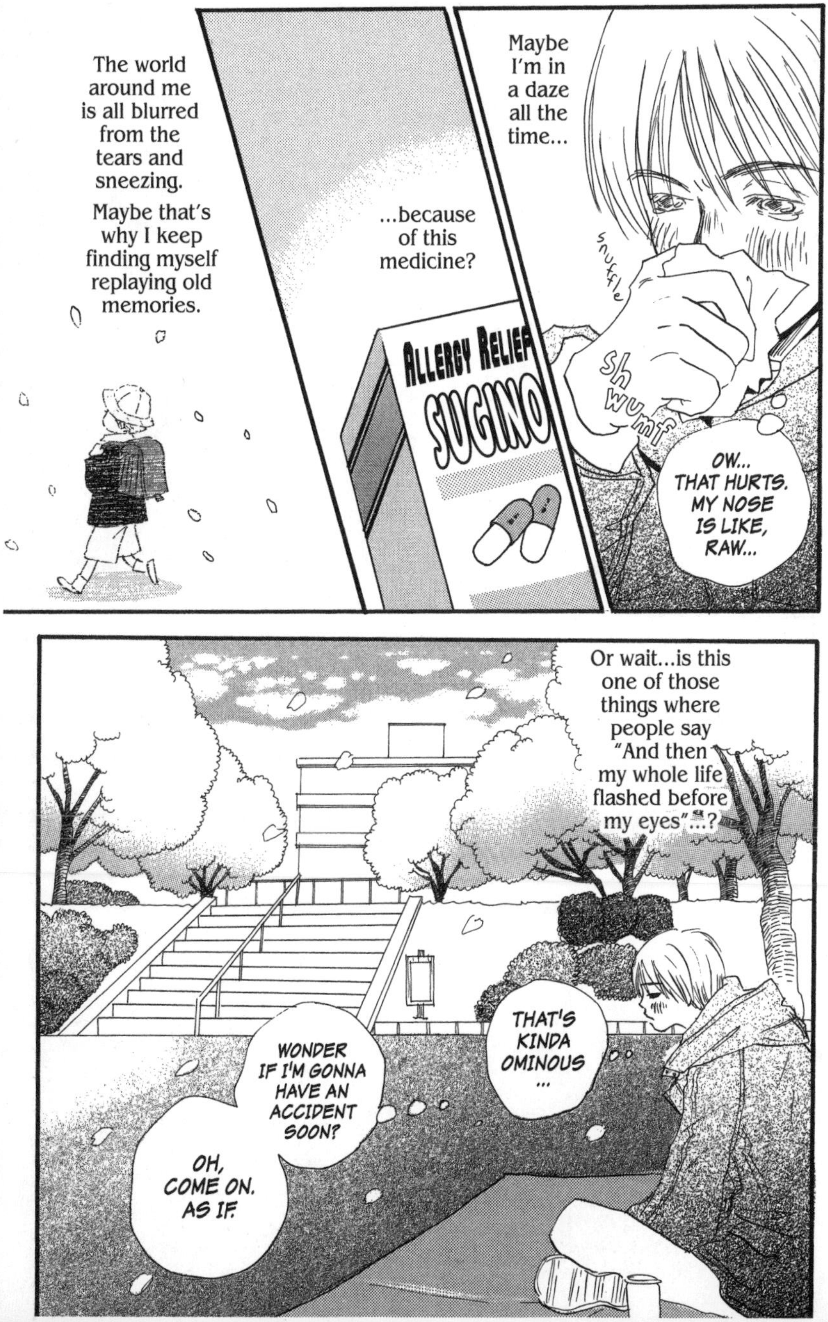
Maybe I'm in a daze all the time...
snuffle
Sh
wumf
OW... THAT HURTS. MY NOSE IS LIKE, RAW...
...because of this medicine?
ALLERGY RELIEF
SUGINO
The world around me is all blurred from the tears and sneezing.
Maybe that's why I keep finding myself replaying old memories.
Or wait...is this one of those things where people say "And then my whole life flashed before my eyes"...?
THAT'S KINDA OMINOUS...
WONDER IF I'M GONNA HAVE AN ACCIDENT SOON?
OH, COME ON. AS IF.

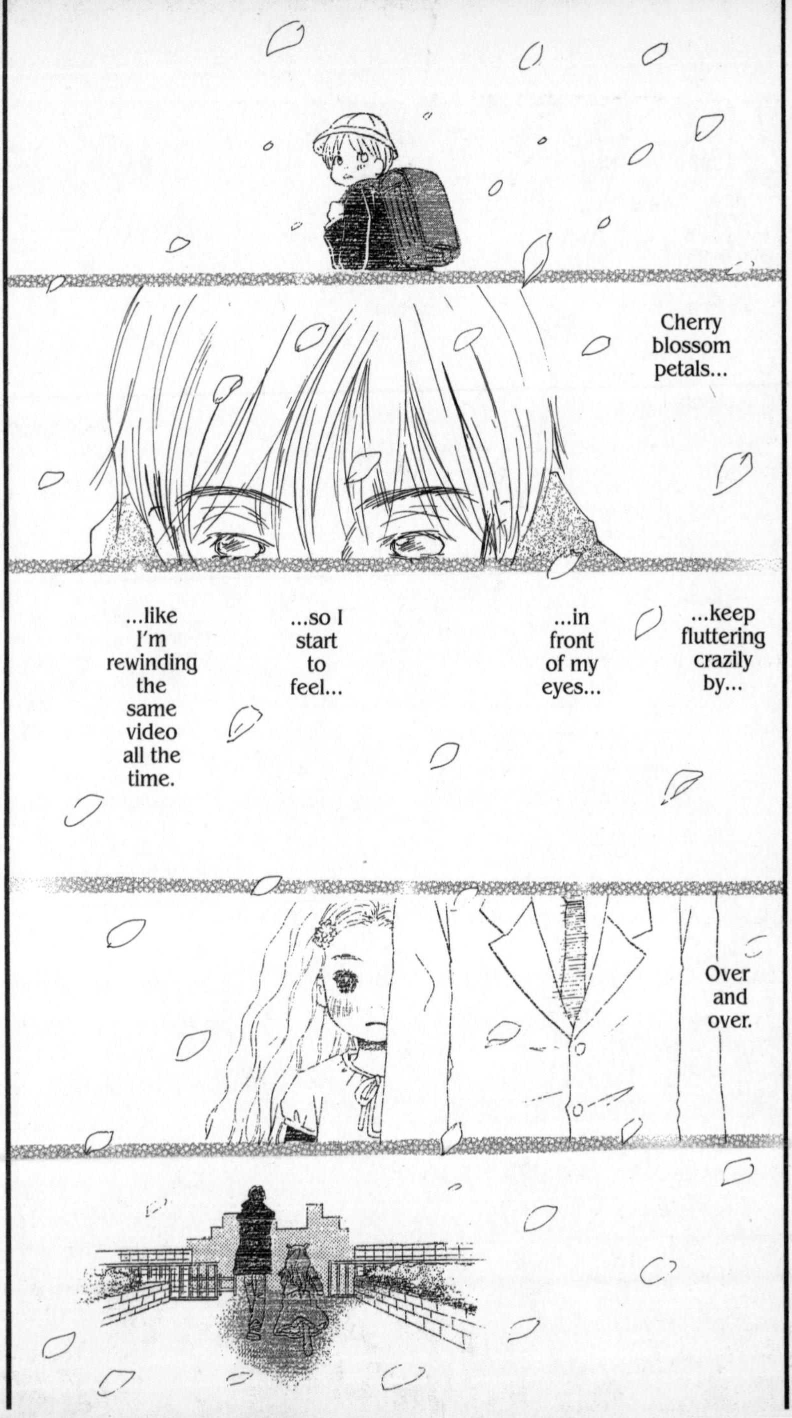
Cherry blossom petals...
...keep fluttering crazily by...
...in front of my eyes...
...so I start to feel...
...like I'm rewinding the same video all the time.
Over and over.

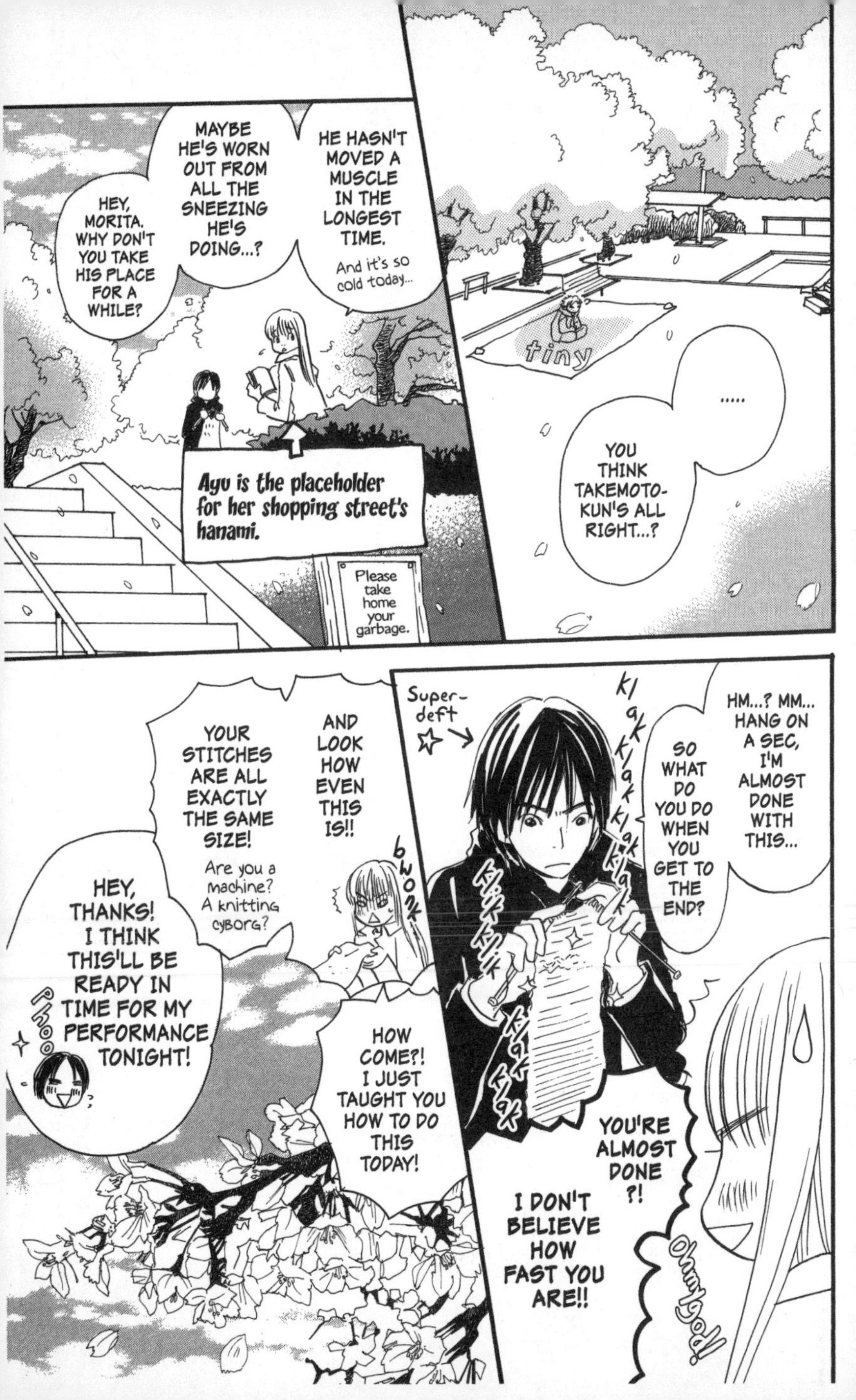
tiny
.....
YOU THINK TAKEMOTO-KUN'S ALL RIGHT...?
HE HASN'T MOVED A MUSCLE IN THE LONGEST TIME.
And it's so cold today...
MAYBE HE'S WORN OUT FROM ALL THE SNEEZING HE'S DOING...?
HEY, MORITA. WHY DON'T YOU TAKE HIS PLACE FOR A WHILE?
Ayu is the placeholder for her shopping street's hanami.
Please take home your garbage.
HM...? MM... HANG ON A SEC, I'M ALMOST DONE WITH THIS...
SO WHAT DO YOU DO WHEN YOU GET TO THE END?
Super-deft
klak klak klak klak klak
klik klik klik
klak klak klak
YOU'RE ALMOST DONE?!
I DON'T BELIEVE HOW FAST YOU ARE!!
Ohmygod!
AND LOOK HOW EVEN THIS IS!!
YOUR STITCHES ARE ALL EXACTLY THE SAME SIZE!
Are you a machine? A knitting cyborg?
bwonk
HOW COME?! I JUST TAUGHT YOU HOW TO DO THIS TODAY!
HEY, THANKS! I THINK THIS'LL BE READY IN TIME FOR MY PERFORMANCE TONIGHT!
Phoo

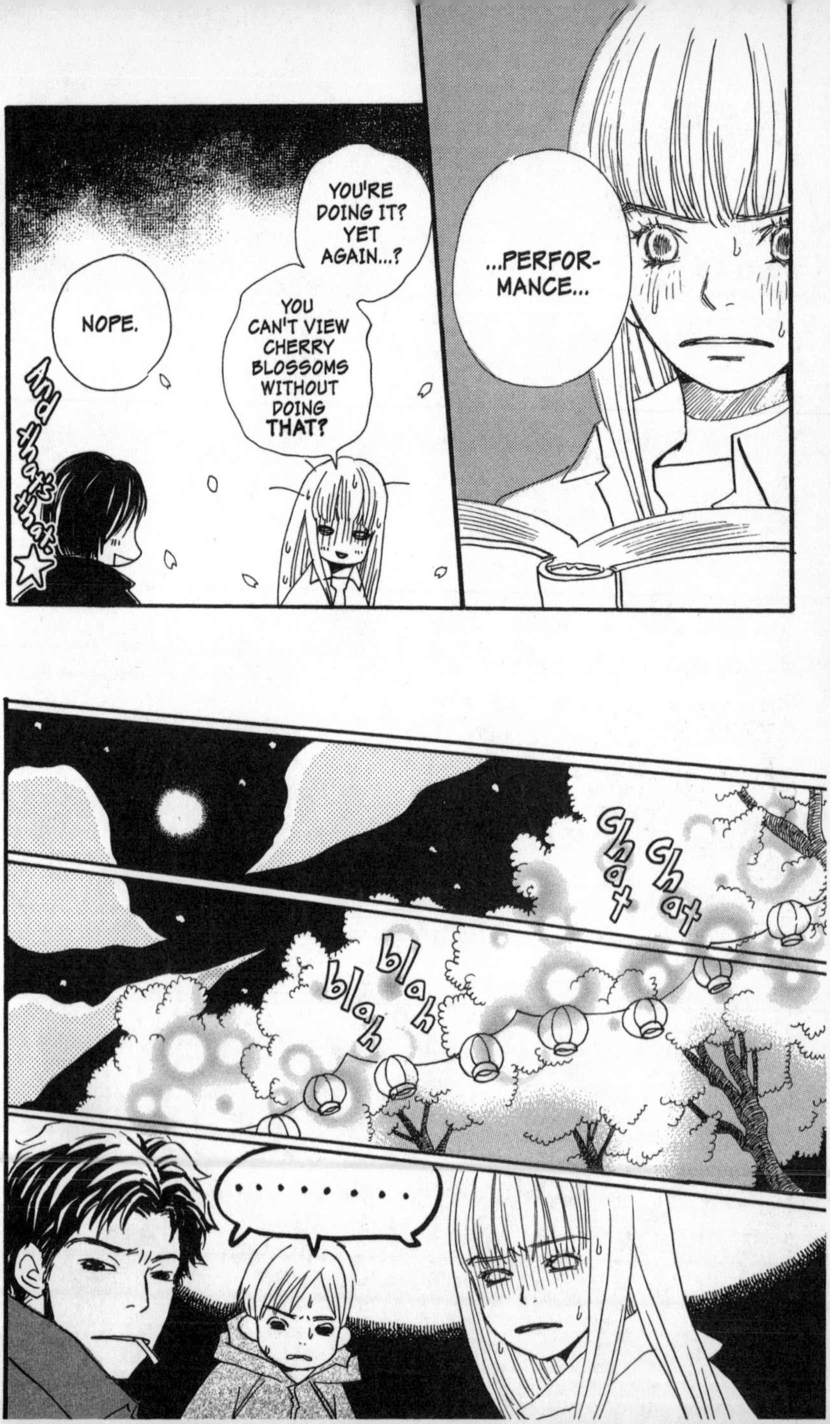
...PERFORMANCE...
YOU'RE DOING IT? YET AGAIN...?
YOU CAN'T VIEW CHERRY BLOSSOMS WITHOUT DOING THAT?
NOPE.
And that's that. ☆
Chat chat
blah blah
....

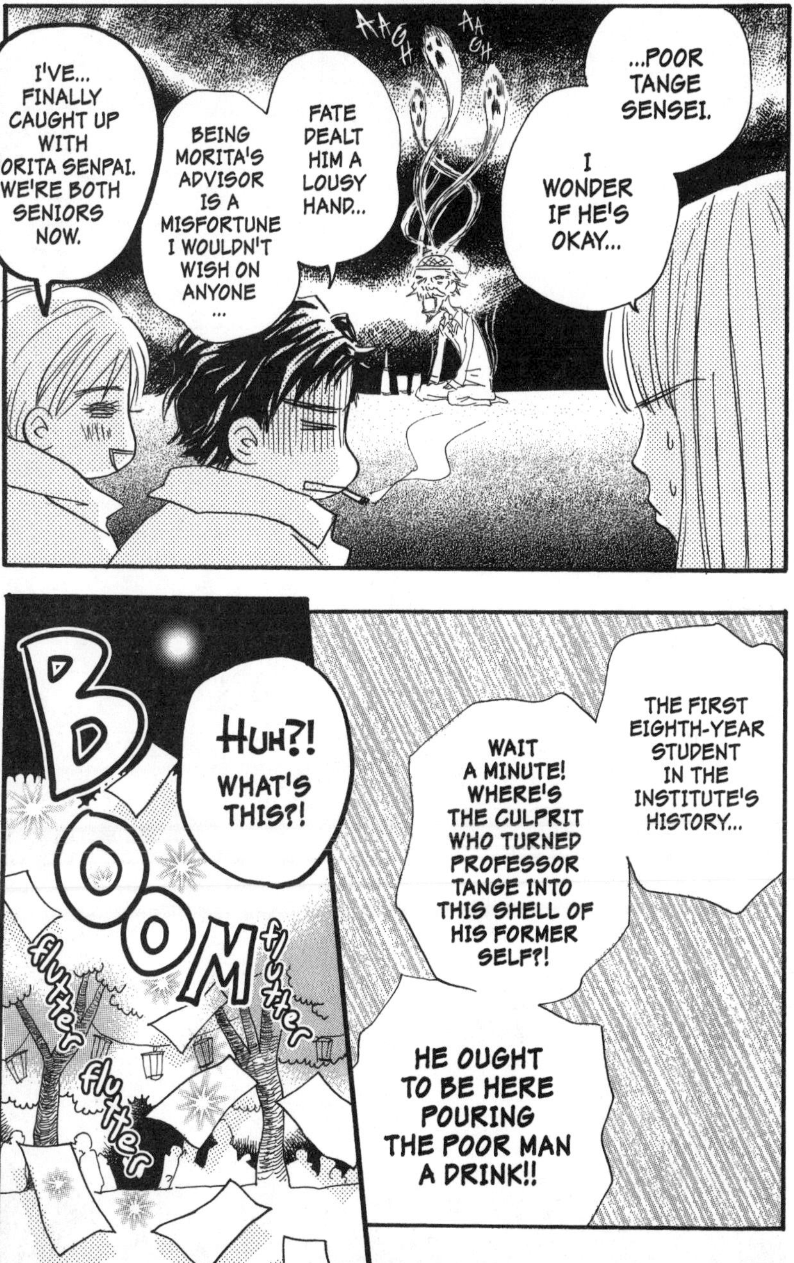
...POOR TANGE SENSEI.
I WONDER IF HE'S OKAY...
AAGH
AAGH
FATE DEALT HIM A LOUSY HAND...
BEING MORITA'S ADVISOR IS A MISFORTUNE I WOULDN'T WISH ON ANYONE ...
I'VE... FINALLY CAUGHT UP WITH MORITA SENPAI. WE'RE BOTH SENIORS NOW.
THE FIRST EIGHTH-YEAR STUDENT IN THE INSTITUTE'S HISTORY...
WAIT A MINUTE! WHERE'S THE CULPRIT WHO TURNED PROFESSOR TANGE INTO THIS SHELL OF HIS FORMER SELF?!
HE OUGHT TO BE HERE POURING THE POOR MAN A DRINK!!
HUH?! WHAT'S THIS?!
BOOM
flutter
flutter
flutter

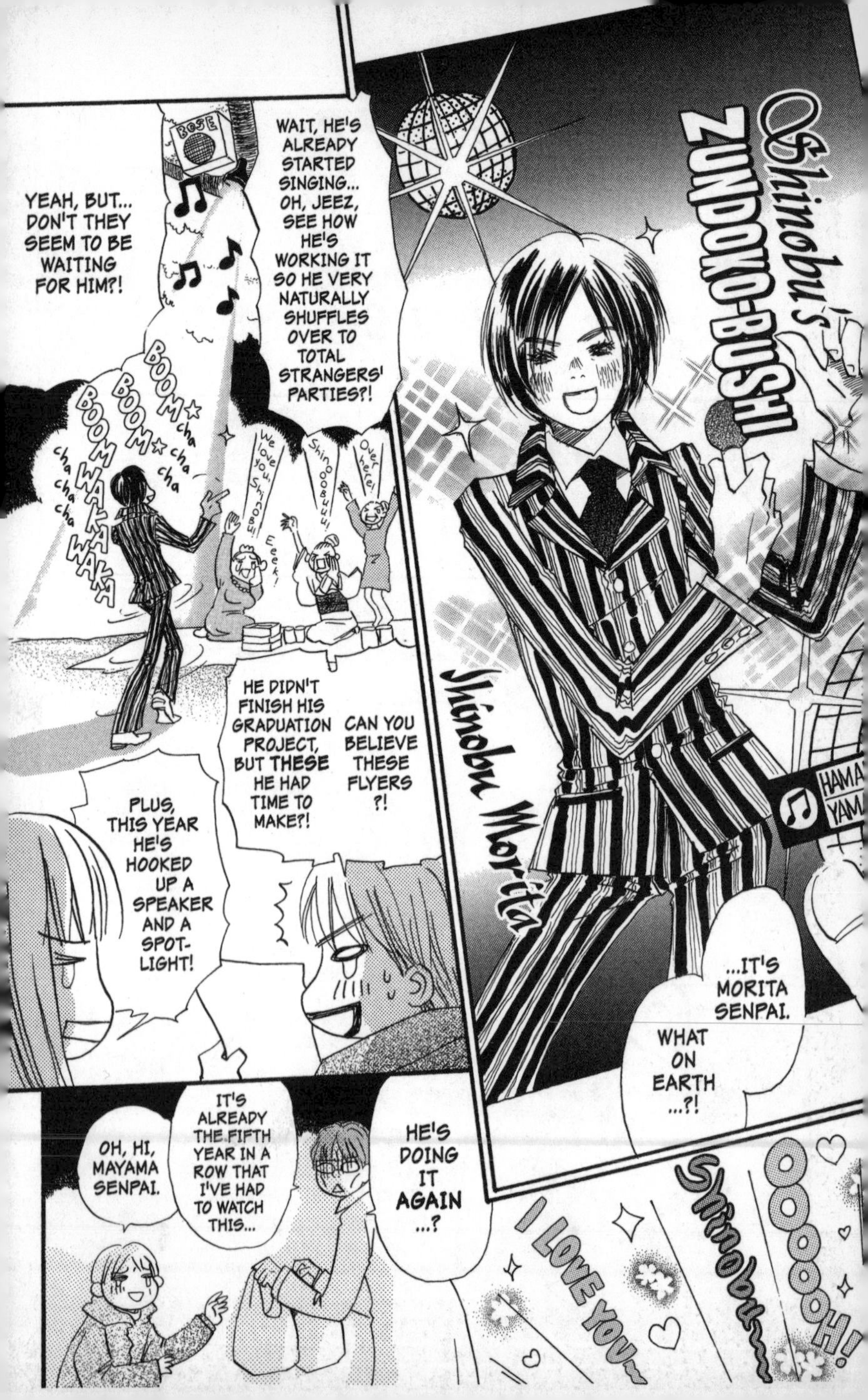

Shinobu's
ZUNDOKO-BUSHI
Shinobu Morita
HAMA YAM
...IT'S MORITA SENPAI.
WHAT ON EARTH ...?!
OOOOOOH!
Shinobu~~
I LOVE YOU~
BOSE
WAIT, HE'S ALREADY STARTED SINGING... OH, JEEZ, SEE HOW HE'S WORKING IT SO HE VERY NATURALLY SHUFFLES OVER TO TOTAL STRANGERS' PARTIES?!
YEAH, BUT... DON'T THEY SEEM TO BE WAITING FOR HIM?!
BOOM☆ cha cha
BOOM☆ cha cha
BOOM WAKA WAKA WAKA cha cha cha
Over here!
Shinoooobuuu!
We love you, Shinobu!
Eeek!
CAN YOU BELIEVE THESE FLYERS?!
HE DIDN'T FINISH HIS GRADUATION PROJECT, BUT THESE HE HAD TIME TO MAKE?!
PLUS, THIS YEAR HE'S HOOKED UP A SPEAKER AND A SPOT-LIGHT!
HE'S DOING IT AGAIN ...?
IT'S ALREADY THE FIFTH YEAR IN A ROW THAT I'VE HAD TO WATCH THIS...
OH, HI, MAYAMA SENPAI.

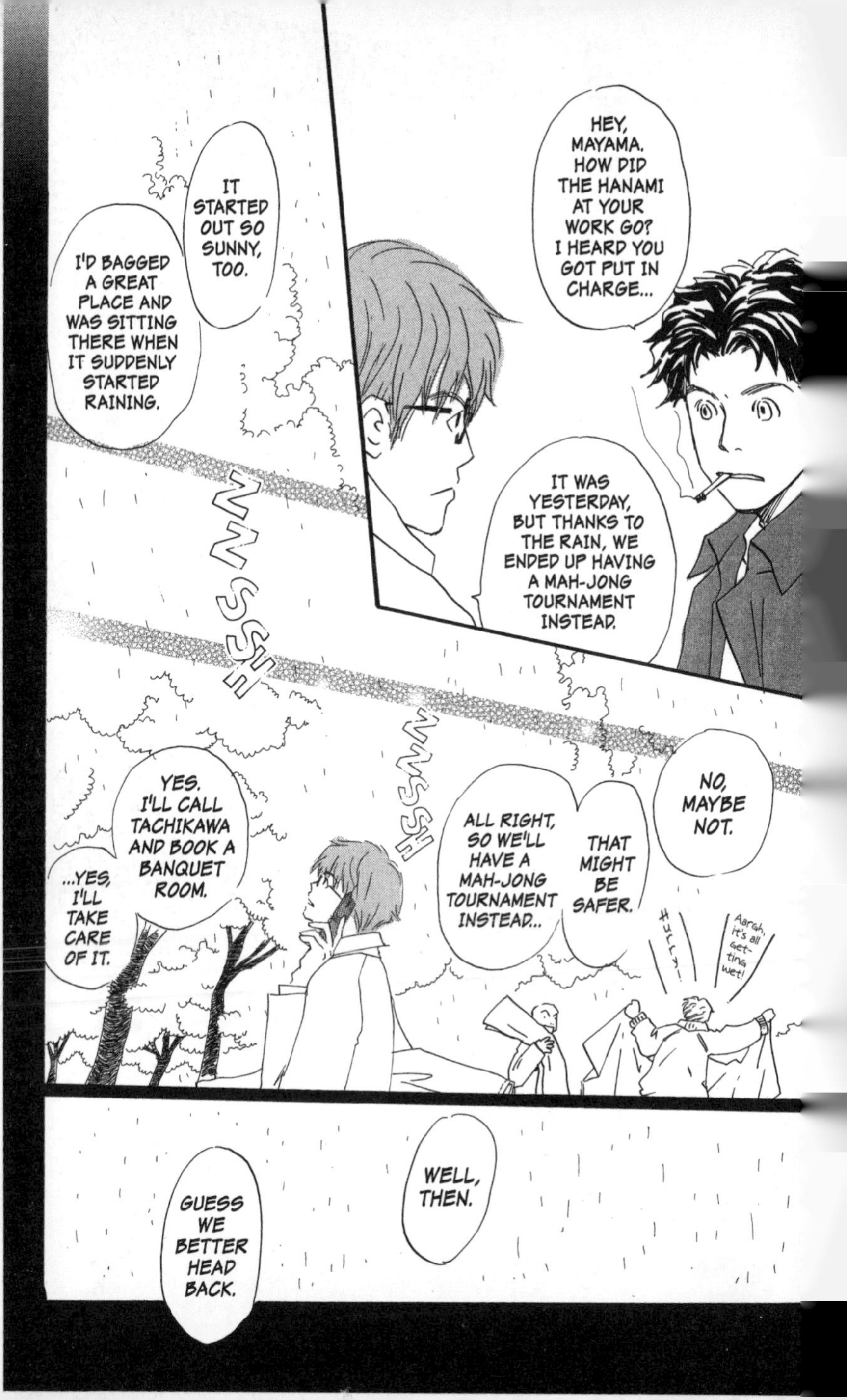
HEY, MAYAMA. HOW DID THE HANAMI AT YOUR WORK GO? I HEARD YOU GOT PUT IN CHARGE...
IT WAS YESTERDAY, BUT THANKS TO THE RAIN, WE ENDED UP HAVING A MAH-JONG TOURNAMENT INSTEAD.
IT STARTED OUT SO SUNNY, TOO.
I'D BAGGED A GREAT PLACE AND WAS SITTING THERE WHEN IT SUDDENLY STARTED RAINING.
HSSNN
NO, MAYBE NOT.
THAT MIGHT BE SAFER.
Aargh, it's all getting wet!
Hurry!
ALL RIGHT, SO WE'LL HAVE A MAH-JONG TOURNAMENT INSTEAD...
HSSNN
YES. I'LL CALL TACHIKAWA AND BOOK A BANQUET ROOM.
...YES, I'LL TAKE CARE OF IT.
WELL, THEN.
GUESS WE BETTER HEAD BACK.

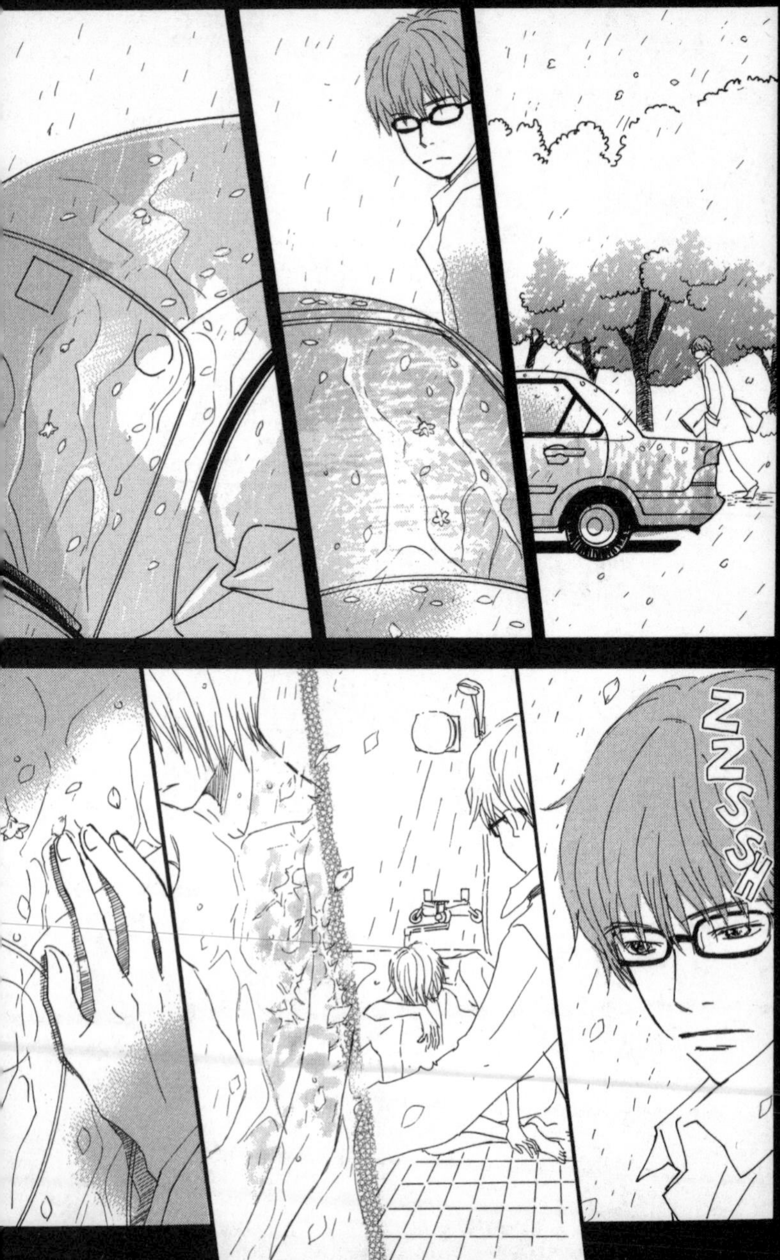
NNSSH

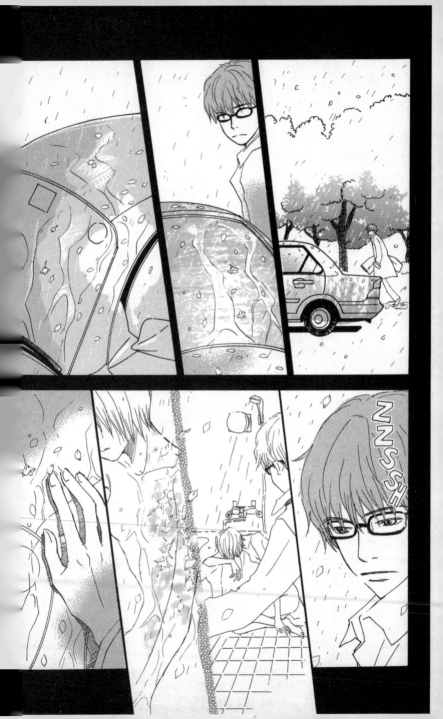

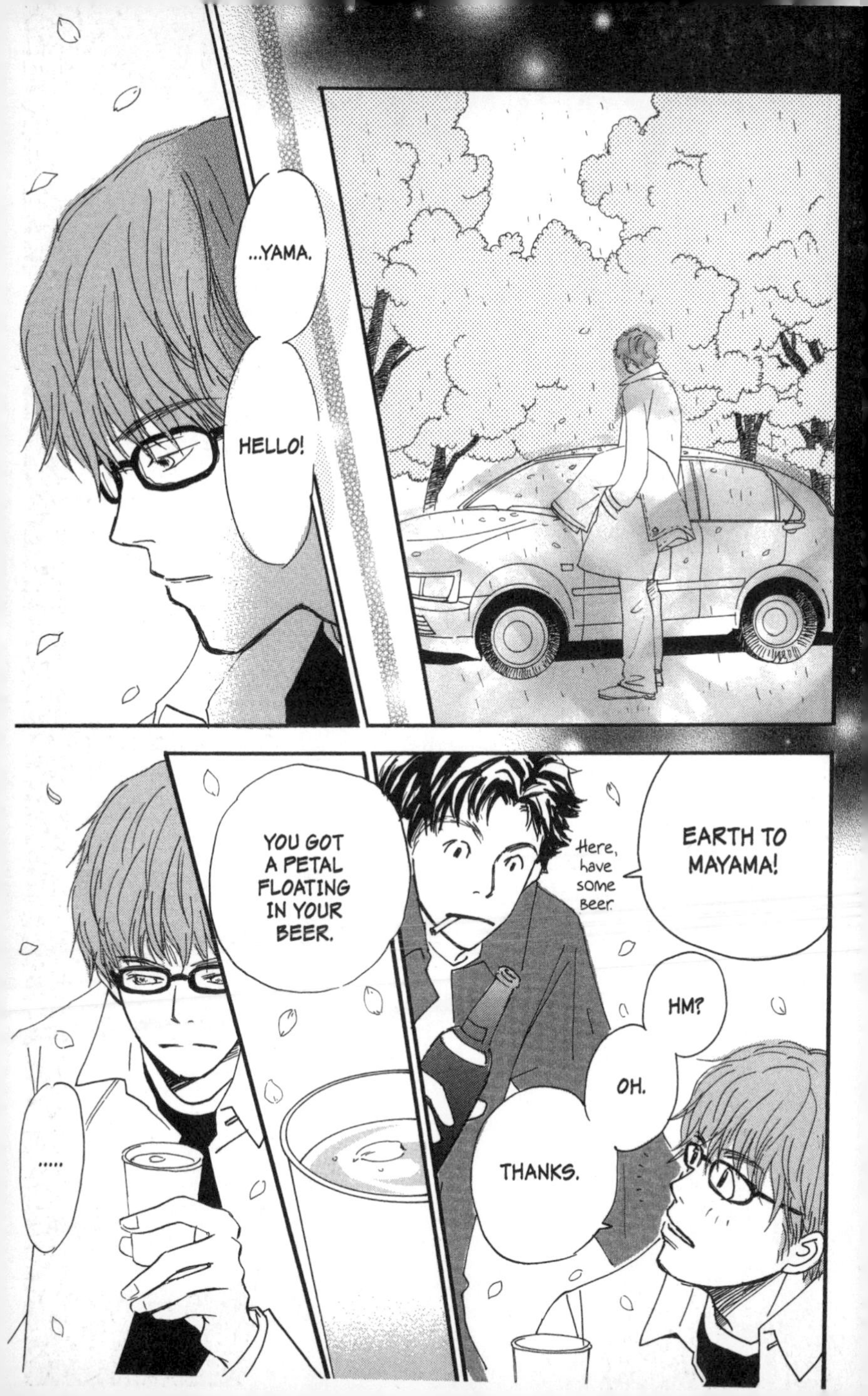
...YAMA.
HELLO!
EARTH TO MAYAMA!
Here, have some beer.
HM?
OH.
THANKS.
YOU GOT A PETAL FLOATING IN YOUR BEER.
.....

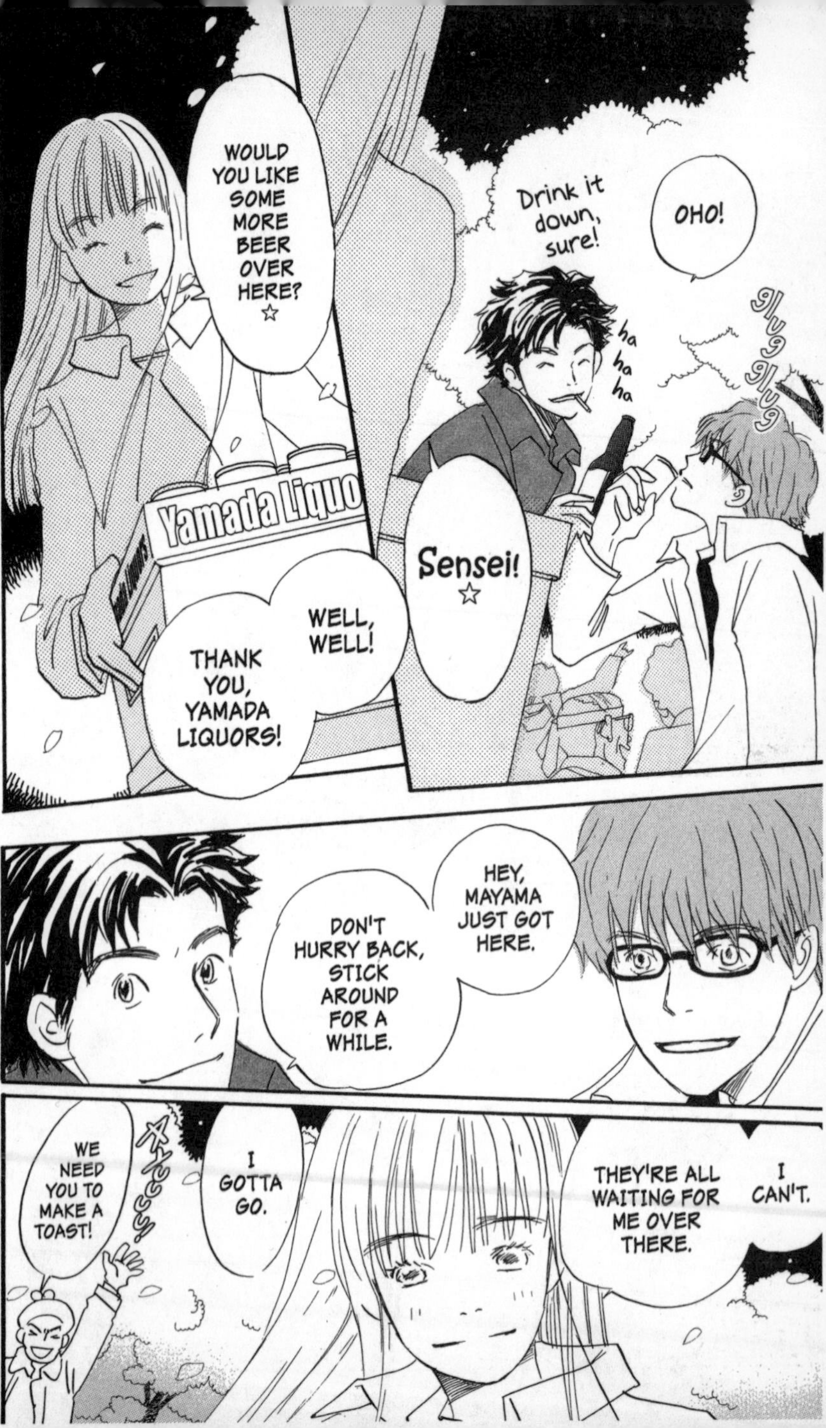
OHO!
Drink it down, sure!
glug glug
ha ha ha
Sensei! ☆
WOULD YOU LIKE SOME MORE BEER OVER HERE? ☆
Yamada Liquo
WELL, WELL!
THANK YOU, YAMADA LIQUORS!
HEY, MAYAMA JUST GOT HERE.
DON'T HURRY BACK, STICK AROUND FOR A WHILE.
I CAN'T.
THEY'RE ALL WAITING FOR ME OVER THERE.
I GOTTA GO.
WE NEED YOU TO MAKE A TOAST!

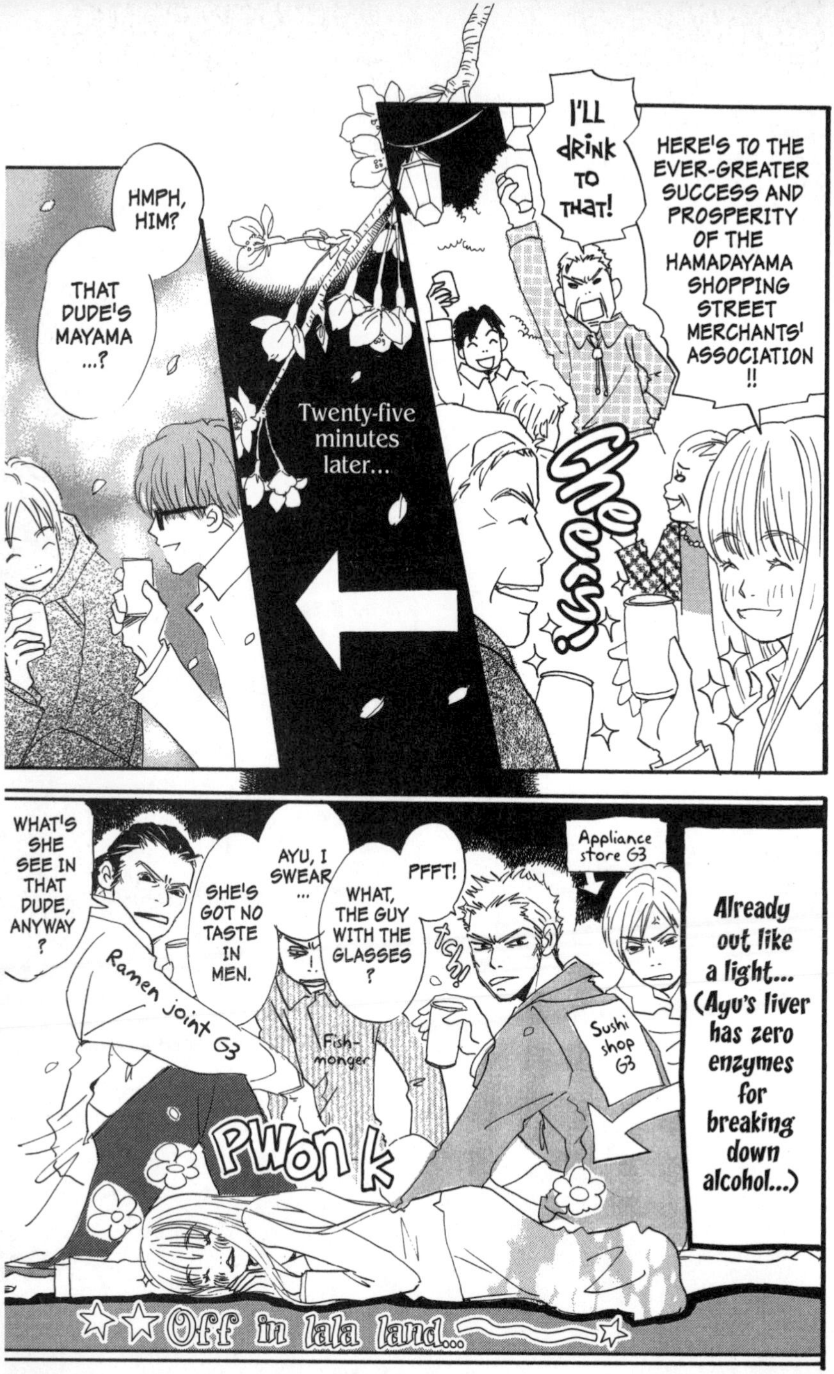
HERE'S TO THE EVER-GREATER SUCCESS AND PROSPERITY OF THE HAMADAYAMA SHOPPING STREET MERCHANTS' ASSOCIATION !!
I'LL DRINK TO THAT!
Cheers!
Twenty-five minutes later...
HMPH, HIM?
THAT DUDE'S MAYAMA ...?
Already out like a light... (Ayu's liver has zero enzymes for breaking down alcohol...)
Appliance store G3
PFFT!
WHAT, THE GUY WITH THE GLASSES ?
AYU, I SWEAR ...
SHE'S GOT NO TASTE IN MEN.
WHAT'S SHE SEE IN THAT DUDE, ANYWAY ?
tch!
Sushi shop G3
Fish-monger
Ramen joint G3
PWON k
☆☆Off in lala land...~~☆

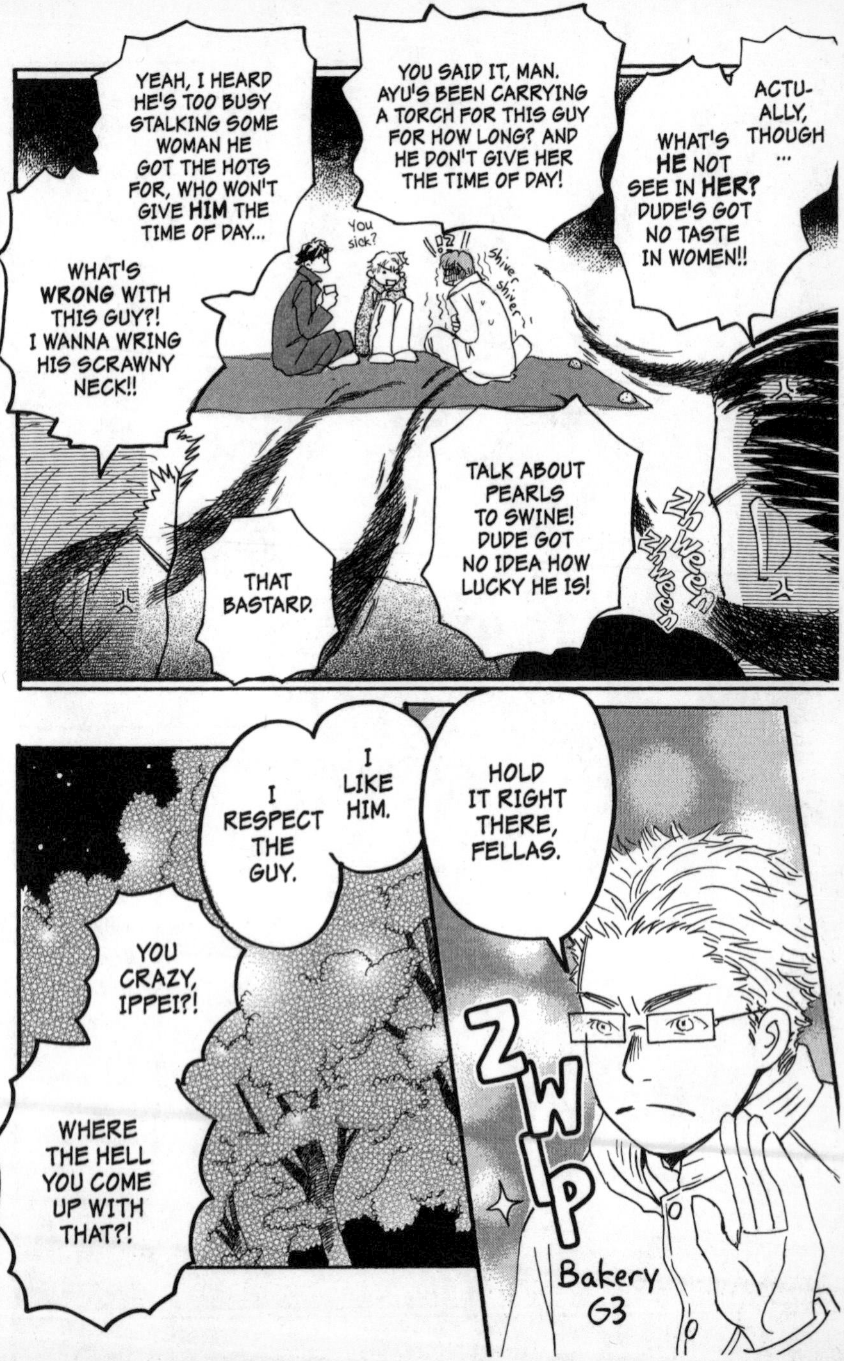
ACTUALLY, THOUGH...
WHAT'S **HE** NOT SEE IN **HER?** DUDE'S GOT NO TASTE IN WOMEN!!
YOU SAID IT, MAN. AYU'S BEEN CARRYING A TORCH FOR THIS GUY FOR HOW LONG? AND HE DON'T GIVE HER THE TIME OF DAY!
YEAH, I HEARD HE'S TOO BUSY STALKING SOME WOMAN HE GOT THE HOTS FOR, WHO WON'T GIVE **HIM** THE TIME OF DAY...
Shiver shiver
You sick?
WHAT'S **WRONG** WITH THIS GUY?! I WANNA WRING HIS SCRAWNY NECK!!
Zhween zhween
TALK ABOUT PEARLS TO SWINE! DUDE GOT NO IDEA HOW LUCKY HE IS!
THAT BASTARD.
HOLD IT RIGHT THERE, FELLAS.
ZWIP
Bakery 63
I LIKE HIM.
I RESPECT THE GUY.
YOU CRAZY, IPPEI?!
WHERE THE HELL YOU COME UP WITH THAT?!

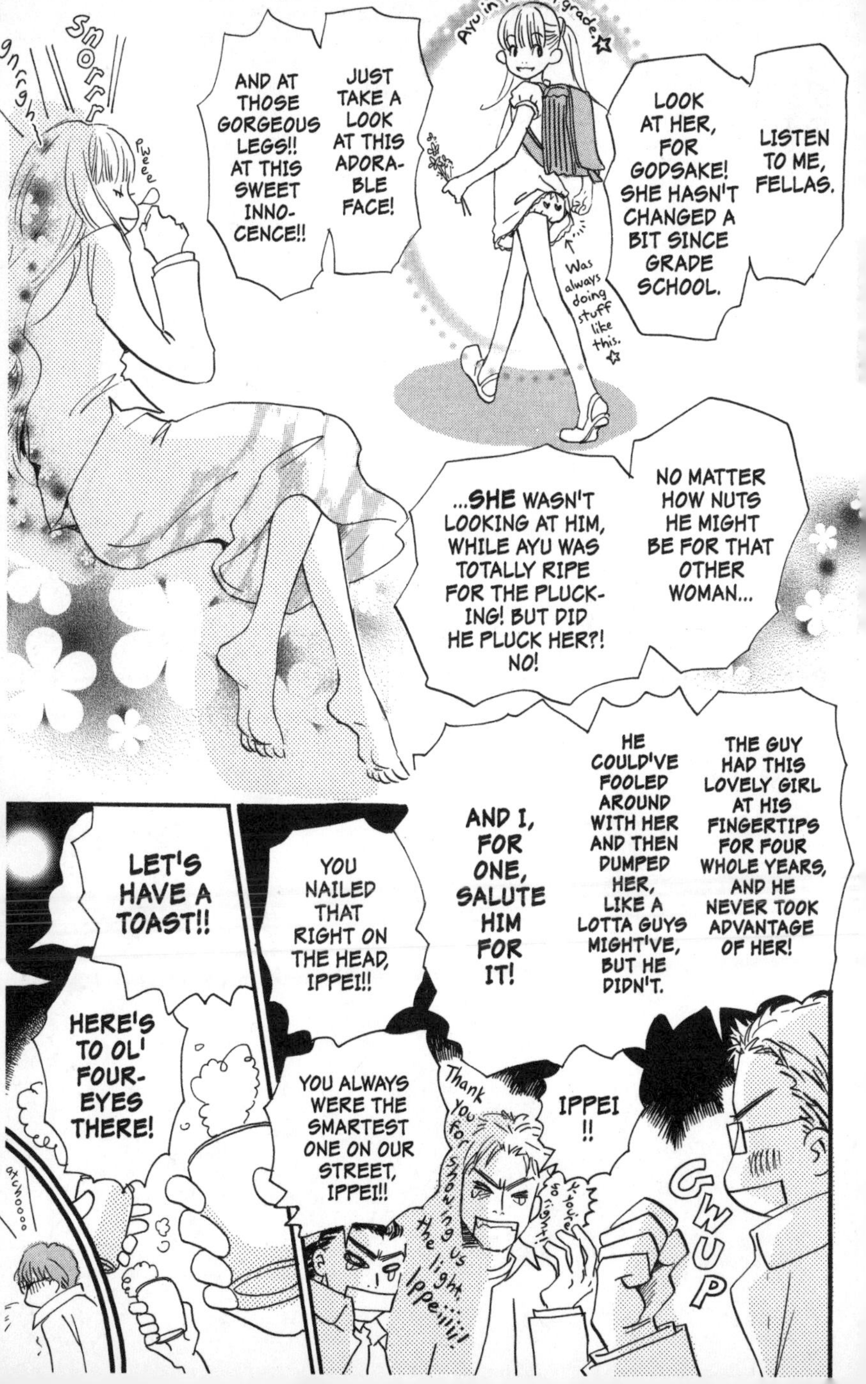
LISTEN TO ME, FELLAS.
LOOK AT HER, FOR GODSAKE! SHE HASN'T CHANGED A BIT SINCE GRADE SCHOOL.
Ayu in fourth grade.☆
Was always doing stuff like this.☆
JUST TAKE A LOOK AT THIS ADORA-BLE FACE!
AND AT THOSE GORGEOUS LEGS!! AT THIS SWEET INNO-CENCE!!
Snorrr
gnrrgh
Pweee
NO MATTER HOW NUTS HE MIGHT BE FOR THAT OTHER WOMAN...
...SHE WASN'T LOOKING AT HIM, WHILE AYU WAS TOTALLY RIPE FOR THE PLUCK-ING! BUT DID HE PLUCK HER?! NO!
THE GUY HAD THIS LOVELY GIRL AT HIS FINGERTIPS FOR FOUR WHOLE YEARS, AND HE NEVER TOOK ADVANTAGE OF HER!
HE COULD'VE FOOLED AROUND WITH HER AND THEN DUMPED HER, LIKE A LOTTA GUYS MIGHT'VE, BUT HE DIDN'T.
AND I, FOR ONE, SALUTE HIM FOR IT!
YOU NAILED THAT RIGHT ON THE HEAD, IPPEI!!
LET'S HAVE A TOAST!!
IPPEI!!
GWUP
Y-you're so right!
Thank you for showing us the light, Ippei!!!
YOU ALWAYS WERE THE SMARTEST ONE ON OUR STREET, IPPEI!!
HERE'S TO OL' FOUR-EYES THERE!
atchoooo

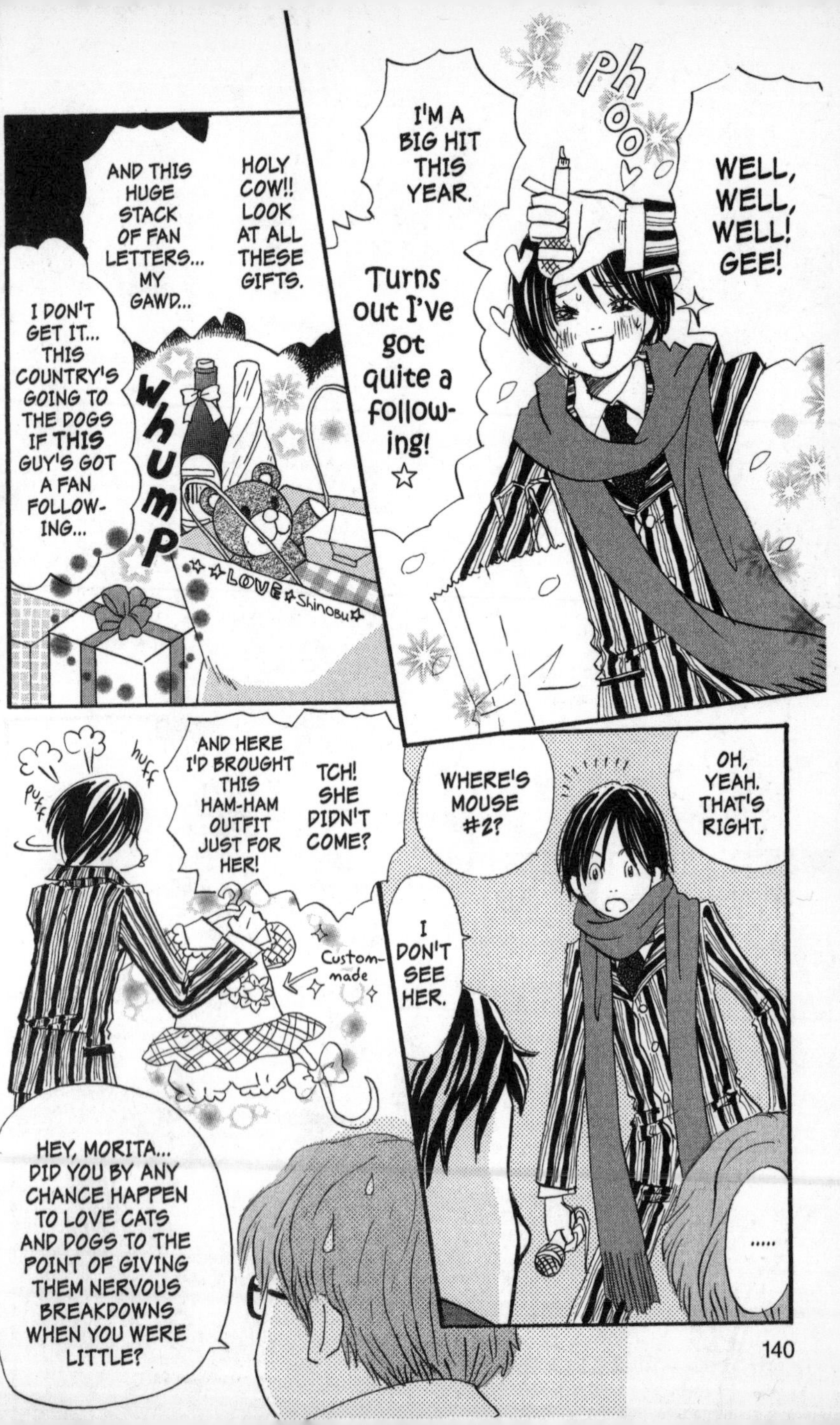

WELL, WELL, WELL! GEE!
Phooo
I'M A BIG HIT THIS YEAR.
Turns out I've got quite a following! ☆
HOLY COW!! LOOK AT ALL THESE GIFTS.
AND THIS HUGE STACK OF FAN LETTERS... MY GAWD...
I DON'T GET IT... THIS COUNTRY'S GOING TO THE DOGS IF THIS GUY'S GOT A FAN FOLLOWING...
WHUMP
☆☆LOVE☆Shinobu☆
OH, YEAH. THAT'S RIGHT.
WHERE'S MOUSE #2?
I DON'T SEE HER.
.....
TCH! SHE DIDN'T COME?
AND HERE I'D BROUGHT THIS HAM-HAM OUTFIT JUST FOR HER!
huff
puff
Custom-made
HEY, MORITA... DID YOU BY ANY CHANCE HAPPEN TO LOVE CATS AND DOGS TO THE POINT OF GIVING THEM NERVOUS BREAKDOWNS WHEN YOU WERE LITTLE?

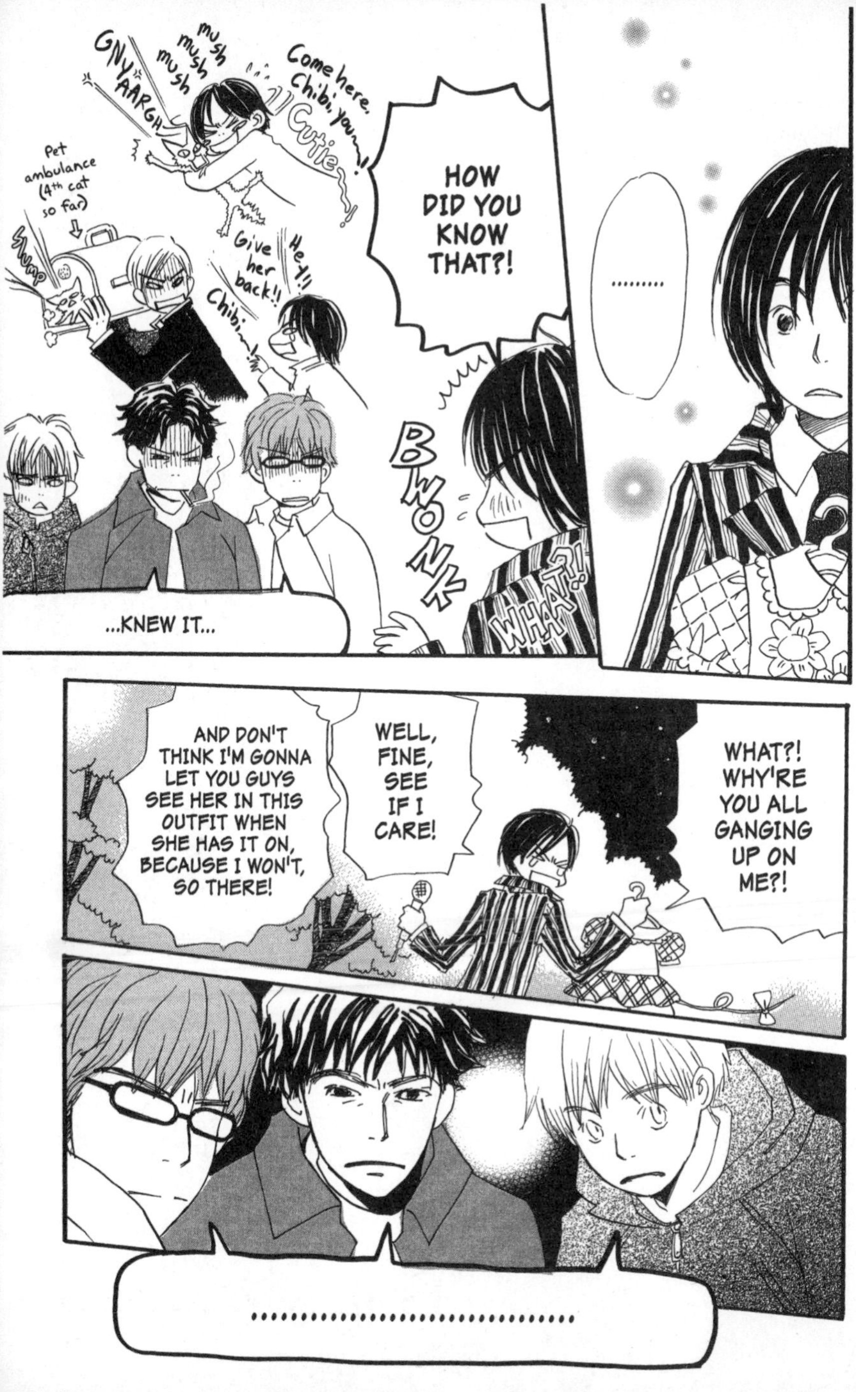
....
HOW DID YOU KNOW THAT?!
BWONK
WHAT?!
Come here, Chibi, you...!!
Cutie~!
mush mush mush
GNYAARGH
Pet ambulance (4th cat so far)
Slump
Give her back!!
Hey!!
Chibi~!
...KNEW IT...
WHAT?! WHY'RE YOU ALL GANGING UP ON ME?!
WELL, FINE, SEE IF I CARE!
AND DON'T THINK I'M GONNA LET YOU GUYS SEE HER IN THIS OUTFIT WHEN SHE HAS IT ON, BECAUSE I WON'T, SO THERE!
....

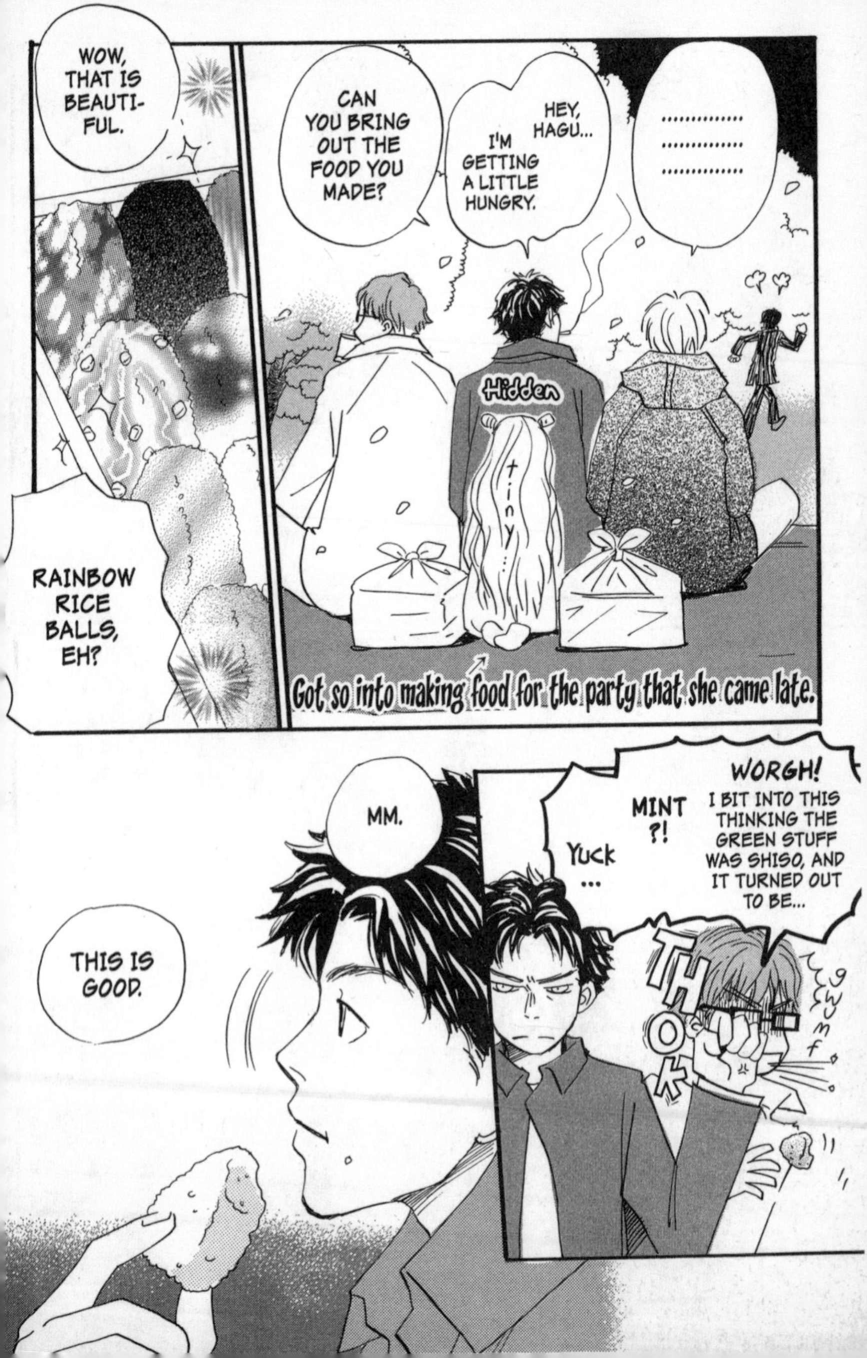
....
HEY, HAGU... I'M GETTING A LITTLE HUNGRY.
CAN YOU BRING OUT THE FOOD YOU MADE?
Hidden
tiny...
Got so into making food for the party that she came late.
WOW, THAT IS BEAUTI-FUL.
RAINBOW RICE BALLS, EH?
WORGH! I BIT INTO THIS THINKING THE GREEN STUFF WAS SHISO, AND IT TURNED OUT TO BE...
MINT ?!
Yuck ...
THOK
gwumf
MM.
THIS IS GOOD.

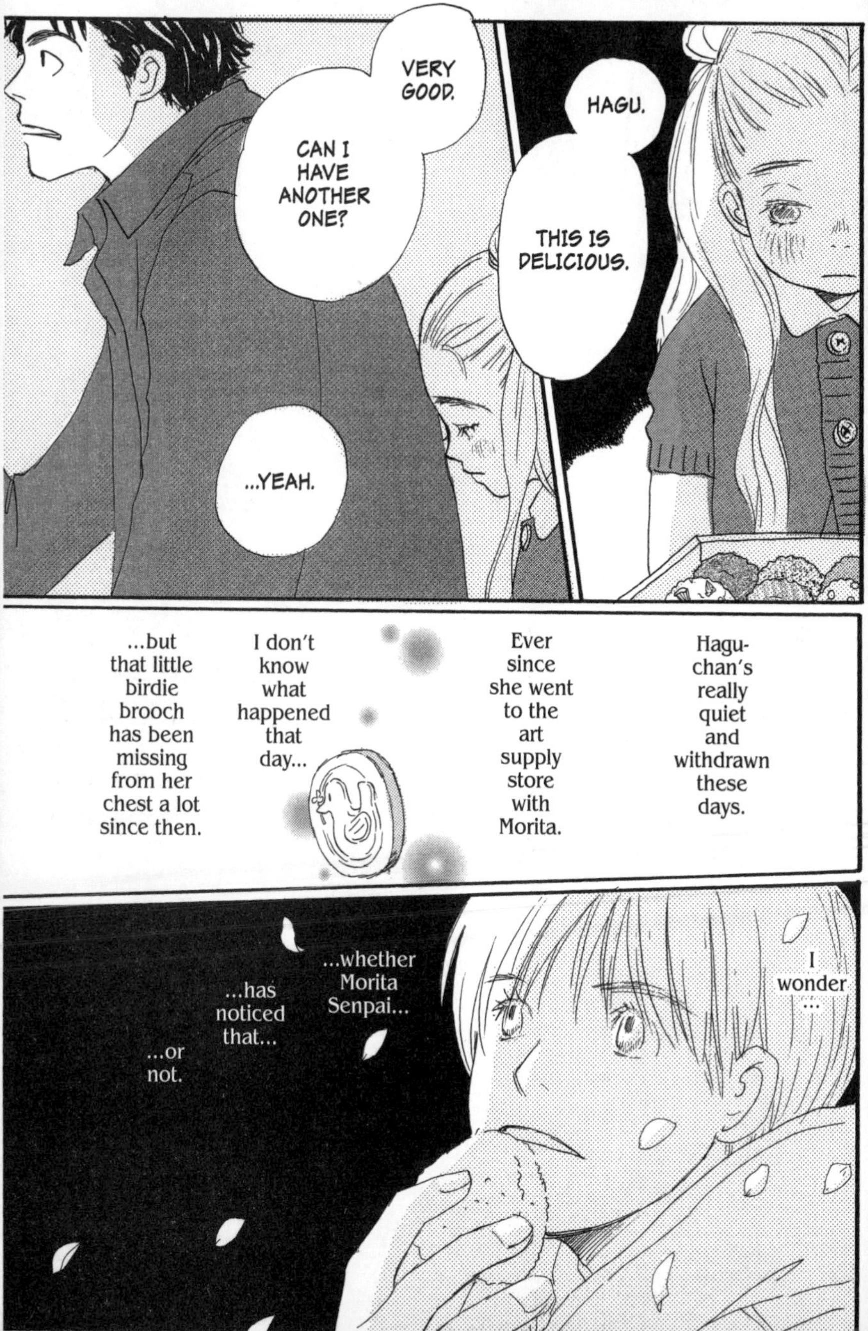
HAGU.
THIS IS DELICIOUS.
VERY GOOD.
CAN I HAVE ANOTHER ONE?
...YEAH.
Hagu-chan's really quiet and withdrawn these days.
Ever since she went to the art supply store with Morita.
I don't know what happened that day...
...but that little birdie brooch has been missing from her chest a lot since then.
I wonder...
...whether Morita Senpai...
...has noticed that...
...or not.

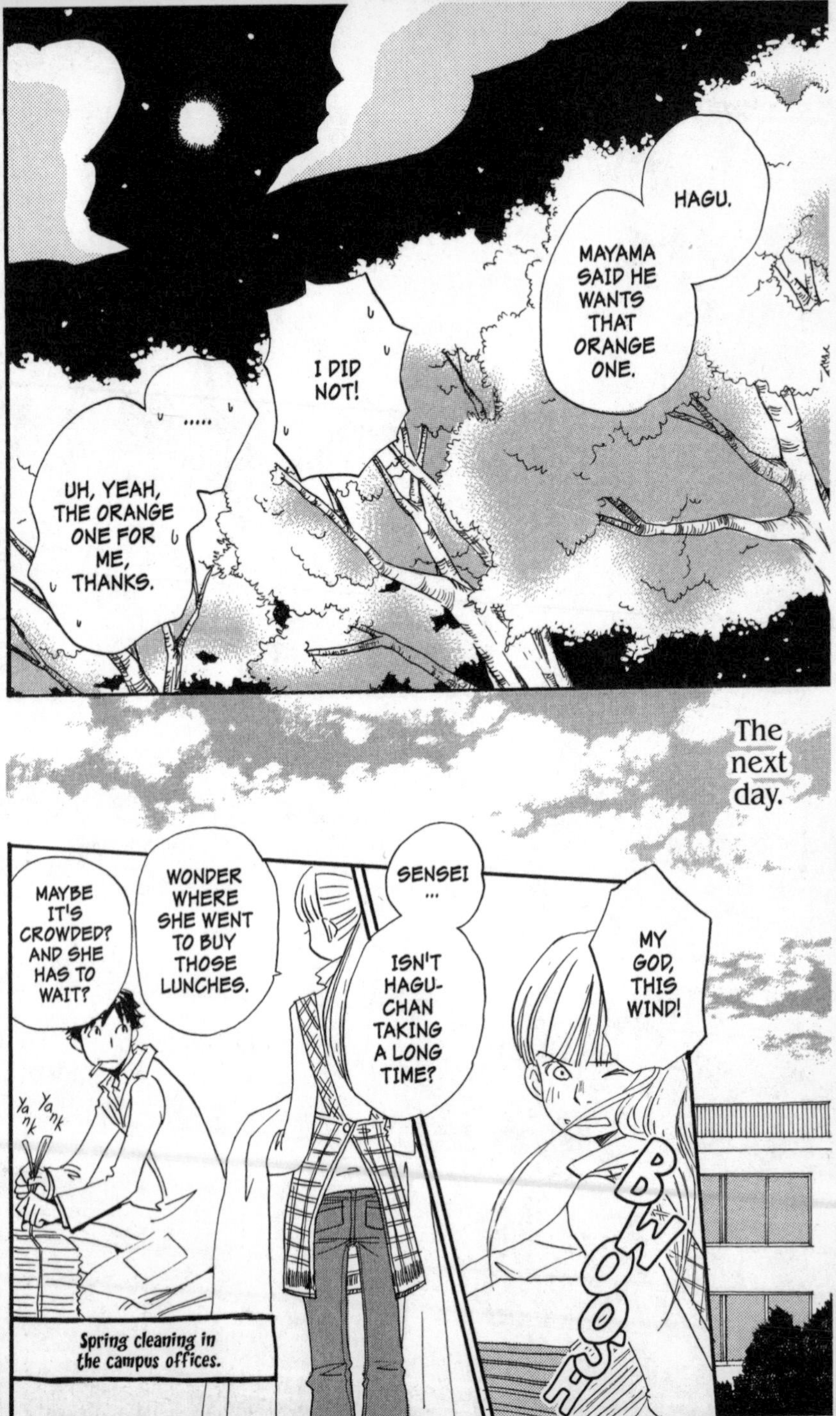
HAGU.
MAYAMA SAID HE WANTS THAT ORANGE ONE.
I DID NOT!
.....
UH, YEAH, THE ORANGE ONE FOR ME, THANKS.
The next day.
MY GOD, THIS WIND!
BWOOSH
SENSEI ...
ISN'T HAGU-CHAN TAKING A LONG TIME?
WONDER WHERE SHE WENT TO BUY THOSE LUNCHES.
MAYBE IT'S CROWDED? AND SHE HAS TO WAIT?
Yank Yank
Spring cleaning in the campus offices.

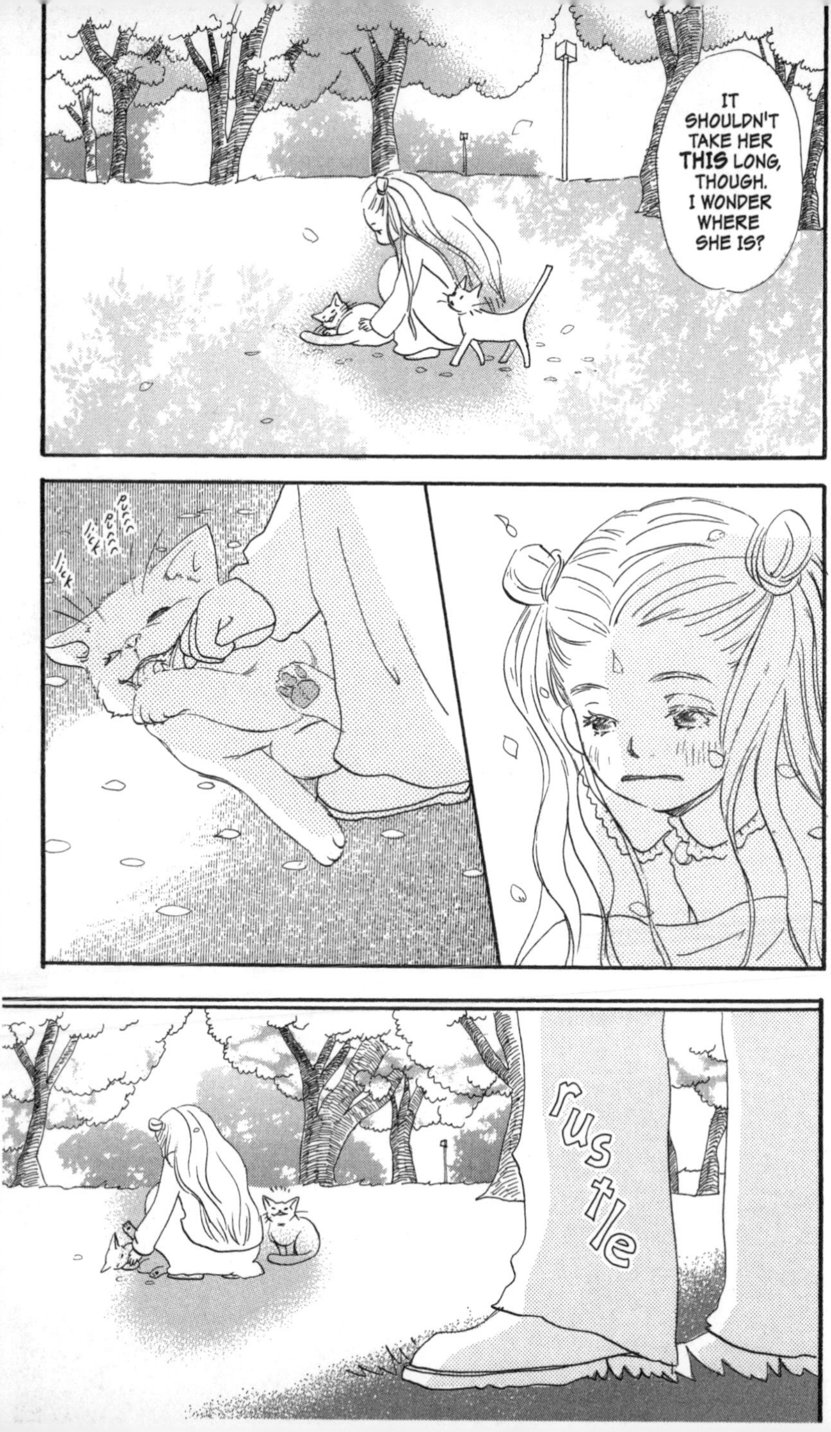
IT SHOULDN'T TAKE HER **THIS** LONG, THOUGH. I WONDER WHERE SHE IS?
purrr purrr
lick lick
rustle

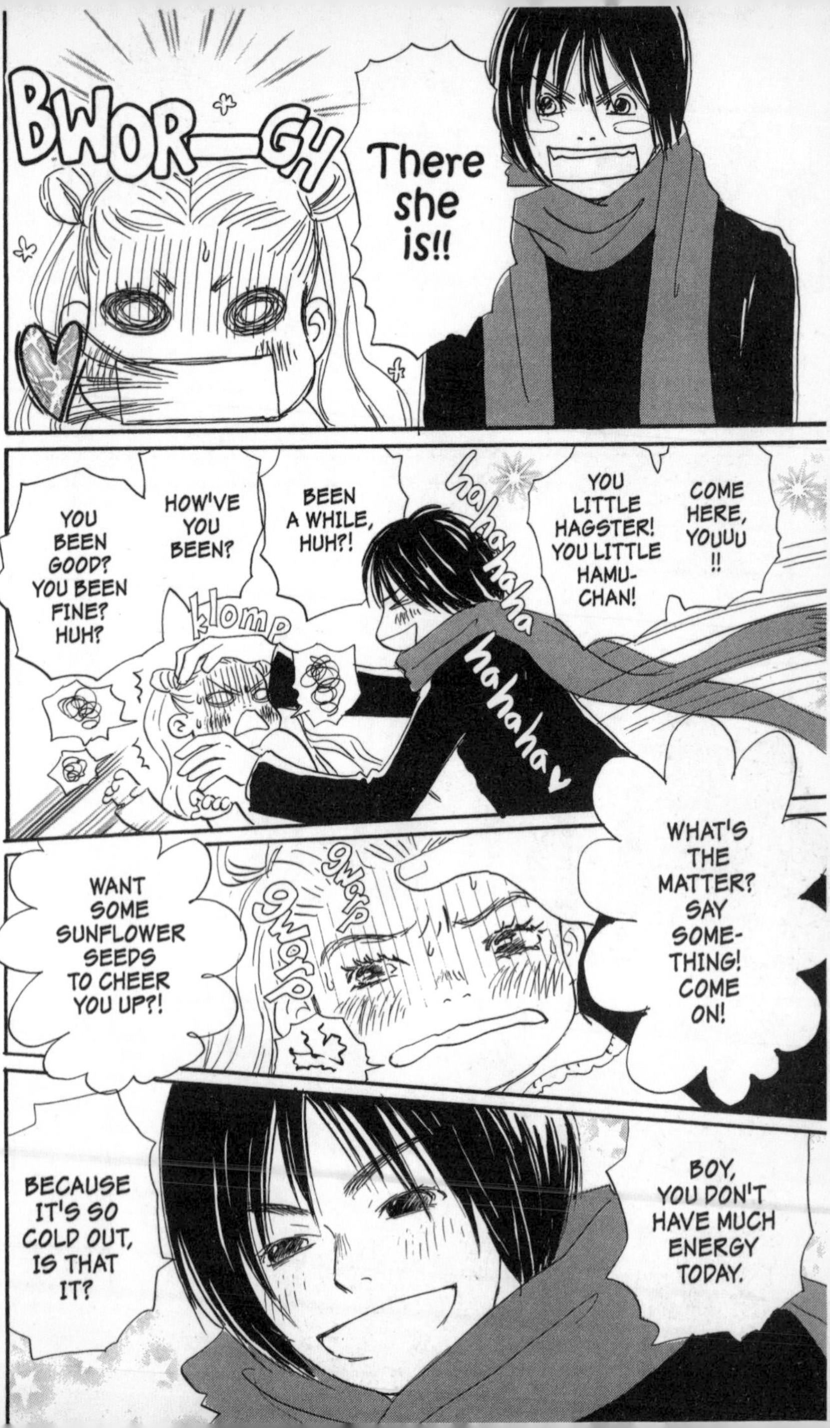
There she is!!
BWOR—GH
COME HERE, YOUUU!!
YOU LITTLE HAGSTER! YOU LITTLE HAMU-CHAN!
hahahaha
BEEN A WHILE, HUH?!
HOW'VE YOU BEEN?
YOU BEEN GOOD? YOU BEEN FINE? HUH?
klomp
hahahaha♥
WHAT'S THE MATTER? SAY SOME-THING! COME ON!
gworp
gworp
WANT SOME SUNFLOWER SEEDS TO CHEER YOU UP?!
BOY, YOU DON'T HAVE MUCH ENERGY TODAY.
BECAUSE IT'S SO COLD OUT, IS THAT IT?

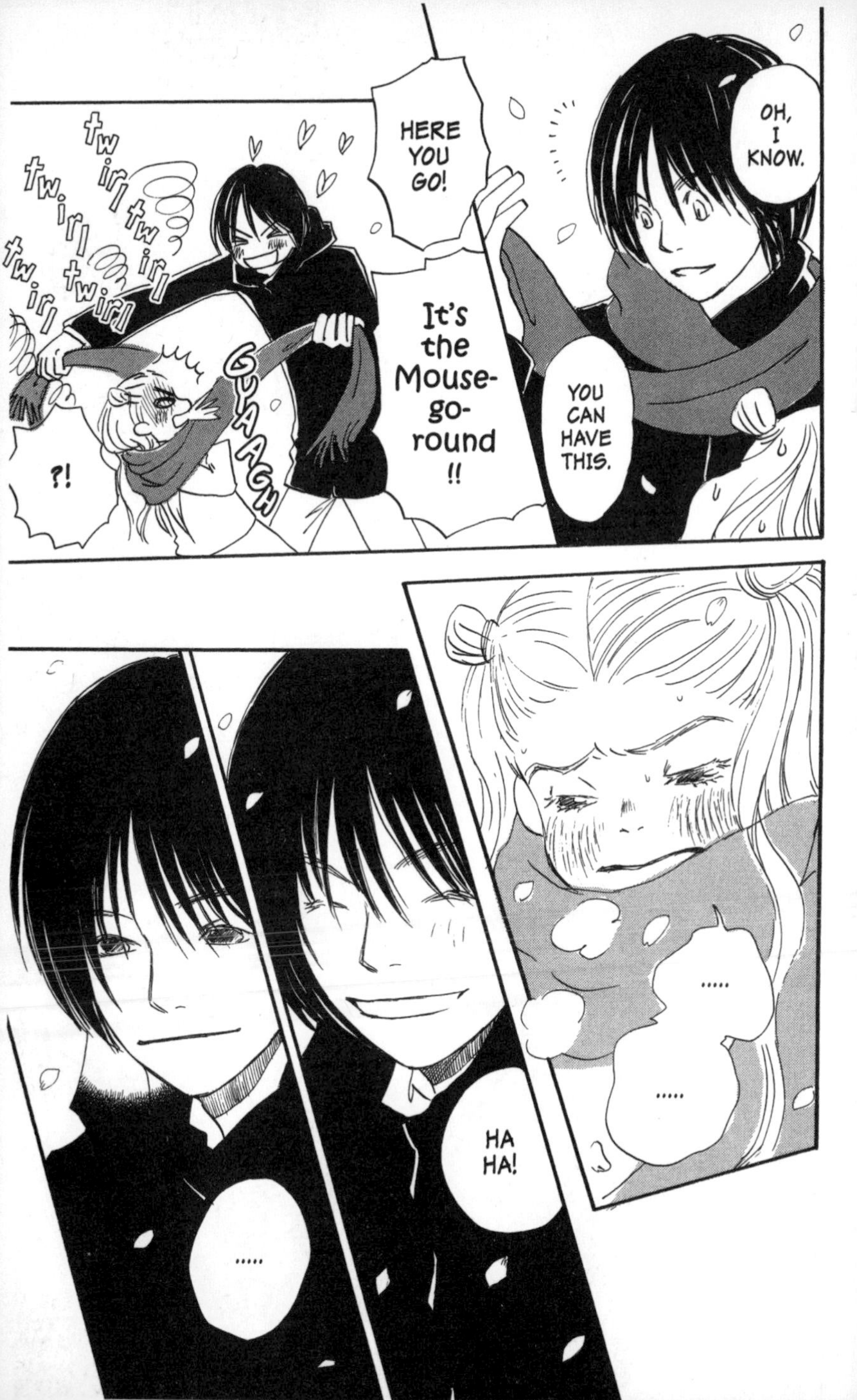
OH, I KNOW.
YOU CAN HAVE THIS.
HERE YOU GO!
It's the Mouse-go-round!!
twirl twirl twirl twirl twirl
GYAAAGH
?!
.....
.....
HA HA!
.....

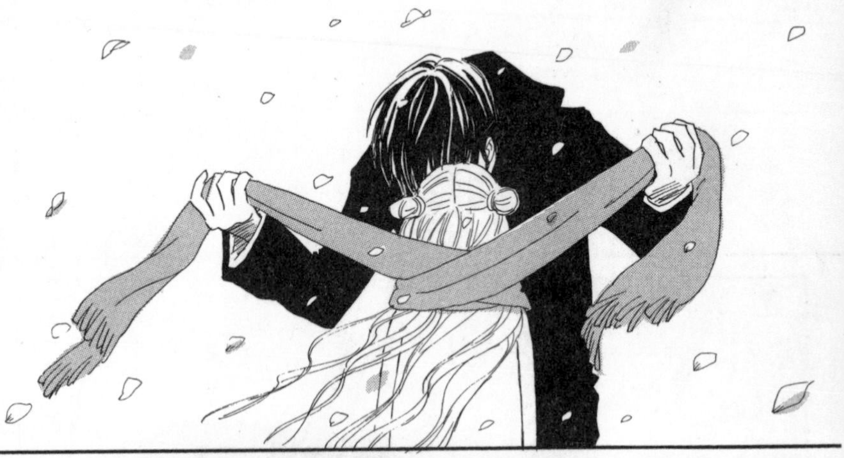

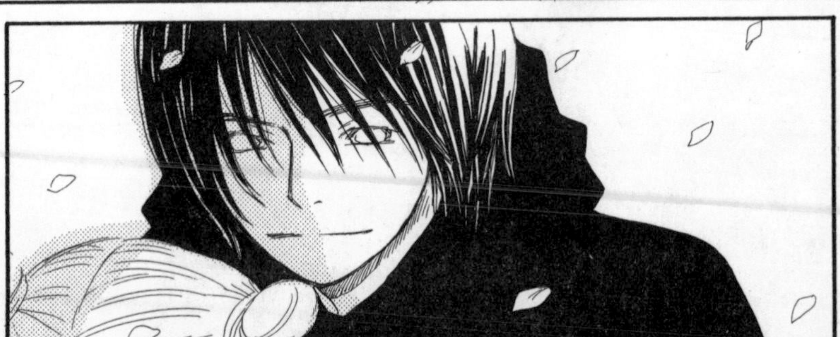

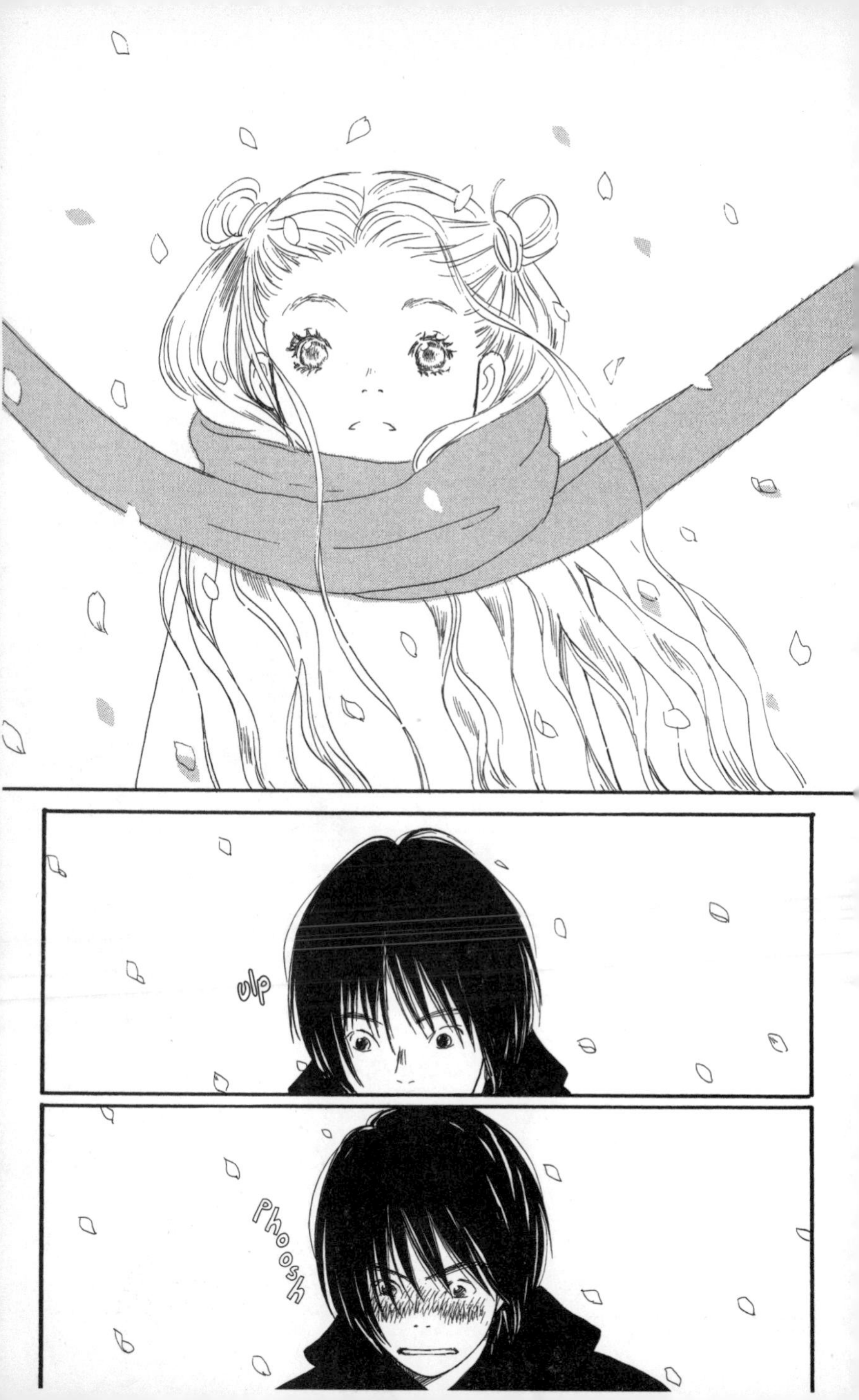
ulp
Phoosh

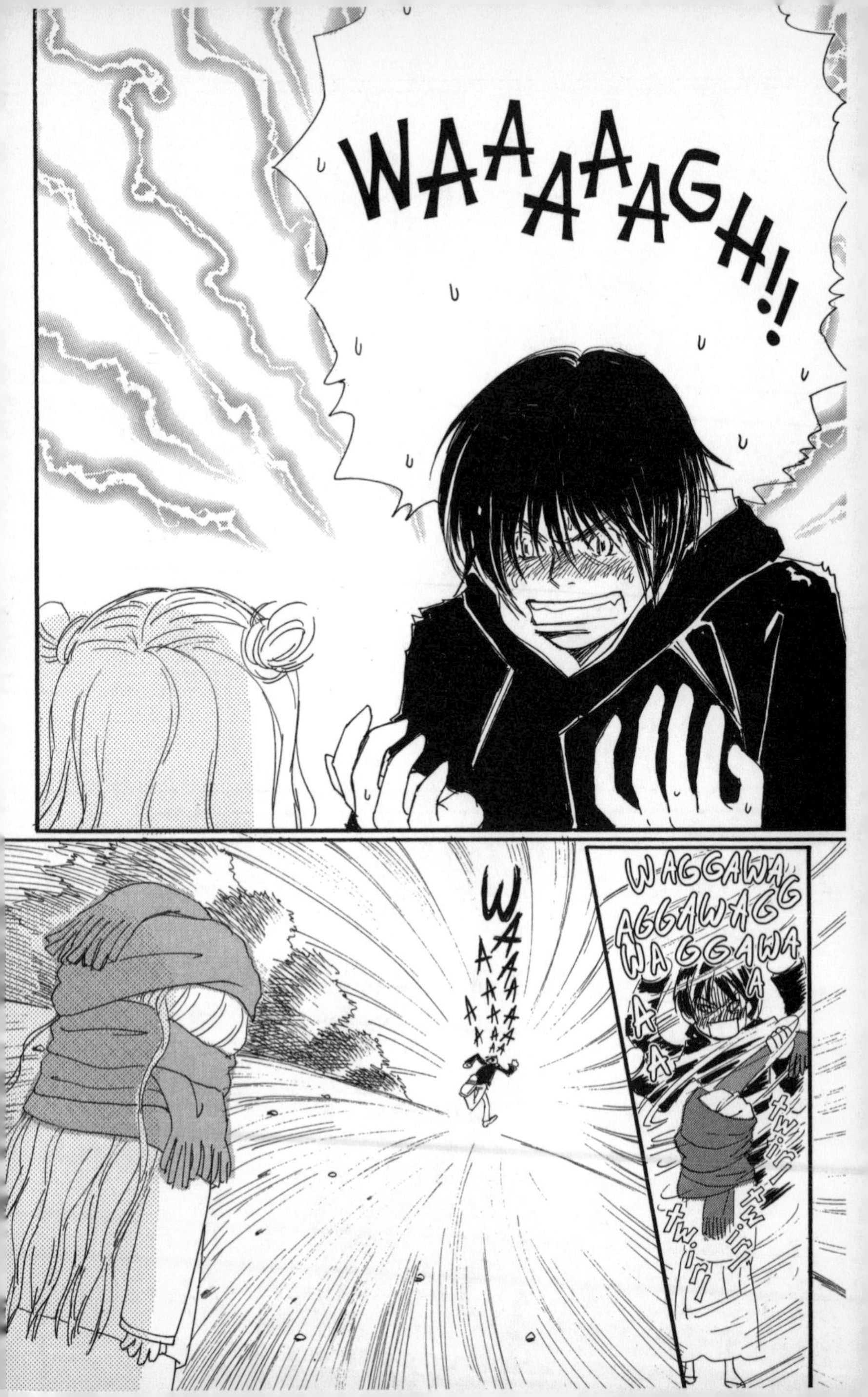
WAAAAAGH!!
WAGGAWAG
AGGAWAGG
WAGGAWA
A
A
A
A
twirl twirl
twirl
WAAAAAAAAAAAA

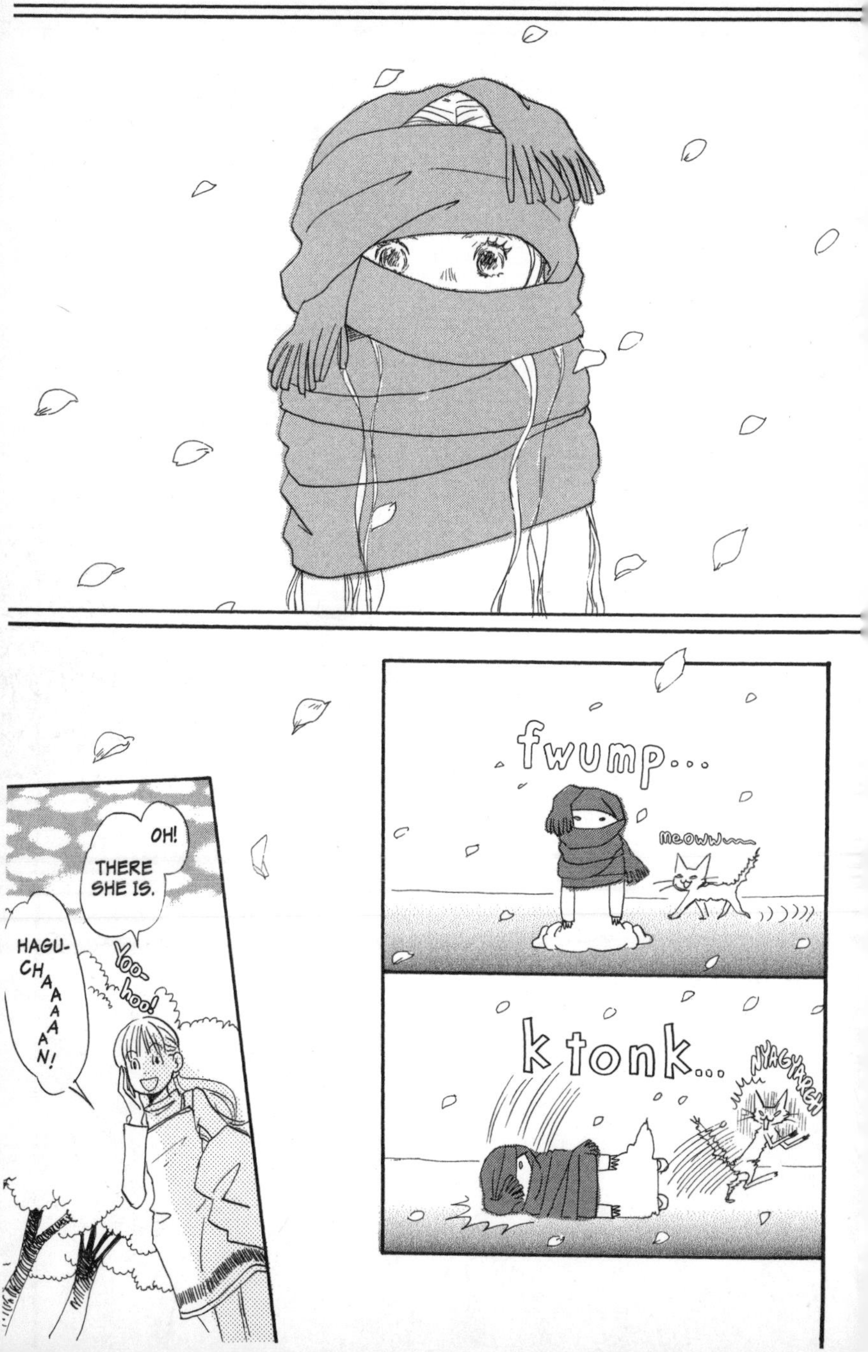
fwump...
meowww
ktonk...
NYAGYARCH
OH! THERE SHE IS.
Yoo-hoo!
HAGU-CHAAAAAAN!

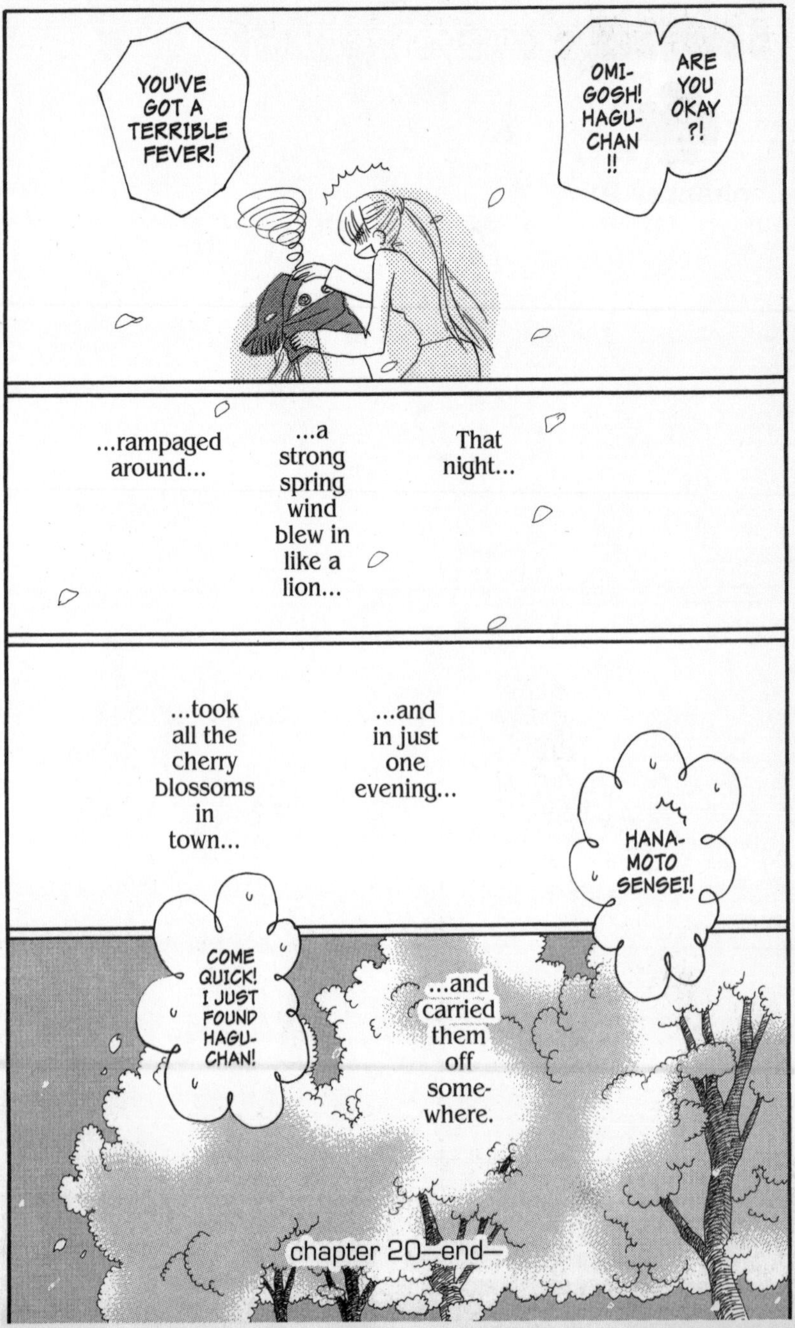
OMIGOSH! HAGU-CHAN!!
ARE YOU OKAY?!
YOU'VE GOT A TERRIBLE FEVER!
That night...
...a strong spring wind blew in like a lion...
...rampaged around...
...and in just one evening...
...took all the cherry blossoms in town...
HANAMOTO SENSEI!
COME QUICK! I JUST FOUND HAGU-CHAN!
...and carried them off somewhere.
chapter 20—end—

honey and clover

honey
and
clover

chapter 21

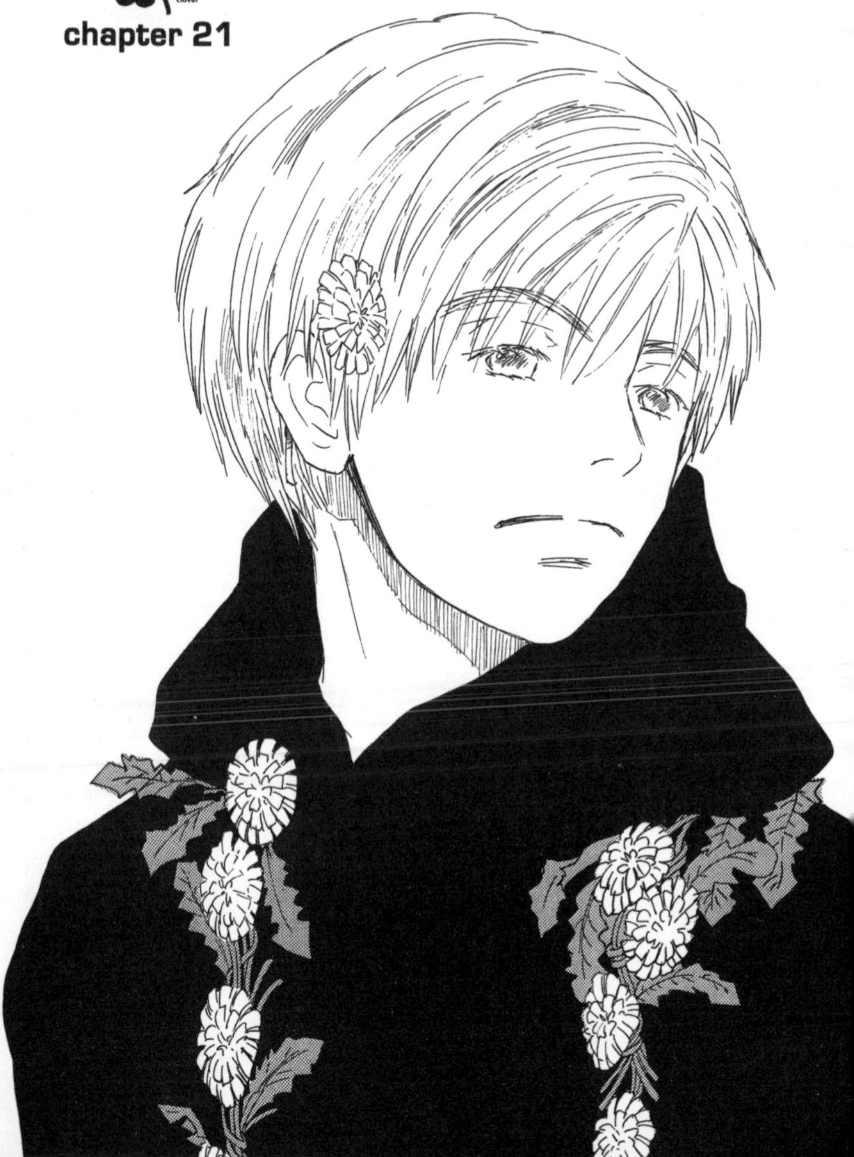

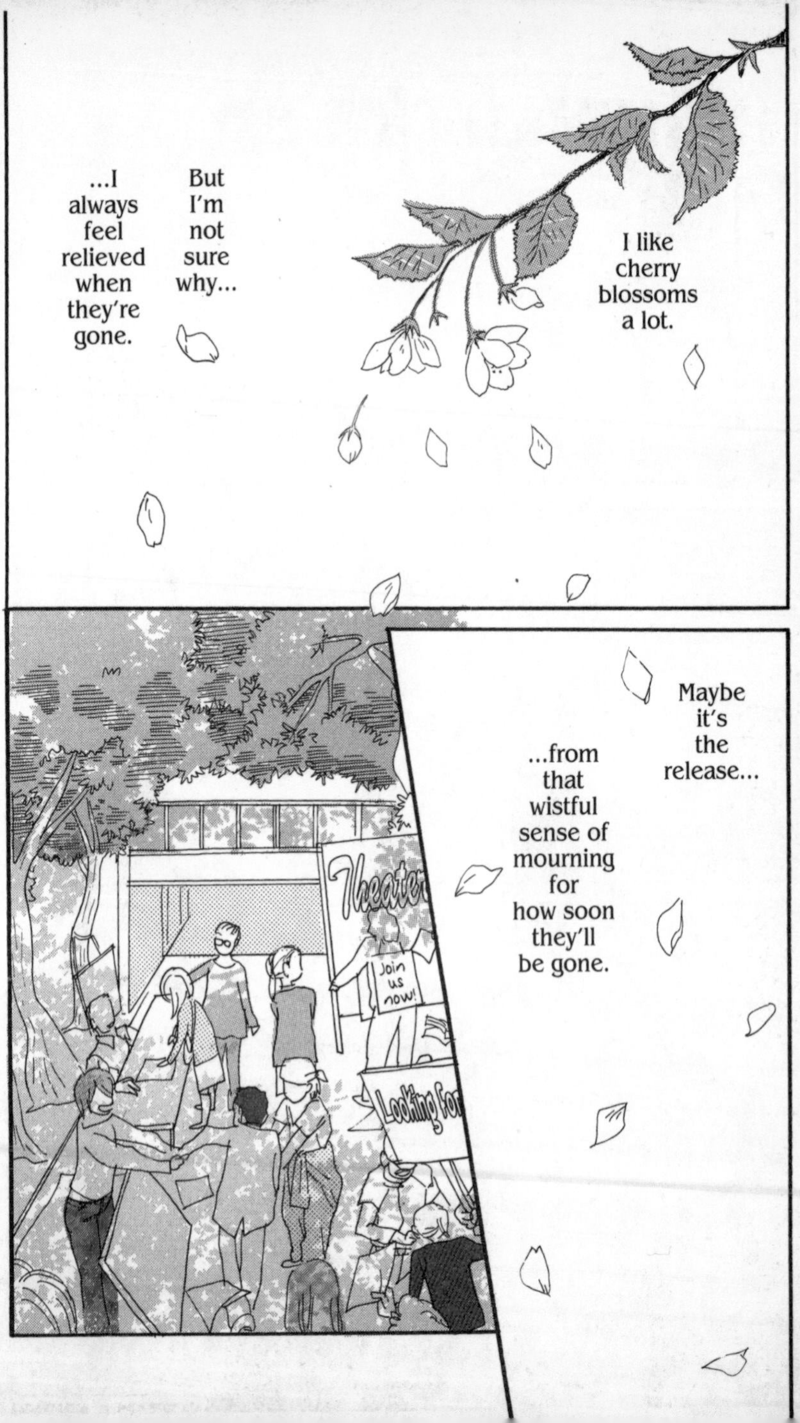
I like cherry blossoms a lot.
But I'm not sure why...
...I always feel relieved when they're gone.
Maybe it's the release...
...from that wistful sense of mourning for how soon they'll be gone.
Theater
Join us now!
Looking For

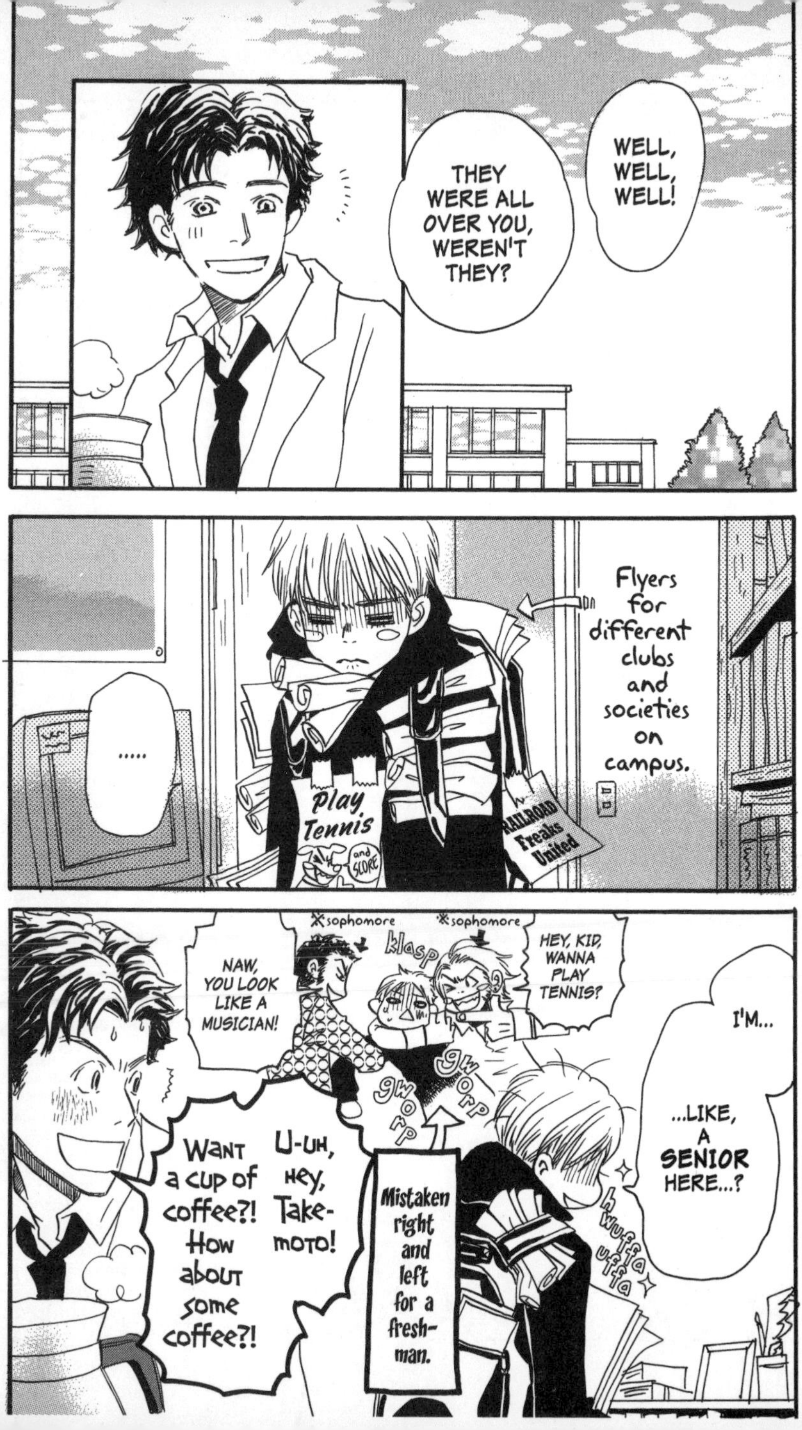
WELL, WELL, WELL!
THEY WERE ALL OVER YOU, WEREN'T THEY?
Flyers for different clubs and societies on campus.
.....
RAILROAD Freaks United
Play Tennis
and SCORE
I'M...
...LIKE, A SENIOR HERE...?
hwuffa uffa
※sophomore
HEY, KID, WANNA PLAY TENNIS?
klasp
※sophomore
NAW, YOU LOOK LIKE A MUSICIAN!
gworp gworp
Mistaken right and left for a freshman.
U-UH, HEY, TAKE-MOTO!
Want a cup of coffee?! How about some coffee?!

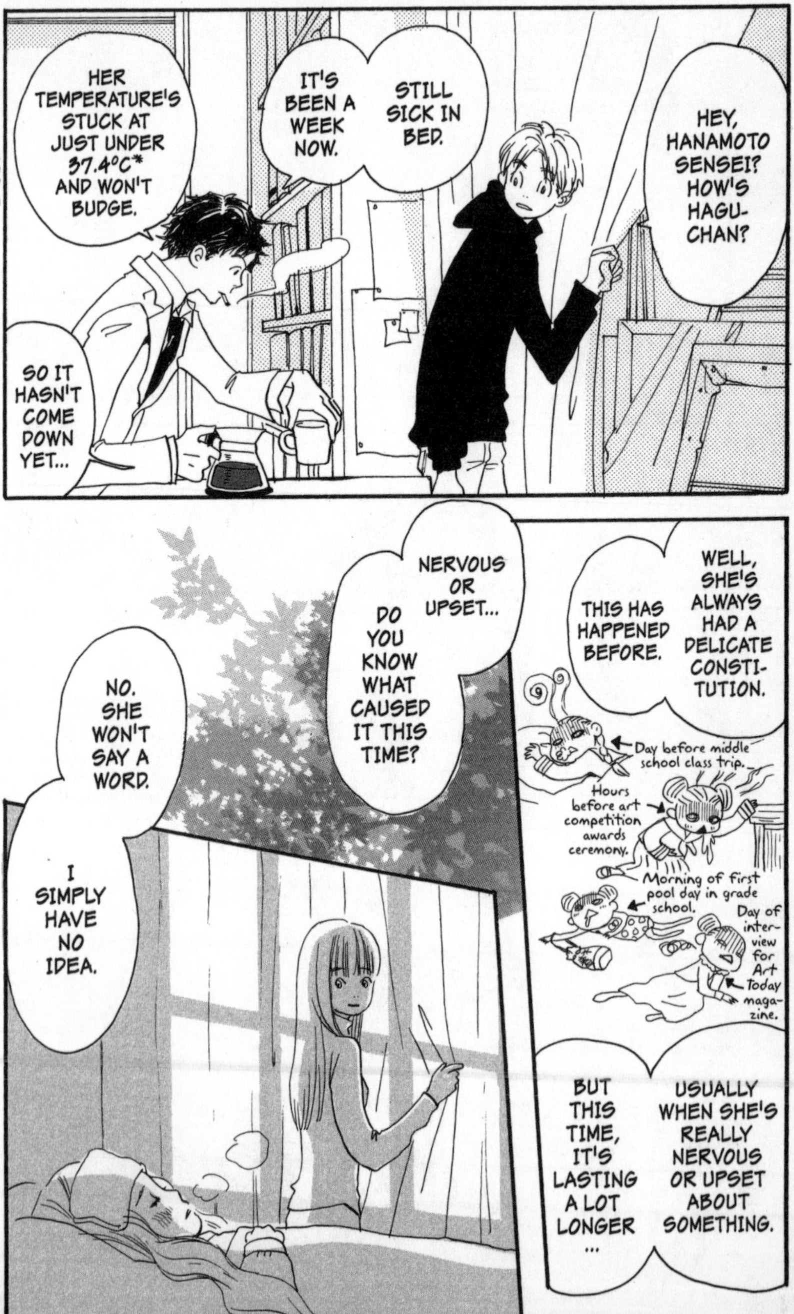
HEY, HANAMOTO SENSEI? HOW'S HAGU-CHAN?
STILL SICK IN BED.
IT'S BEEN A WEEK NOW.
HER TEMPERATURE'S STUCK AT JUST UNDER 37.4°C* AND WON'T BUDGE.
SO IT HASN'T COME DOWN YET...
WELL, SHE'S ALWAYS HAD A DELICATE CONSTI-TUTION.
THIS HAS HAPPENED BEFORE.
Day before middle school class trip.
Hours before art competition awards ceremony.
Morning of first pool day in grade school.
Day of interview for Art Today magazine.
USUALLY WHEN SHE'S REALLY NERVOUS OR UPSET ABOUT SOMETHING.
BUT THIS TIME, IT'S LASTING A LOT LONGER...
NERVOUS OR UPSET...
DO YOU KNOW WHAT CAUSED IT THIS TIME?
NO. SHE WON'T SAY A WORD.
I SIMPLY HAVE NO IDEA.

*100°F

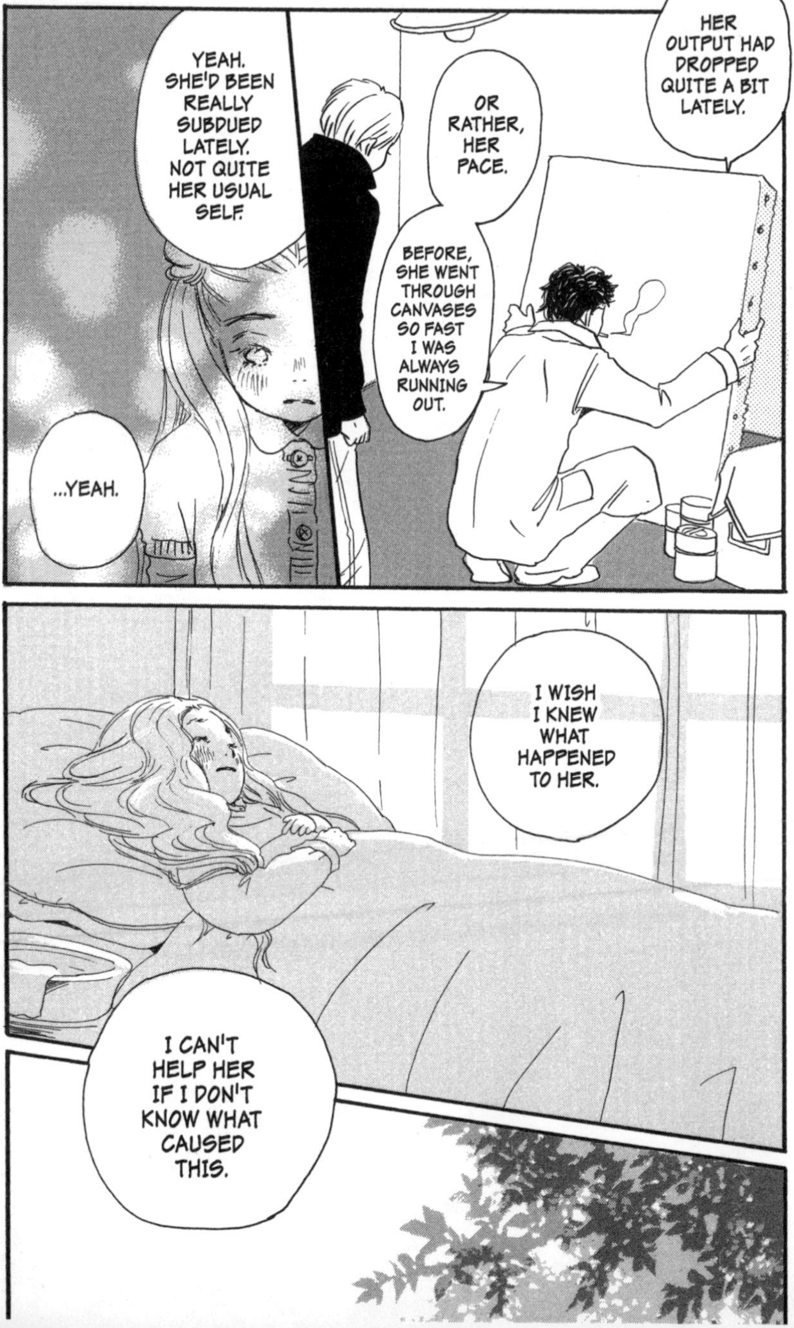
HER OUTPUT HAD DROPPED QUITE A BIT LATELY.
OR RATHER, HER PACE.
BEFORE, SHE WENT THROUGH CANVASES SO FAST I WAS ALWAYS RUNNING OUT.
YEAH. SHE'D BEEN REALLY SUBDUED LATELY. NOT QUITE HER USUAL SELF.
...YEAH.
I WISH I KNEW WHAT HAPPENED TO HER.
I CAN'T HELP HER IF I DON'T KNOW WHAT CAUSED THIS.

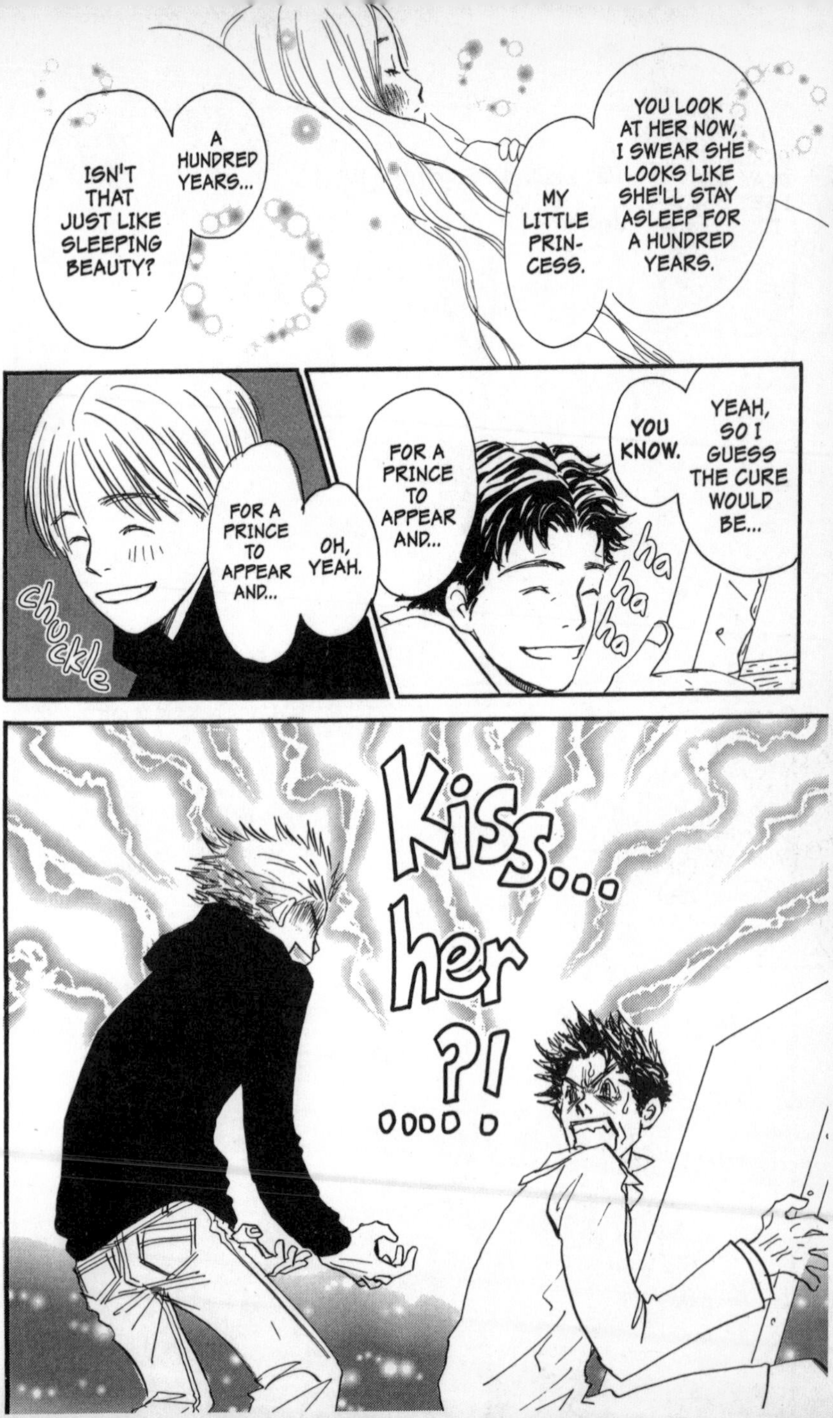
YOU LOOK AT HER NOW, I SWEAR SHE LOOKS LIKE SHE'LL STAY ASLEEP FOR A HUNDRED YEARS.
MY LITTLE PRIN-CESS.
A HUNDRED YEARS...
ISN'T THAT JUST LIKE SLEEPING BEAUTY?
YEAH, SO I GUESS THE CURE WOULD BE...
YOU KNOW.
ha ha ha ha
FOR A PRINCE TO APPEAR AND...
OH, YEAH.
FOR A PRINCE TO APPEAR AND...
chuckle
Kiss... her ?!

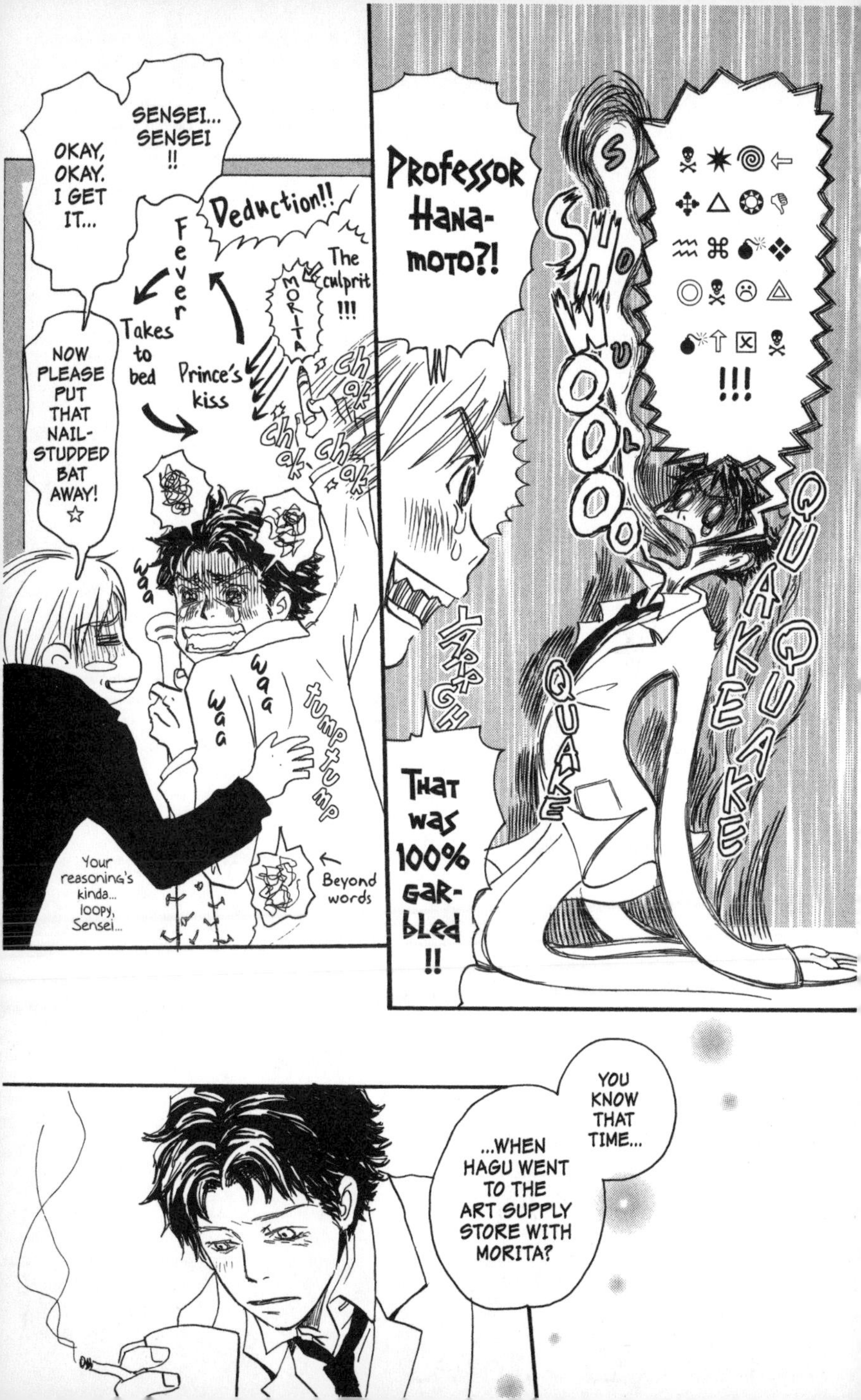

Professor Hana-moto?!
!!!
SHOWOOOO
QUAKE QUAKE QUAKE
YARRGH
That was 100% gar-bled!!
SENSEI... SENSEI !!
OKAY, OKAY. I GET IT...
Deduction!!
Fever
Takes to bed
Prince's kiss
The culprit !!!
MORITA
NOW PLEASE PUT THAT NAIL-STUDDED BAT AWAY! ☆
chak chak chak chak
waa waa waa
tump tump
Beyond words
Your reasoning's kinda... loopy, Sensei...
YOU KNOW THAT TIME...
...WHEN HAGU WENT TO THE ART SUPPLY STORE WITH MORITA?

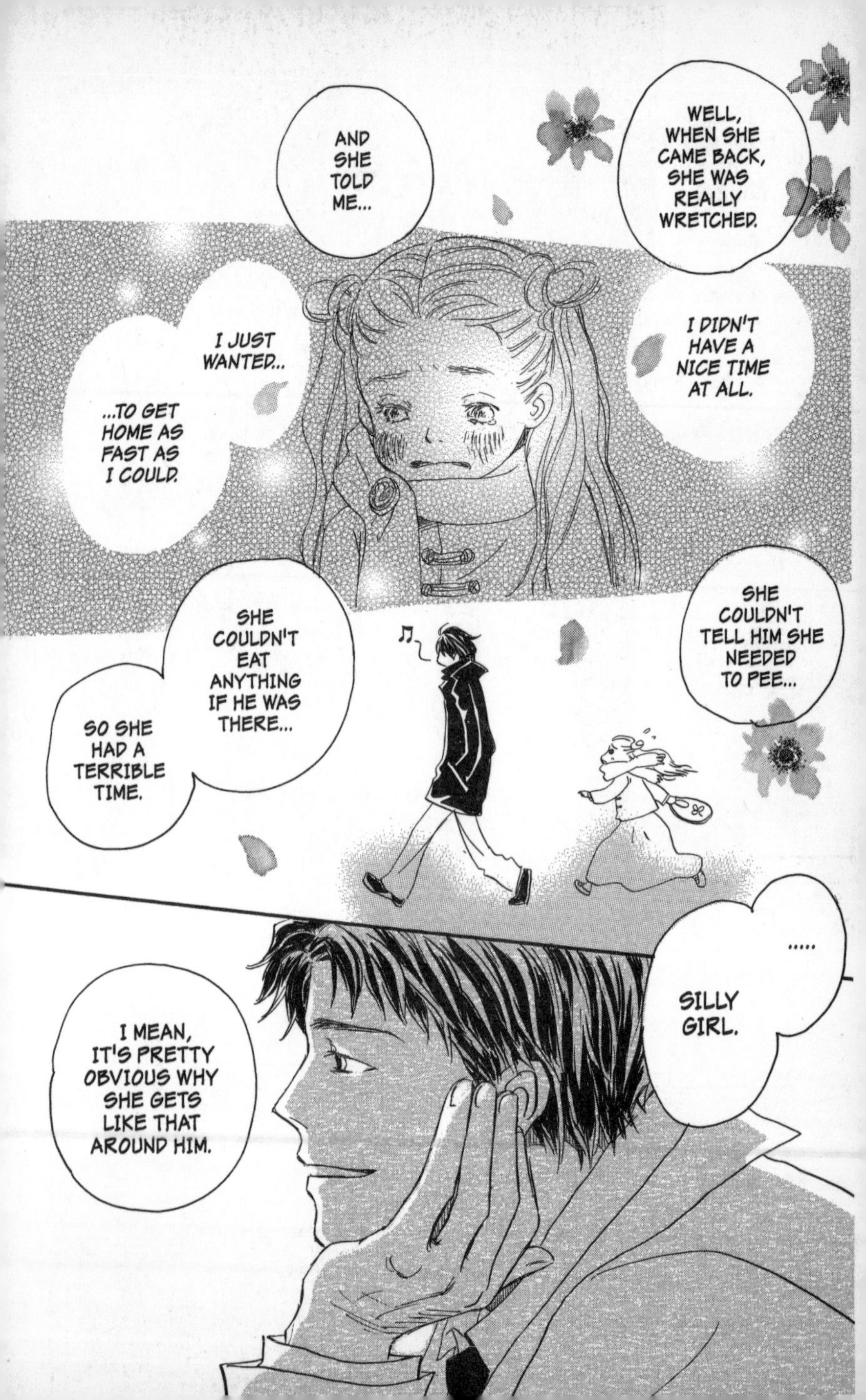
WELL, WHEN SHE CAME BACK, SHE WAS REALLY WRETCHED.
AND SHE TOLD ME...
I DIDN'T HAVE A NICE TIME AT ALL.
I JUST WANTED...
...TO GET HOME AS FAST AS I COULD.
SHE COULDN'T TELL HIM SHE NEEDED TO PEE...
SHE COULDN'T EAT ANYTHING IF HE WAS THERE...
SO SHE HAD A TERRIBLE TIME.
.....
SILLY GIRL.
I MEAN, IT'S PRETTY OBVIOUS WHY SHE GETS LIKE THAT AROUND HIM.

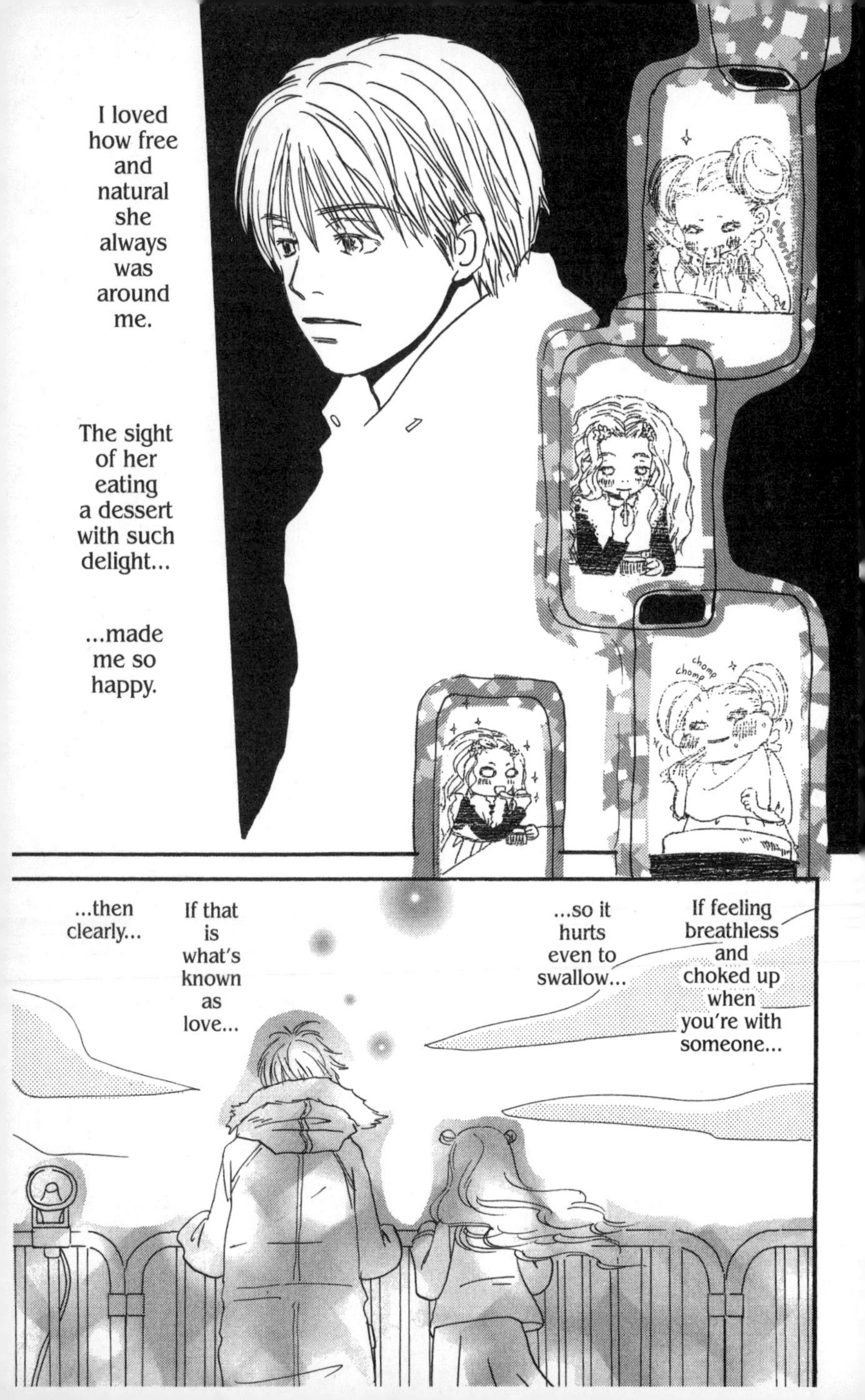
I loved how free and natural she always was around me.
absorbed
The sight of her eating a dessert with such delight...
...made me so happy.
chomp chomp
If feeling breathless and choked up when you're with someone...
...so it hurts even to swallow...
If that is what's known as love...
...then clearly...

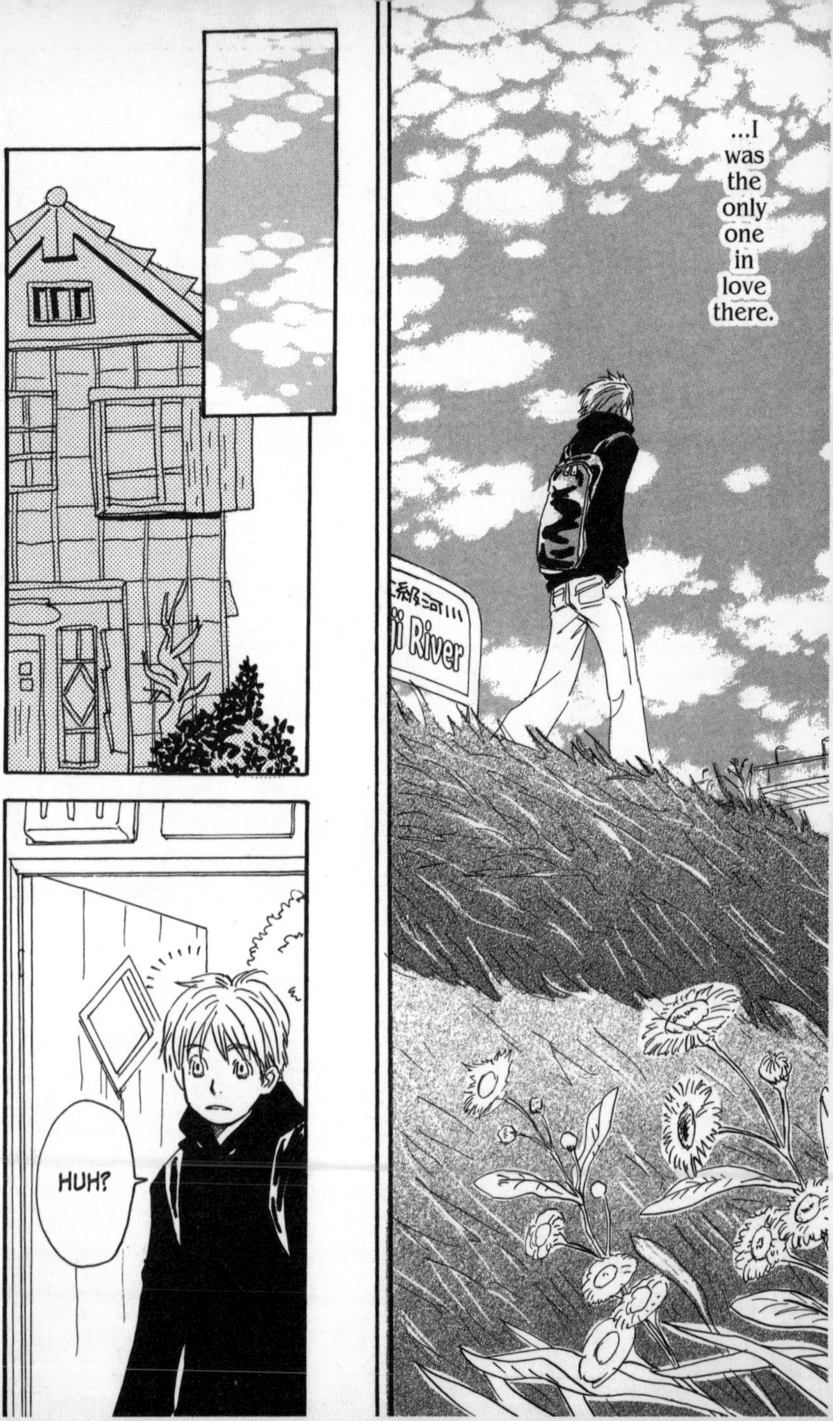
...I was the only one in love there.
ji River
HUH?

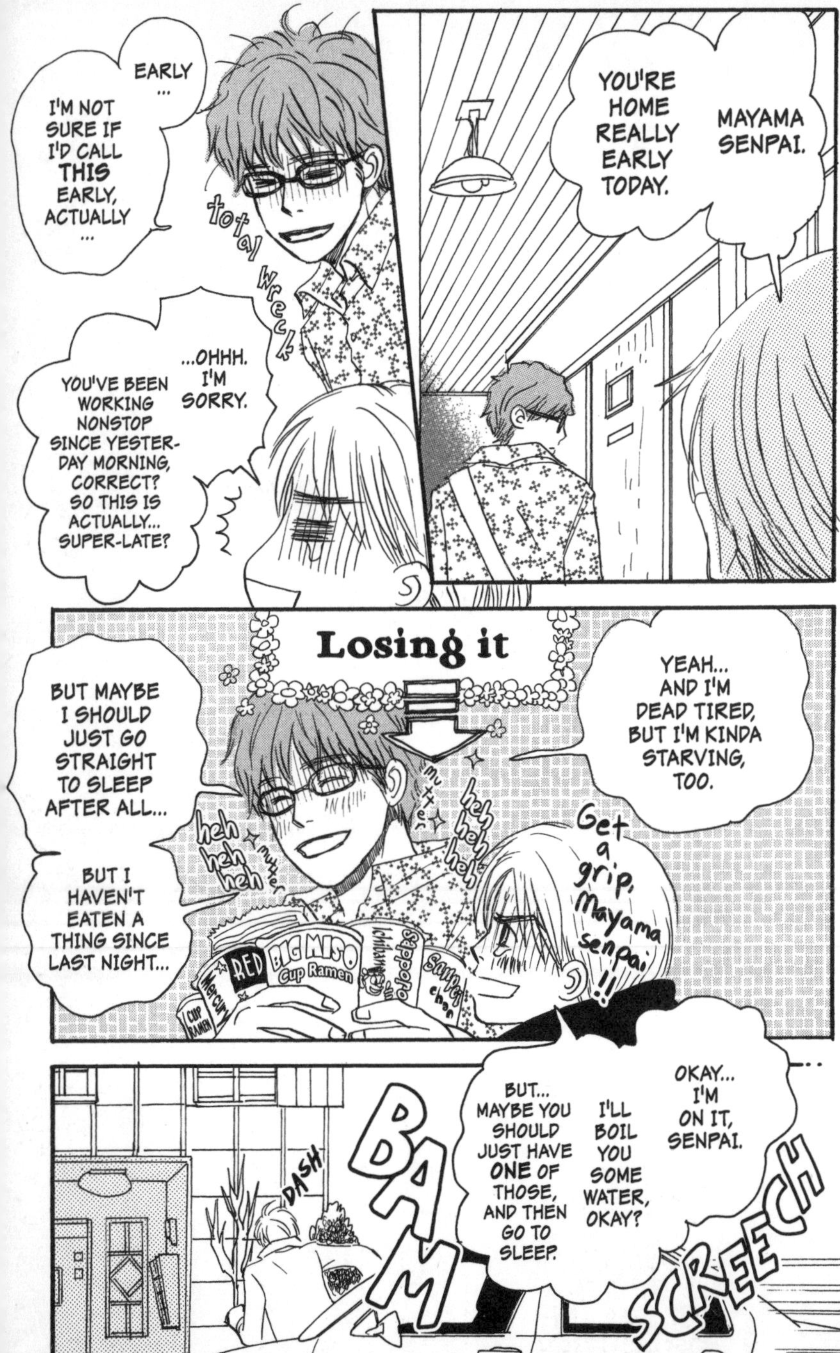
MAYAMA SENPAI.
YOU'RE HOME REALLY EARLY TODAY.
EARLY...
I'M NOT SURE IF I'D CALL THIS EARLY, ACTUALLY...
total wreck
...OHHH. I'M SORRY.
YOU'VE BEEN WORKING NONSTOP SINCE YESTERDAY MORNING, CORRECT? SO THIS IS ACTUALLY... SUPER-LATE?
Losing it
YEAH... AND I'M DEAD TIRED, BUT I'M KINDA STARVING, TOO.
heh heh heh
mutter
BUT MAYBE I SHOULD JUST GO STRAIGHT TO SLEEP AFTER ALL...
heh heh heh
mutter
BUT I HAVEN'T EATEN A THING SINCE LAST NIGHT...
Get a grip, Mayama senpai!!
RED
BIG MISO Cup Ramen
Mercury
CUP RAMEN
Sapporo
OKAY... I'M ON IT, SENPAI.
I'LL BOIL YOU SOME WATER, OKAY?
BUT... MAYBE YOU SHOULD JUST HAVE ONE OF THOSE, AND THEN GO TO SLEEP.
SCREECH
BAM
DASH

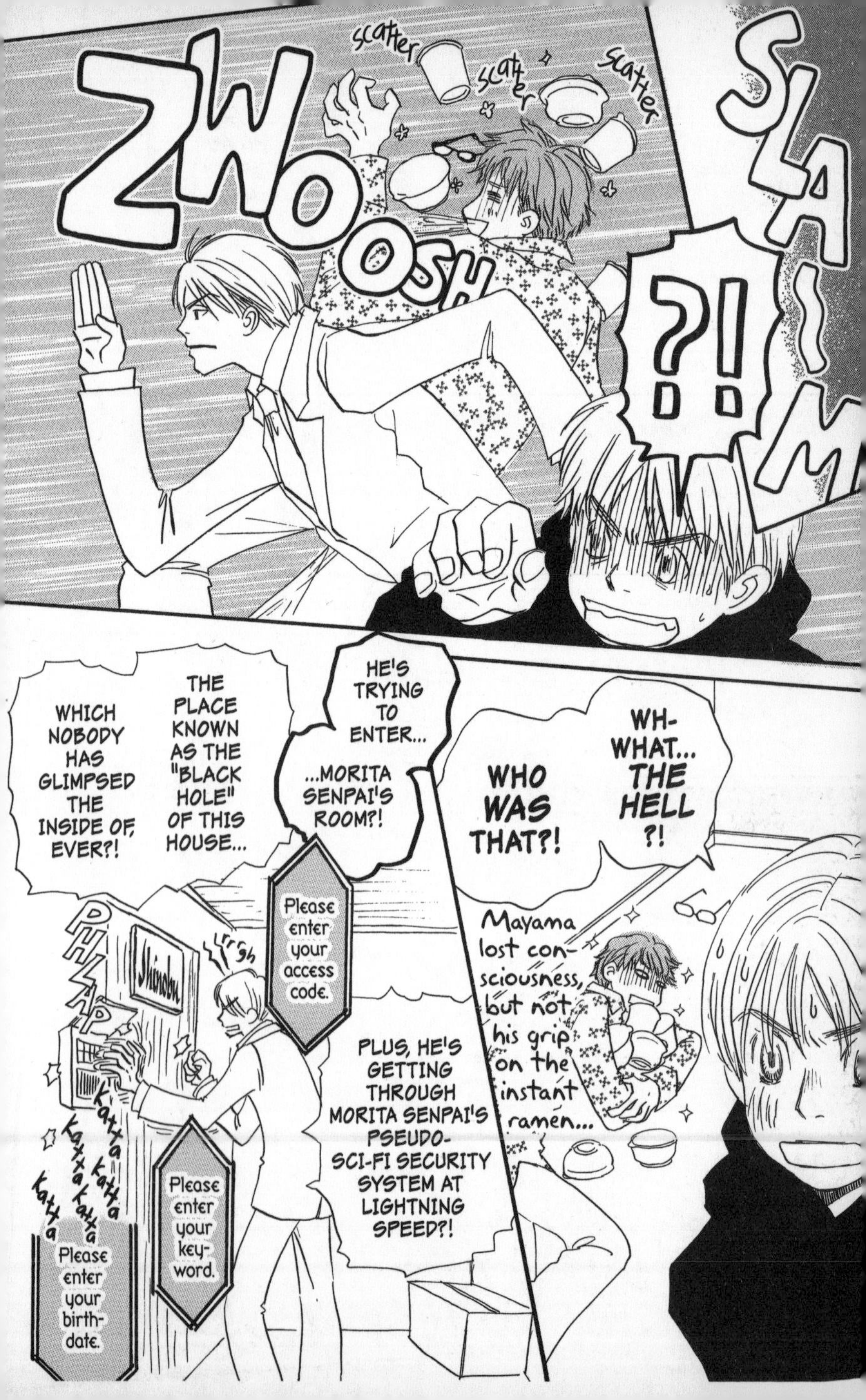
SLAM
?!
ZWOOSH
scatter
scatter
scatter
WH- WHAT... THE HELL?!
WHO WAS THAT?!
Mayama lost consciousness, but not his grip on the instant ramen...
HE'S TRYING TO ENTER...
...MORITA SENPAI'S ROOM?!
THE PLACE KNOWN AS THE "BLACK HOLE" OF THIS HOUSE...
WHICH NOBODY HAS GLIMPSED THE INSIDE OF, EVER?!
Please enter your access code.
rrgh
Shinobu
PHLAP
PLUS, HE'S GETTING THROUGH MORITA SENPAI'S PSEUDO-SCI-FI SECURITY SYSTEM AT LIGHTNING SPEED?!
Please enter your keyword.
katta katta
katta katta
katta
Please enter your birthdate.

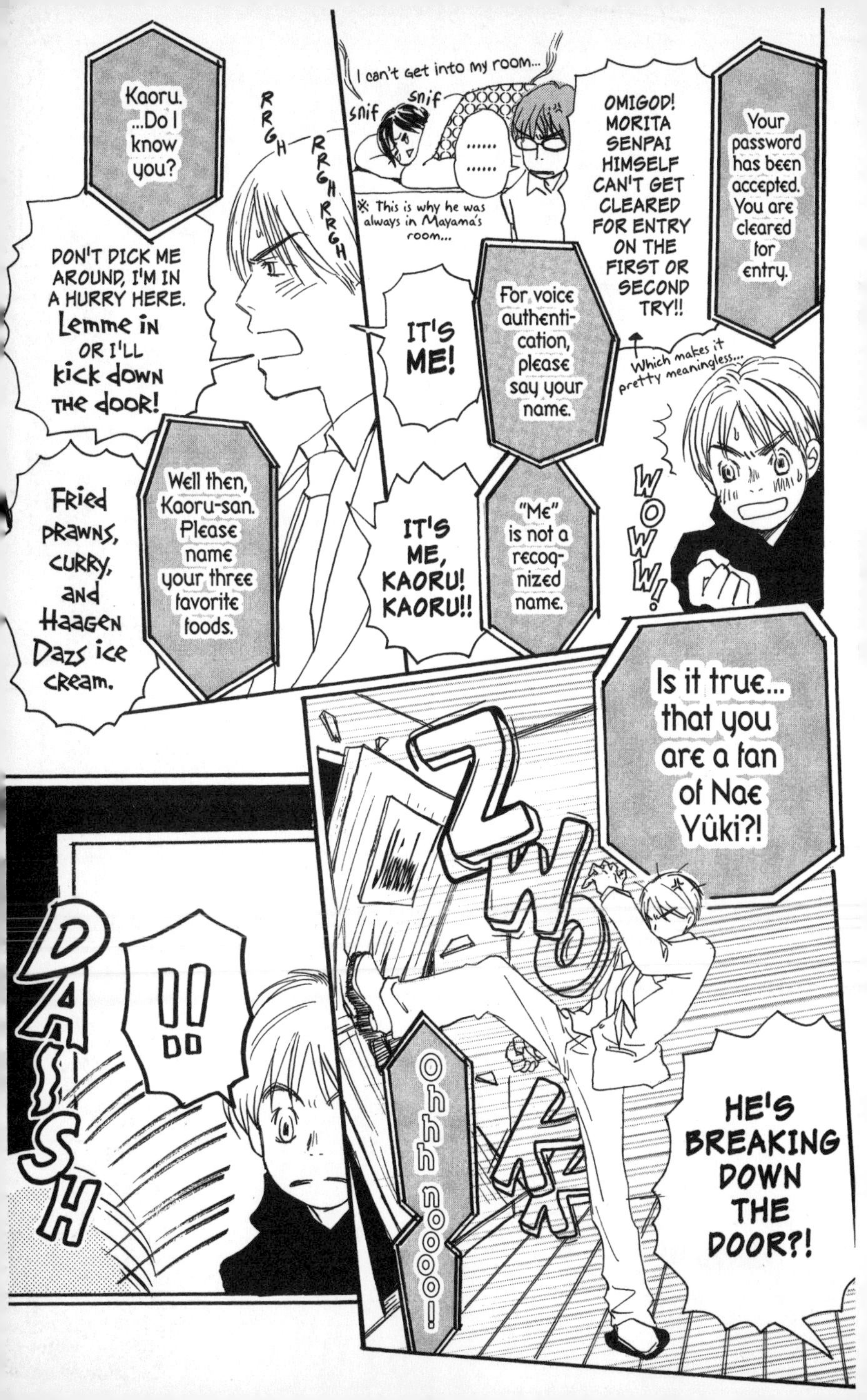
Your password has been accepted. You are cleared for entry.
OMIGOD! MORITA SENPAI HIMSELF CAN'T GET CLEARED FOR ENTRY ON THE FIRST OR SECOND TRY!!
Which makes it pretty meaningless...
WOWW!
I can't get into my room...
snif
snif
......
......
※ This is why he was always in Mayama's room...
For voice authentication, please say your name.
IT'S ME!
"Me" is not a recognized name.
IT'S ME, KAORU! KAORU!!
RRGH RRGH RRGH RRGH
Kaoru. ...Do I know you?
DON'T DICK ME AROUND, I'M IN A HURRY HERE. Lemme in OR I'LL kick down the door!
Well then, Kaoru-san. Please name your three favorite foods.
Fried prawns, curry, and Haagen Dazs ice cream.
Is it true... that you are a fan of Nae Yûki?!
HE'S BREAKING DOWN THE DOOR?!
Ohhh noooo!
!!
DASH

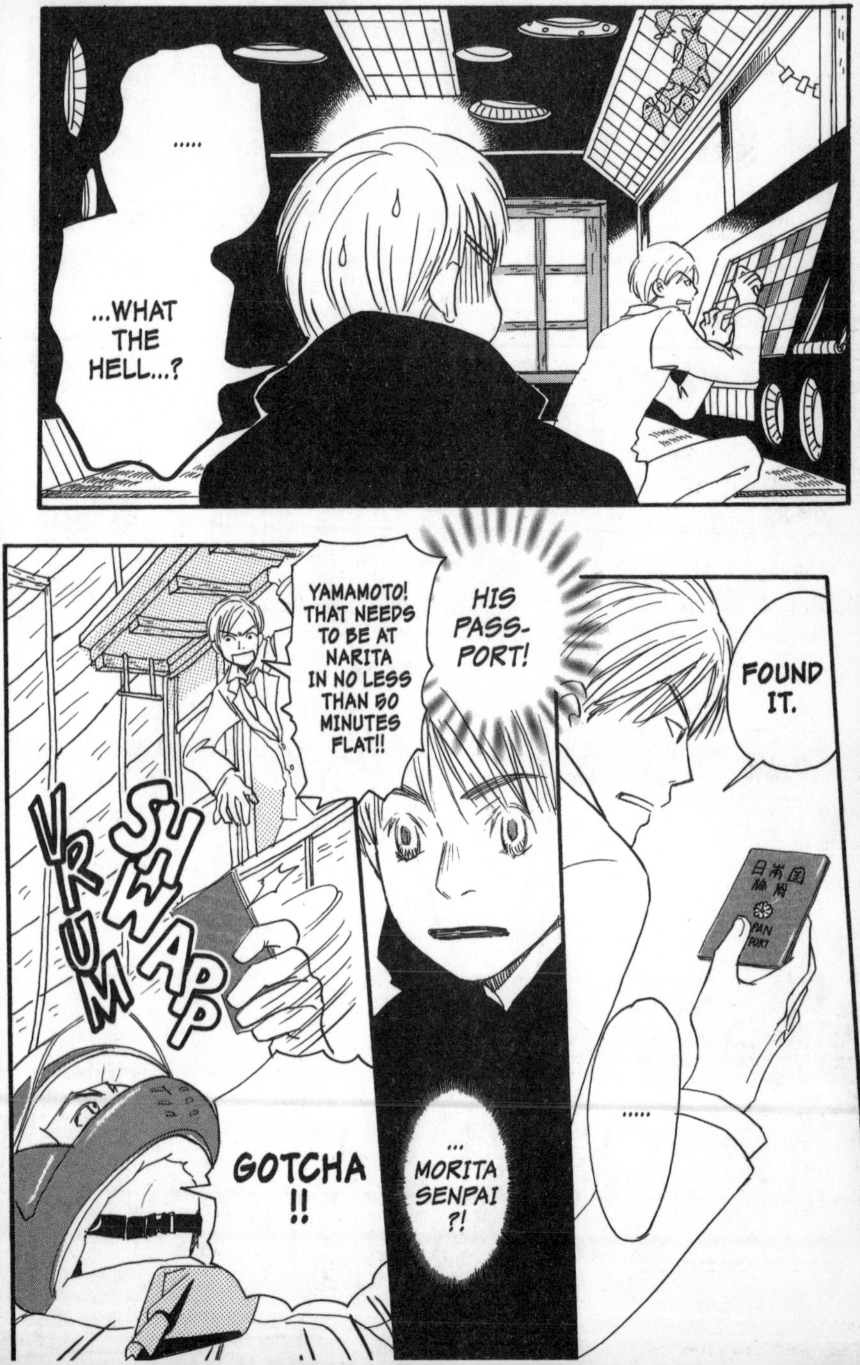
.....
...WHAT THE HELL...?
FOUND IT.
HIS PASS-PORT!
YAMAMOTO! THAT NEEDS TO BE AT NARITA IN NO LESS THAN 50 MINUTES FLAT!!
SHWAP
VRUM
.....
...MORITA SENPAI?!
GOTCHA!!

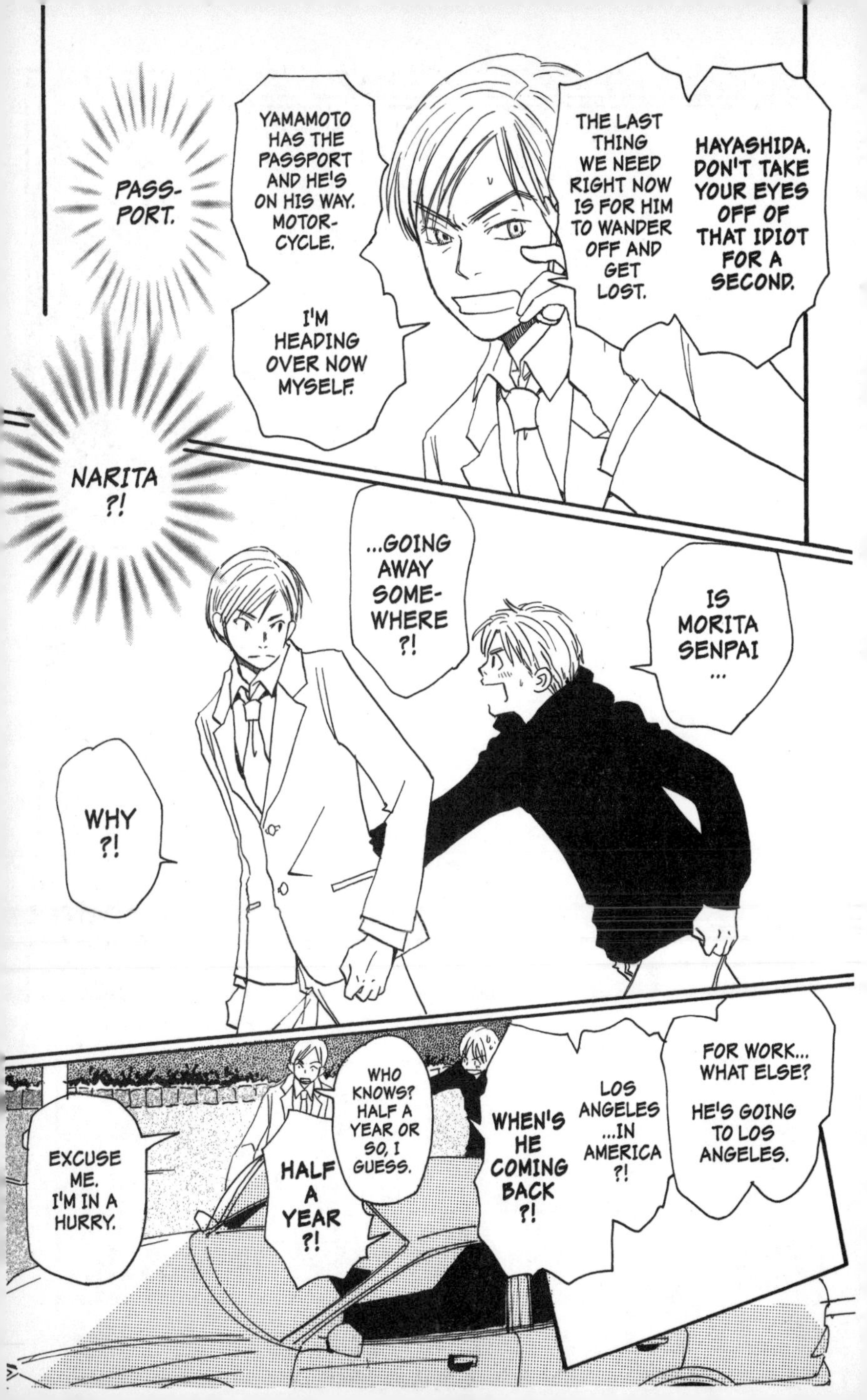
HAYASHIDA. DON'T TAKE YOUR EYES OFF OF THAT IDIOT FOR A SECOND.
THE LAST THING WE NEED RIGHT NOW IS FOR HIM TO WANDER OFF AND GET LOST.
YAMAMOTO HAS THE PASSPORT AND HE'S ON HIS WAY. MOTOR-CYCLE.
I'M HEADING OVER NOW MYSELF.
PASS-PORT.
NARITA ?!
IS MORITA SENPAI ...
...GOING AWAY SOME-WHERE ?!
WHY ?!
FOR WORK... WHAT ELSE?
HE'S GOING TO LOS ANGELES.
LOS ANGELES ...IN AMERICA ?!
WHEN'S HE COMING BACK ?!
WHO KNOWS? HALF A YEAR OR SO, I GUESS.
HALF A YEAR ?!
EXCUSE ME. I'M IN A HURRY.

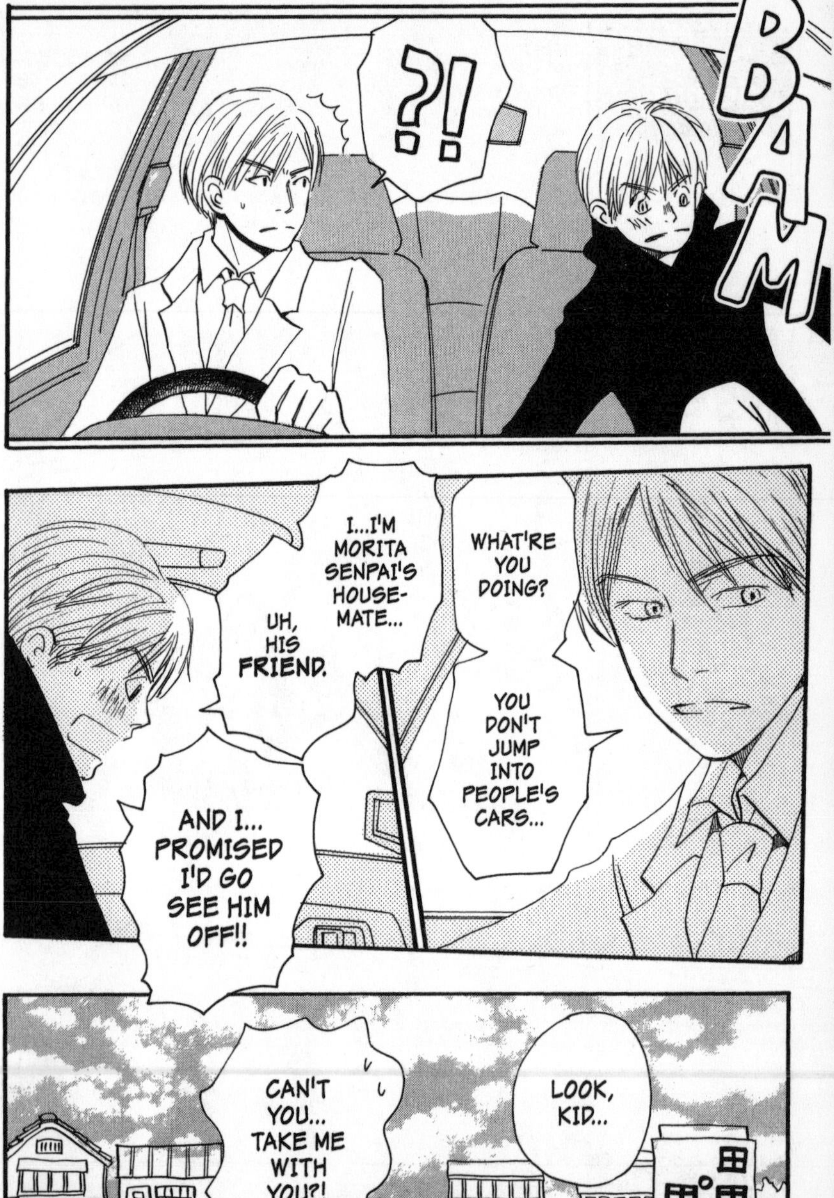
BAM
?!
WHAT'RE YOU DOING?
YOU DON'T JUMP INTO PEOPLE'S CARS...
I...I'M MORITA SENPAI'S HOUSE-MATE...
UH, HIS FRIEND.
AND I... PROMISED I'D GO SEE HIM OFF!!
LOOK, KID...
CAN'T YOU... TAKE ME WITH YOU?!

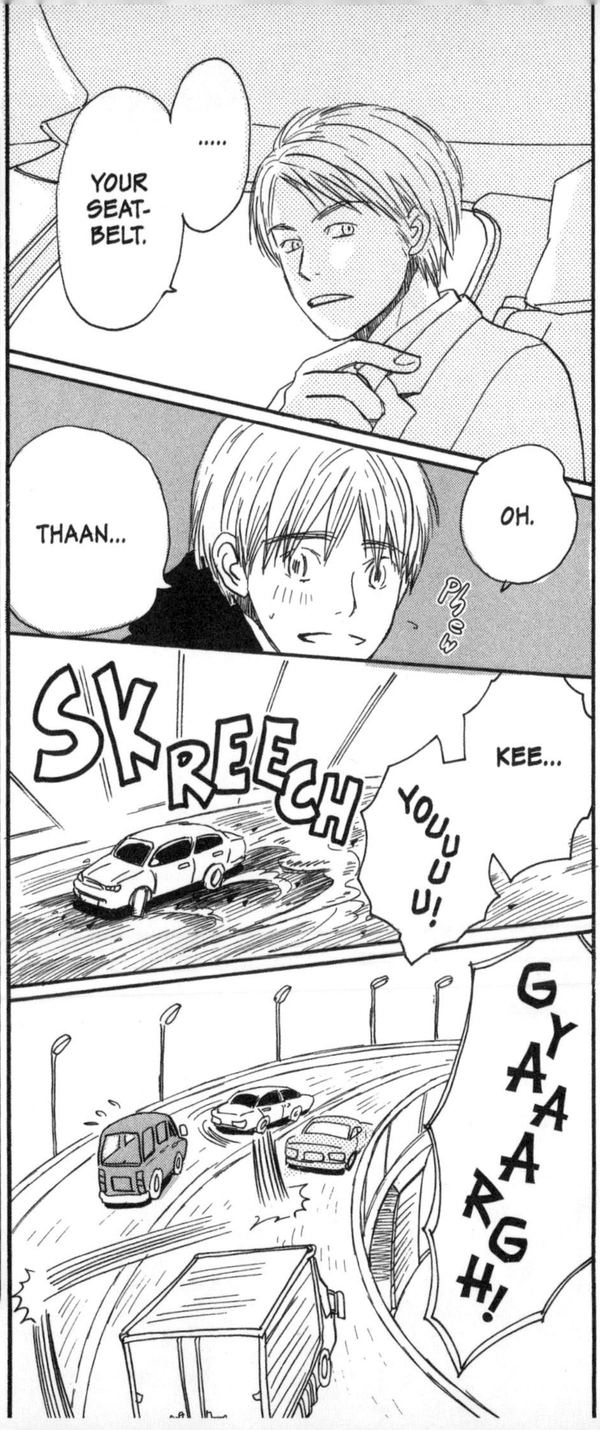
.....
YOUR SEAT-BELT.
OH.
Phew
THAAN...
KEE...
YOUUUUUU!
SKREECH
GYAAAARGH!

I love cleaning!

I've just completed a manga installment. My room is fantastically dirty... I have to clean it...

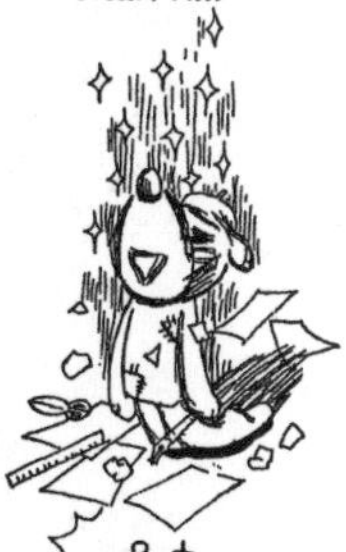

But first... FOOD! I need to eat!!

Chica Umino

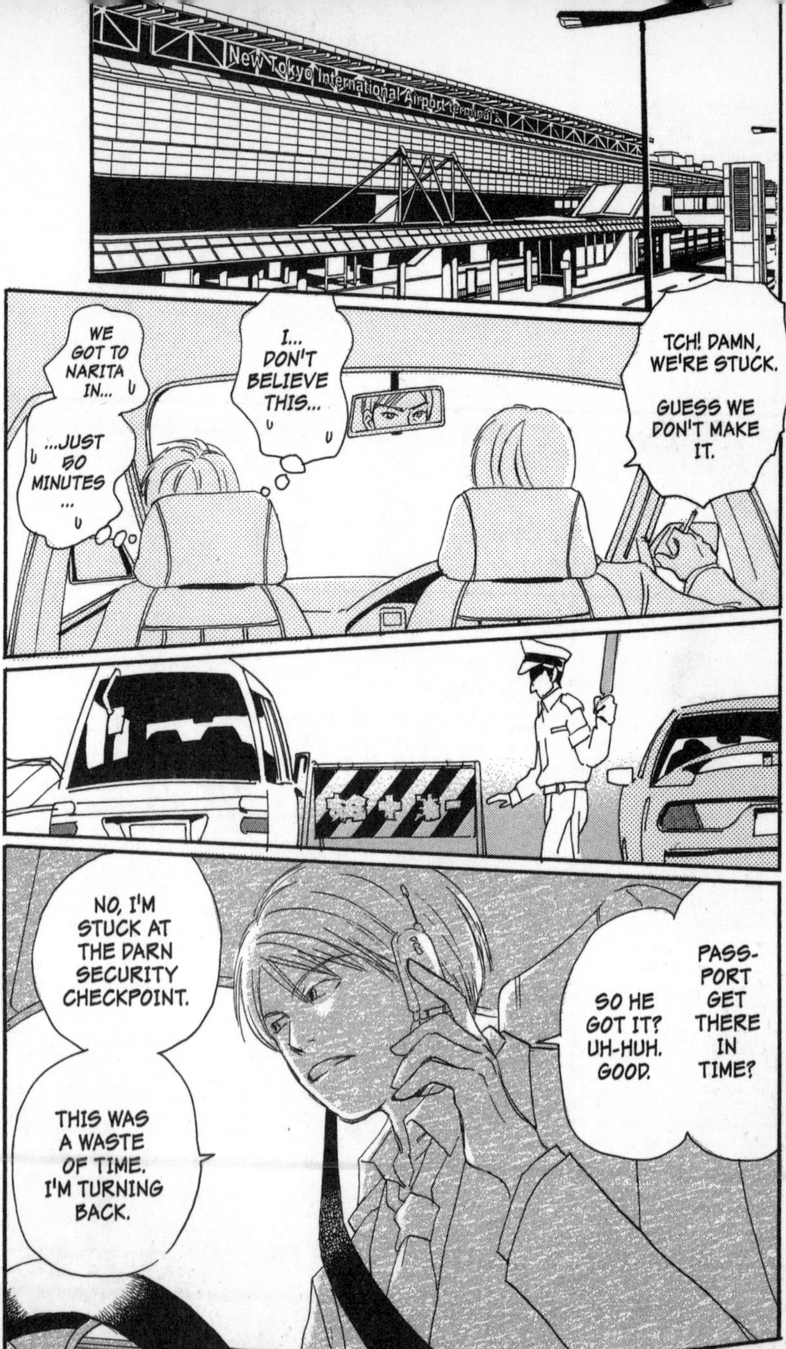
New Tokyo International Airport terminal 2
TCH! DAMN, WE'RE STUCK.
GUESS WE DON'T MAKE IT.
I... DON'T BELIEVE THIS...
WE GOT TO NARITA IN...
...JUST 50 MINUTES ...
PASS-PORT GET THERE IN TIME?
SO HE GOT IT? UH-HUH. GOOD.
NO, I'M STUCK AT THE DARN SECURITY CHECKPOINT.
THIS WAS A WASTE OF TIME. I'M TURNING BACK.

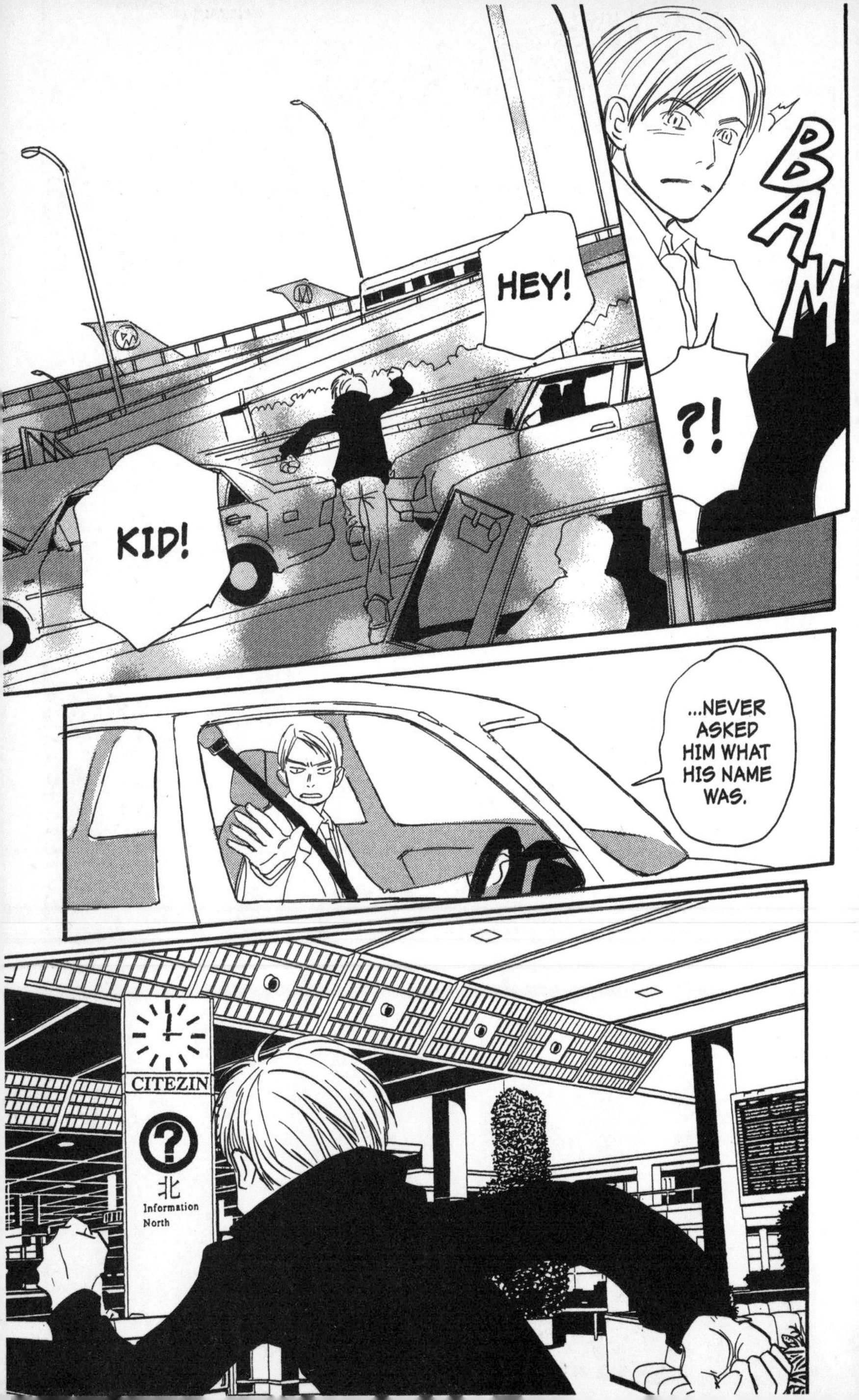
BAM
?!
HEY!
KID!
...NEVER ASKED HIM WHAT HIS NAME WAS.
CITEZIN
北
Information
North

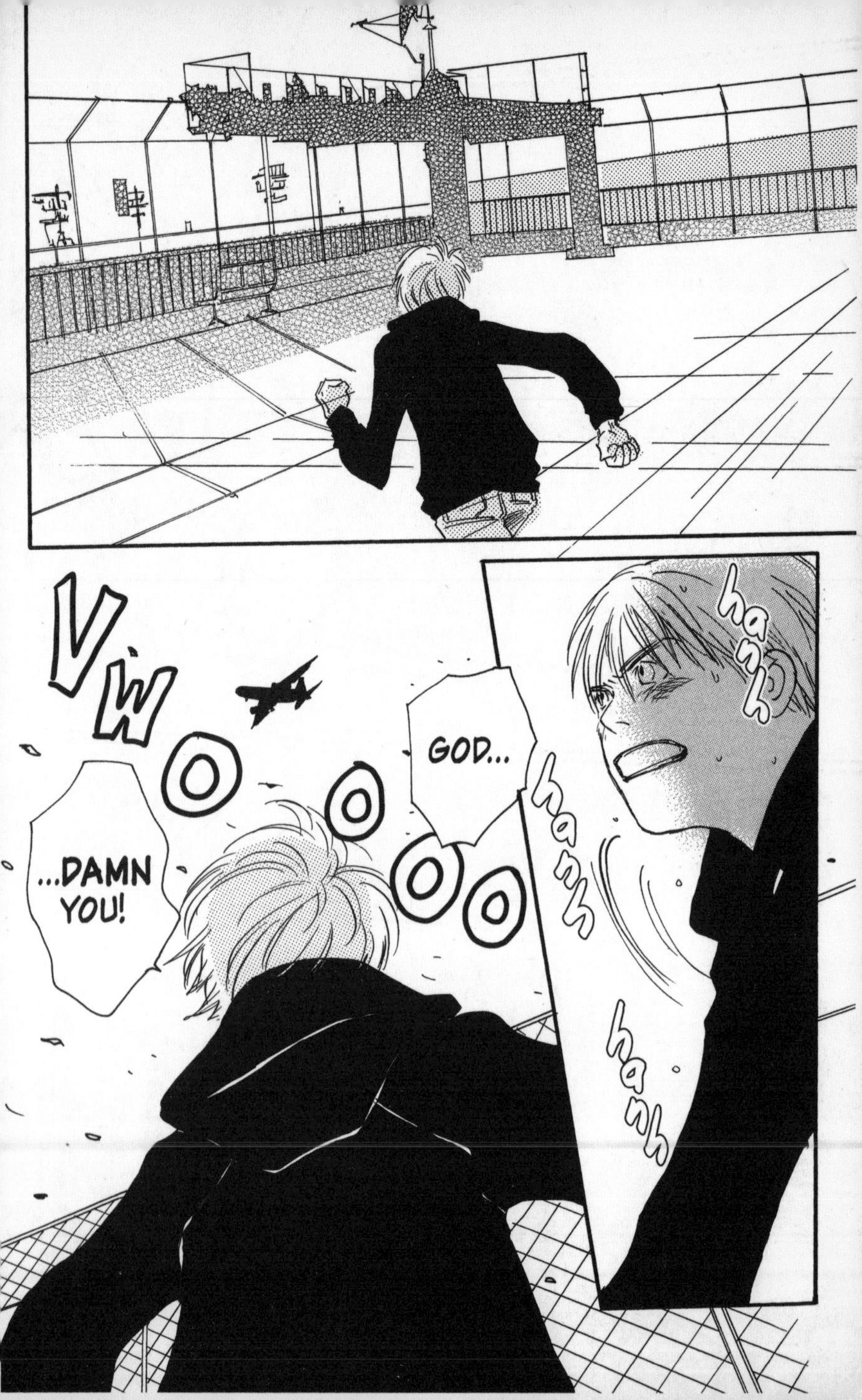
hanh
hanh
hanh
GOD...
VWOOOOO
...DAMN YOU!

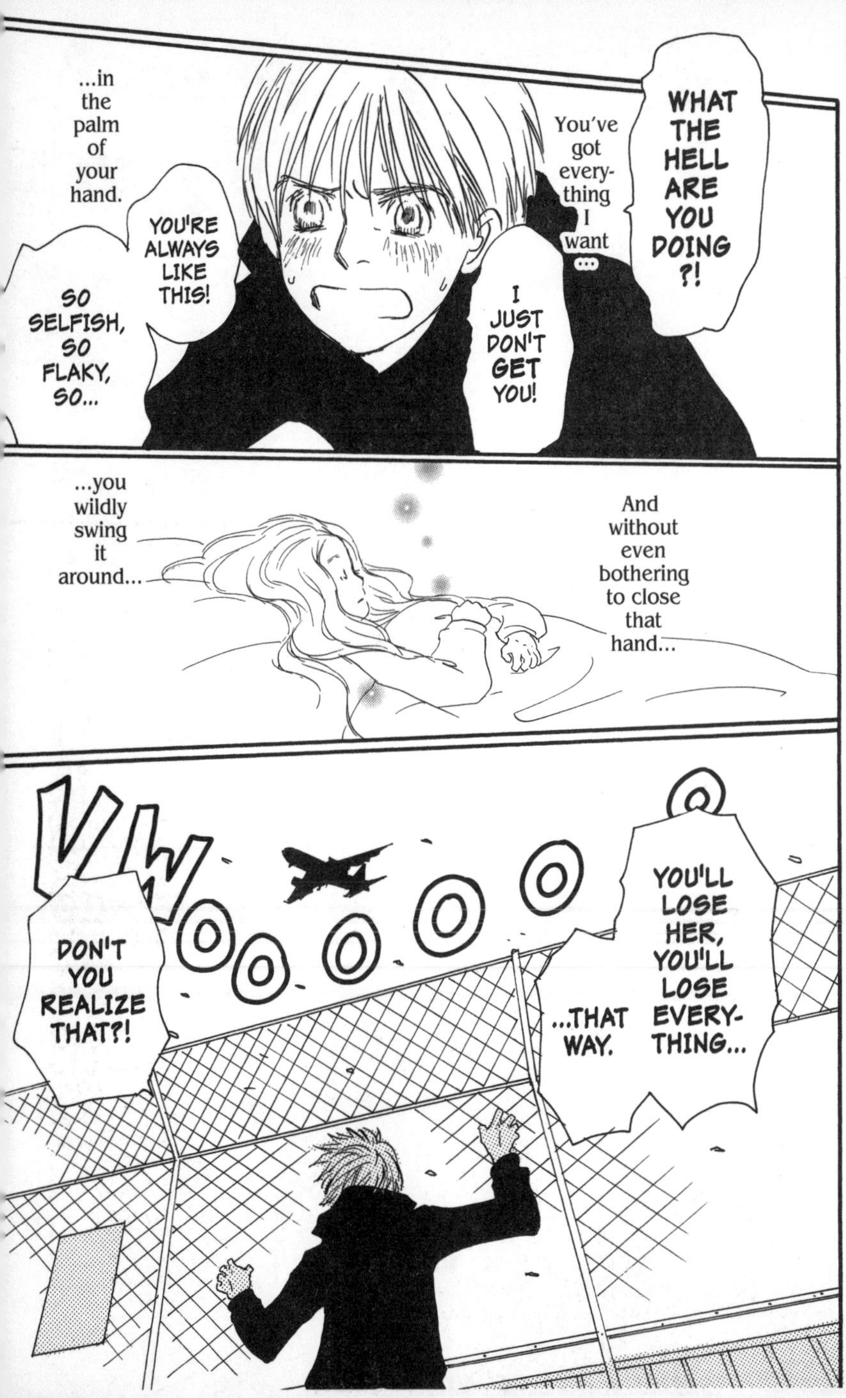

WHAT THE HELL ARE YOU DOING?!
You've got everything I want...
...in the palm of your hand.
I JUST DON'T GET YOU!
YOU'RE ALWAYS LIKE THIS!
SO SELFISH, SO FLAKY, SO...
And without even bothering to close that hand...
...you wildly swing it around...
VWOOOOOOO
YOU'LL LOSE HER, YOU'LL LOSE EVERYTHING...
...THAT WAY.
DON'T YOU REALIZE THAT?!

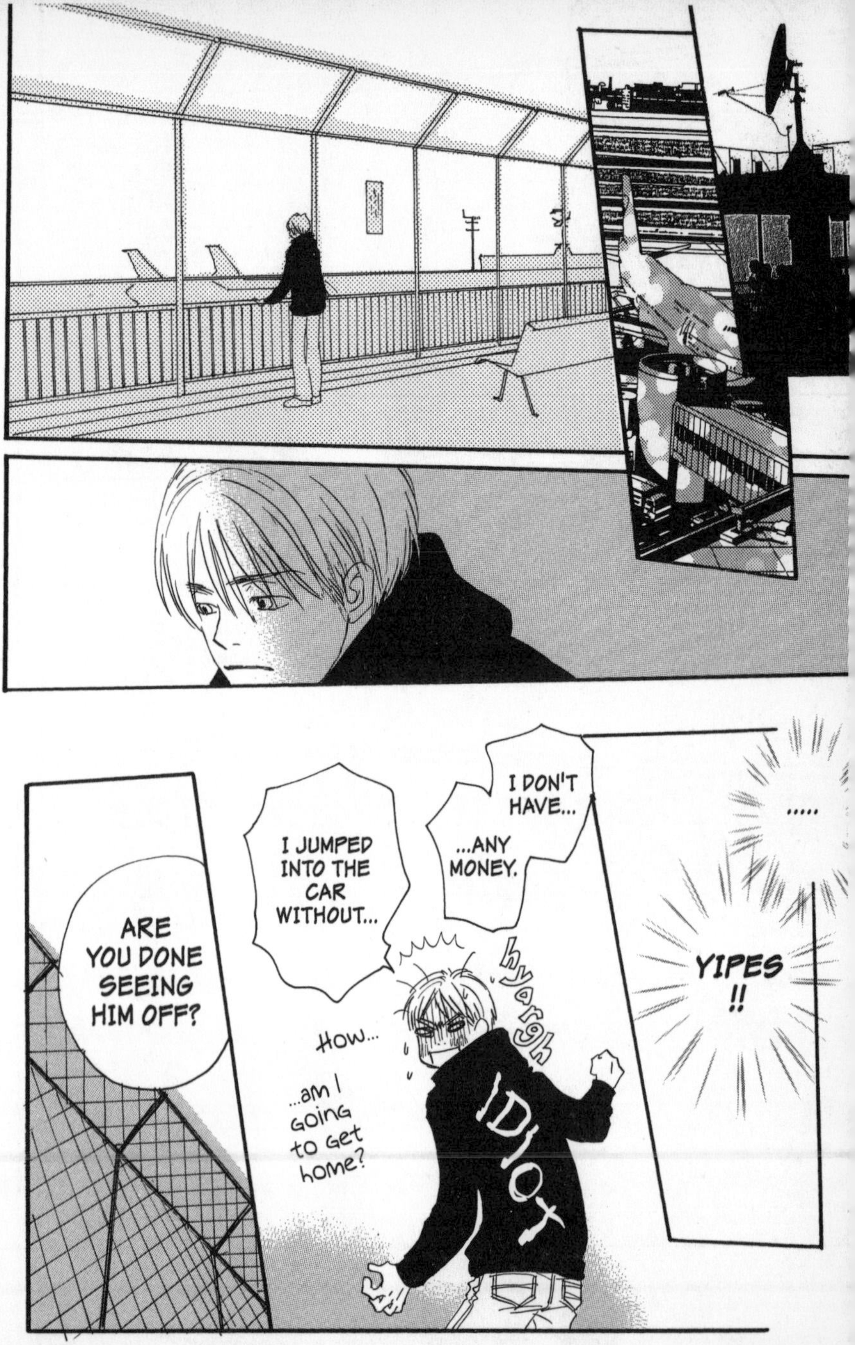
.....
YIPES !!
I DON'T HAVE...
...ANY MONEY.
I JUMPED INTO THE CAR WITHOUT...
hyargh
IDIOT
How...
...am I going to get home?
ARE YOU DONE SEEING HIM OFF?

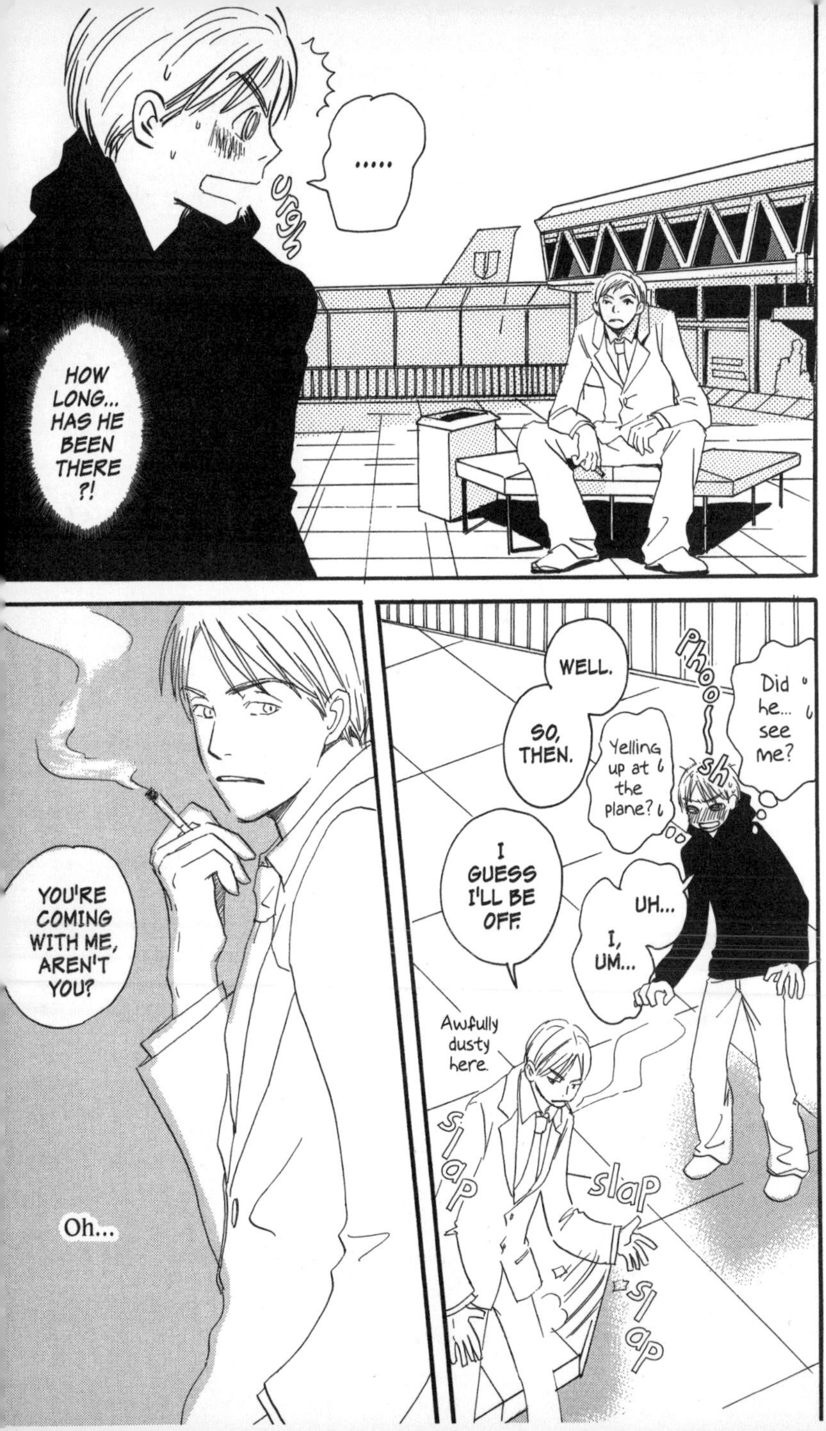
.....
urgh
HOW LONG... HAS HE BEEN THERE?!
Phoo~sh
Did he... see me?
WELL.
SO, THEN.
Yelling up at the plane?
I GUESS I'LL BE OFF.
UH...
I, UM...
Awfully dusty here.
slap
slap
slap
YOU'RE COMING WITH ME, AREN'T YOU?
Oh...

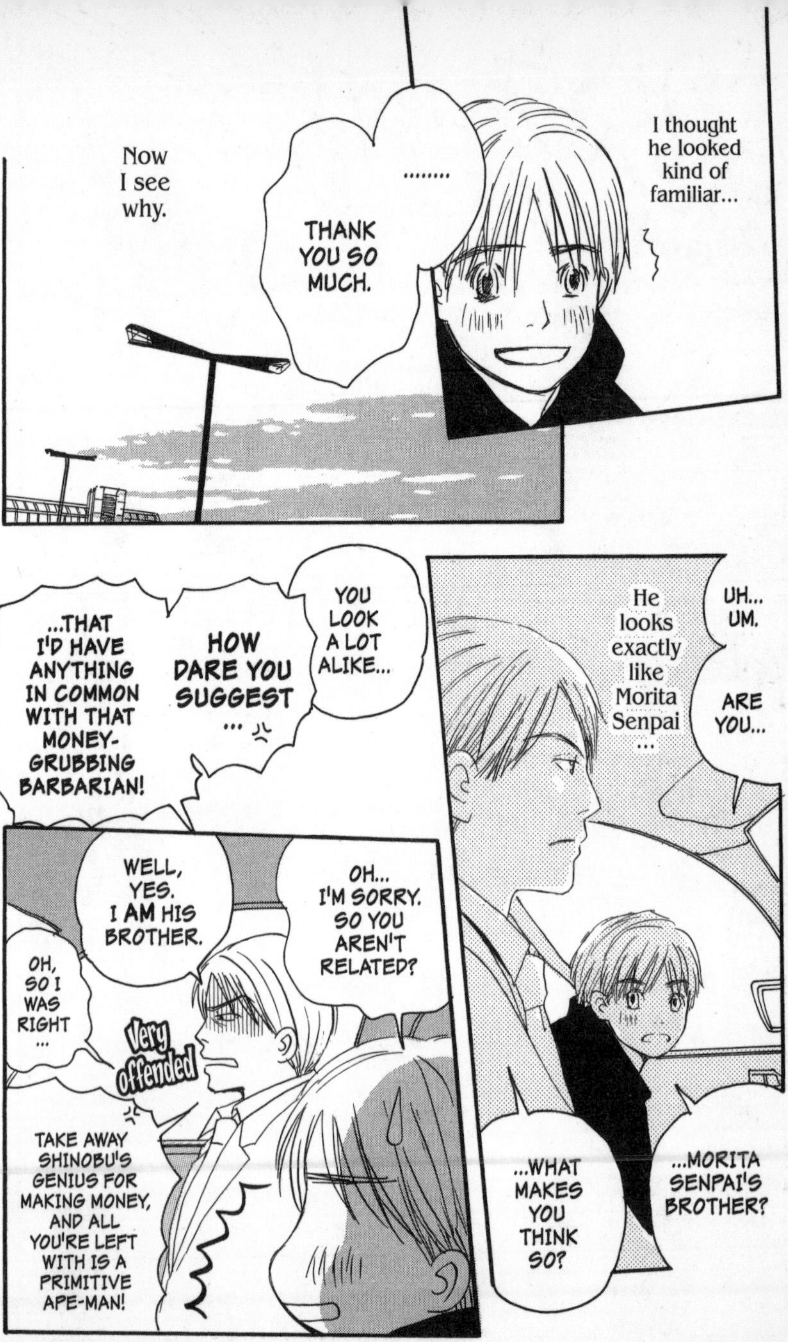
I thought he looked kind of familiar...
....
THANK YOU SO MUCH.
Now I see why.
UH... UM.
ARE YOU...
He looks exactly like Morita Senpai ...
...MORITA SENPAI'S BROTHER?
...WHAT MAKES YOU THINK SO?
YOU LOOK A LOT ALIKE...
HOW DARE YOU SUGGEST ...
...THAT I'D HAVE ANYTHING IN COMMON WITH THAT MONEY-GRUBBING BARBARIAN!
OH... I'M SORRY. SO YOU AREN'T RELATED?
WELL, YES. I AM HIS BROTHER.
OH, SO I WAS RIGHT ...
Very offended
TAKE AWAY SHINOBU'S GENIUS FOR MAKING MONEY, AND ALL YOU'RE LEFT WITH IS A PRIMITIVE APE-MAN!

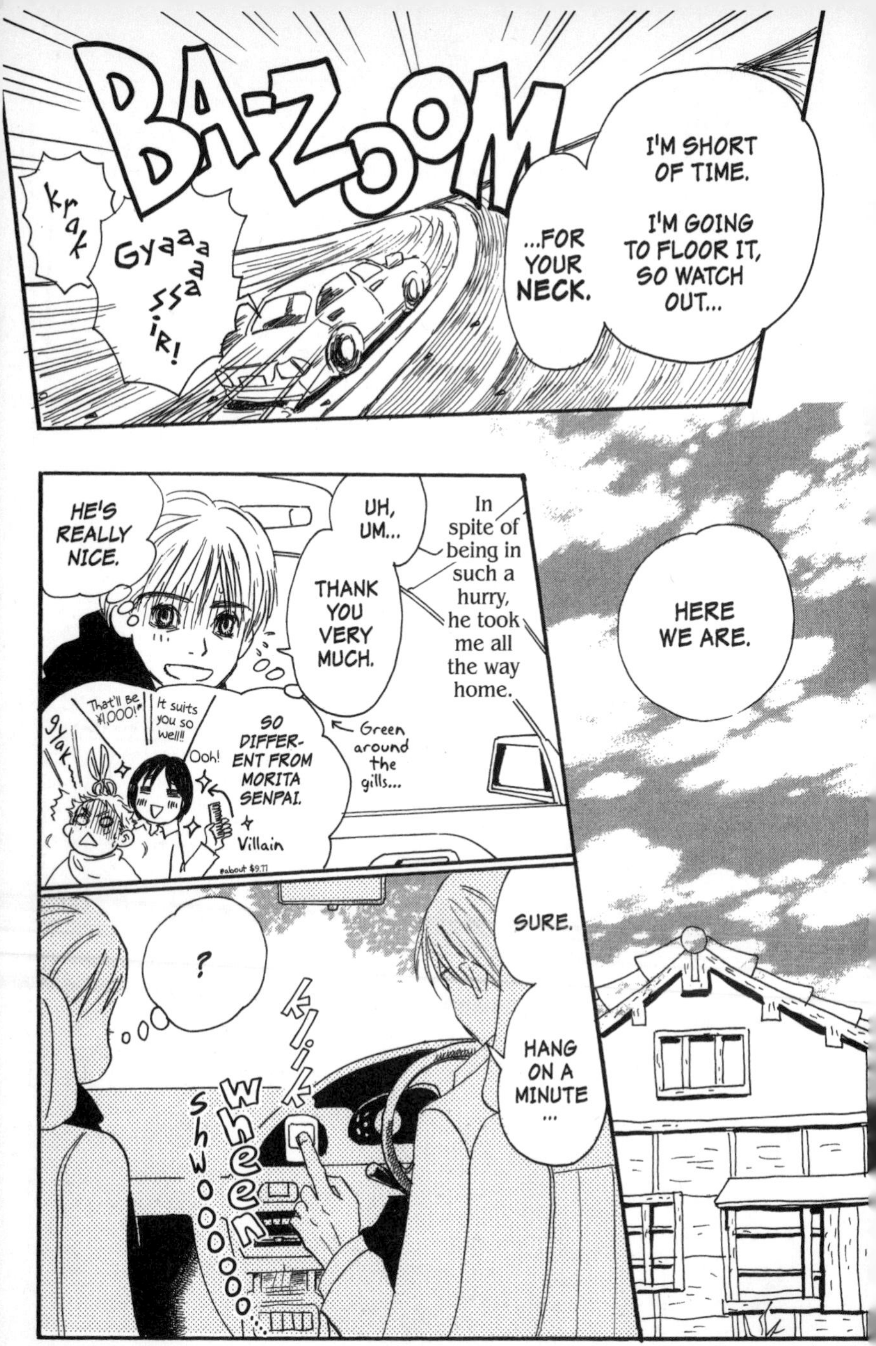
I'M SHORT OF TIME.
I'M GOING TO FLOOR IT, SO WATCH OUT...
...FOR YOUR NECK.
BA-ZOOM
Gyaaaaassaaiir!
krak
HERE WE ARE.
In spite of being in such a hurry, he took me all the way home.
UH, UM...
THANK YOU VERY MUCH.
HE'S REALLY NICE.
Green around the gills...
SO DIFFERENT FROM MORITA SENPAI.
It suits you so well!!
That'll be ¥1,000!*
Ooh!
gyak
Villain
*about $9.11
SURE.
HANG ON A MINUTE...
?
klik
wheen
shwoooooooo

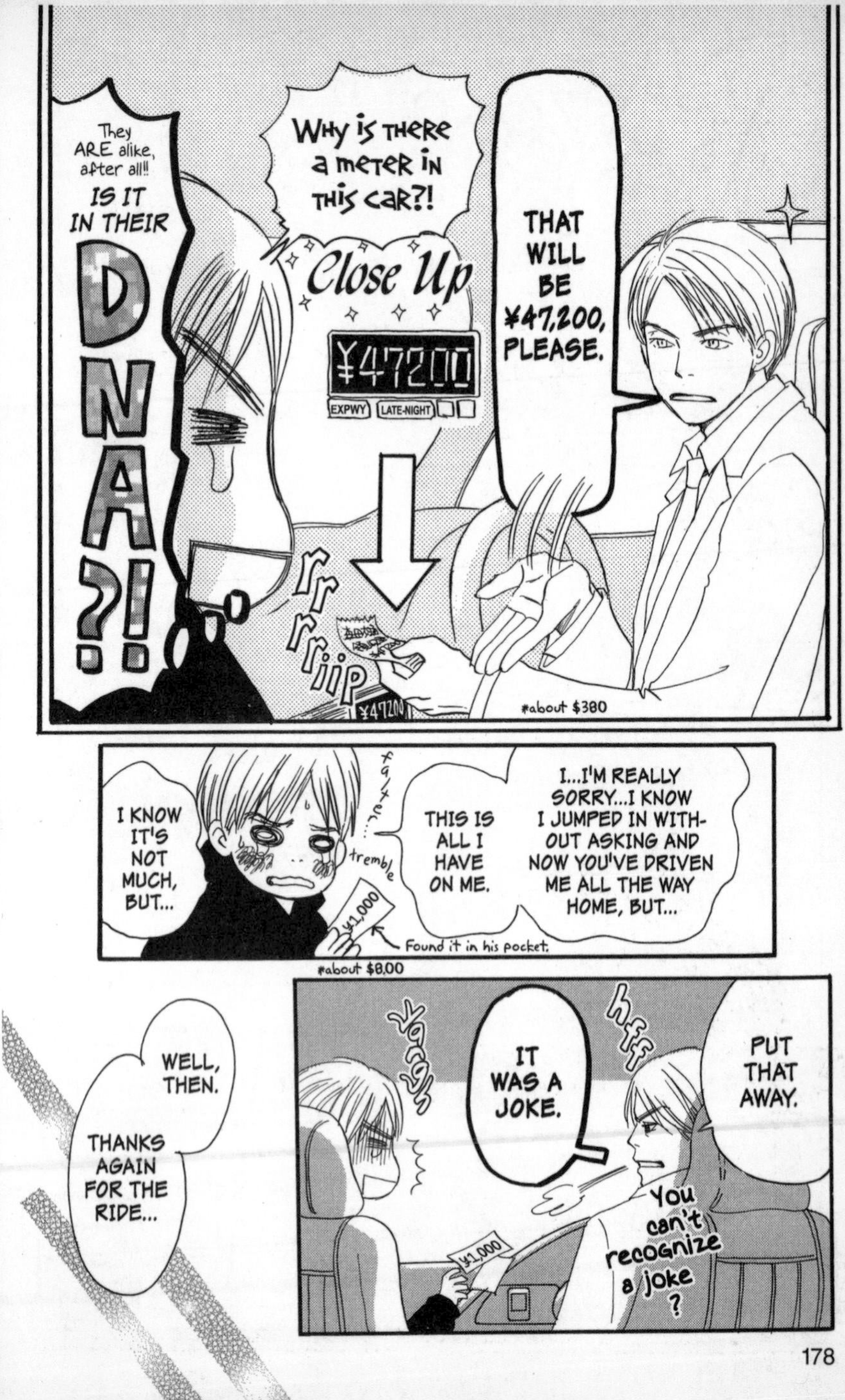
THAT WILL BE ¥47,200, PLEASE.
Why is there a meter in this car?!
Close Up
¥47200
EXPWY
LATE-NIGHT
rrrriip
They ARE alike, after all!!
IS IT IN THEIR DNA?!
*about $380
I...I'M REALLY SORRY...I KNOW I JUMPED IN WITH-OUT ASKING AND NOW YOU'VE DRIVEN ME ALL THE WAY HOME, BUT...
THIS IS ALL I HAVE ON ME.
falter...
tremble
I KNOW IT'S NOT MUCH, BUT...
¥1,000
Found it in his pocket.
*about $8.00
PUT THAT AWAY.
hff
IT WAS A JOKE.
You can't recognize a joke?
¥1,000
WELL, THEN.
THANKS AGAIN FOR THE RIDE...

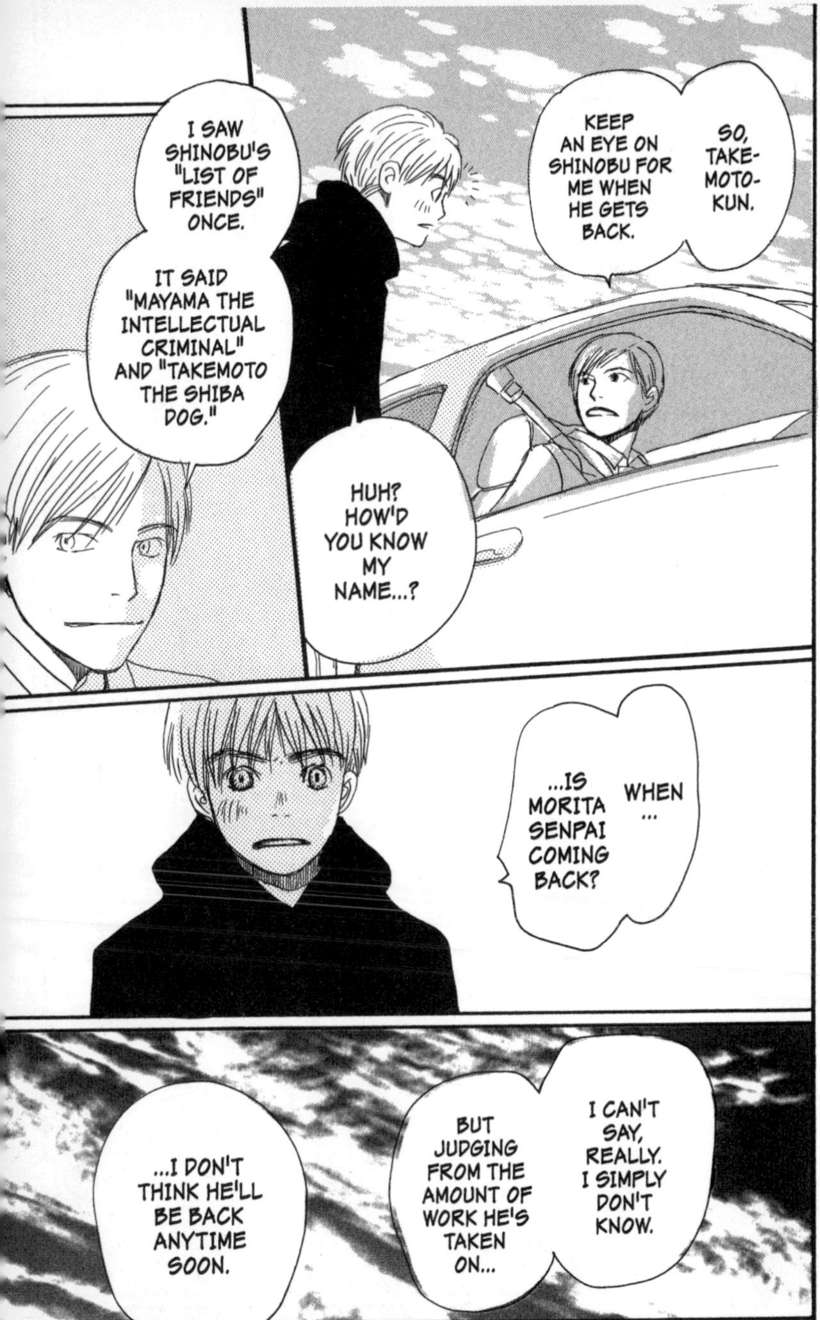

SO, TAKE-MOTO-KUN.
KEEP AN EYE ON SHINOBU FOR ME WHEN HE GETS BACK.
HUH? HOW'D YOU KNOW MY NAME...?
I SAW SHINOBU'S "LIST OF FRIENDS" ONCE.
IT SAID "MAYAMA THE INTELLECTUAL CRIMINAL" AND "TAKEMOTO THE SHIBA DOG."
WHEN...
...IS MORITA SENPAI COMING BACK?
I CAN'T SAY, REALLY. I SIMPLY DON'T KNOW.
BUT JUDGING FROM THE AMOUNT OF WORK HE'S TAKEN ON...
...I DON'T THINK HE'LL BE BACK ANYTIME SOON.

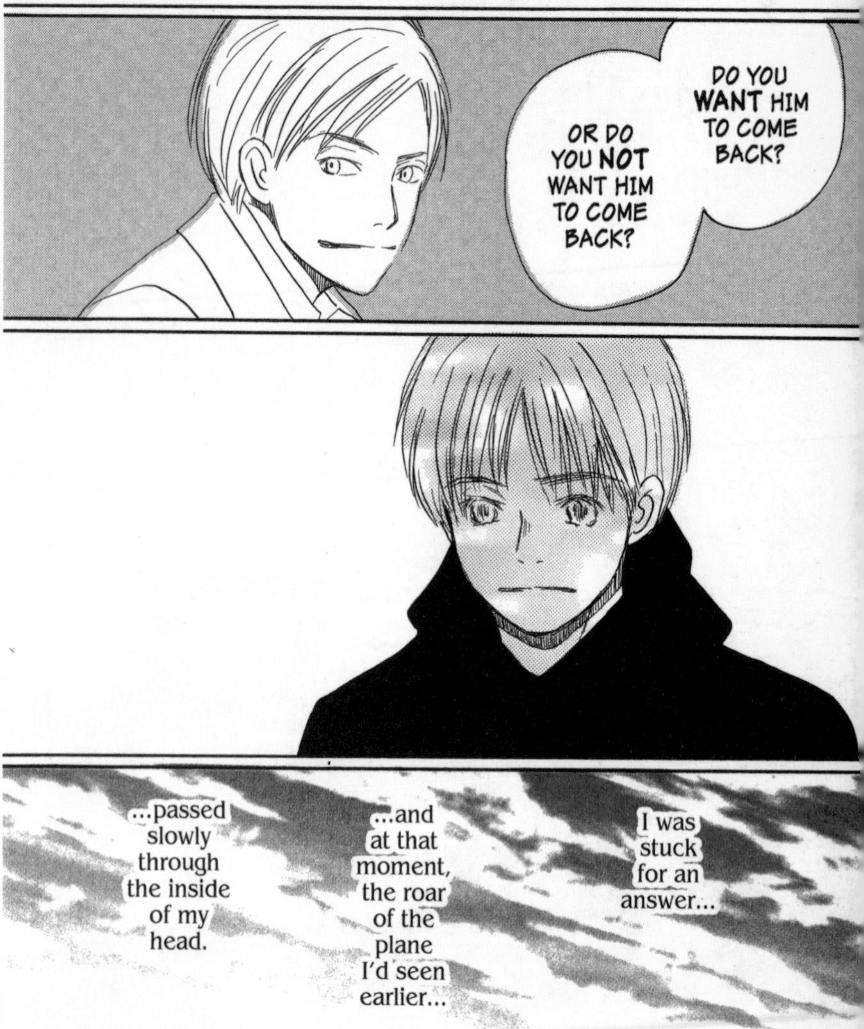
DO YOU WANT HIM TO COME BACK?
OR DO YOU NOT WANT HIM TO COME BACK?
I was stuck for an answer...
...and at that moment, the roar of the plane I'd seen earlier...
...passed slowly through the inside of my head.

chapter 21—end—

honey and clover

—Bonus Chapter—

Pukkun & Milky Tea

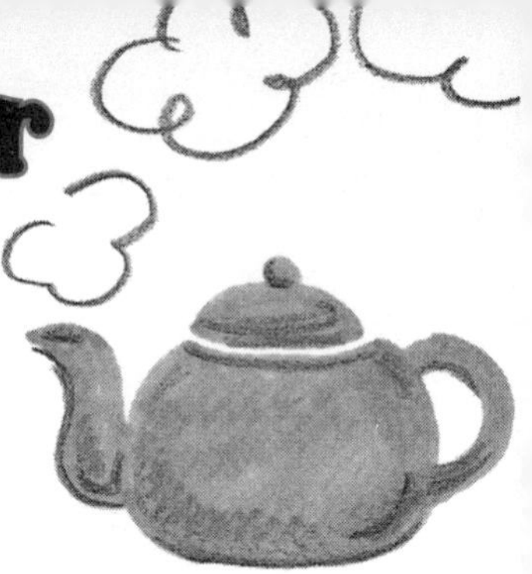

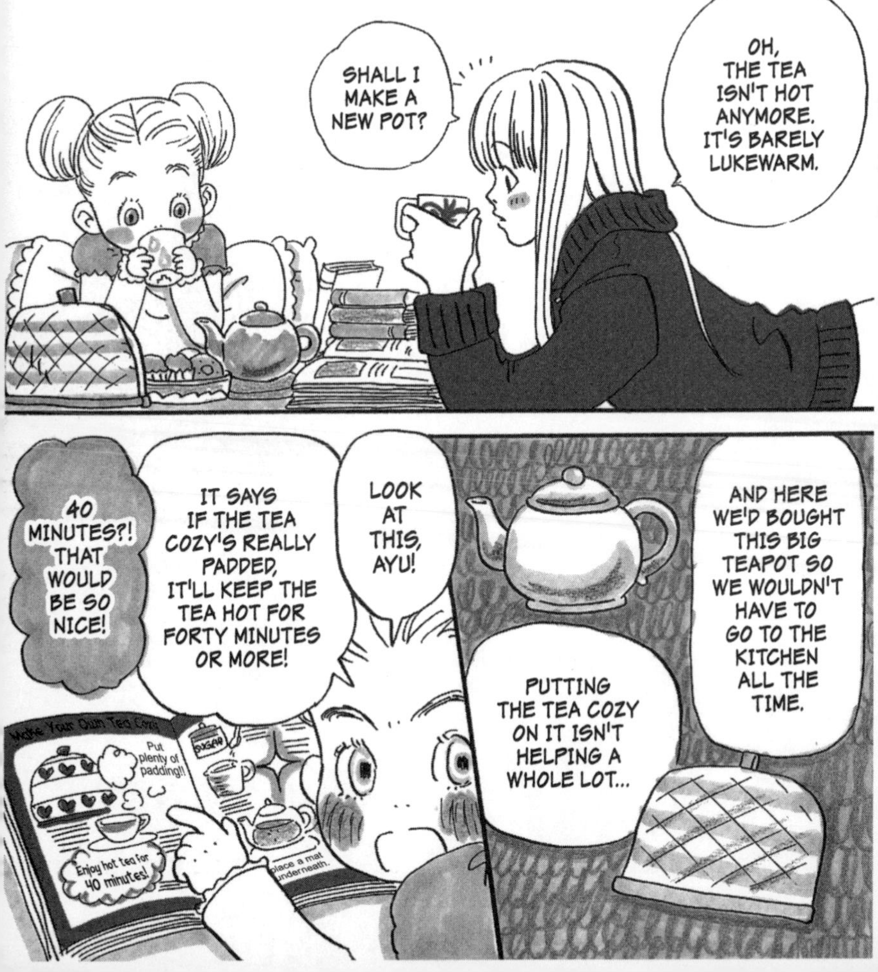

OH, THE TEA ISN'T HOT ANYMORE. IT'S BARELY LUKEWARM.
SHALL I MAKE A NEW POT?
AND HERE WE'D BOUGHT THIS BIG TEAPOT SO WE WOULDN'T HAVE TO GO TO THE KITCHEN ALL THE TIME.
PUTTING THE TEA COZY ON IT ISN'T HELPING A WHOLE LOT...
LOOK AT THIS, AYU!
IT SAYS IF THE TEA COZY'S REALLY PADDED, IT'LL KEEP THE TEA HOT FOR FORTY MINUTES OR MORE!
40 MINUTES?! THAT WOULD BE SO NICE!
Make Your Own Tea Cozy
Put plenty of padding!!
SUGAR
Enjoy hot tea for 40 minutes!
place a mat underneath.

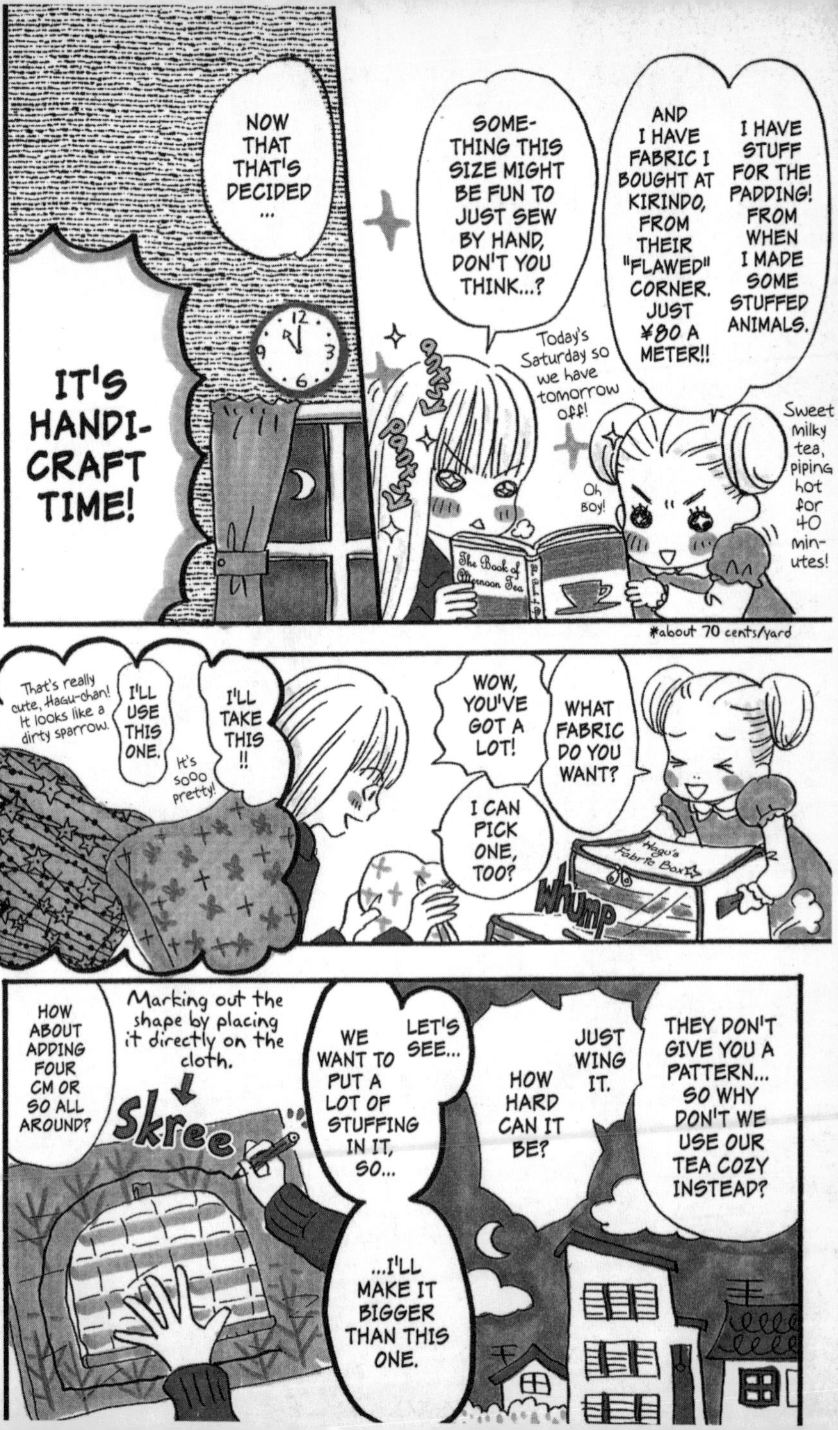
I HAVE STUFF FOR THE PADDING! FROM WHEN I MADE SOME STUFFED ANIMALS.
AND I HAVE FABRIC I BOUGHT AT KIRINDO, FROM THEIR "FLAWED" CORNER. JUST ¥80 A METER!!
Sweet milky tea, piping hot for 40 minutes!
SOME-THING THIS SIZE MIGHT BE FUN TO JUST SEW BY HAND, DON'T YOU THINK...?
Today's Saturday so we have tomorrow off!
Oh boy!
The Book of Afternoon Tea
*about 70 cents/yard
NOW THAT THAT'S DECIDED ...
IT'S HANDI-CRAFT TIME!
WHAT FABRIC DO YOU WANT?
WOW, YOU'VE GOT A LOT!
I CAN PICK ONE, TOO?
Hagu's Fabric Box☆
WHUMP
I'LL TAKE THIS !!
It's sooo pretty!
I'LL USE THIS ONE.
That's really cute, Hagu-chan! It looks like a dirty sparrow.
THEY DON'T GIVE YOU A PATTERN... SO WHY DON'T WE USE OUR TEA COZY INSTEAD?
JUST WING IT.
HOW HARD CAN IT BE?
LET'S SEE...
WE WANT TO PUT A LOT OF STUFFING IN IT, SO...
...I'LL MAKE IT BIGGER THAN THIS ONE.
Marking out the shape by placing it directly on the cloth.
Skree
HOW ABOUT ADDING FOUR CM OR SO ALL AROUND?

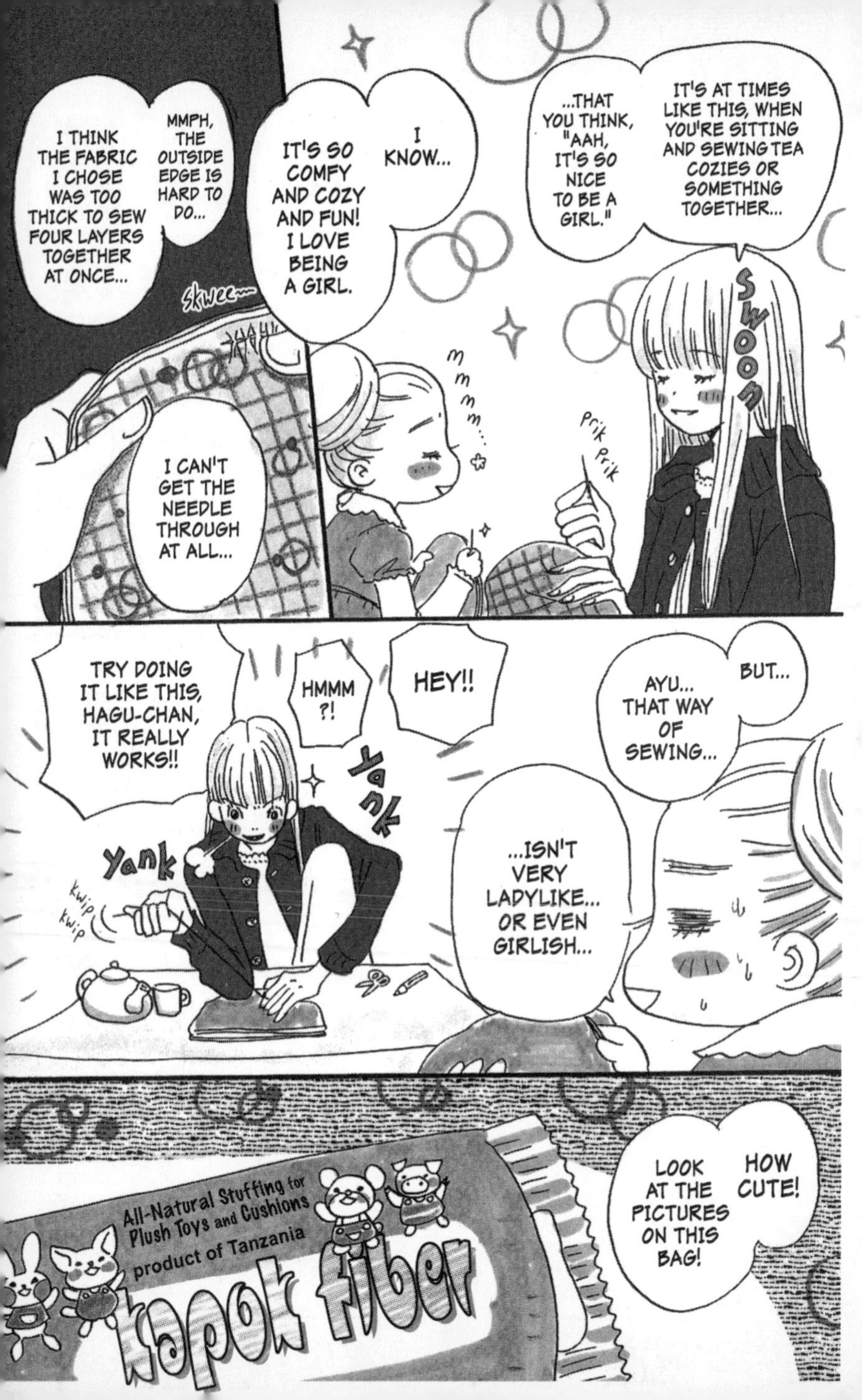
IT'S AT TIMES LIKE THIS, WHEN YOU'RE SITTING AND SEWING TEA COZIES OR SOMETHING TOGETHER...
...THAT YOU THINK, "AAH, IT'S SO NICE TO BE A GIRL."
SWOON
Prik Prik
I KNOW...
IT'S SO COMFY AND COZY AND FUN! I LOVE BEING A GIRL.
mmmm...
MMPH, THE OUTSIDE EDGE IS HARD TO DO...
I THINK THE FABRIC I CHOSE WAS TOO THICK TO SEW FOUR LAYERS TOGETHER AT ONCE...
skwee~~
I CAN'T GET THE NEEDLE THROUGH AT ALL...
BUT...
AYU... THAT WAY OF SEWING...
...ISN'T VERY LADYLIKE... OR EVEN GIRLISH...
HEY!!
HMMM ?!
Yank
TRY DOING IT LIKE THIS, HAGU-CHAN, IT REALLY WORKS!!
Yank
kwip kwip
HOW CUTE!
LOOK AT THE PICTURES ON THIS BAG!
All-Natural Stuffing for Plush Toys and Cushions
product of Tanzania
kapok fiber

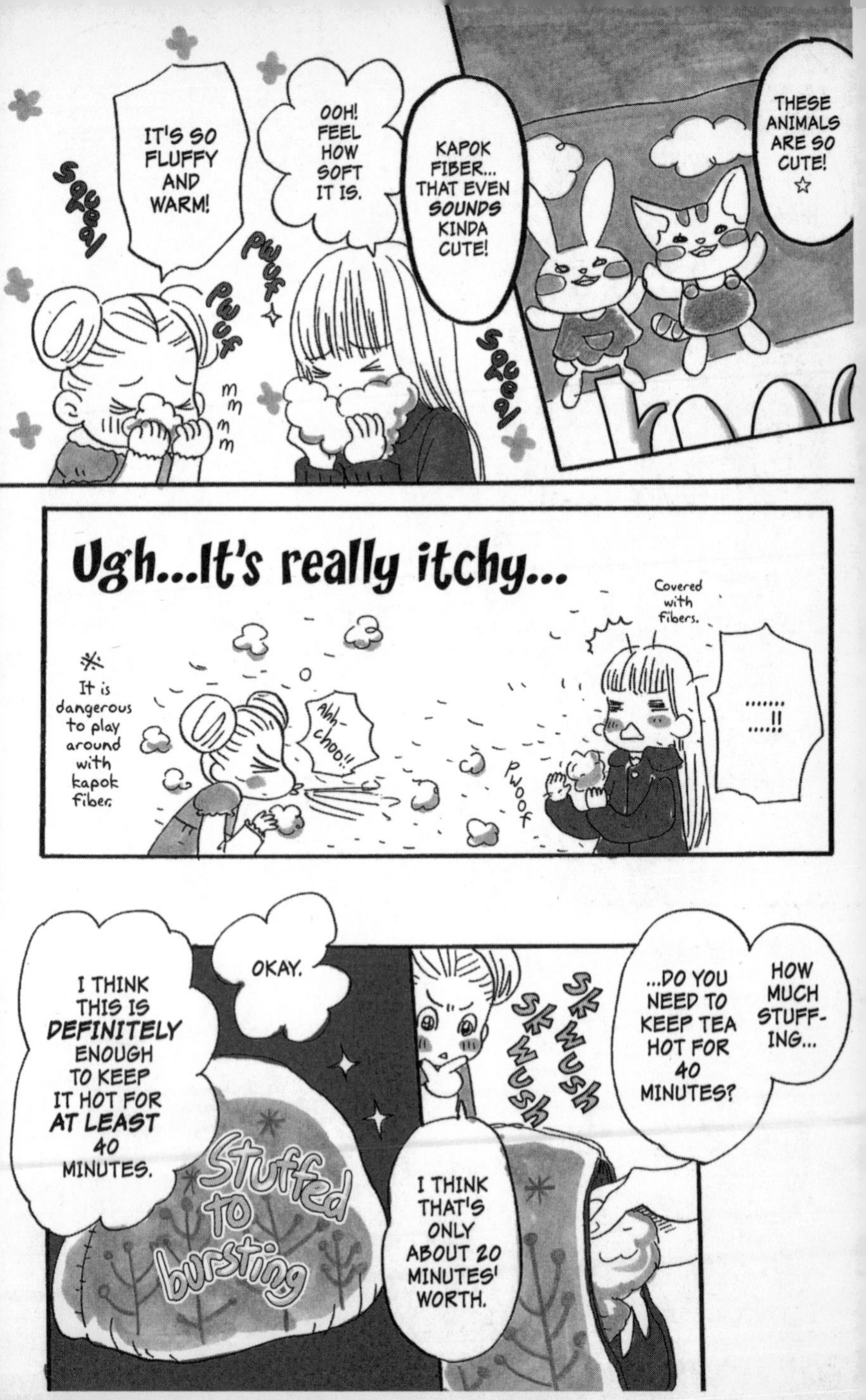
THESE ANIMALS ARE SO CUTE! ☆
KAPOK FIBER... THAT EVEN SOUNDS KINDA CUTE!
OOH! FEEL HOW SOFT IT IS.
Squeal
Pwuf Pwuf
IT'S SO FLUFFY AND WARM!
Squeal
mmmm
Ugh...It's really itchy...
Covered with fibers.
....!!
Pwoof
Ahh-choo!!
※ It is dangerous to play around with kapok fiber.
HOW MUCH STUFFING...
...DO YOU NEED TO KEEP TEA HOT FOR 40 MINUTES?
SKWUSH SKWUSH
I THINK THAT'S ONLY ABOUT 20 MINUTES' WORTH.
OKAY.
I THINK THIS IS DEFINITELY ENOUGH TO KEEP IT HOT FOR AT LEAST 40 MINUTES.
Stuffed to bursting

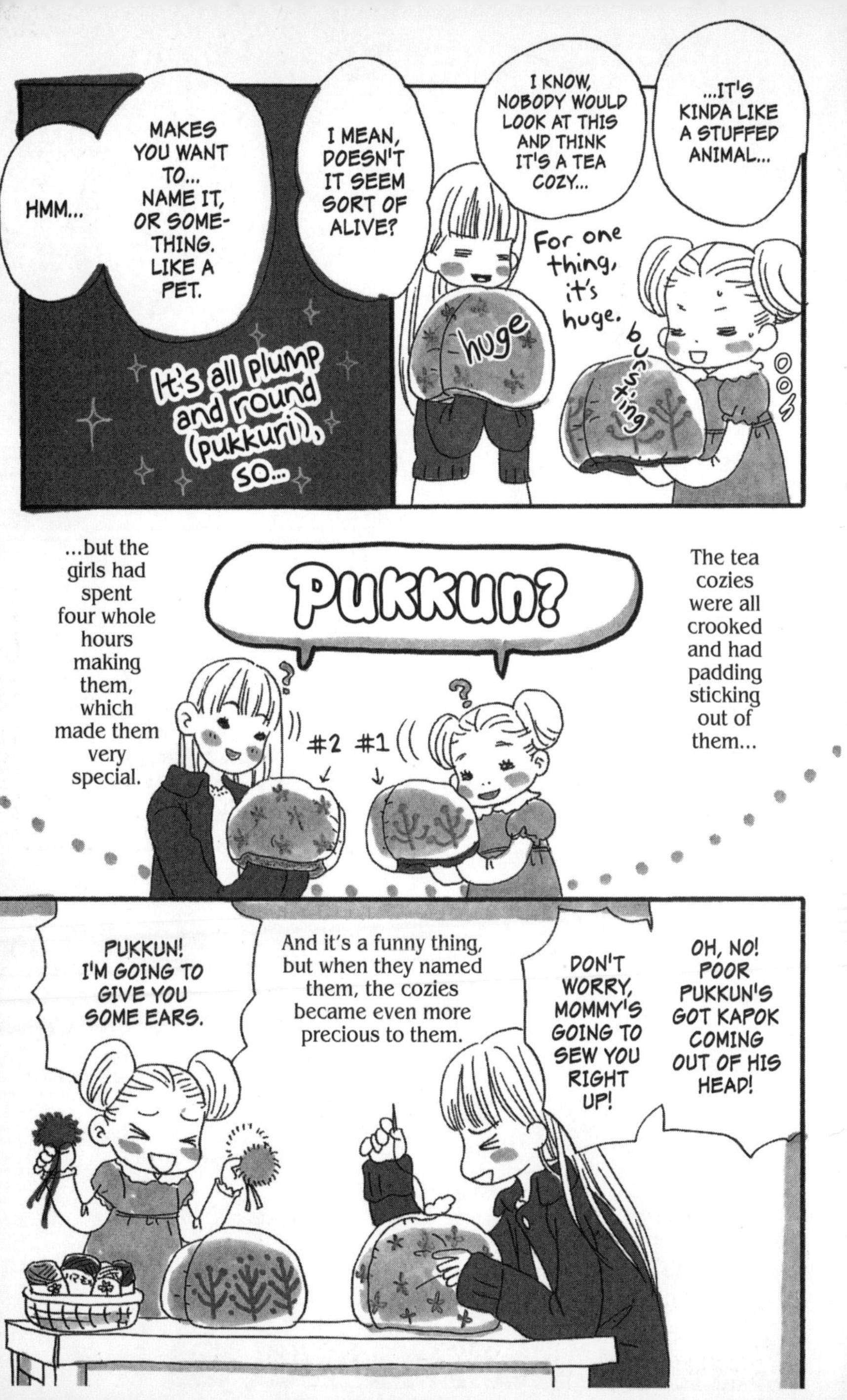
...IT'S KINDA LIKE A STUFFED ANIMAL...
I KNOW, NOBODY WOULD LOOK AT THIS AND THINK IT'S A TEA COZY...
For one thing, it's huge.
huge
bursting
ooh
I MEAN, DOESN'T IT SEEM SORT OF ALIVE?
MAKES YOU WANT TO... NAME IT, OR SOME-THING. LIKE A PET.
HMM...
It's all plump and round (pukkuri), so...
The tea cozies were all crooked and had padding sticking out of them...
Pukkun?
#2 #1
...but the girls had spent four whole hours making them, which made them very special.
OH, NO! POOR PUKKUN'S GOT KAPOK COMING OUT OF HIS HEAD!
DON'T WORRY, MOMMY'S GOING TO SEW YOU RIGHT UP!
And it's a funny thing, but when they named them, the cozies became even more precious to them.
PUKKUN! I'M GOING TO GIVE YOU SOME EARS.

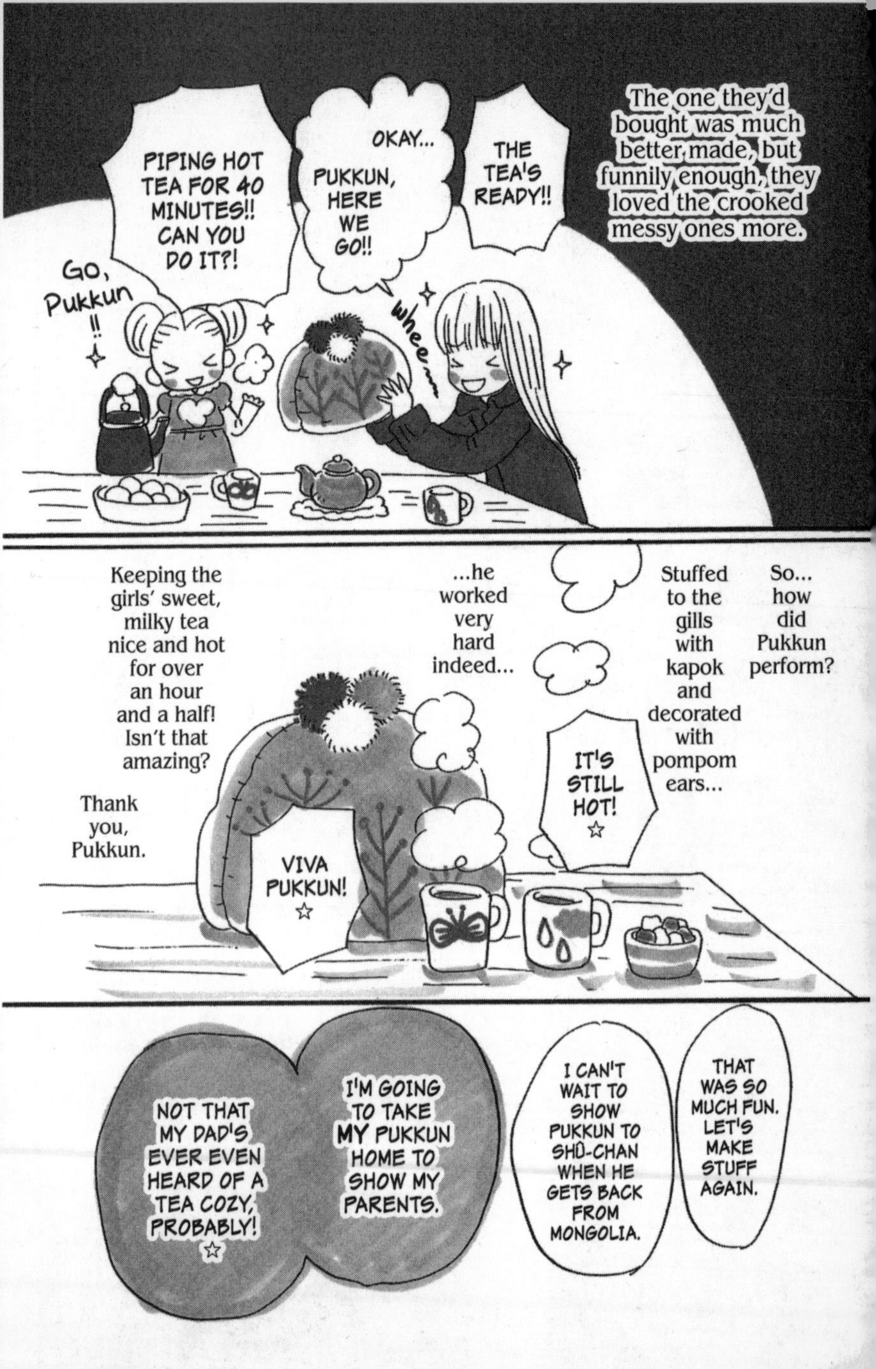
The one they'd bought was much better made, but funnily enough, they loved the crooked messy ones more.
THE TEA'S READY!!
OKAY... PUKKUN, HERE WE GO!!
PIPING HOT TEA FOR 40 MINUTES!! CAN YOU DO IT?!
Go, Pukkun!!
whee~
So... how did Pukkun perform?
Stuffed to the gills with kapok and decorated with pompom ears...
...he worked very hard indeed...
IT'S STILL HOT! ☆
Keeping the girls' sweet, milky tea nice and hot for over an hour and a half! Isn't that amazing?
VIVA PUKKUN! ☆
Thank you, Pukkun.
THAT WAS SO MUCH FUN. LET'S MAKE STUFF AGAIN.
I CAN'T WAIT TO SHOW PUKKUN TO SHÛ-CHAN WHEN HE GETS BACK FROM MONGOLIA.
I'M GOING TO TAKE MY PUKKUN HOME TO SHOW MY PARENTS.
NOT THAT MY DAD'S EVER EVEN HEARD OF A TEA COZY, PROBABLY! ☆

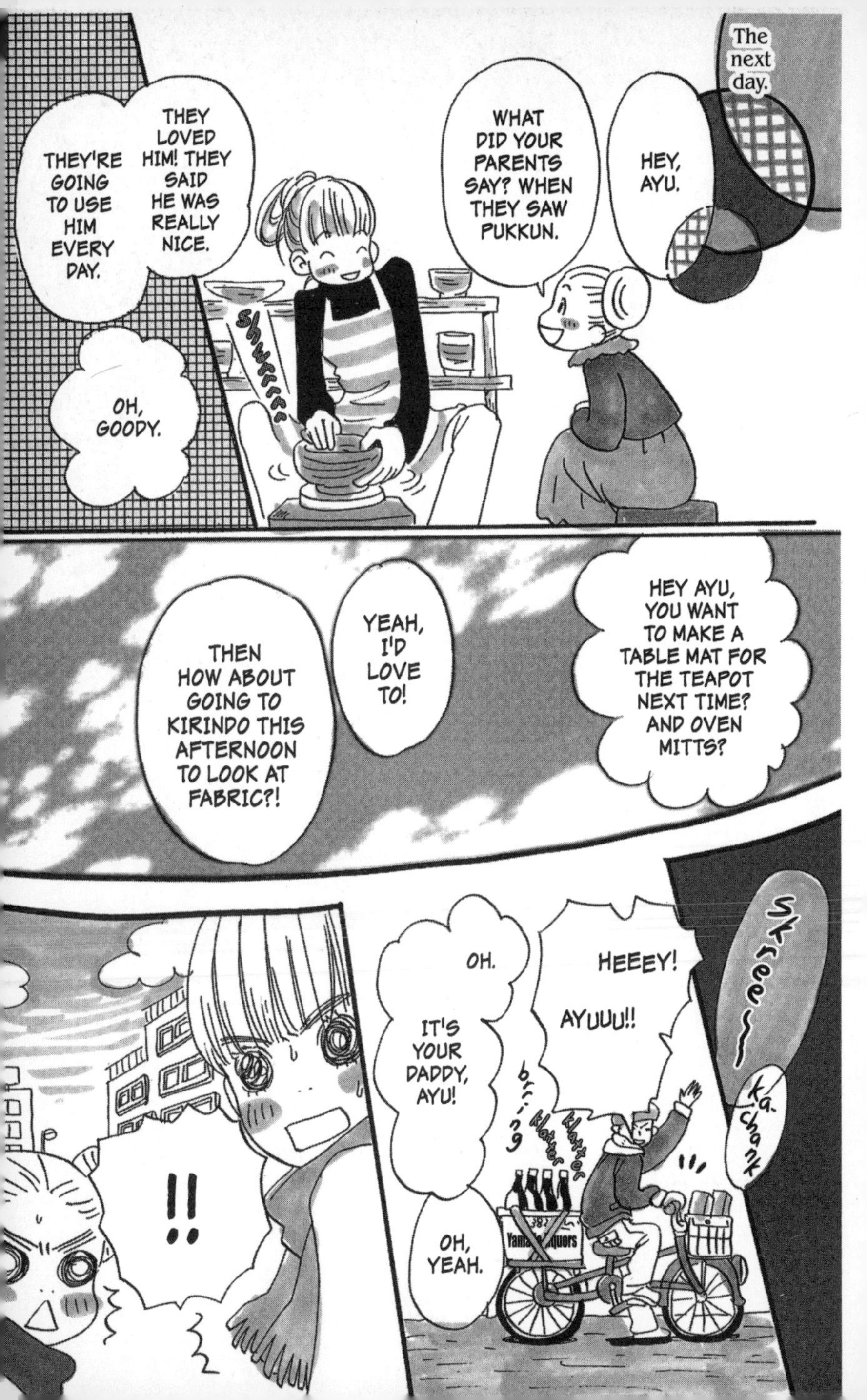
The next day.
HEY, AYU.
WHAT DID YOUR PARENTS SAY? WHEN THEY SAW PUKKUN.
THEY LOVED HIM! THEY SAID HE WAS REALLY NICE.
THEY'RE GOING TO USE HIM EVERY DAY.
shwrrrrr
OH, GOODY.
HEY AYU, YOU WANT TO MAKE A TABLE MAT FOR THE TEAPOT NEXT TIME? AND OVEN MITTS?
YEAH, I'D LOVE TO!
THEN HOW ABOUT GOING TO KIRINDO THIS AFTERNOON TO LOOK AT FABRIC?!
Skreee—
ka-chank
HEEEY!
AYUUU!!
klatter
klatter
bri-i-ng
OH.
IT'S YOUR DADDY, AYU!
OH, YEAH.
!!

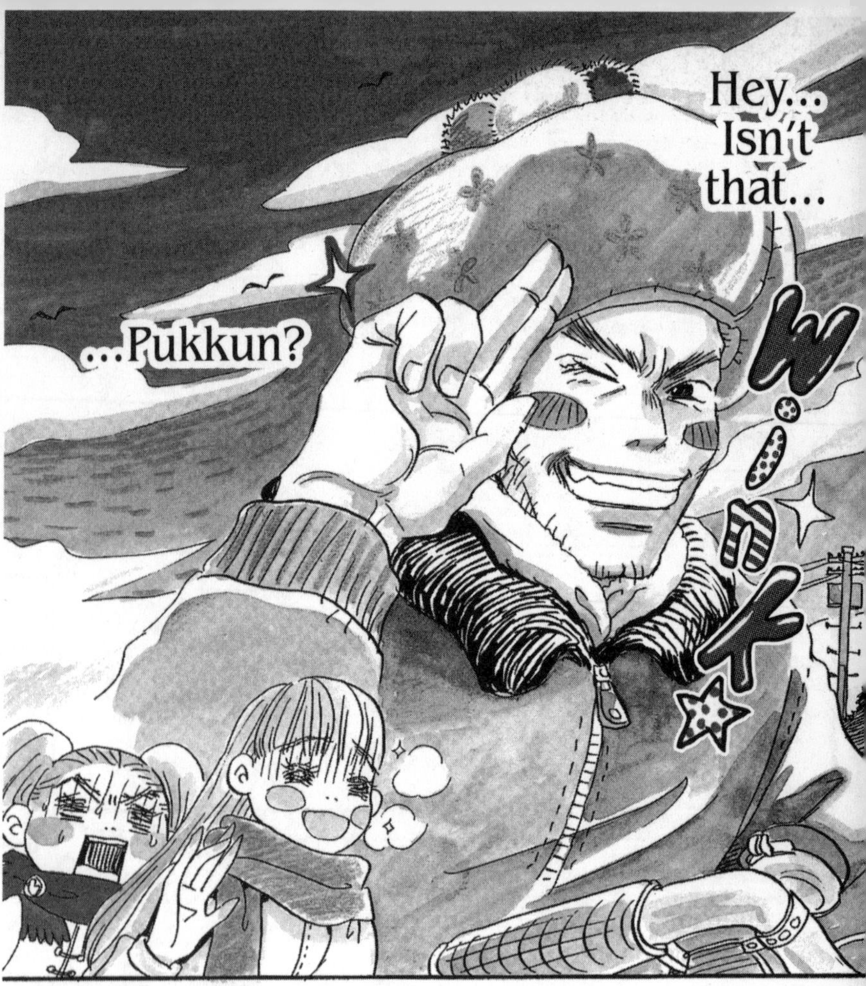
Hey... Isn't that...
Wink
...Pukkun?

"Thanks, Ayu, it's really nice...

But I think it might be a little bohemian for your old dad." ☆

Good-bye, Pukkun... And thank you, Pukkun...

The winter sun shone gently on the two girls who, even as they waved back in shock at Ayu's father, couldn't help thinking to themselves that Pukkun kinda suited him...☆

—End—

This bonus chapter originally appeared in issue No. 2 of Bessatsu YOUNG YOU, 2002.

OTAKU☆ House Call ☆

Hello, this is Chica Umino. Thank you so much for picking up this volume of *Honey and Clover*.

This title, my first to be published in the graphic novel format, is now up to Volume 3.

You, who are holding this volume in your hand as you read this, are the reason I was able to come this far.

I am really, truly grateful to you for your support.

THANK YOU SO MUCH.

And now, for the bonus manga.

In the Volume 2 bonus, I mentioned a mapping-nib holder bearing the Cagliostro coat-of-arms that went missing.

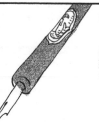

It was discovered very soon after (stuck in the tape holder)...

...and safely returned to its owner, Jukuchô. ☆

Hare-chan   Jukuchô   Here.   Umino   yaaay!

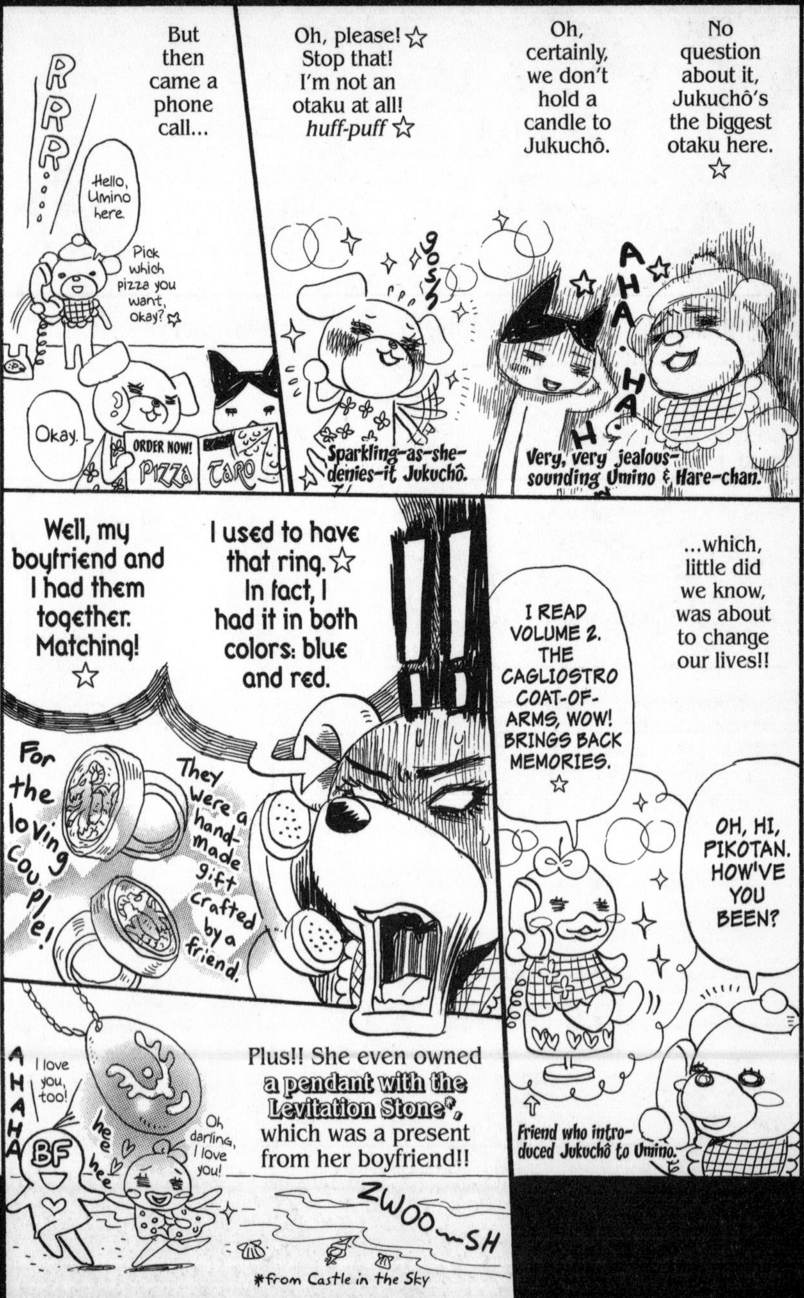
No question about it, Jukuchô's the biggest otaku here. ☆
Oh, certainly, we don't hold a candle to Jukuchô.
AHAHAHA
Very, very jealous-sounding Umino & Hare-chan.
Oh, please! ☆ Stop that! I'm not an otaku at all! huff-puff ☆
gosh
Sparkling-as-she-denies-it Jukuchô.
But then came a phone call...
RRRR...
Hello, Umino here.
Pick which pizza you want, okay? ☆
Okay.
ORDER NOW! PIZZA TARO
...which, little did we know, was about to change our lives!!
OH, HI, PIKOTAN. HOW'VE YOU BEEN?
I READ VOLUME 2. THE CAGLIOSTRO COAT-OF-ARMS, WOW! BRINGS BACK MEMORIES. ☆
Friend who introduced Jukuchô to Umino.
!!
I used to have that ring. ☆ In fact, I had it in both colors: blue and red.
Well, my boyfriend and I had them together. Matching! ☆
For the loving couple!
They were a hand-made gift crafted by a friend.
Plus!! She even owned a pendant with the Levitation Stone*, which was a present from her boyfriend!!
AHAHAHA
I love you, too!
BF
hee hee
Oh darling, I love you!
ZWOO~SH
*from Castle in the Sky

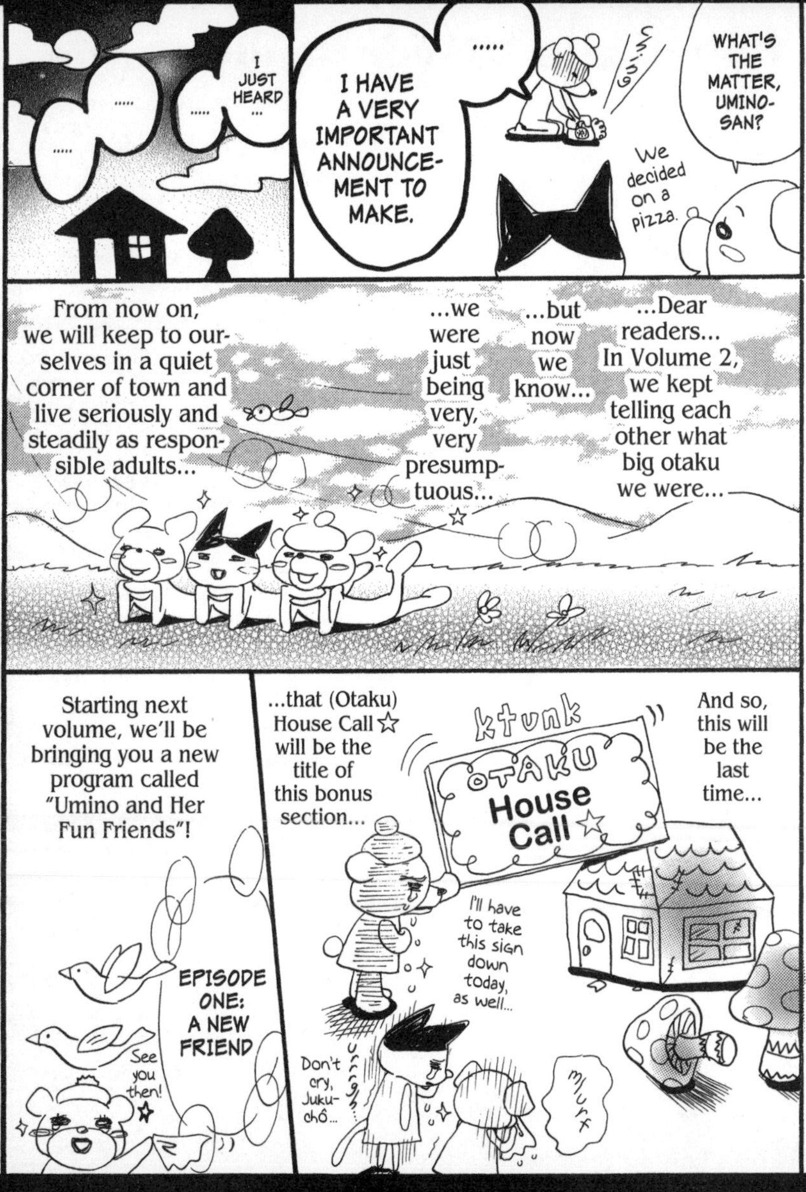
WHAT'S THE MATTER, UMINO-SAN?
We decided on a pizza.
.....
I HAVE A VERY IMPORTANT ANNOUNCEMENT TO MAKE.
I JUST HEARD ...
.....
.....
.....
...Dear readers... In Volume 2, we kept telling each other what big otaku we were...
...but now we know...
...we were just being very, very presumptuous...
From now on, we will keep to ourselves in a quiet corner of town and live seriously and steadily as responsible adults...
And so, this will be the last time...
ktunk
...that (Otaku) House Call☆ will be the title of this bonus section...
OTAKU House Call☆
I'll have to take this sign down today, as well...
Don't cry, Juku-chô...
Starting next volume, we'll be bringing you a new program called "Umino and Her Fun Friends"!
EPISODE ONE: A NEW FRIEND
See you then!

END

★★ I'm keeping an Internet diary!
http://www2.diary.ne.jp/user/162279/

Honey and Clover Study Guide

Page 11, panel 2: Char siu
Cantonese style pork roast, with a marinade made from soy sauce, honey, oyster and/or hoisin sauce and five spice powder.

Page 11, panel 2: Tanmen
In Japan, a salty ramen soup served with stir-fried vegetables on top. The Chinese version is just broth and noodles.

Page 34, panel 4: Asakusabashi
A wholesale shopping district known mostly for its doll and craft shops.

Pg 38, panel 5: Silverberries
Silverberries are the edible fruit of the *Elaeagnus pugens* and are related to the ancestor of the olive. The fruits are dry and mealy when fresh and resemble small dates when dried. The North American variety is *Elaeagnus commutata*.

Page 44, panel 3: Amazake
Amazake is a traditional drink made from fermented rice. Street vendors once sold a warming beverage of simmered amazake and water topped with grated ginger.

Page 61, panel 2: Ryōgoku
A neighborhood in Sumida, Tokyo, known as a center of the sumo world. It houses many sumo stables and is the location of the Tokyo sumo stadium.

Page 61, panel 2: Rainbow Bridge
The Rainbow Bridge is a suspension bridge that connects Odaiba (a man-made defensive island converted into a shopping district) to the rest of Tokyo. It is painted white to complement the Tokyo skyline.

Page 61, panel 2: Odaiba
An artificial island in Tokyo Bay that began as a part of six fortresses built in 1853 to protect Tokyo from attack by sea. In the '80s and early '90s, Odaiba was re-built to be a showcase of futuristic living but was largely abandoned when the economy collapsed. Today the district is a popular destination for tourists and Tokyo residents, with many shopping malls, a hot spring, a beach, a science museum, a giant Ferris wheel, and more.

Page 61, panel 3: Kasai
Kasai Rinkai Park was built on reclaimed land in Tokyo Bay, and opened in 1989. The park includes a bird sanctuary, an aquarium, and a Ferris wheel.

Page 97, panel 2: Signature seal
Similar to the Chinese chop, these sticks carved at one end with a name are used in place of or in addition to a signature on various documents. There are both personal seals and registered seals (used for official business transactions).

Page 100, panel 2: Coming of Age Day
Coming of Age Day (成人の日) is a national holiday in Japan held on the second Monday in January. It celebrates everyone turning 20 in the coming year, and most participants wear formal kimono or suits. In Japan, 20 is the age at which you can vote and drink.

Page 100, panel 4: *Shichi-go-san*
七五三 literally means "seven-five-three" and is a festival to celebrate 3-year-old children, 5-year-old boys, and 7-year-old girls, although the practice varies by region. Traditionally the children are dressed in kimono and taken to a shrine where they receive bags of *chitose-ame*, long candies that symbolize long life. *Chitose* means "1,000 years old."

Page 108, panel 2: Del
The typical Mongolian garment for both men and women. The basic design has changed little over the centuries, although the decorations and collar style have shifted with time.

Page 109, panel 3: Naadam
A traditional Mongolian festival sometimes called *eriin gurvan naadam*, which means "three manly games." The games include wrestling, horse racing, and archery. Women participate in the archery and girls in the horse races, but the wrestling is restricted to men. The largest Naadam is held in the capital city of Ulaanbaatar July 11-13, during the national holiday.

Page 124, panel 3: Oden
A Japanese comfort soup served in winter. It consists of a variety of ingredients such as tofu, boiled eggs, daikon radish, konyakku (a vegetable gelatin), and fish cake simmered in a dashi broth. Oden is often sold at food carts or convenience stores.

Page 132, panel 1: Zundoko-bushi
A song that dates back to at least 1945, with multiple versions released as pop songs since then, always titled "So-and-so's Zundoko-bushi". Morita's version is based on Hikawa Kiyoshi's version.

Page 142, panel 3: Shiso
Also called perilla or beefstake plant. It is a member of the mint family and tastes like a mild cross between mint and basil. It is used in all sorts of Japanese dishes, including as a pizza topping and in pesto sauce.

Page 165, Nae Yûki
A Japanese actress who has appeared in such films as *Letters from Iwo Jima*, *MPD Psycho*, *Ultraman*, and *White on Rice*.

The magic is getting worse. Paper and other art supplies keep going missing in my room...
I think I have no choice but to master a magical
spell that, when chanted, lights up the hiding place
of whatever I'm looking for.

-Chica Umino

Chica Umino was born in Tokyo and started out as
a product designer and illustrator. Her beloved
Honey and Clover debuted in 2000 and received the
Kodansha Manga Award in 2003. *Honey and Clover*
was also nominated for the Tezuka Culture Prize
and an award from the Japan Media Arts Festival.

Shojo Beat

HONEY AND CLOVER
VOL. 3
The Shojo Beat Manga Edition

This manga volume contains material that was originally published in English in *Shojo Beat* magazine, May-July 2008. Artwork in the magazine may have been slightly altered from that presented here.

STORY AND ART BY CHICA UMINO

English Translation & Adaptation/Akemi Wegmuller
Touch-up Art & Lettering/Sabrina Heep
Design/Yukiko Whitley
Editor/Pancha Diaz

Editor in Chief, Books/Alvin Lu
Editor in Chief, Magazines/Marc Weidenbaum
VP of Publishing Licensing/Rika Inouye
VP of Sales/Gonzalo Ferreyra
Sr. VP of Marketing/Liza Coppola
Publisher/Hyoe Narita

Printed in Canada

Published by VIZ Media, LLC
P.O. Box 77010
San Francisco, CA 94107

Shojo Beat Manga Edition
10 9 8 7 6 5 4 3 2 1
First printing, September 2008

VIZ media

store.viz.com

love ★ com
By Aya Nakahara

Class clowns
Risa and Ôtani
join forces
to find love!

Manga available now

High School DEBUT

By Kazune Kawahara

When Haruna Nagashima was in junior high, softball and comics were her life. Now that she's in high school, she's ready to find a boyfriend. But will hard work (and the right coach) be enough?

Find out in the *High School Debut* manga series—available now!